Saying and Doing in Zapotec

Bloomsbury Studies in Linguistic Anthropology

Series Editors

Sabina Perrino, Paul Manning and Jim Wilce

Presenting and exploring new and current approaches to discourse and culture, **Bloomsbury Studies in Linguistic Anthropology** examines the most recent topics in this field. Publishing contemporary, cutting edge research, this series investigates social life through everyday discursive practices, making these practices visible and unveiling processes that would remain concealed without careful attention to discourse.

The series titles focus on specific themes to advance the field both theoretically and methodologically, such as language contact dynamics, language revitalisation and reclamation, and language, migration and social justice. Positioning linguistic anthropology at the intersection with other fields, this series will cast light on various cultural settings across the globe by viewing important linguistic ethnographies through an anthropological lens. Standing at the frontier of this growing field, **Bloomsbury Studies in Linguistic Anthropology** offers a balanced view of the current state of the discipline, as well as promoting and advancing exciting new directions for research.

Forthcoming Titles

Graphic Politics in Eastern India, Nishaant Choksi
Language and Revolutionary Magic in the Orinoco Delta, Juan Luis Rodriguez
Language Revitalization and Indigenous Remaking in Amazonia, Michael Wroblewski

Saying and Doing in Zapotec

*Multimodality, Resonance, and the
Language of Joint Actions*

Mark A. Sicoli

BLOOMSBURY ACADEMIC
LONDON • NEW YORK • OXFORD • NEW DELHI • SYDNEY

BLOOMSBURY ACADEMIC
Bloomsbury Publishing Plc
50 Bedford Square, London, WC1B 3DP, UK
1385 Broadway, New York, NY 10018, USA
29 Earlsfort Terrace, Dublin 2, Ireland

BLOOMSBURY, BLOOMSBURY ACADEMIC and the Diana logo
are trademarks of Bloomsbury Publishing Plc

First published in Great Britain 2020
This paperback edition published in 2021

Copyright © Mark A. Sicoli, 2020

Mark A. Sicoli has asserted his right under the Copyright,
Designs and Patents Act, 1988, to be identified as Author of this work.

For legal purposes the Acknowledgments on p. xiii constitute an extension
of this copyright page.

Series design by Ben Anslow
Cover image © Bloomberg Creative Photos / Getty Images

All rights reserved. No part of this publication may be reproduced or transmitted
in any form or by any means, electronic or mechanical, including photocopying,
recording, or any information storage or retrieval system, without prior
permission in writing from the publishers.

Bloomsbury Publishing Plc does not have any control over, or responsibility for,
any third-party websites referred to or in this book. All internet addresses given
in this book were correct at the time of going to press. The author and publisher
regret any inconvenience caused if addresses have changed or sites have
ceased to exist, but can accept no responsibility for any such changes.

A catalogue record for this book is available from the British Library.

Library of Congress Cataloging-in-Publication Data

Names: Sicoli, Mark A., author. Title: Saying and doing in Zapotec: multimodality, resonance, and the language of joint actions / Mark A. Sicoli. Description: London; New York: Bloomsbury Academic, 2020. | Series: Bloomsbury studies in linguistic anthropology | Includes bibliographical references and index. | Summary: "A multimodal ethnography of language as living process, this book demonstrates methods for the integrated analysis of talk, gesture, and material culture, developing a fresh way to understand human language through a focus on jointly achieved social actions to which it is part. Based on findings from a participatory, multimedia language documentation project in a highland Zapotec community of Oaxaca, Mexico, Mark A. Sicoli brings together goals of documentary linguistics and anthropological concern with the everyday means and ends of human social life with theoretical consequences for the analysis of linguistic and cultural reproduction and change. This book argues that resonances emergent in the whole of multiparticipant, multimodal interaction, are organizational of human social-cognitive process important for understanding both the shape linguistic utterances take in interaction (dialogic resonance) and the relationships built between distinct sign modes (intermodal resonance). In this way, Saying and Doing in Zapotec develops a new theory, characterizing the logic of resonance in human interaction as semiotic process that connects and juxtaposes interactional moves into assemblages of relations, resonances and collaborations that build an emergent lifeworld for a language"– Provided by publisher.
Identifiers: LCCN 2020020662 (print) | LCCN 2020020663 (ebook) |
ISBN 9781350142169 (hardback) | ISBN 9781350142176 (ebook) | ISBN 9781350142183 (epub)
Subjects: LCSH: Anthropological linguistics–Mexico–Santa Maria Lachixío. | Zapotec language–Dialects–Mexico–Santa Maria Lachixío. | Zapotec language–Social aspects–Mexico–Santa Maria Lachixío. | Zapotec Indians–Mexico–Santa Maria Lachixío. | Santa Maria Lachixío (Mexico)–Languages.
Classification: LCC P35.5.M6 S36 2020 (print) | LCC P35.5.M6 (ebook) | DDC 497/.68–dc23
LC record available at https://lccn.loc.gov/2020020662
LC ebook record available at https://lccn.loc.gov/2020020663

ISBN: HB: 978-1-3501-4216-9
PB: 978-1-3502-0411-9
ePDF: 978-1-3501-4217-6
eBook: 978-1-3501-4218-3

Series: Bloomsbury Studies in Linguistic Anthropology

Typeset by Deanta Global Publishing Services, Chennai, India

To find out more about our authors and books visit www.bloomsbury.com
and sign up for our newsletters.

Para Benné Xe'yyò noo Benné Zhílìì
Beè mbálle á
And all relations that connect our worlds

Contents

List of Illustrations	viii
Preface	xi
Acknowledgments	xiii
Orthography and Abbreviations	xv
1 Introduction	1
2 Offer	37
3 Recruit	71
4 Repair	99
5 Resonate	133
6 Build	167
7 Living Assemblages	207
Notes	229
References	233
Index	249

Video Repository: https://www.bloomsbury.com/cw/saying-and-doing-in-zapotec/videos/

Illustrations

Figures

1.1	Visible, audible, and multimodal request formations	13
1.2	Passing the bowl co-temporal with acceptance of offer to rinse dishes	14
1.3	Turkey Corral	15
1.4	Picnic in the milpa	16
1.5	Basic semiotic process (after Enfield [2013] and Kockelman [2011, 2013])	20
1.6	Playback dialogue at Casa Hernández García	27
1.7	Region of the fieldwork in Sierra Sur of Oaxaca, Mexico	34
1.8	Zapotec Service Station, Santa María Lachixío	35
2.1	An assistant standing next to bride and groom keeps track of gifts on paper as a guest watches the procession of gifts	41
2.2	Wedding gift exchange, July 2014. The *Benné Òlla* (orator) mediates between the receivers of gifts (*Toòmbálle* [godfather] and *Noòmbálle* [godmother]) and the givers of gifts, here in view of the *Novio* (groom) and *Novia* (bride) (and about sixty guests)	42
2.3	Benné Òlla addresses Noòmbálle with gesture and body posture iconic of the smallness/humility of the gift	43
2.4	The groom reframes the gift as not four turkeys but two for the godfather and two for the godmother	51
2.5	Mary gathers dishes	65
3.1	A material recruitment for water	77
3.2	Tortilla making in a Lachixío kitchen	78
3.3	A family takes a break from weeding in the milpa	84
3.4	Recruitment of water at a family dinner	89
3.5	Mariana passes directive to Rodrigo who issues verbal directive to Inez in synchronicity with Pedro's material directive with the cup	91
3.6	Sign-object interpreted through three interpretants that produce an intermodal discord between energetic interpretants that reproduce the value of the sign-object and representational interpretants that contest it and subsequently transform it by scale shifting	93
3.7	Material affordance of empty cup used as directive interpreted through three interpretants that subsequently accept, reject, and then transform the action represented in the sign-object	94
4.1	The retrospective and prospective dimensions of conversational repair (after Dingemanse and Enfield 2015: 105)	104
4.2	Repair initiation formats by position	106
4.3	Lachixío Zapotec open and restricted repair initiation	108

4.4	Lachixío Zapotec repair initiation as request versus offer	109
4.5	Sofia head/gaze points toward window while Mary's gaze is down (left), and Sofia redoes her turn with a second head/gaze point with Mary in joint attention (right)	115
4.6	Sofia (left) turns to Andrea saying, "Many spines here are getting on me"	117
4.7	Trouble in unseen head/gaze point, Remedy with hand point into visual field	119
4.8	David grabs parts assemblage after repair on Daniel's recruitment	121
4.9	Neither participant diverts their embodied activity as Andrea (left) offers repair *Fréssa la?* (Strawberries?)	123
4.10	Angeles, Elvia, and Andrea turn heads in synchrony toward Jorge	127
4.11	Sofia turns her head and gazes toward her implicit place reference (line 5)	129
5.1	Francisco, Regina, and Aurelia sit side by side talking	140
5.2	Adrian turns to look at the mountain after feeling the cool wind announce the rain, and Giovani follows the direction of his gaze	149
5.3	Pablo's head point north (B) resonated by Pedro's head point (C) north blended to nod (D)	154
5.4	Sofia sets a tortilla on the comal as Mary assesses the smoke	156
5.5	Efraín helps his grandfather work the oxen to weed the milpa	159
5.6	Chiasmatic resonance between parents	163
6.1	Felicita and Francisco talk about fastening rope to the strap	171
6.2	Francisco's index finger points to fold saying, "Leave just a little bit" (27), and then he turns his hand to depict the cinching of the fold wrapping two fingers through ring and squeezing folded strap held by Felicita	175
6.3	Felicita and Francisco take reciprocal roles working together to seize a ring at the end of a saddle cinch. Felicita holds the strap in place while Fernando seizes it with rope	178
6.4	A family works together to build a turkey enclosure	180
6.5	Two solutions to fastening the planks	181
6.6	Andrea gestures to right indicating the place she is suggesting they put another post	182
6.7	Andrea assesses the trouble to be because of a prior joint commitment at the beginning of the project, saying, "Too bad we didn't dig the ground that we just made it like this" while catching a falling board (line 11)	183
6.8	Pedro steps between Nazaria and Andrea placing hand on planks (line 32)	186
6.9	Spaces of a focused orientation: Adam Kendon's F-Formation (2009: 235): Participants (P) orienting to a space of common perceptual access (O) defining residual space (R) outside the perimeter of focused participants	187
6.10	Pedro runs hand to right and left along boards while saying, "Yes it will just sit there now"	188

6.11	Pedro and Nazaria collaborate to iterate Solution 1	190
6.12	Andrea comes back with a rope and Pedro and Nazaria take notice	191
6.13	Andrea steps between Pedro and Nazaria placing hand on planks	194
6.14	Andrea makes repeated C-shaped gestures left-to-right while saying "one-by-one" indicating tying the boards iteratively while Pedro and Nazaria gaze at her gestures	196
6.15	Pedro picks up a rope beginning to formulate an idea	199
6.16	Pedro stands and pulls his rope out abandoning his idea (line 138)	205

Tables

4.1	Basic format types for other-initiation of repair (after Dingemanse and Enfield 2015)	105
4.2	Repair Initiators and Their Frequencies in 13.75 Coded Hours of Conversation	106
4.3	Repair Initiation Forms and Their Frequencies in 13.75 Coded Hours of Conversation	107

Preface

Saying and Doing in Zapotec is a multimodal ethnography of a language as living process. The project brings together goals of documentary linguistics and anthropological concern with the everyday means and ends of human social life to examine how language form and function is shaped through the multimodal joint actions that build social, intersubjective, and material worlds. Based on a participatory video documentation of language use in a highland Zapotec community of Oaxaca, Mexico, this book develops our understanding of human language through a focus on the jointly achieved social actions to which any language is part with theoretical consequences for understanding language, reproduction, and change. As part to the interparticipant, multimodal wholes of interaction, language displays an ontology that is in itself incomplete—an evolved *openness* to the copresent modalities and multiple participants sharing the timespaces of its use. The joint actions this book engages concern everyday obligations for living a human life—to offer for another and recruit from another—where offering and recruiting produce human affordances for emergent scales of action that collaboratively build and repair our social relations, understandings, and material culture.

This book argues that resonances emergent in the whole of multi-participant, multimodal interaction are organizational of human social-cognitive process important for understanding both the shape utterances take in interaction (dialogic resonance) and the relationships built between semiotic modalities (intermodal resonance). The simultaneities of copresence and iterated sequences of co-relevant language forms in interactions produce emergent resonances that connect diverse sign types into assemblages of relations that build a lifeworld for a language. Across the participants and modalities of multimodal assemblages, semiotic actions inform each other in relationships of harmony and discord. The larger wholes emergent with the resonances between the participants, modalities, and things of human interaction both enable and constrain the form, function, meaning, and use of the component parts, including language. Recognizing the organizing logic of resonance in language use obligates its study in concert with co-relevant sign modes through holistic, participatory, and interactional methods fit to the scale of social life where language form and function accrue through everyday joint actions.

The book brings together multiple trajectories of my scholarship. I began collaborating with people of Lachixío for language documentation as a master's student in American Indian Linguistics at the University of Pittsburgh. This grounded more general interests across linguistics, and anthropology begun as an undergraduate at the University of California, Santa Cruz, when the *Writing Culture* critique of Clifford and Marcus (1986) was still a fresh topic of conversation. I worked to integrate disciplinary perspectives as a PhD student combining anthropology and linguistics at the University of Michigan. My dissertation focused on several linguistic orders achieved in the layering of pitch and voice qualities mainly through analysis of narrated speech content. I embraced a turn from methods that relied primarily on audio recording and text narratives to those of multimodal interaction through video analysis while a postdoctoral researcher in the Language and Cognition Department of the Max Planck Institute in Nijmegen, the Netherlands. The book is built specifically around videos recorded by and with the help of Lachixío community members over three summers of fieldwork (2007–09) with participatory analysis over subsequent years. I began building the video corpus modeled after an MPI *Field Manual* entry by Enfield, Levinson, de Ruiter, and Stivers (2007) toward building multimodal corpora of spontaneous everyday interaction, and while thinking about the pragmatics of speech acts, and its problems in cross-cultural perspectives since psychological and linguistic anthropologist Michelle Rosaldo reflected on speech act theory as both "inspiration" and "butt" (1982: 203).

My idea for writing an ethnography of language as social action that would also be a language documentation resource was enabled by a fellowship from the NEH-NSF Documenting Endangered Languages (DEL) program to preserve and transcribe for analysis the growing video corpus on the conduct of social life in Lachixío (FN50065-10). For these reasons *Saying and Doing in Zapotec* can be read for diverse purposes; it is a scholarly argument, a documentary resource, and a teaching tool: it is a multimodal ethnography of a language living through the contingencies, commitments, and moral obligations of social life. It is a primary reference source for an endangered Zapotec language built with participatory methodologies through which indigenous perspectives are central in the narrative, depicted in the poetics, phonetics, morphology, syntax, and resonances represented in the transcriptions, in explicit accounts of community members, and in interactive video resources for more immersive teaching and learning. And it engages philosophical debates that connect the social and natural sciences' common concerns with the phenomenology of more-than-human systems, and the ontology of action between human and nonhuman participants, where life, mind, objects, and institutions are reproduced and transformed through the mutual self-reinforcement of the resonances that energize their assemblages. The ethnographic and multimodal focus on the language of joint actions within the holistic framework of a temporally ongoing semiosis is an important intersection of theory and methods for both linguistics and anthropology, and one that is resonant with and informing of developing inquiry into the biosemiotics of life. The generic focus on multimodal actions that join social actors into the real-time collaborative projects of social life provides a means for both thick ethnographic interpretations of local conduct and a relatively stable field to compare cultural and linguistic variability, and which makes sensible the resonances at work in language reproduction and language change.

Acknowledgments

This book would not exist without the generosity of my friends, family, and colleagues. I am greatly indebted to the warm hospitality of the people of Lachixío who have welcomed me into their homes to share meals and teach me about language, culture, and social life in the Oaxacan *Sierra Sur*. By consenting to video and audio recording, patiently answering many questions, and offering many explanations over the years since 1997, they have enabled this work. I aim to honor them with a book that amplifies the nestings of language and social life emergent from the rhythms and resonances of their everyday interactions. I particularly want to thank my *compadres* Daniel Hernández Morgan and Felipa García Hernández. So many others have also offered understandings through dialogues, especially Giovani Hernández, David Hernández, Adrián Hernández Réyes, Abad García, Inocencia Hernández, Angélica Hernández, Pablo Vásquez, *Toò* Mario Hernández García, and *Toò* Fabiano Hernández García. I am also deeply indebted to my collaborators Pedro Martínez García, who was a videographer, and María Morales Morales, who helped me with transcription and translation, thanks in part to NEH DEL FN50065-10, and to both as interlocutors. To the many more participants than I can list, *Chettza lá wa* 'Thank you all.'

I thank the *Centro de las Americas* at the University of Virginia for sponsoring a manuscript workshop, and Laura Ahearn and Emiliana Cruz for visiting Charlottesville to participate, read, and comment on the draft manuscript. I am grateful to my UVA colleagues for the supportive environment and engaging discussions that inspired developments of this project: Sonia Alconini, Ira Bashkow, Ellen Contini-Morava, Fred Damon, Eve Danziger, Lise Dobrin, Carrie Douglass, David Edmunds, Gertrude Fraser, Richard Handler, Jeff Hantman, Jim Igoe, Kasey Jernigan, Adria LaViolette, Dan Lefkowitz, Susan McKinnon, George Mentore, China Scherz, John Shepherd, Sylvia Tidey, Pati Wattenmaker, Kath Weston, Jarrett Zigon, and especially *Toò* Roy Wagner for your responses to drafts and for the long conversation that perdures beyond copresence.

Lourdes De León, Eve Danziger, Mark Dingemanse, Nick Enfield, Fred Erickson, Candy Goodwin, Chuck Goodwin, Deborah Tannen, Matt Wolfgram, Chip Zuckerman, Alessandro Duranti, and Roy Wagner provided helpful comments on drafts, as did students in my Multimodal Interaction and Language as Social Action seminars at Georgetown University and the University of Virginia.

I have appreciated opportunities to give talks that developed this project, and I am grateful to the audiences whose questions improved the arguments and presentation. I've benefited from discussions with Stephen Levinson, Jack Du Bois, Tanya Stivers, John Heritage, Elinor Ochs, Terra Edwards, Denise Brennan, Heidi Hamilton, Laurie King, Sylvia Onder, Mubbashir Rizvi, Joanne Rappaport, Anna Trester, Anna De Fina, Isolda Carranza, Penny Brown, Olivier LeGuen, Joe Blythe, Eric Campbell, Dan Everett, Terrence Kaufman, Robin Queen, Anna Babel, Judith Irvine, Bruce Mannheim, Sarah

Thomason, members, and visitors to the Language and Cognition Department of MPI Nijmegen. Rosemary Beam de Azcona and Juan José Bueno Holle provided important critical reads of the Zapotec transcriptions and glossing.

Student assistants at the University of Alaska, Georgetown University, and the University of Virginia helped with many tasks. Special thanks to Joslyn Burchett, Summer Chambers, Vernon Chow, Kristine DeLeon, Daniel Ginsberg, Quinn Legallo-Malone, Jin Lee, Yesha Malla, Peri Oxford, Dave Prine, Raquel Rosenbloom, April Michelle Thomas, Amelia Tseng, Kaycia Voorman, Angela Lynn Yates, Julia Warner, and Kennedy Castillo who also helped with some line drawings.

I am grateful to the series editors Sabina Perrino, Paul Manning, and Jim Wilce, Andrew Wardell and Becky Holland of Bloomsbury Press, five anonymous reviewers, and Aimee Hosemann for indexing, and Isabel Haviland for proofreading.

And thank you, Kelly, for your loving support and for helping me make times to write; Silvio, for your interest and help with illustrations; and Luca, whose preschool schedule provided just enough time and structure to make the final push to publication.

Orthography and Abbreviations

Each transcript block has five tiers: (1) attention to phonetics with conversation analysis (CA) transcription conventions, (2) action descriptions in which the pipe symbol within a description <|> indexes the onset of the action aligned to Tier 1, (3) morpho-phonemic representation, (4) morpheme-by-morpheme gloss, and (5) English free translation.

In transcriptions, the tones of Lachixío are written with acute accent above a vowel for high tone, grave accent above a vowel for low tone, or a sequence of the two for rising or falling tone across geminate vowels each tone in Lachixío Zapotec requiring its own mora. Vowels that show no tone marking are unspecified for tone (mid), or underspecified receiving their tone from, for example, the spreading of high tone to the end of the stem. On the geminate vowels of the phonetic tier of transcription blocks, high tone is only written on the first vowel and spreads progressively to the second, and low tone is only written on the second vowel representing a phonetic ML fall for what is a phonemically simple low tone (as indicated in the morpheme tier). The orthography uses *x* and *zx* to indicate voiceless and voiced retroflex fricatives and *tx* for the retroflex affricate. The voiceless palatal fricative is written *xh*, the voiced *zh*, and the palatal affricate *ch*. Voiceless sonorants are *jl*, *jr*, and *jn*. Perceptually they give the impression of being preaspirated. These come about through morphological concatenation of the Habitual aspect prefix /r-/ with resonant-initial verbs. Combination of Habitual /r-/ with d-initial verbs yields an interdental fricative [θ] written <jd>. Glottal stop is written with the raised comma (apostrophe) /'/. Unintelligible syllables are indicated with zero <0>. The palatal nasal which is phonologically predictable adjacent to the high-front vowel /i/ is written in the transcription line as in Spanish ñ. Geminate consonants and vowels are predictable from the minimal word constraint requiring two mora in monosyllables [(C)VV] and a durational stress timing that builds heavy-light trochees in disyllables [(C)VXCV], where X is filled from the specifications of the post-tonic C if that C is voiceless or sonorant, and with the tonic V if the post-tonic C is voiced. Doubled orthographic digraphs are represented with trigraphs (e.g., tx → ttx). This gemination is a semiotic index of the morphological nucleus of the phonological phrase and is written in the transcription line but not in the morpheme breakdown that represents phonemic structure. In morphological breakdown and glosses hashtag /#/ indicates word boundary in compounds (see Sicoli 2007 for a fuller description of Lachixío Zapotec stress, word, and syllable structure).

In conversational transcription (line 1 of transcription blocks),
colon indicates extended length of a segment,
square brackets co-index overlapping speech between lines,
raised circles °...° indicates quieter speech,
downward arrow ↓ is for lowered pitch,

upward arrow ↑ is for raised pitch,
percent signs %...% bracket speech that is whispered/voiceless,
number sign (hashtag) #...# is for breathy voice,
outward pointing brackets <...> is for slower speech, and
inward pointing brackets >...< is for faster speech.

Glossing Conventions occurring in examples are listed here. These generally follow Leipzig glossing rules with some simplification and innovation in pronouns.[1]

1S	first person singular
1PLI	first person plural inclusive
1PLX	first person plural exclusive
2S	second person singular
3ANIM	third person animal
3DIS	third person distal (also used for respect)
3INAN	third person inanimate
3F	third person feminine
3M	third person masculine
3O	third person inanimate
ACT3O	indefinite subject acting on object
ACT	active
CAUS	causative
CMP	completive
CLAS	classifier
COMP	comparative
DEF	definite
DIM	diminutive
EXCL	exclamative enclitic
HAB	habitual
IMP	imperative
IND	indefinite article
INT	interjection
K+AF	knowing affirmation enclitic
PL	plural
POS	possessive
POT	potential
PRO	pronoun root/base
Q	polar question enclitic
RECP	reciprocal
SEQ	sequential
SIM	simulative
STA	stative

1

Introduction

Andrea:	Too bad we didn't dig the ground—that we just made it like this.
Elvia:	Not like this?
Andrea:	I see that like this it's truly coming along badly.
Nazaria:	Think it will really stay up?
Andrea:	This may not stay up.
Elvia:	It will stay up.
Nazaria:	It will stay up?
Elvia:	It will stay up.

1.1 Language and Joint Actions in Lachixío

On the night of July 23, 2009, a coyote (*bichoò*) got into the turkey enclosure at the house of a family living on the flats near the southeast edge of the Zapotec village of Santa María Lachixío and killed a bird. The loss of the turkey was serious. Turkeys (*becchò*) are ritually valuable and form the iconic center of a system of gift exchange known in Oaxaca as *guelaguetza* and locally in Lachixío as *eeliettzá*. The turkeys are themselves the symbols of debts owed to other villagers, and the currency of loans that could be given to others as gifts. Determining that the turkey was killed because their enclosure was inadequate, the family gathered materials to build a new one. The transcription provided at the beginning of this chapter is a free translation of a few turns of dialogue that were woven into the family collaboration that produced, in the end, a new dwelling. The construction was recorded on video by my collaborator Pedro, whose family was the one affected by the loss. Their joint action built a complex artifact, one that itself emerged as the effects of constituent joint actions between participants who offered for and recruited from each other, and who built upon each other's semiotic productions to repair and resonate attention and interpretations.

Yet looking at this dialogue transcribed in this way, the reader is left to wonder about many things. Besides wondering what the Zapotec language formulations were since only an English translation is presented, the talk assumes many open links to the multiple modalities of the activity. What does "like this" refer to? Don't we need to see Andrea pointing to understand *the point* of her speech here? What evidence does Andrea "see" that looks like it is coming along badly? What are the three people doing in relation to each other and the developing corral structure so that their talk can be formulated the way it is? The joint actions of human life, where multiple parties share time, space, and purpose, occur in multimodal gatherings co-populated by talk, body movements, and actions with material artifacts that already exist, or that come into being along with the language of the interaction. Still, the vast majority of representations of language use and grammatical description only represent language in textual forms, as if the verbal dimension were a self-contained, self-explanatory system.

This book is about how joint actions that build worlds build languages. Examining the Lachixío Zapotec language in everyday use, it focuses theoretical attention on multimodal relationships emergent as people weave their talk and embodied actions to build social relations, displays of mutual understanding and contestation, and the material formations of their worlds. As Herb Clark (2006) has observed, language is often, though not exclusively, a vital element for both the conduct *and* the coordination of the joint actions achieved between people in interaction. The video-recorded collaboration from which the short transcript was extracted is examined in its multimodal order in Chapter 6. But in only the few turns of talk as presented here, we find several functions of language as social action that are examined in this book. Through the collaborative practices of interaction, ideas or actions are *offered* for others, *recruiting* responses that accept or reject, and *building* social relations in the joint action of the offer-response whole. Participants collaborate in *repair* sequences to build and fix the jointly constructed common ground of intersubjectivity, like Elvia's interjection *Not like this?*, and her statement, *It will stay up*, contradicting Andrea's assessment, *This may not stay up*, and answering Nazaria's confirmation request, *It will stay up?* A response is also *recruited* by Nazaria's question of whether others think the enclosure will stay up. We see further that the linguistic form of Nazaria's question is made of material that *resonates* with the form of Andrea and Elvia's prior utterances. The resonant moves of questioning, agreement, and disagreement are created in the accrual of form across interactional moves where the field of commonality built through repetition brings to focus the differences between them.

As the ends of their joint actions, aspects of their world were built: a physical structure on the landscape for turkeys to sleep at night, a limit to the world of the coyote, a "vault" for a family's ritual wealth, future security for the birds and the humans, the potential for future gift exchanges that would build social relationships between this family and other families in Lachixío, and the ongoing tuning of family relations through working together, negotiating plans, and resolving conflicts around their developing project. What was also built are numerous exemplars of the Lachixío Zapotec language connected to this emergent world. Joint activity like this is widely instructive of how the Lachixío Zapotec language lives through its sociality. When we revisit this event in Chapter 6, we will see that collaborations and conflicts were worked out through coordinated talk, gesture, and action with objects, and how those actions actually left their marks on the form of the material artifact produced. Different structural aspects of the enclosure represented different ideas, disagreements, attempts at persuasion, and resolutions all achieved in the family's multimodal interaction directed toward the ends of care for their turkeys.

The question of representation I engage is one that contrasts ways of knowing about a language and what such differences can mean for language documentation, description, linguistic and anthropological theory, and ethnographic methods. Lachixío Zapotec conversationalists often contrast the source of knowledge for their claims about the world as something that is "said" (*nii*), which can be opinion, hearsay, or received knowledge, and something that is "seen" (*ri'yya*) for empirical knowledge gained through sensory perception beyond received or produced words. In my own effort to work with the reader to produce knowledge of Lachixío Zapotec that is more holistically sensed rather than simply read as text, this work engages the language in its *doing* through collaborative joint actions in multimodal interactions. As a part of participatory actions that make worlds, the signs of a language are open to sensory modes of experience and semiotic dimensions for action with which they are interwoven. The pragmatic nexus in which we find languages shares qualities with what ecologists have called *assemblages* involving multispecies gatherings in often collaborative interactions. None of the species in an assemblage can be plucked out as an independent whole without the loss of our ability to understand its ontology in an interdependent world from which comes consequence and to which any species' life processes create consequence, not only for itself but for others as well. I attempt in this book to examine and depict the Lachixío Zapotec language as—like any language—an always incomplete part of multimodal and multi-participant assemblages in which its grammatical forms have been shaped through accrued usage. This involves bringing together methods of video analysis, grammatical analysis, and ethnography, depicting language beyond a text transcription to attend to its multimodal-multi-participant relations, and complementing readers' experiences with illustrations, figures and direct access to online video examples.

I started this chapter with a bit of talk transcribed without aspects of its speech environment to make the point that language, by its semiotic nature, is open to the multimodal assemblages through which it helps build worlds. We can also see this openness of language if we ask the reciprocal question of how the material world resulting from human joint activities presupposes talk that brought it into being. We can look at a material artifact, a relationship, or a social institution and ask what kind of talk was jointly produced along with its creation. How did the talk leave its marks on material objects? How does such activity itself leave marks on our languages in the shapes and functions of morphology and grammatical constructions? Focusing on the language of joint actions, I examine here how social, intersubjective, and material worlds are emergent from fundamental joint actions that offer, recruit, repair, resonate, and build in collaboration. Descriptions of language and our theories of language can benefit by explicit attention to the dialogic processes of multimodal attunement through which exemplars of language emerge in collaborative action. Through attunement processes, participants tie grammatical dimensions of language to other available semiotic dimensions like gaze, gestures, and actions with objects to pragmatic ends (see, for example, Kendon 1990a; Goodwin 2017). To understand language as part of a multimodal ecology, I take an approach that studies language through actual uses, and without privileging either the verbal or the nonverbal as analytical primaries, but rather attending to the spatiotemporal interfacing of multiple embodied dimensions of emplaced interactions (Duranti 1992). Further informed by subsequent work in multimodal interaction, my approach goes beyond the verbal-nonverbal distinction to examine resonance relationships built between modalities and participants made visible through a semiotic framework and methodologically potentiated through affordances of digital video for playback analysis. Building on my previous work on the multidimensionality of the "verbal" to create parallelisms and contrasts in configurations of words juxtaposed with their intonations and voice qualities (Sicoli 2007, 2010a; Sicoli 2015b), we hail the readers' attention to the built resonances between participants and modalities and the emergent harmonies and discords of their relations.

My project is also a response to recent calls for documenting "language in cultural life" (e.g., Himmelman 2008), and thus, though different in scope, broadly shares some goals with the ethnography of communication (Gumperz and Hymes 1964; Bauman and Sherzer 1974). It also responds to several recent calls of funding agencies including Documenting Endangered Languages (DEL) and the Endangered Languages Documentation Programme (ELDP). I work to show that approaching living language as it is bound up in matters of sociocultural life is fundamentally consequential for how we represent and build theories about language, and understand how it is reproduced and transformed through the accumulated uses of interaction. To do so I turned to participatory research methods to build and analyze a fifty-hour video corpus of everyday life events in Lachixío ranging from cooking and eating together to daily chores, agricultural team work, craft making, and construction projects. With this move this project also works toward reciprocal goals both bringing ethnography to bear on language documentation and grounding ethnography through multimodal analysis of the talk and embodied actions through which people make sense of, and at the same time build, a world of meaningful action with others. My goal in developing this multimodal ethnography of language in joint actions is to demonstrate some ways to interpret complexity in social interactions that can aid linguistic scholarship and the project of interpretive anthropology, bringing them together in ways that reveal and inform overlapping concerns of linguists and anthropologists, especially at a time when the turn to multimodality is affecting both disciplines.

Modern linguistics largely came to limit itself to aspects of language more easily writable in alphabetic systems, inheriting the legacy of philology and its object of "texts." It was only toward the end of the twentieth century that sign languages began to be attended to as full languages and that voice qualities and intonation gained the sustained attention of linguists. In anthropology, traditional print formats for ethnographies have effected a similar reduction. Books and articles expect the written word and privilege representations of human action that can easily be spelled out in the single dimension of a text line—a technologically mediated habit of representation critiqued in the contemporary turn to multimodal anthropology (Collins, Durington, and Gill 2017). While the turn by this name is relatively recent and amplified by the use of new media, the critique of monodimensional linguistic science has emerged several times before. Edward Sapir as early as 1937 pointed to the importance of multidimensional interaction in the creation of culture. Even so, the details of the *interpersonal relations adjusted to by individuals in interactional encounters* that he suggested be "the problem of the future" (Sapir 2002: 12) are still easily lost between field research and its disseminated products.

There have been many technological barriers to studying copresent interactions. The potential of sound film technology for studying gesture and embodied practice was pointed to as early as the 1930s by Malinowski (1935: 26), yet film has had limited uptake for examining interaction being both heavy and expensive to use in the field. And early pioneers of the use of film in the *Natural History* approach to interaction like Bateson and Birdwhistell found their analytical results and alternative formats of data presentation difficult to publish and critiqued as a hyper-structuralism (Lempert 2012). The development of analog video also posed challenges to multimodal analysis by giving up the affordances of the sequenced still frames of sound film that afforded focus on the alignment of visible action, visible touch, and audible action through pausing, slowing, and rocking back and forth the medium. Such actions with analog video rather turned the patterned visual information into the noise of "snow" that some readers will remember from VHS and Beta devices of the 1970s and 1980s. Most discourse analysts through the analog video period based their analyses on interactions reduced to audio recordings (Erickson 2004b), though there were important exceptions—for example, C. Goodwin 1980 and M. Goodwin 1980, Erickson 1982, Duranti 1992, Ochs 1982, Haviland 1993, among some others.

Decisions to still so often represent embodied interactions as audio-only are partly the result of technological challenges, but are also based in ideologies of language as mono-modal and autonomously carried in the oral-auditory channel, which itself was supported in technologies of communication from writing to telephones and radios. For many field researchers, audio-only recording and content-based text transcription continue to be standard representations of copresence even as digital video inscription has become cheap and lightweight, and in many cases in ubiquitous use among research subjects themselves (Sicoli, 2021). This continued reduction appears to be an effect of institutional habit. In language description, for example, the Boasian trilogy of the grammar, dictionary, and text collection is still an iconic goal among many twenty-first-century documentary linguists, even though the published form of the Boasian "texts" represented mostly monologues dictated to linguists phrase by phrase so they could be transcribed in the field in the absence of recorders. Furthermore, texts commonly came to be represented as decontextualized stories with prose formatting that mimicked European folktale collections bound as separate chapters in volumes (see Hymes 1981 for critique). We should ask why today, when it is relatively easy to build a record of a language living through multi-participant and multimodal means, and when participatory research methodologies make it possible for research subjects to build such a record themselves as autoethnographic, that we only target "texts" inscribed through technology that erases most of the living ecology of the speech event—how and why the speech emerged as part of joint actions in multimodal interaction, why it mattered, and how that matter relates to their linguistic forms. By engaging Lachixío Zapotec through a focus on joint actions in multimodal, multi-participant interactions, this work aims to represent an order of language that is unrecoverable through the words and rules of language descriptions that level the representation of living and dead languages to the same form but rather of a Zapotec language living with and through the people of Lachixío in the early twenty-first century.

By adopting this approach, I do not aim to discredit forms of linguistic documentation using the elicitation of words and targeting grammatical contrasts through interviews and experimentation. I use such methods myself as part of a set of methodologies important for linguistic fieldwork, particularly important for survey and laying a ground for more engaged and participatory research. Working with a "last speaker" or "rememberer" may, in fact, be limited to such methods and is valuable. What I find to be ideologically tainted and imperative to move beyond is the institutional habit of documenting a living language in the philological way we have come to know dead languages of history: words, rules, and texts.[1] Where speakers are conversationally competent and getting things done in their world *together* with their language(s), limiting documentary work to eliciting words and phrases and "getting some texts" from a speaker should be recognized as a strange sort of language game we impose, and one which retains the form of colonial projects of a past anthropology and linguistics. We cannot assume grammatical patterns that emerge in such a game to unproblematically transport across the many social scales and practical ends of language use. Early in my career (1998 on the Project for the Documentation of the Languages of Meso-America in Catemaco, Mexico) I had the opportunity to record narratives with single speakers talking to microphones and with two speakers—a father and a son—with one narrating for the other. The differences I discovered were robust and resonate through this current work. They involved speaker fluency and moral responsibility to their listener demonstrated in instances of reference repair (Chapter 4) that would go unchallenged in a monologic setting, and the collaboration of resonance building (Chapter 5) that displayed speaker knowledge of their language and the coproduction and tracking of the common ground needed to interpret the narrative. It mattered greatly that a speaker was responsible to a competent listener for everything they offered (Chapter 2) and that the active listener could at any moment become speaker offering something to the developing joint project and recruiting attention, interpretation, and further action from another speaker (Chapter 3). I started to think about more dialogic field methods in an unpublished paper "On the Importance of an Addressee." The importance of multi-participant and material coproduction continues to influence my thinking about how interaction is an order of purposive joint activity where languages are shaped and reproduced that is not accessible for study in monologic materials and methods focusing on the knowledge of single speakers. While my project shares some goals of a grammar and text collection, the order of language represented is bound up with the purposes of actual interactions that mattered in the lives of participants building with each other from the affordances of multimodal engagements.

For researchers who have started using video in fieldwork for language documentation and multimodal ethnography, analytical frameworks of individual competence are not theoretically equipped to deal with the *semiotic carrying capacity* of the multidimensional and multi-participant (often more than dyadic) interactions that they find. Philosophers of language developed semantic theory on mostly propositional sentences in isolation, and pragmatics on always-dyadic made-up dialogues. I speak to a wide range of researchers of language and culture with this work in which I demonstrate some practical methods to address multimodal complexity in a video corpus. In doing so, I open language theory to the work of social relations undertaken in the practical encounters of day-to-day life, the work of building mutual understanding among dialogic participants, and the building of worlds including enduring objects, and the cognitive habits of grammatical, lexical, and discursive formations that emerge in multimodal interaction and perdure through future uses.

This project then is a multimodal ethnography of the arts and resources taken up and shaped through the doing together of language as part of social life. These arts and resources both involve language and are beyond language. Joint actions involve joint commitments to some interactive project between people, their public signs, and the objects they engage with together. Such meaningful configurations of different types of signs, brought into relationships for purposes, require that we think beyond metaphors of text and context that have become pervasive in linguistics and more broadly across the humanities and social sciences, where context is somehow an addition around language, or preexists it as something to which language can be added (or taken away for separate analysis). Rather I want to think about how in embodied interactions that emerge over time and across multiple modalities talk, gestures, and actions with objects are what C. Goodwin (2017, 2011) describes as "mutually elaborating." Signs are arranged as meaningful relationships in which simultaneous and sequenced actions are brought to bear on each other. These relations are not the product of a single person but intimate engagements between participants that can be human or nonhuman, animate or inanimate. Multimodal fields of action require from us theory and methods that can bring multiple species of meaningful actions (e.g., talk, techniques of body movement, and the technology of material culture) into a single framework: one that is flexible enough to handle the shifting dimensionalities and contradictions of copresence, where talk may be temporally co-performed with gesture one moment, substitute for it in another, and be replaced by some bodily action or a meaningfully constituted object in the next. To do so I turn to the processual and dialogic view of meaning encapsulated in the *semiosis* of Charles Sanders Peirce and to a discussion of complex living assemblages emergent across scales of time, modalities, and resonances of joint actions.

1.2 From Context to Living Assemblages

The metaphor I want to think with is inspired, in part, by Anna Tsing's (2015) use of "polyphonic assemblages" to think about interspecies ecologies that connect different types of agents into "enabling entanglements" that collaboratively build emergent worlds. An "assemblage" is the term biologists have turned to in complicating a concept of ecology beyond simplified models of nature as driven by "competition" and "selection," and those of species and individuals as essentially complete entities. It has been found more explanatory to rather think of how, in complex living systems, the action of life forms "facilitate" (Bulleri, Bruno and Benedetti-Cecchi 2008) the life processes of other life forms through "niche construction," creating dynamic feedbacks that connect organisms and things into meaningful relations to which they are *open* and without which they are *incomplete*.

In philosophy a concept of assemblage as an arrangement or layout of heterogenous elements is developed by Deleuze and Guattari 1987 as the organizing logic of their work *A Thousand Plateaus* (Nail 2017). Assemblages are not to be seen as closed functional systems, in the way organisms (and languages) have been thought of, but as the mechanism of events gathering elements into relationships. Connections among difference produce the possibility of what any element can be and become in an emergent assemblage. The appeal to biology is in part to communicate that species in multispecies assemblages are constituted in the relationships *between them* rather than as their own essential unity. Multispecies assemblages share emergent properties with the multimodal-multi-participant assemblages of the joint actions of human interaction. Tsing's term "polyphonic" resonates with terms I have coined in my previous work to characterize relations between dimensions of communication where multiple information channels inform each other in relations that are "harmonic" or "discordant" with each other (Sicoli 2007, 2013).

Assemblages and their concrete elements are not approachable with ontological questions of essence (what-questions), but rather in the how, where, and when of the step-by-step processes of relating that afford what elements become capable of doing in the now of their arrangement (Nail 2017). The ongoing renewing and transformation of assemblages requires analytical attention to temporal and multimodal dimensions of their arrangement and the resonances that emerge between their parts.

1.3 Time

Social actions are tied into many scales of time and causality. We may consider an action's *phylogeny* as developed over the time-course of evolution, or its *ontogeny* as developed within an individual's lifetime and related to the scale of their biography. In *Talk and Social Theory*, Erickson's (2004a: 6–7) discussion of time as quantitative *kronos* and qualitative *kairos* cuts across these scales of time and causality. We can represent time as *kronos*, the continuous and measurable succession of time. But we can also think about time as *kairos*, a discontinuous quality of time as a moment for the doing of something. *Kairos* is a temporal dimension of being at some particular moment in time that makes it propitious for some action—time as experienced (time to eat, time to play, time to sleep, time to work, time to answer a question, accept an offer, decline an invitation, time to wait, etc.) and as types of events (a meeting, a lecture, a service encounter, a hunt, a traffic stop, a wedding ritual, construction task, dinner, petition, etc.). Kairotic time and kairotic space weave together an institutional scale of action that social theorist Anthony Giddens (1984) called timespaces, following the work of Time Geographers as represented in the work of Hägerstrand (1970). Giddens draws additionally on Erving Goffman's *Interaction Order* of "encounters" to attune to the certainty that institutions are reproduced through such timespaces by inter-agentive processes of *structuration*, and that such moments positioned in iterated process open the possibility for social change. His conception for a dynamical relation between structure and practice in interaction parallels in several ways Sapir's conception of the relationship between individuals and cultural patterns fifty years earlier, though only published posthumously (Sapir 2002). There are scalar relations between an "interaction order" and perdurant social institutions like languages, identity formations, and systems of social inequality like rank, class, and gender.

However, it is not exactly clear in Giddens's work how the causal processes at one scale can affect those at another, as it was difficult to see when Goffman first introduced the "Interaction Order" in his 1982 presidential address to the American Sociological Association (Lempert 2012). While we may look out from an encounter within a *kairotic* timespace and see institutional structuring of interactions laid out for us in ways that constrain and enable action, it is difficult to see how the action of separate individuals can qualitatively change an institution. This is also a problem with Bourdieu's accounting of *habitus* (1972, 1980). While Bourdieu shows well, for example, that a working-class habitus may be misfit to standard language norms of educational routines, his accounts omit the details of how, for example, children's interactions in particular classroom settings afford or inhibit their learning (however, see Heath 1983 and Erickson 2004a, among others). One thing that is missing from Giddens and Bourdieu is how the kairotic moments of particular settings are built up from lower-order kairotic moments of joint action in which multiple scales and dimensions of time are implicated. The temporal scalar relationship is what Favareau (2008: 187) described as grounded in the "immediate next" combing Bateson's concern with cybernetically auto-adaptive systems (1972), Sack's concern with public activity in the joint building of information and meaning (Sacks 1972), and C. Goodwin's work on distributed cognition (e.g., Goodwin 2011). Expected and relevant moves link individual social action through the "contingent responsivity" of turn-taking and into a collaborative emergent system symbiotically creating "the very structures upon which subsequent interaction may be created and contained in a real-time unfolding 'ecology of mind'" (Favareau 2008: 179). Turns are built that respond to prior action and are themselves prior action and material for next turns (Sacks, Schegloff, and Jefferson 1974). Each move provides participants with a test of fit, and a place to make adjustments to fit as part of an emergent ecology it also helps to build (Schegloff 2006). The reference to Bateson's "ecology of mind" (1972, 2002) indexes a shift in studies of cognition from conceiving of mind as an individual's computation to mind as biosemiotic relationships between actors and environment—an ontology that is emergent with the whole of the ecology rather than a prior property of its component parts. Where mind is theorized as the computational property located in an individual, the social and material worlds beyond individuals are unreachable across the Cartesian void between an inside mind and outside world. But where mind is conceived of as relationally semiotic in part-whole relations of living assemblages built up through linked actions across multiple entities, we can develop a framework in which the joint actions of individuals in collaborations scale up to the social institutions we inherit and can reproduce, repair, disrupt, and change.

Multiple dimensions of time are important for language and interaction though not all of these have phenomenological experience outside of scholarly discourse. A contrast between *diachrony* (change over time) and *synchrony* (an atemporal state of relations) has organized research into language structure and language change since Saussure (1986). Synchrony represents an ideal abstraction useful for structural analysis but the actual production, perception, and interpretation of a sentence takes place in a timescale that has been referred to as the microgenetic (Enfield 2013). Even the reading of a syntactic tree that diagrams a synchronic hierarchy of relations takes place in time and depends on a history of literacy and dominant cultural metaphors where time progression is inscribed left to right and top to bottom. Diachrony as the analytical difference between two synchronic states of a language at one time and another is a difference between abstractions but again without phenomenology or ontology outside of academic discourse, though in human experience, a sense of diachronic difference can be gained from interacting with past representations and from mapping language form and function across the age-grades of living experience. The term "diachronic" is morphologically composed of *dia-* "through, across" and the *kronos* of time succession capturing well the goal of some historical linguistic projects examining language change across time. In this project though, I am rather interested in the being of language *in time* as kairotic encounters where collaborative actions are built from multimodal materials made available in local historical process, and where complex living assemblages scaffold possibilities of intersubjectivity.

While synchrony and diachrony are analytical abstractions rather than language experience, these analytical frames are projected from the timescales experienced in human practice. Already mentioned is the *kairos* of timespace geography involving the habitualized repetitive practices of everyday life where we inhabit moments for the doing of expected action. Another timescale is what Enfield (2013) has referred to as *enchrony* in his book *Relationship Thinking* and which itself resonates with the biosemiotic account I drew from Favareau earlier. Enfield defines enchrony as a causal/temporal frame of "sequences of interlocking or interdependent communicative moves that are taken to be co-relevant" (2013: 29). An enchronic frame has both prospective and retrospective dimensions pivoting on the relationship between two interactional moves. Each move in an interaction shows two faces of relevance. Embodied as a sign, a move is evaluated for its "effectiveness," to give rise to a next move that in relation to the previous move may be evaluated for its "appropriateness" (2013: 32). As a temporal domain for the evaluation of a *fittedness* between interactional moves, enchrony is also a domain of moral accountability to the specific participants of an interaction. Thus analysis at this scale of language in interaction is also a site of everyday ethics.

Enfield describes the enchronic as a distinct causal frame for a particular granularity of analysis (local bidirectional causation of moves) among other causal/analytical frames (phylogenetic, ontogenetic, microgenetic). He suggests that enchrony is the scale we should privilege as the "primary locus of social action," the "central causal-conditional locus for the learning of language" and of "selectional processes" at work in maintaining conventions and producing language change. To his exposition I add two trans-scalar dimensions: the first is the importance of timespace geography (the fact that one event can be interpreted as an icon of another), and the second being the emergence of an institutional scale. A primary task for theory is not only to characterize the level of causality represented at some scale on which we focus our analytical lens but of how action at one scale affects another. Where such cross-scale directionality has been imagined in social theory, as in Foucault's (1972) *Discourse*, or Fairclough's (1995, 1989) *Critical Discourse Analysis*, the general illustration is how power from institutions can pervade interactions through its representatives in a top-down way (see Erickson 2004a for critique). But to understand the creation of new institutions, social change, and linguistic reproduction and change, we must also be able to relate the local issue of the moral relevance of coupled actions at an enchronic scale to their effects on the perdurant scale of sociocultural institutions, which are reproduced through social actions. Actions across enchronic frames scale up through recurrent timespaces to create and transform social institutions embodied in languages, identity formations, and social relations.

What Enfield calls the "experience near" level of enchrony connects through timespace geographies to institutions because they are inhabited by subjectivities whose goals in interaction may represent relationships to sociocultural institutions to various degrees of mimesis or contestation. But part of the complexity of social life is that our goals may be multiple, conflicted, and nonconscious. The focus on turn-taking as a model of enchrony in action does not by itself capture two other dimensions of copresent interaction. One is a quality of Erickson's (2004a) backward and forward pointing "now" moment of copresent interactions that affords communicative behaviors such as simultaneous listenership feedback and the "interactive construction of the utterance" (Goodwin 1979). During the microgenetic timescale of listener feedback a speaker may adjust her ongoing utterance to the other speaker's signs of recognition. The other is that time affords the emergence of resonances of and by both sequential and simultaneous arrangements—resonances that connect modalities, participants, and actions into harmonies and discords.

1.4 Multimodality

Multimodal interaction involves social actions achieved through the combination of multiple sensory modalities. These often integrate the audible and visual but may also include the tactile (haptic and proprioceptive) (M. Goodwin 2017; M. Goodwin and Cekaite 2018), olfactory (Majid et al. 2018), and as pointed to by Edward T. Hall (1959, 1990), thermo-reception, the sensing of body heat in near contact. Video analysis of multimodal interaction can make available to analysts the audible, visible, and visibly tactile. Configurations involving two modalities may be thought of as crossmodal (Lempert 2012), though meaningful configurations are more broadly multimodal, involving the temporal intersection of several modalities across multiple information channels, and potentially achieved through the nesting of modalities "within" channels because certain senses themselves afford a simultaneous layering of communicative signals that inform each other. Such nestings allow audio configurations in which prosody is co-performed with lexical-syntactic structure, and visual configurations that unite hand shapes, movements, and facial gestures into the utterances of a sign language. Temporal relations of simultaneity, like these, and sequencing are both important affordances of timespace that can be appropriated for building complex multimodal signs in interaction. Multimodal interaction thus requires accounts of language beyond considering speech as text occurring within some context. Speech can in fact be a context for some other action. Scholars noting this limitation have turned to co-text (Agha 2007) capturing an idea of appearing together and correlation, and beyond this to ideas of distributed cognition and mutual elaboration (C. Goodwin 2000). The basic observation is one of "dimensionality" in meaning systems broadly pointed to some years ago by Charles Hockett (1987) where the sequencing and prosodic layering of speech have greater dimensionality than the linearity of writing, and the visual affordances of sign language have greater dimensionality than oral-auditory speech. In the perspective I take in this book, the intercorporeal scene of encounter is one where a *semiotic carrying capacity* (Sicoli 2013) emerges from the degrees of freedom presented by diverse modalities which people have variable access to, and power to appropriate and use relevantly within the flow of interaction. To represent language in the reduced linear form of its orality where the encounter was, for participants, actually characterized by perceptual access to each other's bodies and actions with objects is to be guilty of a creative erasure that distorts its form. This recognition raises moral questions for fieldworkers and analysts. Social actors interpret and formulate sign configurations appropriating whatever dimensionalities they can control as an actor with a contingent ability to effect the world through assemblages where agency itself is distributed among the human and nonhuman participants gathered together. In this way social actors are like Lévi-Strauss's *bricoleur* whose game is "always to make do with 'whatever is at hand'" (1966: 17).

In analyzing multimodal interaction I build on premises summarized in Duranti (1992: 660) following the work of Birdwhistell (1970), Goffman (1971c), Kendon (2009b) among others of the Natural History of the Interview project (McQuown 1971) and developed by linguistic anthropologists and other contemporary scholars concerned with multimodal interaction:

1. Any study of interactional routines such as greetings should start from actual uses of speech-in-interaction rather than from ideal linguistic structures or linguistic taxonomies.
2. If we want to understand the respective roles played by verbal and nonverbal channels, we should not hold preconceived notions about the primacy of one code over another; we should instead carefully examine the sequential as well as interlocking properties of their interfacing.
3. Communicative acts should always be located in the social space that those acts utilize and help reconstitute along culture-specific distinctions. (Duranti 1992: 660)

There are multiple ways talk and action can elaborate each other. Consider Figure 1.1 which depicts a mother's embodied request for her daughter to fill a pitcher of water (discussed in Chapter 3). A social action like this request can be achieved by only

```
Mother:      Would you get me another pitcher of water?

Daughter:    OK.
```

Figure 1.1 Visible, audible, and multimodal request formations.

visible means (just the action represented in the line drawing of the mother presenting an empty pitcher to be filled). Or it can be achieved through talk, like the exchange, "*Mother*: Would you get me another pitcher of water? *Daughter*: OK." By gesture alone, or talk alone, we would have a paradigmatic relationship. Each is a potential substitute for the other. Gesture and talk may also be in a syntagmatic relationship where the gesture precedes or succeeds the talk.

Beyond substitution and sequence, the saying and doing can be simultaneous in a multimodal configuration (i.e., Enfield's "composite utterance" 2009). In the image in Figure 1.2, a woman's passing of a bowl is co-temporal with her verbal acceptance of the other woman's prior offer to rinse the dishes. Throughout the multimodal transcripts of the book, I have worked to capture both co-temporal and sequential relations by aligning utterances and brief action descriptions complemented in some cases with photos or line drawings. My multimodal transcriptions occur in blocks like in Figure 1.2 with all of the transcribed text in fixed width font to allow for interlinear alignments. These alignments often involve the actions of multiple speakers within a single line; thus, it is important to note that the block does not necessarily indicate the turn of a single speaker or one individual's composite utterance, but rather it tries to represent the development of an assemblage over a stretch of interactional time. The first line of the block is in a practical orthography in bold text that additionally represents semiotically relevant speech features in this publication format. For example, upward arrows bracket the phrase to mark the respectful falsetto voice register of Lachixío (Sicoli 2007, 2010a). This line also represents conversational

```
22 Lidia:  ↑nyàá tze'e ínza é txee Máarì↑
           -|L passes bowl to M
           nyàá      tze'e=inza=é       txe     mari-L
           good      dip=water=3o       then    Mary-CLAS
           ↑Fine rinse it then Mary↑.

23 Mary:   ↑Áwwà Lídyà↑
           ↑yes Lydia↑.
```

Figure 1.2 Passing the bowl co-temporal with acceptance of offer to rinse dishes.

features of overlap, emphatic lengthening, rate of speech, hesitation, and self-repair. Below this is the line of action description (sometimes several lines) indicating which actor is performing an action in relation to whom or what, with the pipe symbol <|> indexing, when relevant, the onset of the action with respect to a constituent in the line above. The bottom line is what is called a "free translation" in bold italics. For me this is a "radical translation" (cf. Quine 1960; Becker 1995; Mannheim 2015) using what I know about Zapotec and English to produce an appropriate *feeling* translation for the reader, but one that does not attempt to level or erase the Zapotec discourse patterning under English norms. Between the visible action and the translation are two lines representing the morphological concatenations and their glosses for a literal representation of the lexical-syntactic structure. These lines are in 50 percent text density in gray to allow the reader to scan over them to the focus on the talk, visible action, and free translations tiers, but to also have proximal immediate access to the morpheme-by-morpheme grammatical representation without the visual overload that would result from unvaried text in such block arrangements. Analysis and argumentation in my prose refer to each of these dimensions of representation. At the same time I have assembled the transcribed examples so they will be read as part of the ongoing argument and narrative of the book, as complement rather than supplement.

The participation frame of the request in Figure 1.2 may be considered dyadic (between two participants), even though the kitchen was inhabited by another woman and two men. Dimensions of complexity are of course multiplied when we move beyond dyadic conversation to multiparty conversation as we will do in much of the

Figure 1.3 Turkey Corral.

book. Many of the examples in the chapters are multi-participant such as Figure 1.3 (Chapter 6) and Figure 1.4 (Chapter 2).

1.5 Resonance

Resonance in human interaction both connects and juxtaposes parallel interactional moves (dialogic resonance), and builds relations between talk, gestures, and actions with objects (intermodal resonance). Dialogic, intermodal, and interpersonal resonances are important to understanding both the shape utterances take in dialogic practice and the way talk, gestures, and actions with objects of a multimodal world come to bear on each other in semiotic assemblages. This project builds on a history of work in linguistic anthropology that has demonstrated the importance of contextualization as both producing of and produced in linguistic action (Duranti and Goodwin 1992), and is part of a dialogue with the recent work of Goodwin (2017) on *co-operative action* and Du Bois (2014) on *dialogic syntax*, which all together heralds a paradigm shift for studying the perdurant forms and practices of language as jointly produced in an order of interindividual action beyond the isolated sentence. Resonance draws analytical attention to a simple but pervasive logic through which people jointly build meaning by coupling sentences, utterances, or actions so that component parts will resonate. In this way prior action can be linked from current action, building a field of similarity for the interpretation of difference. The logic of resonance is characterized by what anthropologist Roy Wagner (2017, 2019) has called the "double-proportional

Figure 1.4 Picnic in the milpa.

comparison"—a figure ground reversal where two things are compared twice. First the resonating parts are brought together for a mind through their similarity, and then again for their difference. The double comparison that characterizes the logic of resonance is also operational in the way words, intonations, gestures, and tool use are coalesced into assemblages and interpreted through relations made legible by their arrangements in the goal directed activities of interaction.

My approach to the logic of resonance developed from attention to the pervasive dialogic repetition of Zapotec discourse observed during fieldwork in Oaxaca, Mexico, my readings of the semiotic process in the philosophy of Charles Peirce, and neo-Peircean insights on how the semiotic process is made visible through conversational practice (Kockelman 2007; Enfield 2013; Favareau 2015), and built upon foundations laid in work of Roman Jakobson on parallelism, Dell Hymes's verse structure, and John Du Bois's (2014) framework of *Dialogic Syntax*, which examines the resonances people build across spoken utterances. I say more about these intellectual histories in Chapter 5.

Resonance in physics describes parallel activation of form qualities in a synchronous vibration of copresent objects. Resonance can be found in the ringing quality of a bell where standing waves of energy are co-activated in alignment, and in how the quality of one bell's ringing can activate (or animate) another nearby. Resonance like this can be passive, but for humans the building of resonances can be a moral imperative to the ends of social and intersubjective connection. To resonate is to build signs that connect to and evoke the other through a parallelism of form that displays the common experience under development in the saying and doing of conversation as joint activity.

Elements of multimodal assemblages elaborate each other through resonances that I describe as *harmonic*, and which may thus amplify sign function, or *discordant*, to produce conflicted meanings, or an emergent meaning beyond the components. To reject in words an offer for a drink while holding an empty cup is intermodally discordant and this is particularly important for understanding the formulation and transformation of joint action sequences of offer-response in Lachixío. Multiple examples from the video corpus show that such a discordant response will prompt additional offers. The discordant move to close the offer sequence may be redone by re-assembling the semiotic modes to show the concordance of intermodal harmony, where people tie the verbal rejection of an offer to drink more with a clear visible action of putting down the cup that stops the iteration of offer-response sequences. But discordance can also creatively mobilize contradictory meanings. One can, for example, verbally reject an offer or request while simultaneously moving the body to fulfill it. And beyond this, resonance is important to shaping language as developed in the time flow of interaction. A part or whole of a prior participant's interactional move can be iterated by a subsequent participant as the ground upon which new action figures.

Scholars of various disciplines have come to use the term "resonance" (generally having a meaning of parallel activation) to several ends, so it is important that I relate my own usage to this field. Ethnographers have thought about resonance as a goal of engagement between research subjects, writers, and readers. Leon Anderson (2006: 377) wrote of the ethnographic goal to produce an emotional resonance where "evocative autoethnographers have argued that narrative fidelity to and compelling description of subjective emotional experiences create an emotional resonance with the reader that is the key goal of their scholarship." Anderson's emotional resonance parallels a general goal of this book, wherein, through my incorporation of extended sequences of Lachixío interaction, I hope the reader develops some degree of what Webster (2015) calls a felt iconicity with the Zapotec language in Lachixío social life— what speakers have referred to as the language's *tono*, its tone or spirit (Sicoli 2007). And it is my hope that as the language changes, or if it falls out of use, descendants of the community can recover something of the language's *tono* that could never be captured in a dictionary or grammar undertaken without attention to the resonances of copresent life.[2]

Many scholarly uses of *resonance* share a desire to work with a dimension of human action that functions at multiple scales of time. Scales that relate to, for example, the rhythms of meter in speech, the enchronic adjacency relations wherein repetitions and reformulations become conversational repairs, and joint commitments, and over longer timescales the dialogic parallelism of phrases and ideas known as intertextuality (Kristeva 1980; Tannen 1989). Resonance may also work toward understanding the simply difficult to describe connection we might feel, or try to feel, with another being (human or nonhuman). *Resonance* in all these ways is about building connections in the production of an emergent order whose ontology is intersubjective. For the anthropologist Unni Wikan, "Resonance has to do with empathy and understanding, with what fosters comprehension across clefts and boundaries, with enhancing the relevance of matters seemingly out of touch or reach" (2012: 8).

Literary critics and philosophers have used resonance to metaphorically talk about the way one writer activates the idea of another. The history of science is filled with examples of philosophers who, in responding to the same literary interlocutors, produce responses with recognizable parallels sometimes thought of as independent innovations but which, informed in a historical semiotics, can be seen as built in relation to and thus projected off common prior artifacts of their attention. An example is seen in how Max Fisch (1986) described a resonance between the *Pragmaticism* of Charles Peirce and the *New Science* (and earlier writings) of Giambattista Vico 150 years earlier (Vico 1984 [1744]) (two philosophers important to the project of this book for this very resonance). Though in his extensive writings Peirce does not refer to Vico, and may likely not have read Vico, by Peirce's time, Vico's philosophy had pervaded and influenced much of the European and American philosophical atmosphere. Beyond this they were both formulating responses to Descartes's Cartesian science, and thus thinking with some of the same prior discourse artifacts. Peirce's *pragmaticism*, a holism in which the truth or knowledge of something is grounded in its practical effects and consequences, and Vico's *verum factum*, that "the true is the made," were both critiques of Cartesian thinking influential since Descartes who was contemporary to Vico's world and legacy to Peirce's. The legacy of Cartesian philosophy still underlies the arbitrary focus of grammatical analysis on monologic sentences, because sentences can display an internal logic, and the insipid limiting of the study of mind as if an organ residing in the brain of an individual (aka the mind-brain). As we will see in our examination of conversational repair (Chapter 4), many and often all words from one turn find their logical relation not within a sentence, but in dialogic relations that connect participants into coordinated actions (a coactiviation). These actions can happen at the same time or be sequenced relative to each other, and associated utterances are sometimes smaller than and sometimes larger than a sentence. We will also see how content question words, for example, frequently occur alone and link to constituents of other individuals' talk and action. The study of such interpersonal grammatical relations must insist upon ways to talk about the emergent intersubjectivities that are not born in the Cartesian episteme.

Dialogic Syntax examines the resonances people build across utterances, and has principally been applied to spoken discourse. *Frame resonances* are built through repeating the form of prior speech and *focal resonance* contrasts items across frames (Du Bois 2014). These often work together as focal resonance contrasts items in a frame made salient for comparison through its own parallel construction. I develop a wider understanding of the logic of resonance that builds connection not only across utterances and participants but also between modalities, and for which a basic understanding of the semiotic process called *semiosis* is necessary in ways that go beyond the commonplace adoption of Peirce's semiotic categories of icon, index, symbol (see Sicoli 2014 for critique) to the more holistic phenomenology of the life of signs characterized in Peirce's philosophy.

1.6 Semiosis

Semiosis is a process of interpretation in which a sign gets taken by some form of life to represent an object. I start with a broad definition of semiosis beyond its human characterization because, while semiosis attains emergent qualities for humans that result in language and joint action, semiosis is arguably as old as life, coterminous with the life-non-life division of the natural world (Hoffmeyer 1996; Deacon 2013). All life represents its world. Peirce argued that signs themselves are even alive (like a seed) because they can grow and reproduce through interpretive (semiotic) process. With particular reference to the symbol, Peirce wrote: "Every symbol is a living thing, in a very strict sense that is no mere figure of speech. The body of the symbol changes slowly, but its meaning inevitably grows, incorporates new elements and throws off old ones" (CP 2.222). Signs represent by coming to be interpreted by a subsequent sign in a semiotic chain of process. Signs can lie in wait to be noticed (like correlations of scientific fact, written inscriptions, archaeological artifacts, or temporal-spatial relationships in video inscriptions), or they can involve sudden change, as when a tree falls in the forest. In the ethnography *How Forests Think*, Eduardo Kohn (2013: 33) gives such an example of a hunter felling a tree near a monkey to startle it from its perch. I'll take Kohn's ethnographic example as a starting point but quickly appropriate it for my own purpose here (illustrating itself the capability for change that signs achieve through iteration and variation).

For the monkey, some happening is taken to be a sign of something. The falling tree was for the monkey (in the least) a sign of an action, or object, to move away from. Moving away is the monkey's interpretation of the sign. In the vocabulary of semiosis, this would be called an *interpretant* as it is a subsequent sign projected from and oriented to the sign-object of the falling tree. Specifically it would be an energetic interpretant (which contrasts with affective interpretants like an emotion of fear, or representational interpretants which could be an episodic memory or, for humans, a proposition about a sign-object relation) (Kockelman 2007). Beyond this semiosis is talked about as occurring in chain sequences (although *nets* or *webs of signification* may in fact be a better metaphor especially where multiple agents perceive publicly accessible signs from their different relational points of connection to an assemblage). In this interspecies semiotic chain, the falling tree was once an idea to a hunter, where in the kairotic timespace of hunting he encountered the treed-monkey and thought of a solution to his pragmatic goal of hunting it. Perhaps he learned this trick when hunting with his father as a child, in which case he would be creating an icon of an earlier event in episodic memory (just as the kairos of doing hunting today is interpreted in its iconic resonance to earlier hunting episodes experienced empirically or through the hearsay of narrative). The falling tree was an energetic interpretant of his idea (afforded by the object's form, relations to surrounding forms, and relation to gravity) before it was interpreted again by the monkey's moving away. The monkey's moving itself became a new sign in the sights of the hunter for subsequent action.

The basic semiotic process has been represented as in Figure 1.5. The arrow from left to right indicates causal/temporal direction. Semiosis involves a sensing agent for whom a sensory relationship to an environment affords the perception of a sign.

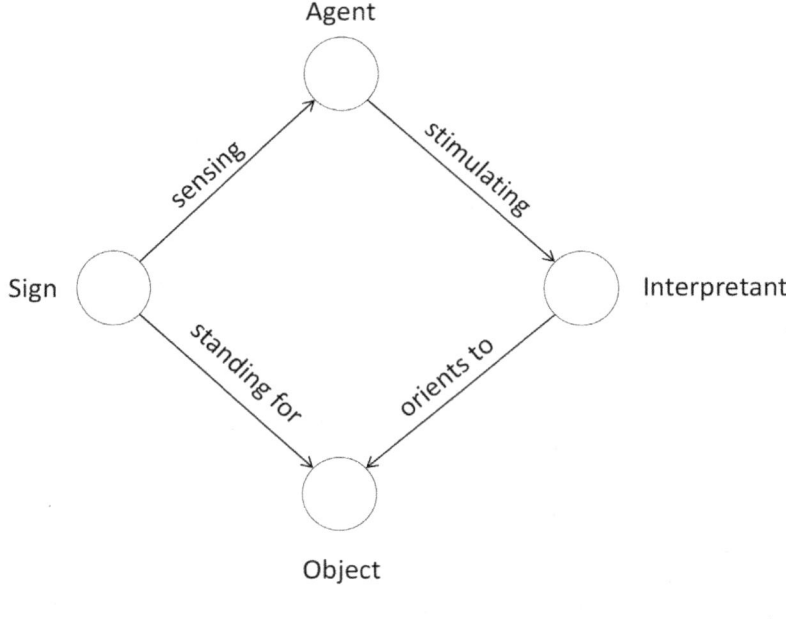

Figure 1.5 Basic semiotic process (after Enfield [2013] and Kockelman [2011, 2013]).

The agent takes the sign to stand for an object if it produces an interpretant that also orients to the same object. The interpretant may be any number of reactions including ones that are energetic (like movement), representational (like a thought, or naming of thing or action), or affective (like a feeling).

Peirce (1955) showed that we can focus on semiotic process from the three different perspectives of the *sign*, the *object*, or the *interpretant* to develop three trichotomies of signs. From the first perspective, the sign-vehicle itself has a quality as a *qualisign*, and may further have existence as a *sinsign* (token), and pattern as a *legisign* (type). From the second perspective—of the object's relation to the sign—the sign-object relationship can be one of likeness as an *icon*, contiguity or causality as an *index*, or convention as a *symbol*. From the perspective of the interpretant of the sign-object relation, a sign interpreted as a possibility is a *rheme*, a sign of verifiable actuality is a *dicent* sign (like a proposition and its truth conditional relation to a world, or a footprint), and an interpretant that represents its object in its character as sign (where for instance verification is achieved through internal relations) is an *argument*. Each of these triads emerges within Peirce's nested metaphysical categories of Firstness (quality), Secondness (timespace contiguity), and Thirdness (habit, generally developed over iterations in time). Each trichotomy is also importantly characterized by emergent or phasal relations where First and Second give rise to an emergent Third order. For example, in the phases of speech perception, the recognition of a word token as a symbol is perceived in its Firstness as an icon of past exemplars of its type. The moment of its recognition as another such occurrence, and its relations of adjacency and copresence within its utterance, is indexical. From relations of icons and indices emerge a symbolic function. The word's grammatical and pragmatic regularities are accrued over usages, and the present usage will in the future be iconically related to new exemplars. Each new relation can become the grounds for adjustment in the symbolic system.

The diagram in Figure 1.5 has a fourth node in the sensing and instigating agent. We can also look at semiotic relationships from this perspective as Kohn (2013) has done to help nudge anthropology beyond human agency, and which Kockelman (2007) has shown involves multiple dimensions for agency in both the *residential agency* to use a meaning-making resource and a *representational agency* to make propositions about an object. Agency can be distributed unevenly in timespaces and may not be available, or available to the same degree, to all the different participants. We can look at semiosis from the perspective of the types of agents involved and see that power is represented in this process at its most basic level. Contrasts in power are in fact amplified when we recognize that the semiotic process chains across the different perceiving and acting subjectivities in joint encounters with signs, and through the memory of their bodies, into future timespaces. This makes semiosis important to anthropologists' and cognitive scientists' interest in the agency of objects (Keane 2003 and Latour 2005, and for review of Peirce and anthropological theory see Sicoli and Wolfgram 2018). In Chapter 6, I turn to questions of the distribution of agency in multimodal assemblages examining how material things like ropes and planks become agents in interaction.

In multimodal interaction, webs of semiosis bind agents and cross modalities along the dimensions which are available to participants, and which particular agents have the power to control, and to possibly represent propositions over. Agents may also be bound up in semiosis when "interpellated" as a sign, as in Judith Butler's (2002) account drawing on Althusser's (1971) hailing, a semiotic process through which ideology can impose identity on another in response to (as interpretant to and as joint action with) the hail. A related process provides the spark of life for objects in more-than-human interactions. Semiosis gives us means for dealing with the phenomenology of multimodal complexity. The whole represented in semiosis is one that is part of our lived experience and which is especially deeply implicated in the interpretations of ethnography. The semiotic process represents a whole, but one that is open to its development across multiple scales of time and space. I see semiosis as an important starting point for the study of language, culture, and society, but even more immediately as a framework to approach the many types of relationships in multimodal interactions.

There are several benefits to adopting semiosis as a framework to engage the emergent complexity of multimodal interaction and the intersecting vectors of time in the encounters of social life. Enfield points to three of these (51–3). First is its *generality* for understanding signs whether they be in reading dark clouds as a sign of rain or making an inference from a statement like "It's cold in here" to interpret the utterance as a request to shut the window. Second is *inclusiveness* by capturing insights from structural linguistics, historically grounded approaches to language and culture, and behaviorally oriented approaches like conversation analysis in a way that connects rather than encapsulates these fields into the silos of separate discourses. Third is *learnability* in that the meaning of a sign is abstracted over iterated occurrences of a sign's uses across enchronic timescales. To this I add that meaning is affective across time geographic scales and beyond this semiosis allows us to develop a concept of mind that connects thought as individual act with thought as dialogically emergent relations in material interactions, to bridge from individual to social cognition, and to build worlds. Two biosemiotic concepts of importance for such world-building processes are *semiotic scaffolding* and *niche construction*. These have important resonances as well with place-based relationship building recognized in indigenous scholarship (Jacob 2016; Snelgrove, Kaur Dhamoon, and Corntassel 2014), and some readers will sense a resonance with what Donna Haraway discusses in *When Species Meet* as the need to treat the worlding relations of the "contact zones" of encounter in terms of "co-presence, interaction, interlocking understandings and practices, often with radically asymmetrical relations of power" (Pratt 1992: 6–7, cited in Haraway 2008: 216). The use of "contact zones" is itself a metaphor with a source in the linguistic study of the emergent hybridities of language contact systems, elsewhere leading to develop understandings of the contact-induced change mechanism of *negotiation* in the histories of creole languages (Thomason 2001) and the deconstruction of distinct languages in timespaces of superdiversity (Blommaert, Rampton, and Spotti 2015).

1.6.1 Semiotic Scaffolding and Niche Construction

Multimodal interaction shapes language in part through processes of semiotic scaffolding and niche construction. In his influential book, *Biosemiotics: An Examination of the Signs of Life and the Life of Signs* (2008a), and related essay "Semiotic Scaffolding of Living Systems" (2008b), Jesper Hoffmeyer developed the notion of semiotic scaffolding for the endosemiotic communication within and between cells in organisms and exosemiotic interpretive processes in the semiosphere that connects all life on earth. Hoffmeyer described semiotic scaffolding as

> the network of semiotic interactions by which individual cells, organisms, populations, or ecological units are controlling their activities can thus be seen as scaffolding devices assuring that an organism's activities become tuned to that organism's needs. And just as the scaffold raised to erect a building will largely delimit what kind of building is raised, so too do the semiotic controls on biological activities delimit when and how such fine-tuned activity should take place. To conceptualize and analyze the myriad of semiotic scaffolding mechanisms operative at and across different levels in natural systems is the core subject matter of biosemiotics. (Hoffmeyer 2008b: 154)

This framing of the subject matter of biosemiotics as involving focus "at and across different levels of natural systems" has an important parallel with the question I raised earlier that a primary task for theory is how action at one scale affects another. Hoffmeyer connects his discussion of semiotic scaffolding to linguistics and psychology drawing on Vygotsky (1986) to exemplify the dynamics of scaffolding processes found in child development. A well-known example of scaffolding is found in "known answer questions" in child socialization and teacher-student interactions. Hoffmeyer also discusses a form of linguistic scaffolding providing an example where a child is "talked through" a tricky challenge, and later might conduct a similar dialogue with self when renavigating such a task, the speech prompting memory and shaping behavior (see also Vygotsky 1986). These are important examples, though I would like to point out that a referentialist ideology of language scaffolds Hoffmeyer's thinking here, leading him to miss the kinds of examples of scaffolding language I take up in this book that are largely *multimodal*. Nonetheless Hoffmeyer's semiotic scaffolding shares qualities with what has been described as *frame attunement* mechanisms in the interaction literature (Kendon 2009b) including the regulatory functions of nods, gaze, and gestures, and where language is itself context as with formulaic language, poetic structure, tense-aspect-mood morphology, and the parallelism of resonance as developed here. Furthermore, we will see across the structure of the chapters of this book the semiotic scaffolding of emergent orders of action where social actions that *offer* and *recruit* scaffold additional orders of relationships, intersubjectivities, and materialities. All such scaffolding actions or devices constrain and enable what communicative and collaborative goals can be realized between participants connected through phenomenal worlds with built potentials for intersubjective action.

Important for understanding semiotic scaffolding process is development of our understanding of niche construction as reciprocal causation (a concept rather contrary to the container metaphor the term "niche" would otherwise evoke). Building on observations of another forebearer of biosemiotics Kinji Imanishi (1941), Peterson et al. (2018) argue that we should think about the "reciprocal causation" of niche construction "with respect to behavior and experience at the level of evolution in daily life (Imanishi 2002 [1941]), which is the scale at which niche constructive behaviors affecting selection pressures operate" (see also Fuentes 2016). As I demonstrate in this book, the resonating iteration of actions, both within interactions and across moments right for the doing of some relevant action, is important to understanding the building of habits, forms, and conventions in the process of sociocultural reproduction and change. In language, culture, and life, reciprocal relations in the experience near interactional domain of participatory semiosis shape and reshape the future of the materials we take up in our saying and doing.

The biosemiotic concept of *facilitation* further emplaces language as part of multimodal, multi-participant assemblages and operationalizes *niche construction* as relationship building rather than container forming. Bulleri, Bruno and Benedetti-Cecchi (2008) have argued that in complex life systems, the action of life forms "facilitates" by creating relations with and for other life forms through "niche construction" processes that make possible dynamic feedbacks that connect organisms and their consequential (sign) actions into meaningful relations to which they are *open* and without which they (and our understanding of them) are *incomplete*. Rather than reduce interspecies relations to a hierarchy of "competition," Bulleri et al. argue for the importance of positive interactions between species, where one creates a niche that facilitates the life process of another. Within multimodal interaction different species of sign actions can similarly facilitate each other and at the scale of their joint action produce new affordances for intersubjective engagement. Embodied, acoustic, and material elements brought into temporal and spatial relationships facilitate the effectiveness of each other reciprocally. This is to say that for mutual understanding or successful collaboration to occur, the potential for intersubjectivity must be established through building a phenomenal world connecting participants. The phenomenal world of an organism has been termed its *umwelt* by Jacob Von Uexküll (1934), characterized in the semiotic dimensions of an environment perceivable through use value and importantly including the affordances of objects and the actions of other organisms where *umwelten* may come to overlap, intersect, and resonate. It is not enough that there is ultimately an objective world. Our subjective experiences of some part-world must be made to resonate to establish a relationship that affords further intersubjective construction. Some examples we will see include the issuing of a summons before other recruitment, establishment of visual perception before deictic and/or pointing gesture is effective, and how the lack of shared visual ground in such cases frequently results in the repair of the reference. Additionally, the facilitation of frame resonance draws perceptual attention to grammatical differences brought in focus on such a field of similarity. Regular construction of such interdimensional and intermodal relationships in day-to-day joint action shapes the elements involved: lexicon, grammar, poetics, gesture, and the communication of attention take form through such mutually facilitative relationships they have evolved to be open to (see Whorf 1941 for such reciprocal shaping relations between habits of culture and habits of language).

Reciprocal causation and mutual mutability in biosemiotic concepts of semiotic scaffolding and niche construction provide us with some means for transcending the Cartesian container metaphor in which language has become trapped by "context." Language is not just elaborated by context, or just constituted by context, but many dimensions of language are themselves context, and are both contextualizing and contextualized. In the analysis of multi-participant, multimodal interaction as facilitating and niche-constructing, there is no *a priori* way to claim which would be a container and which would be the content. And where relationships are mutually elaborating, it is not correct to ask the question in such terms. As an attempt to understand how language takes shape or emerges as life process, I work to represent relations of facilitation, niche construction, and reciprocal causation, through drawing attention to the inter-indexical relations grounded in temporal alignments and sequencing in and between transcription blocks and broader multimodal arrays of text, action descriptions, and images used in this book.[3] I have also elaborated the blocks with prose (just as the blocks elaborate the prose) analysis that was informed through iterative ethnographic methods, observations, and understandings themselves informed and elaborated by multiparty interactions of Lachixío community members through participatory playback methods. The semiotics of multimodality is not about getting more. It is not adding context to language, though it is sometimes misunderstood as such. Rather, multimodal semiotics works to understand the emergence of an order beyond and different from its componentry or their simple sum and how, in a multimodal order, the components from which it emerged are themselves transformed.

1.7 Field Methods and Data Presentation

As a multimodal ethnography, this book invites the reader to build, along with its exposition, representations of a Zapotec language in the joint actions of Lachixío social life. The tour is guided by analysis of the semiotic processes that build connections in resonances between participants' talk, body movements, and actions with objects represented in the video corpus Lachixío community members and I built through participatory methods. The fifty-hour video corpus is archived in the Lachixío Zapotec Conversations Archive, Max Planck Institute for Psycholinguistics (Sicoli 2010b) (with additional video from subsequent visits). As a work in language documentation as well as an ethnography, this book represents, at the time of writing, the most developed representations of my work with Lachixío language and culture. The rigor of my approach examines the symbols of joint actions by looking beyond the symbols to the many semiotic relations that contribute to their emergent, multifunctional, and dense composites of meaning. As I showed in section 1.4, many of these interparticipant and crossmodal connections can be read across the tiers of transcript blocks, images, and prose, which together provide a type of "thick description" as anthropological linguistic response to Geertz's programmatic writing on doing ethnography (1973) and subsequent experimental responses to the epistemological dilemma of writing ethnography (Clifford and Marcus 1986). Many responses in sociocultural anthropology focused on interpretation between the writer of ethnography and their fieldwork interlocutors, and the writer and their scholarly audience, rather than (also) on how research subjects interpret each other. This third perspective is a documentary goal of this work bringing to focus participants' perspectives made noticeable through the visible, audible, and visibly tactile public signs of the interpretive processes elaborated in responses that transform prior public sign-action.

Insofar as this work is also a response to the project of interpretive anthropology, it can be seen as making a similar case to Michael Moerman's *Talking Culture* in which he tried to integrate "culturally contexed conversation analysis and interpretive anthropology" (1988: 86). Thirty years later his argument has been taken up more among conversation analysts and linguistic anthropologists than among his intended audience of cultural anthropologists. As I am writing for multiple audiences, I should clearly differentiate my approach which rather than conversation analysis starts with the affordances of time, multimodality, and semiosis for affecting resonances. Thus I see attention to joint actions as they take place in the real-time alignments and sequences of multimodal interaction to be a necessary rather than simply a useful engagement for thinking about the ontology of language in human life. A challenge is bringing the detail of interactional transcripts into the arguments in a way that they are experienced by a reader and not simply referenced. I think Moerman's message was not taken up more generally in interpretative anthropology because of the book's failure to integrate the transcript data with the narrative of his ethnography. Appended after his exposition as appendix A and referenced abstractly in the text, a reader is made to flip back and forth constantly between the appendix and the narrative, and as I have seen in seminars, many readers are likely to simply take the word of the writer rather than engage the sequence of interaction directly. Malinowski had a similar dilemma when writing *Coral Gardens and their Magic* (1935), and he split the ethnography into cultural and linguistic volumes. And more contemporary uses of transcripts in articles important for linguistic anthropologists, such as Jane Hill's influential study of heteroglossia in the "Voices of Don Gabriel" (1995), are also challenging to read, especially from outside of the subfield, because transcripts are appended to and not integrated with the ethnographic narrative. To his credit, Moerman, like researchers in ethnography of communication inspired by Gumperz, and Hymes, shows us that an interpretive anthropology is indeed aided by close attention to the details of dialogic interaction. I want to suggest that it is additionally important to go beyond the transcription of talk to representing an emergent ontological order where talk, bodies in motion, and the artifacts of use are mutually informing, open to, and bound to each other in the interconnected configurations of multimodal assemblages. This speaks as well to my colleagues in linguistic anthropology and field linguistics who are reluctant to acknowledge the reduction of language effected in representing copresence through audio-only transcription. The audio-only format erases from view the many degrees of freedom that allow the mutual elaboration and the, at times, relative independence of modalities to produce potentially multiple and often contradictory ends. Where talk may code propositions that bodies are contradicting we must recognize that the assumed harmony between modalities that researchers have used to excuse the lack of attention to the non-oral/aural is grounded in pervasive and limiting language ideologies. In practice, emergent intermodal relations are variable, at times resonating harmonically and at other times discordantly. A similar reduction has occurred in conducting discourse analysis of texting and online chats through text only representations (the text record) that erase the embodied practices with the devices mediating the discourse.

    I believe data-heavy ethnographies should still be readable. For this reason, and because a goal of mine is to show the relevance of multimodal interaction analysis of joint actions for linguistics, anthropologists, biosemioticians, and cognitive scientists (and thus beyond the "regular" audience of ethnomethodological conversation analysts), my transcription system, while paralleling the temporal-indexical concerns of, for example, Lorenza Mondada (2014), is not aiming to exhaustively represent all such indices but rather to make relevant relations between talk, bodily movements, and actions with objects visible in a way that does not overload the reader with information that might lead to less receptivity rather than more. What I have selected to represent is most often guided by concern for how responses illustrate participants' orientation to the signs and sign relations emerging in their focused encounter, and especially to harmonic and discordant resonances. I have worked to integrate the transcripts with the ongoing narrative and argumentation so they may be read as integral. For this reason the transcripts are most often presented as exemplar and analysis before or sometimes in lieu of prose metacommentary. Beyond the interdigitated transcript blocks, I have worked to also integrate transcript data with my prose in a dialogic literary fashion, citing participants' voices frequently. The prose also conveys dimensions that reach beyond the transcripts to prior actions, intertextualities, and knowledge from my other sources of information, which included participant-observation and interviews over twenty years engaging with the community through fieldwork, and with collaborative

Figure 1.6 Playback dialogue at Casa Hernández García.

attention to the corpus through a method I call "playback dialogues" where people in Lachixío viewed videos together and discussed the interaction. Several of these were video-recorded as well, as in Figure 1.6. These playback dialogues are a hybrid genre between spontaneous conversation, interviews, and data sessions where speakers discussed action sequences with each other first and subsequently with me.

Technologies of digital video and film allow for playback, and time-aligned transcription schemes can help approach the tangled relations composing the fleeting public signs people bring to bear on the contingencies of interaction. The reader must wonder how present the camera was in any given scene during recording. In my experience the camera and tripod can act like a participant with variable involvement. There are in fact transcripts in which an exchange between people refers to the camera and moments where someone remembers the camera and looks at it. When the camera becomes a focus of joint attention, a dialogue emerges which can be interesting itself as a spontaneous conversation, even if it is one that would not have occurred without the camera. At other times the quiet eye of the camera is a forgotten participant, not being a very good interactor itself. Human interaction has its stakes, priorities, and moral obligations. When a question is asked, an answer is expected. When a repair is issued, a remedy is relevant. Even with a camera participating in the scene people respond to each other to service their social obligations. These are often so engaging to the participants that the camera is forgotten, for a while. So in any of the mostly hour-long recordings that make up the corpus, while there could be several moments of attention on the camera, especially at the beginning, there are always stretches where the camera is a much smaller participant, more like a fly on a wall.

Even after many years visiting Lachixío, my presence in speech scenes often becomes a reference in the talk or evokes other dimensions of my work for participants where I have video-recorded psycholinguistic tasks and conducted more formal linguistic elicitation. Recognizing a social world that has its own trajectories before and after my visits, I worked with a collaborator Pedro Martínez García and a network of other participants connected through kin and geographic relationships. Pedro and his compatriots decided what aspects of life to record, and this in turn substantially influenced the direction of this research. Pedro and I discussed technical details like the use of available light in filming, sound quality, and the importance of videographic framing of interactions to capture the listener as well as the speaker in the ecology of interaction. I also provided equipment and a stipend for him to record everyday life and gifts for people working with him. Roughly half the videos of the corpus were recorded by Pedro in which he visited families over subsequent days, usually recording an hour at a time because of the length of tape in the mini-DV cassette format of the cameras we used at the time. During many of my own recordings of interactions, I did not linger in the scene but set up the camera and left, returning later. While I have often tried to be absent when recording natural conversations for this project, I have engaged participants in the videos in subsequent dialogues about them.

As a tool for linguistic ethnography and cultural description, video analysis affords the close, and repeated, examination of the multimodal scenes of joint actions.[4] When combined with ethnography, the details of social encounters are revealing of the hierarchies, expectations, roles and responsibilities at play among the speakers—factors intimately linked to the production and maintenance of social relations and linguistic forms that perdure beyond the interaction. This recognition requires a practical integration of methods of linguistics and anthropology.

1.8 Plan of the Book

I have ordered the chapters to be instructive of an emergent sequence from the social, to the intersubjective, and to a perduring materiality. Chapters 2 through 6 are titled for joint actions that I take to be obligations of human life through which language takes its shape and worlds are built: offer, recruit, repair, resonate, and build. The chapters move through layered emergences in three phases, which is partly inspired by emergent relations between grammatical complexity and social motivations sketched in Michael Tomasello's the *Origins of Human Communication* (2008), emergence in usage-based theories of language development where complexity emerges in phases that build on children's prior achievements (Lieven 2014), and parallel accounts of the importance of emergence in the biosemiotics of living systems (Deacon 2013; Hoffmeyer 1996). We first examine joint actions of *offers* (Chapter 2) and *recruitments* (Chapter 3) for the way they are instrumental in building and navigating social relations, obligations, and reputations. Then we examine how offering and recruiting are components of the interactional efforts that build, display, and maintain intersubjectivity through sequences of *repairs* (Chapter 4) and the dialogic poetics of *resonance* (Chapter 5) across speakers' moves that connect them into the higher order of dialogic syntax. The emergent relationship between actions that offer and recruit and actions that repair and resonate is that of an implicational hierarchy. While we can imagine a communication system characterized by offers and recruitments but without repair or resonating sequences (e.g., food sharing among apes or corvids), we cannot conduct repair or collaboratively build resonating sequences without already doing the more basic pragmatic actions of its constituents—offering and recruiting. Finally, we turn to collaborations that *build* a material world (Chapter 6), focusing on interactions to build and repair objects of material culture. Of particular interest is how material objects take on living qualities and effect a persuasive momentum through an end-directed dynamic that involves accruing joint commitments in an assemblage of social cooperation. We see how offers, recruitments, repairs, and resonance building combine to produce a material world that bears the indices of the natural history in its emergence, and how that history in turn shapes grammatical forms. Chapter 7, "Living Assemblages," is an epilogue that reprises the phenomenological and biosemiotic engagement of this book, presenting a retrospective and prospective discussion of how our attention to joint actions of human sociality is revealing of a language as lived experience bound up in the means and methods of world building that goes beyond the social world, to the durative aspects of our material environment, and the perdurant qualities of an institution.

1.8.1 Chapter Summaries

In Chapter 2 we examine several examples of everyday offers. In one case a visitor is offered supper. In a contrasting case a visitor offers to wash the dishes. We track the forms of offers as they are proffered, responded to, and reissued with adjusted terms by multiple people present in the social situation learning both about Lachixío grammar and its involvement in building social relations and reputations. We also examine a video of the offering of gifts at a wedding in Lachixío. Together both show that offers in everyday interaction and ritual gift giving follow a common logic and morality that includes obligations to give, to accept, to give back in kind, and to give on (Mauss 1925). What we can also see through a close focus on Lachixío discourse practice is that offers are commonly reiterated by multiple participants of an interaction. Offers, both as actions and as linguistic formulations, resonate through participants to scale up from individual action to the social action of a family, building family reputations in interactions. Where resonating subsequent offers pressure the recipient to accept, they often differ from first offers in Lachixío being reformulated to rhetorically reduce the thing offered to seem smaller and reduce the on-record obligation (the social debt) incurred in accepting: an offer of one taco is reduced to half-a-taco, four turkeys gifted to a couple rephrased as two for the man and two for the woman, and a first offer to "scrub" the dishes that was left hanging (no uptake from the recipient that would complete the joint action), later reformulated as an offer to only "rinse" them, which does get accepted.

Chapter 3 examines recruitments of another's action. Recruitments include speech acts like directives, requests, and hints, and may involve talk, gestures like a palm-up display, various combinations, and often the exchange of something. Like offers, recruitments involve the creation and mobilization of social relationships that include the navigation of rights and responsibilities between people, the power that enables one to solicit action from another, and of another to grant action appropriately, and of objects to stand in as signs of intentions, desires, and relationships. We look at three sequences that are characterized by recruitments that were reissued multiple times, allowing us to track the parallelisms and transformations of the grammatical and multimodal formulations of recruitments as public signs that display social relationships of entitlement and contingency. In one example, a mother recruits her daughter to fetch a pitcher of water for the kitchen and the daughter complies. But when the mother issues a second embodied request for more water, the daughter misunderstands and fails to grant the request. The mother issues subsequent recruitments varying the grammatical inflection in phases that reveal a hierarchy of morpheme choices related to the entitlement of one person to recruit the action of another. A second example shows a family taking a break from work in the agricultural fields and represents an inverse entitlement relationship where a child's baby talk requests for a cup of soda are repeatedly ignored, only granted when the child shifts to a grammatical formulation of recruitment that matches his low entitlement in the family and task hierarchies. In the final sequence, we witness a recruitment for a glass of water at a family dinner shift its shape from a hint to offering the terms of a solution to a problem that another is in a position to remedy, and then to explicit directive grammatical forms. Different family members iterate different formulations as the recruitment is passed from one to another along age and gender hierarchies until finally the youngest woman is left to grant the request. Her compliance is multimodally complex, revealing the creative use of a resonance relationship I call *intermodal discord* to both comply with the directive in one modality and push back against the gender hierarchy through another. She complies in action but contests in words. The discordant relations of the multimodal assemblage point to a mechanism of cultural change in process.

In Chapter 4, we examine how intersubjectivity can be an interactional achievement displayed, checked, and contested by participants in their interrelated moves. We focus specifically on how participants collaborate in sequences of conversational repair and elucidate the lexical and grammatical affordances of Lachixío Zapotec for conducting repair, which includes description of ontological (wh-) questions, polar (yes/no) questions, repair dedicated constructions, dialogic repetition, and the concerted use of signs across modalities. Conversational repair has a universal form in human interaction that can be set into play in any turn where repair is initiated. The repair initiation then becomes a pivot that focuses attention retrospectively to some trouble in a prior turn (or sequence) and also points forward to a prospective remedy to be undertaken (Schegloff 2000; Dingemanse and Enfield 2015; Sicoli 2016a). Repairs are interindividual sequences where action with language is co-structured between multiple participants as a joint action. The involved parties must surrender some of their autonomy to the collaboration, a joint commitment to action with a goal of re-achieving a good enough mutual understanding to move the interaction forward. This chapter shows repairs to be an emergent joint activity built up from lower-order joint actions of offers and recruitments. Repair initiations are formed either as requests that oblige the receiver to remedy the trouble or as offers where the repair initiator offers a possible solution for another's confirmation or rejection. The concept of emergence is important to consider how the more basic joint actions of offers and recruitments, when constrained within the sequence organization of repair, take function beyond the component parts to adjust the ground of an interactionally emergent mind always in a state of becoming through the dialogic process of semiosis. Repairs are also initiated and remedied through a great deal of partial or modified repetition. Like in the previous chapters the resonances between such connected moves provide privileged insights into the workings of the Lachixío Zapotec language as used in daily life.

Chapter 5 reflects on how repetition and parallelism between the signs formulated by social actors in dialogue were important dimensions of the offers, recruitments, and repairs we examined. In this chapter, we focus on joint activity that builds resonances in dialogic interaction, drawing on foundations laid in the work of Jakobson, Hymes, and other linguistic anthropologists' attention to the poetic function of language, and especially on Du Bois's (2014) framework of Dialogic Syntax, which examines the resonances people build across utterances. I develop analysis of Lachixío grammar through examining *resonances* built between participants in the pervasive repetition that characterizes the rhythm of Lachixío discourse. Dialogic syntax can be seen both as an order of social activity with language and as an order of linguistic analysis that examines not what is "transmitted" between individuals but what is emergently built between them. It is a way to let the participants tell the story of their language, through the richness of their jointly produced dialogic resonances made available for analysis by linguistic corpora produced through documentary methodologies. I illustrate the concepts of *frame resonances* that repeat the form of prior speech and *focal resonance* that contrasts items across frames (Du Bois 2014). These often work together as focal resonance contrasts items in a frame made salient for comparison through its own parallel construction. To create dialogic resonance, social actors construct what Peirce (1955) called a *diagrammatic icon*, which he argued to be a basic pillar of human epistemology (see Mannheim 1999 for review). Building resonance is a joint activity in which the chaining process of semiosis is laid bare, as prior sign becomes material for new action with inter-sign indexicalities grounded on iconically parallel constructions. Lachixío interactions ring with the emergent rhythms of speech passed back and forth in the building of harmonic and discordant resonances and through which speakers orient to and diagram their own attention to language form through public signs that also then become available to analysts. Dialogic resonance is important to examine for the epistemological projects of ethnography and documentary linguistics where representing an *emic* or *ethno-* perspective is a goal. Thus analysts may learn how members of the subject community attend to, interpret, appropriate, and contest interactional moves in a poetics of resonance that, like repair, is also grounded in the affordances of turn-by-turn dialogue emergent from joint actions that offer and recruit. Resonance can be initiated in response to any turn, an offer of parallel form which recruits the action of another to notice and infer the relevance of their difference.

In Chapter 6, "Build," we shift scales again to more directly engage multimodal world-building activity where the place, form, and function of offers, recruitments, repairs, and resonances enable and constrain collaborations to build and repair material artifacts. We examine two focused collaborations with objects where interactional troubles emerge and track their resolutions. The affordances for meaningful action here are multimodally distributed across talk, embodied action, and action with objects, and are developed in time through "co-operative action" (Goodwin 2017), working at any moment with the cumulative and material state of affairs that a collaboration has become. We first analyze a video of an elderly couple repairing saddles. A joint commitment to a too-short rope initiates an ill-fated sequence of work that then needs to be undone. Then we engage a video of a family constructing a corral for their turkeys, returning to the episode with which the book began. The finished corral shows two different design features we can see develop interactionally. The video corpus, and its multimodal transcription, gives access to a natural history in which multiple ideas were offered, and joint commitments to objects were both established and contested. Through embodied orientations of attention, and joint commitments to objects, objects are seen to become interactional participants who, with the help of their living collaborators, may self-perpetuate. We follow the emergence of a participant role for a wooden pole as two people jointly work to reproduce its form as a solution to a parallel problem solved earlier in a parallel way. An elder woman contests the move to replicate what she recognizes as a bad idea, but as overt disagreement is rare in Lachixío, her argument and redirection relies largely on disrupting the trajectory of the ongoing joint activity of her collaborators, and the joint commitments it represents. Her redirection is accomplished partly through talk and though gesture, and beyond these representative semiotic modes, she importantly turns to an intrinsic mode of semiotic action where the sign and the object of the sign are one and the same. She manipulates objects directly in the place for her audience. Through the holism of multimodality, we come to understand how joint commitments to objects of joint action scaffolds a social life for objects, and provides insight into the parallel ways languages as cultural objects are built and rebuilt through the joint actions and joint commitments of daily life.

Chapter 7 reprises and elaborates on broader theoretical contributions of this book that I worked to depict through practices of multimodal ethnography and attention to interparticipant and intermodal resonances of the documentary chapters. I elucidate how the holistic study of a language as part to the multimodal-multiparty assemblages of joint actions is parallel to concerns developing across the humanities, social, and natural sciences as they aim to understand the theoretical consequences of engaging with phenomena as part of complex and emergent wholes, when they have commonly been studied as reductions. This last chapter develops a dialogue between the field linguist's goal of documenting language in cultural life, anthropologists' and ethnomethodologists' concerns with world-building and understanding knowledge from a participant's point of view, and the concerns of several foundational scholars of the transdisciplinary field of biosemiotics to connect the life processes of diverse organisms into facilitating, niche-constructing, reciprocal relations (Hoffmeyer 2008a,b; Favareau 2015; Kull 2009). Connecting multimodal interaction with the semiosphere of biosemiotics is the philosophical intersection of phenomenology and the semiotics of living systems. I discuss relations between my notion of multimodal assemblages and biosemiotic relations, drawing on Uexküll's semiotic and phenomenological notion of *umwelt*, as the phenomenal world of an organism characterized in the semiotic dimensions of an environment perceivable through use value and including the affordances of objects and the actions of other organisms.

I compare the biosemiotic concepts of semiotic scaffolding and niche construction to the inter-indexical and iconically resonant worlds of multimodal assemblages to think about nonlinear causal relations between the multimodal whole composed in part by language and the shapes of a language as parts to such a whole. I argue that multimodal, multi-participant interactions represent a dynamic organization that is cocreated, ends-directed, self-repairing, and self-replicating—qualities reflected in the chapters of this book. These qualities for languages and other human artifacts also characterize living systems as "co-emergent autopoiesis" (Varela and Maturana 1998), and through the "teleodynamics" defined by Deacon (2013) as synergistically generated in the interaction of participants that contribute their energy to the emergence of a new order of relations. I conclude that language emerges as part of the larger scale teleodynamics of multimodal interaction when considered phylogenetically in its evolution, ontogenetically in its development, and continuously in daily life activity. Building on trajectories of scholarship in linguistic anthropology, phenomenological anthropology, and biosemiotics, this work contributes to a scale-shift in the study of language, one that makes legible how languages are reproduced and transformed through the joint actions and joint commitments of daily life.

1.9 Lachixío: *Xe'yyò* and *Zhílii*

Before we enter the houses, courtyards, and agricultural fields of families in Lachixío through the multimodal transcripts, images, videos, and ethnographic writing, I will sketch a brief introduction to the community. My fieldwork since 1997 has primarily been in a village called *Xe'yyò* in Zapotec, *Santa Maria Lachixío*, in Spanish and additionally with people of *Zhílii*, San Vicente Lachixío, the neighboring village to the south. I first visited Lachixío with Daniel Hernández Morgan, a past two-term president of the community who I had been working with on a dictionary project as a master's student. His son was graduating from middle school, so we left the field station where we had been working at the time to return to Lachixío for the ceremony. My first participant-observer role then was as family photographer (later roles have included godparent, compadre, trombonist, plumber, chauffeur, consultant, and a connection to the world of scholarly linguistics, ethnohistory, archaeology, among others).

Xe'yyò occupies a highland valley in the southern mountains of Oaxaca located about 7,500 feet with surrounding peaks to about 9,000 feet. Oaxaca is one of the southernmost states of Mexico and has one of the highest percentages of indigenous population and a concentration of diversity with more than sixty indigenous languages spoken in an area about the size of the US state of Indiana, though many people originating in the community are working in other cities of Mexico and the United States. The area of this fieldwork is in the southwest of the state shown within Mexico in Figure 1.7.

The principle mode of production is subsistence agriculture growing the Mesoamerican staples of corn, beans, squash through the facilitating companion-planting assemblage of the Milpa (*iñaa*). In the last few years, there have been a number of experiments with cash crops, particularly hothouse tomatoes for export, and the

Figure 1.7 Region of the fieldwork in Sierra Sur of Oaxaca, Mexico.

maguey cactus sold to Tequila distilleries in the state of Jalisco or the Tobala maguey (*dokko laà*) to craft distilleries in Oaxaca. The Santa María Lachixío valley supports about 350 households, 1,700[5] people. San Vicente, founded in 1776 by people originating in Santa María, and related to a time of Cochineal production in Lachixío's region (Dahlgren de Jordan 1963), now supports 560 households, 3,000 people. Additional economic activities include horticulture and wild food gathering, commercial logging, and out-migration to Mexican urban centers and numerous regions of the United States. A mound complex on the western side of the valley known as *Licchi* (the flats) attests to millennia of occupation. The area has been an important crossroads for trade through these mountains since before the emergence of the Monte Alban State, roughly 2,000 years ago, and this area of southwest Oaxaca is the center of linguistic diversity of the Zapotec-Chatino family of the Otomanguean language stock, with several Chatino languages to the south and several mutually unintelligible Zapotec languages representing three of the five main branches of the Zapotec language family (Smith-Stark 2007). The Spanish had an established parish in Santa María Lachixío by the late sixteenth century with a church constructed and a permanent priest living in Lachixío by the year 1600. Lachixío is still an important crossroads today—for example, hosting, since 2004, the first gas station in this region of the *Sierra Sur* of Oaxaca Figure 1.8).

The Lachixío gas station that opened in 2004 is one place where Zapotec cultural identity is expressed through modern ventures designed to attract transit and tourism. Another is the *Restaurant Santa Maria Lachixío* more recently opened by some of the same entrepreneurs.

While at the time of writing the Zapotec language is still learned and spoken by many children in Lachixío, the community is aware of what is sensed as a trajectory

Figure 1.8 Zapotec Service Station, Santa María Lachixío.

of language shift in the region (Sicoli 2007, 2010a) where eight of the twelve main population centers that spoke West Zapotec languages have become moribund (no children learning the language). The recognition of such history as a trajectory and the potential for language loss in Lachixío were motivations of my long-time collaborator Daniel to take up language documentation work in the 1990s and that brought us into relations. He has articulated his hope that if or when the language is no longer spoken, the recordings and transcriptions we produced together with the help of other community members will be of value for future generations. My collaborator Pedro has similar motivations and is involved in cultural documentation and dance performance. We can hope that maintenance and revitalization efforts in Lachixío will prevent the language from becoming moribund or falling completely out of use, but at the same time the ideological pressure for Spanish monolingualism is strong and has been effective in so many surrounding communities that it is felt as a real possibility, and one that is increasingly being realized in socialization practices that often constitute children now as speakers of Spanish (Sicoli 2020; Sicoli 2011).

I hope this book and the larger documentation corpus on which it is based will be a resource for the community of Lachixío that illustrates for future generations not only how to say things in Lachixío Zapotec but how to do things, and particularly how the people of Lachixío use the language to do things together in the collaborative actions that create a world of lived experience. Let us begin now by turning, in Chapter 2, to a fundamental of social life: the offering of gifts, words, and actions in communal exchange.

2

Offer

That histories bear on the interactional present is well understood,[1] but it is less intuitive, and less examined, how the future bears on the interactional present. Thinking about how futures can exert causal relations on the present, the philosopher Charles Peirce described a "being in futuro" that "appears in mental forms, intentions and expectations." He observed that "the future does not influence the present in the direct, dualistic, way in which the past influences the present. A machinery, a medium, is required" and asked, "What kind of machinery can it be?" (CP 2.86, Peirce 1932). This chapter works to answer this question, exploring how the "mental forms, intentions, and expectations" of joint actions of offer-response connect to future obligations, and future memories of individual and household reputations in Lachixío. What Michael Moerman (1988) referred to as people's "motives for action" are attuned to potential social relations assembled through the joint efforts of participants in interactional moments of a becoming future. In this chapter I argue that in the multimodal analysis of both formal offers, like gift giving at a Lachixío wedding, and everyday offers of things like food, drink, or household help, we make visible emergent social relations instantiated through the chaining of obligations to give, to receive, to give back, and to give on to others. A key analytical observation I make is that the *saying* and *doing* of social actions cannot be expected to mirror each other in stance or purpose, and that analyzing talk alone will often miss what people are doing through an order that emerges in multimodal interaction. Where saying and doing do not mirror each other, I term the concept "intermodal discord," which contrasts with the generally assumed parallelism of "intermodal harmony" (see also Sicoli 2007: 12). In moments of intermodal discord, saying and doing can be at cross purposes, serving multiple and even conflicting social and ritual constraints and motives for action.

In analyzing the language of offers the self-contained sentence of synchronic analysis and the immediate dependency of the adjacency pair of conversation analysis is not enough to approach the machinery, or medium, Peirce suggested is required for the future to have causal influence on the present—a present that includes the linguistic forms of offers, their appropriate responses, and action with, or transfer of, an object. We additionally must develop an understanding of the openness of language to its multimodality built on the affordances of time and space to connect to diverse modes of being across scales and to worlds of motives, reputations, economies, and identities. Deleuze and Guattari (1987) drew on the metaphor of the rhizome, an underground plant network, to think about mediated causality through assemblages.

The horizontally extending structure of rhizomes from which new roots and new shoots can emerge contrasts with the vertical hierarchies of trees with roots that has pervasively guided the linguistic and historical imagination of scholars. The metaphor communicates that any point of a rhizome can be connected to any other thing as "semiotic chains of every nature are connected to very diverse modes of coding (biological, political, economic, etc.) that bring into play not only different regimes of signs but also states of things of differing status" (1987: 7). We may ask if this metaphor resonates enough with the connections emergent across the multimodal assemblages of human interaction to help us think about them. Often becoming entangled like matts of grass, rhizomatic networks are still the products of individual plant species (and often single plants), and thus not of ecologies with multiple participants (and types of participants) connecting to, and through, each other. So while the rhizome metaphor has helped challenge ideologies that privilege uniformity and hierarchy in scholarly questions, and has drawn attention to reciprocity and reticulation, it is not clearly able to bridge the ontological divides between the materialities of language forms, embodied actions, objects given and received, and the social obligations and reputations that perdure beyond a moment of interaction.

Anthropologist Anna Tsing has offered another way to think about connections between diverse modes of being in her ethnography, *The Mushroom at the End of the World* (2015). A more apt metaphor for the ontology is *mycorrhizal relations* through which fungi live along with and interpenetrate the cell structure of plant roots. The key figure in her book, the matsutake mushroom (*Tricholoma matsutake*), may draw carbohydrates from a pine tree and in exchange make minerals available for the tree by creating a soil environment through its own life process, but the relationship only thrives in disturbed landscapes, linking its success to capitalist scales of landscape destruction and life's reclamation. Beyond these interspecies collaborations, mycelium webs connect plants with other plants beneath the forest floor, linking diverse species into webs of relations. These webs permit the sharing of nutrients and even provide a means of communication between plants, a medium for the feedbacks, self-organization, and emergent properties of complex adaptive assemblages (Simard et al. 2012). Through tracking assemblages as "polyphonic," "open-ended gatherings" (Tsing 2015: 23) (rather than bounded systems or communities), Tsing documents how gifts of matsutake mushrooms that work to build social relationships in Japan are tied to people and forests in Japan, China, and the United States (and even Lachixío where *be'yya yoò* the 'earth mushroom' is wild harvested and sold to Japanese buyers in Oaxaca City). I add here that polyphonic and open-ended assemblages of embodied and emplaced interactions are *multimodal* and work to show that the biosemiotic concept of trans-species assemblages is helpful for thinking through how the multiple types of participants in multimodal interactions not only produce meaning and social relations but also build interconnected worlds that reciprocally effect the form of meaningful actions and social relations. As I discussed in the Introduction, Peirce thought of symbols as alive. Both the forms that offers take and the obligations they create are symbolic since we are habituated to ways of formulating, accepting, and rejecting offers, of giving and receiving things of conventional values, and of assuming or establishing sets of social relations through these acts. Thus it is more than a metaphor to turn to trans-species life relations for understanding the medium through which a future of obligation and reputation comes to bear on a present joint action.

The recognition of how the future and the past are linked through offers in the present has long drawn the attention of anthropologists. Pierre Bourdieu (1972), for example, also emphasized the importance of temporality in gift giving in *Outline to a Theory of Practice*. Bronislaw Malinowski emphasized the reputation building involved in gift giving (1922). And Marcel Mauss's *Essay on the Gift* (1990) showed us that the social actions involved in the offering and accepting of gifts bring into being social relationships of solidarity, and future obligations for reciprocity This reciprocity may involve an obligation to give back to the giver, or a generalized reciprocity to give on to others. Mauss argued that the purpose of offers was a moral one "hidden below the surface, and ... one of the human foundations on which our societies are built" (1990: 4). We learn through such works that gift exchange produces a moral and social order of a world connected in time and space through social obligation—that a gift reaches forward in time to create obligation and may itself be the reciprocation of prior actions.

Erving Goffman (1964, 1971c), like Mauss, but attending more to language in social encounters, showed us some ways that interactions can create and nurture social bonds (see also Berking 1999; Cheal 1988; Keane 1997; 2003). One way this is done is through what Goffman called "Tie-Signs" that link action beyond the interaction and which can include "interpersonal rituals" that display relationships, "markers" that claim territory through acts or arrangements with objects, and "change signals" which signify change in a relationship (1971a: 199–204). It is notable that these resonate the Peircean categories of Firstness (Quality), Secondness (Contiguity), and Thirdness (Habit). Goffman even cites Peirce's pragmatist interlocutor, Henry James (1969), to depict "interpersonal rituals" (of eye gaze, distance, orientation, etc.) as an "image" (an icon or First) from which one can get an impression of a social relationship. As a scale for noticing social relations, like picking out those socially "with" another, apart as singletons, close intimates, or social distance, this imagistic perspective is an ecological view of the whole encounter. *Markers* indexically link to the owner/holder/wearer of an object through its bearing (contiguity or Secondness), and *change signals* involve performative acts that bring about new relationships for the individuals involved, like first uses of particular forms of address, first time holding hands, first kiss, and the like (developing new habits of convention or Thirdness). Tie signs like this involve an offer and acceptance, and can involve the exchange of material gifts that serve as markers, displaying certain ritual relations and acts of transformation. These relations and their signs of transformation are multimodal and through the audible and visible practices of participants become noticeable through video analysis.

With this background sketched, we turn to examining how offers in Lachixío are initiated, responded to, and how future relations weigh heavy on the interactional present, even to the point of influencing grammatical formulations and the negotiation of their pragmatics. Lachixío wedding gift-offers share several qualities with mundane offers. Offers are habitually made over multiple iterations, increasing the pressure on the receiver to accept. And like a wedding gift, everyday offers implicate the reputation of entire families, not just individuals. While iterations can increase the pressure to accept an offer in Lachixío, there is also an ethic of humility in the gift. Semiotic work is undertaken to minimize the burden of acceptance (a future burden of obligation to reciprocate). We see this last quality exemplified in second or third offers, or in verbal accountings, that reduce the burden of acceptance to less than the whole of the first offer. These subsequent offers can draw on affordances of the grammar and lexicon to rhetorically reduce the thing offered, or shift the definition of the situation to make accepting the offer less of a personal debt. We will consider three examples. In the first, an initial wedding gift of four turkeys is reframed by stating that it is a distributed gift of two for the husband and two for the wife. In the second, a whole taco first offered to a guest is reduced in the subsequent offer to just half-a-taco. We will also consider that one may pressure the receiver to accept a food offer by saying that everybody here is eating (like at a party). This tactic scales up the definition of the situation, what Goffman (1974) called the frame, rather than scaling down the gift, with the same net effect on the pressure to accept. In the third example, the first offer to "scrub" dishes is reissued with lexical substitutions. The second time it is formulated with a verb for "washing" them, and finally just "rinsing" them, which was the only one accepted.

2.1 Gifts for the Godparents: Two Plus Two Does Not Equal Four

The wedding in Lachixío has several rounds of gift giving in multiple places over three days: first to the bride's parents at their house, then to the marrying couple at the groom's (or groom's parents) house, and to close the wedding, gifts are given to the *Toòmbálle* (godparents) who sponsored the wedding. Gifts of food and drink are also given to guests throughout the days of festivities. The gift exchanges also make visible the social calculus that Mauss argued for with families keeping track of future obligations they are incurring. A person may even take notes linking gifts and givers so they can match a gift when the time comes to repay it (Figure 2.1). This section examines a video of the ritual gift giving to the godparents at a wedding I attended in Lachixío on July 13, 2014. I had just arrived in town for summer fieldwork when I learned that my friend Leon's wedding was going on. Passing by his house I was invited in and offered generous amounts of food and drink. Unprepared with a gift of my own I offered to make a wedding video for the bride and groom as no one else was doing this. I video recorded the dancing and gift exchange and made DVDs for the bride's and groom's families.

My compadre Daniel was *Benné Òlla*, the principal orator for the ceremonies, and I had known the groom and the family of the bride for several years. The bride and groom had actually been living together (*nzokko nóo sa'a'* [STA-sit that relation]) for many years and both were of advanced age. Many couples live together as spouses without going through the great expense of civil or church ceremonies and the obligatory festivities, but now having the means after many years the couple with the help of their godparents[2] put together the resources to make their union legal with the state and official with the church. Their age was the subject of several jokes since it was a bit out of the ordinary to marry so old. Yet the wedding followed the same

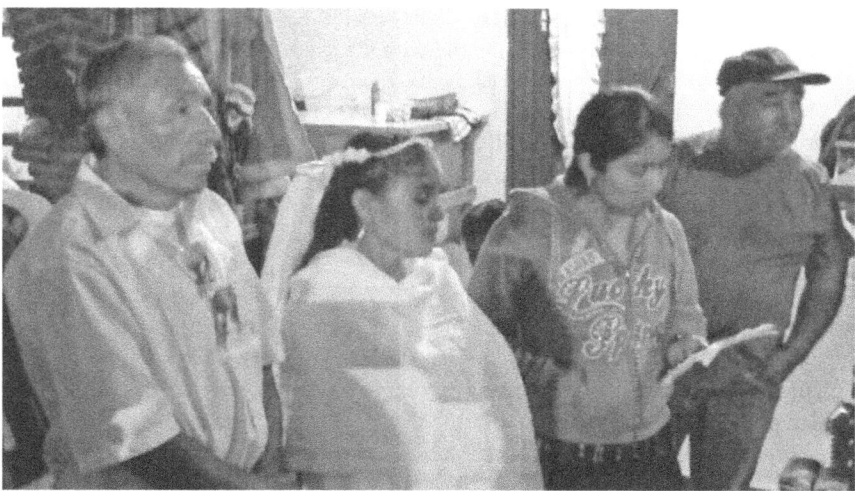

Figure 2.1 An assistant standing next to bride and groom keeps track of gifts on paper as a guest watches the procession of gifts.

customs as would be expected for a younger couple. I had only arrived in the afternoon that Sunday, and so missed the morning ceremony at the church and gift giving at the bride's house the night before but arrived in time for the afternoon reception at the groom's house. The feast was turkey with mole sauce. The dancing was to live music of the local musicians of Lachixío's band. Since I had a car, I helped move the party from Santa María, where the bride and groom lived, to the house of the godparents in San Vicente a few kilometers to the south where there would be the last exchange of gifts for the day along with more music, dancing, and spirits to bring the ceremony to closure.

Offers in the wedding are stylized in comparison with everyday offers. For example, one by one the guests present their gift which is passed from the giver to an assistant, who passes it to the Benné Òlla, who then announces the gift and characterizes it with words that also work to portray the gift as humble. The words minimize the material value of the gift to rather praise the relationship and goodwill it signifies. The gift is an offer that must be formally accepted by the recipient's performance of words and gestures as we will examine later. While more stylized, wedding offers also share several qualities with everyday offers, parallels that I work to draw out for the reader in transcripts and discussion. In both we see an ethic of humility in offering to frame gifts as small, and that orientation toward future social obligations mediates how action is accomplished in the present. As we will see in the transcribed wedding sequence, this background concern comes to the fore when a bigger than normal gift is offered. The gift is not immediately accepted but rather becomes reason to stop the orderly progression of the gift ritual and becomes the explicit subject of talk and remediation.

In the giving of gifts for the godparents (*Toòmbálle*), the groom's sister Alfonsa acted as an assistant to the Benné Òlla Daniel who ultimately presented the gifts. The

Benné Òlla does most of the talking, speaking about the gift, during the exchange. The dialogue of the Benné Òlla shares qualities with the speech of another ritual figure the *Benné Óxxo* (old/wise person) as well as the *Táaòlla* (*Viejitos* in Spanish), the funny, childlike elders who visit from the dead during the autumn celebration of *Toò Zándo* (*Todos Santos/Día de los Muertos* [All Saints' Day/Day of the Dead]). León (the groom) in fact refers to Daniel as Benné Óxxo at one point, and many of the Benné Òlla's improvised descriptions of gifts are comical and feign an ignorance of a gift's everyday use. He and the others have also been drinking mezcal and beer, which was described to me as a ritual obligation.

Figure 2.2 shows the bride and groom in the foreground with the Benné Òlla as he received a gift for the Toòmbálle (godfather). The Benné Òlla addresses the Toòmbálle as *paà* (father) and Noòmbálle (godmother) as *naà* (mother), addressing them in the audience of the bride and groom while holding the gift between them. Body postures used in giving and receiving often indicate the smallness of humility as seen in Figure 2.3 where Benné Òlla has palms facing each other close together and a slight bow when describing a "small" gift to Noòmbálle.

Before examining the transcribed video from this wedding, I want to present a segment from a narrative characterizing an ideal wedding in Lachixío to show how the participants in the video are performing cultural scripts. This will also be important when we consider everyday household offers. When conducting research with the Project for the Documentation of the Languages of Meso-America in Catemaco, Veracruz in 1998, I recorded (audio only) a narrative in Lachixío Zapotec titled *Xaa rekka tòkko elo chiaa* (How to make a wedding) authored by Toò Fabiano Constantino

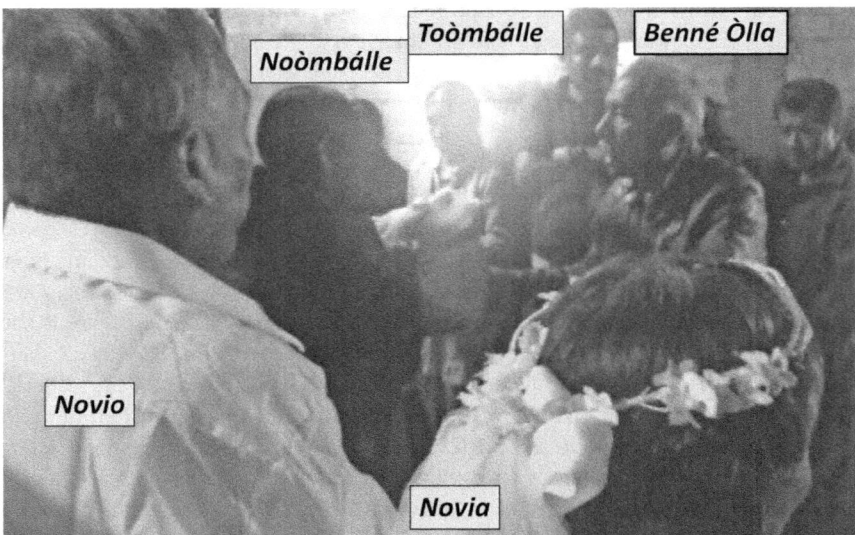

Figure 2.2 Wedding gift exchange, July 2014. The *Benné Òlla* (orator) mediates between the receivers of gifts (*Toòmbálle* [godfather] and *Noòmbálle* [godmother]) and the givers of gifts, here in view of the *Novio* (groom) and *Novia* (bride) (and about sixty guests).

Figure 2.3 Benné Òlla addresses Noòmbálle with gesture and body posture iconic of the smallness/humility of the gift.

Hernández García. The narrative characterizes the multitude of gift exchanges that mark weddings beginning with gifts to the parents of the bride, continuing with gifts to the *novios* (bride and groom), and its ending with gifts to *Beè Toòmbálle*, the godparents over three days of festivities. Before a wedding, *eeliettzá* (guelaguetza exchange) debts are called in by the family and godparents. People who are generally kin and ritual kin (compadres) offer help often in the form of fowl (turkeys and chickens), other food items, and labor for the reception dinner. The guelaguetza system of exchange was described in Beals (1970) as a nonmonetary system of debt prototypically in the form of turkeys which families raise to lend to other families. The term "guelaguetza" has also been appropriated for reference to a popular annual display of Oaxacan culture during the celebration of *Lunes del Cerro* in the state capital, Oaxaca City. Each July dancers from Oaxacan regions perform for audiences that include many international and national tourists. Before this guelaguetza was Zapotec for the cooperative exchange system that still organizes reciprocity in Lachixío and other communities that govern themselves by a customary system of practice known as *usos y costumbres*. In the Lachixío wedding, turkeys are commonly given as gifts during formal exchanges, used in food preparation and serving. The practical wedding gifts are collectively referred to as *eexhki'ñña* for which I just use the free translation of "gifts" in the transcript of Toò Fabiano's narrative.

1 Kwa'a beè ì yokko kwénda beè ì eexhkì'ñña
   kwa'a   bè=ì   -yoko   kwénda   bè=ì   e#xh-kì'na
   be.place PL=3s receive gift.pleasure PL=3s   CLAS#POS-use.item
   They are there to receive the pleasure of the gifts

2 nóo dette' kwénda beè toòmbálle konna beè ozanna' ona'a.
   nó   dete=' kwénda.   bè to#mbále kona bè o-zana='   ona'a
   that give=ACT gift.pleasure PL godparent with PL CLAS-parent=POS woman
   that the godparents are giving with the bride's parents.

3 Txekkye' tòkko tòkkwa beè benné zé'e dette' kwénda eexhkì'ñña.
   txeke' tòko   tòko=a bè benné zé'e dete='   kwénda   e#xh-kì'na
   then   one   one=SEQ PL person there give=ACT gift.pleasure CLAS#POS-use.item
   Then one-by-one the people there give their gifts.

4 Nii zxa, "Máa lò mbálle. Máa lò endò'.
   ni=zxa   má=lò   mbále   má=lò   endò'
   say=3DIS greetings=2s compadre greetings=2s child
   They say, "Good day compadre. Good day child.

5 Níngye' tòkko eexhkì'ñña nóo nzella ye'tta yoò á.
   nínge'   tòko e#xh-kì'na   nó n-zela   ye'ta.yò=á
   this.thing one CLAS#POS-use.item that STA-permit bring.place=1s
   This is one gift that I'm able to bring here.

6 Kí'ñña lò duránte nóo newaññí lò.
   H*-ki'na=lò duránte nó   ne-waní=lò
   POT-use=2s   during that STA-live=2s
   That you use it during your life.

7 Tòkko tzyáà nokkwa nzella ye'tta yoò á née
   tòko tzyáà nokwa n-zela   ye'ta#yò=á   né
   one just this STA-permit   bring#place=1s   because
   Only this one I am able to bring here because

8 nokkwa tzyáà ri'i alkánse á láa lo'kko á waxxhì.
   nokwa tzyáà ri'i alkánse=á lá   lo'=ko=á waxxhì
   this just do   attain=1s NEG   have=1s   much
   just this I can afford as I don't have much.

9 Nokkwa tzyáà nzella ye'tta yoò á. Ri'i lò perdónna
   nokwa tzyáà n-zela   ye'ta.yò=á   ri'i=lò perdóna
   this just STA-permit bring.place=1s make=2s pardon
   Only this I bring. Forgive me

10 nóo nokkwa tzyáà nzella ye'tta yoò á." nii benné.
   nó   nokwa tzyáà n-zela   ye'ta.yò=á   ni bené
   that this just STA-permit bring.place=1s say person
   that only this I am able to bring." say the people.

This narrative was recorded in my second summer of fieldwork sixteen years before the wedding was video recorded in 2014. Toò Fabiano wanted to share descriptions of cultural practices recording several narratives he composed describing rituals, crafts, and with his father, Daniel, several dialogues about life, travels, and Lachixío history. I use the classifier *Toò* with his name and some others in this book for respect. *Toò* is a word used when referring to saints and ancestors, and as a classifier for the holy or sacred. *Toò* before names marks a venerated status achieved in death. Shortly after recording this and other narratives describing Lachixío life and skillfully depicting Zapotec verbal art, Fabiano crossed the border to the United States and worked as a farmworker for the next ten years in California mainly tending and harvesting grapes, tomatoes, and strawberries, often in fields freshly sprayed with pesticides. He died of colon cancer at the age of twenty-nine.

His narrative captures ideals of offering and gift giving in a Lachixío wedding, particularly in the constructed dialogue of what the gift givers say, and which is attributed to general knowledge with the phrase of speaking at the end, *nii bennè* (say the people). We will see these values enacted in the interactions throughout this chapter. Toò Fabiano described the givers approaching one by one and presenting gifts of use value,[3] exchanging a formal greeting, and humbly denoting the gift as small and singular as in 5, "This is one gift," and 7, "just this one," being humble as in 8 "just this I can afford" and even asking forgiveness for not giving more. While the material of the gift is small, its value as a sign carries great social weight. The first line of the transcript captures this: *Kwa'a beè i yokko kwénda beè i eexhki'ñña* (They are there to receive the pleasure of the gifts). I want to draw your attention to two aspects of this. This first is *yokko kwénda* which we translated as "receive pleasure" and which resonates with the description of gifts described by Radcliffe-Brown from his work in the Andaman Islands. On the purpose of gifts he wrote, "The goal is above all a moral one, the object being to foster friendly feelings between the two persons in question" (cited in Mauss 1990: 19). A less noticeable attribute of line 1 is the importance of being in a place *kwa'a* for the giving. Each round takes place in a specific location, the wedding party moving between the house of the bride's family, the house of the groom's family, and the house of the godparents.

I was drawn to a segment of the gift exchange while filming in 2014 because I noticed that the ritual "broke down." What I mean by that is that the orderly progression of gift givers, acts of offering, and acts of accepting stopped. A gift was not accepted and the giving itself became the subject of what Jefferson (1972) called a "side sequence," because it constitutes a departure from the main line of interaction, and which can be characterized specifically as a type of repair (Schegloff 1987). It was clear at the time that some expectation of the ritual had been transgressed, and what was progressing normally became what Goffman (1967: 12) referred to as an "incident" threatening the ritual order, ratified as needing attention, and becoming the object of interactional work to remedy and reestablish the ritual order.[4] Such moments of repair make the conventional expectations of social interaction visible to participants, and through close analysis of video, to analysts.

As we examine the dialogue of the exchange with the godparents, the ideal of the gift represented by Radcliffe-Brown and Toò Fabiano as a humble signifier of friendly feelings is clearly organizational and operating as a background ideology of this wedding ritual. The actions and words of the Benné Òlla, and the godparents, as well as those of the newlyweds emphasize the humility of the gifts and their function as signs of *amistad* (friendship) rather than for a transfer of wealth, although, in the case of turkey exchange, the gift is valuable as turkeys are currency for the ritual guelaguetza exchange, and adult turkeys have required long-term care and investment. The sequence of activity to fix the broken-down ritual in the wedding displays the interactional work of people within an ideological system reminiscent of Foster's (1965) characterization of a cognitive orientation as unspoken "rules of the game" implicit in normative behavior. Foster described notions of social equilibrium in Tzintzuntzan, a Tarascan (Purépecha) indigenous community of Michoacán, Mexico. He argued that the notions of a "limited good" were interpreted as implying that the accumulation of good by one family would be at the expense of another. Such a cognitive orientation underlies the debt that gifts create in wedding exchanges and social life. Receiving a gift obligates one to give in kind and quantity.

In the procession of gifts, four turkeys are offered to the godparents. These were given one by one in sequence. They were accepted one by one until the third turkey, when it became apparent to the recipient and to the Benné Òlla that they were all from the same giver. The unfolding commitments of obligation that grew in the accepting of the first two offers were then stopped in the liminal timespace between offer and acceptance. The third turkey was not accepted, and the orderly ritual procession of gifts came to a halt. Multimodally, there is a discordant relationship between the words of the Benné Òlla referencing the humility of the gift and the quantity of the gift made apparent when the third turkey was presented.

As Toò Fabiano's narrative indicated, the normal gift is one, and as I have been told by others, a generous gift is sometimes two, but three is noticed as a transgression and sent the ritual off its rails. Benné Òlla then asked his assistant how many turkeys are being gifted, and she responded by saying *Tàkko* (four). When Benné Òlla tells Toòmbálle this, he responds, *Taa Paà* (Who father?). Looking to the crowd they discover the gifts came from the groom's family. The groom then stepped forward to speak (accompanied by other people close to the center of the wedding). The groom stated that if the Benné Òlla would grant permission for its giving, this gift represented his will. He then reframed the gift as not "four" but rather two for the godfather and two for the godmother, a verbal move that gives the appearance of reducing the size of the gift and the debt it represents. The groom insists using the ritual construction *Áà kwà' nekka né tombále* (Yes, it is like this godfather), repeating it several times until Benné Òlla advises Toòmbálle to just accept them all. When Toòmbálle finally accepts, he resonates a parallel response, *Nóo nekka nokkwa* (that it be this) and gestures graciousness with an open hand. When the acceptance is made, closing the joint action of offer-acceptance, the ritual again began to walk forward through the stepwise progression of offer and acceptance.

In these transcripts participants are labeled *Benné Òlla* for the orator (Daniel), *Toòmballe* for the godfather (Benito), *Noòmbálle* for the godmother (Francisca), *Alfonsa* for the assistant (sister to the groom), *Novio* for the groom (León), and *Novia* for the bride (Carmela). References to individuals in the transcription of embodied action are BO Benné Òlla, T Toòmballe, N Noòmballe, A Alfonsa, No Novio, Na Novia. We enter about twenty minutes into the ceremony with Benné Òlla contrasting the smallness of a gift object with the greatness of its signification then beginning a new gift sequence by the greeting *Máa lò* in 2, like in Toò Fabiano's narrative. One of the striking aspects of Daniel's improvisation as Benné Òlla is the lucidity of his own semiotic analysis of gift giving, which very clearly rivals Radcliffe-Brown and Marcel Mauss. In 1 he states that the gift object is small but of much significance, in 5 he refers to the gift explicitly as a *sign*, and in 8 and 9 he indicates that the value of the gift comes "in the passing," and then marks this as common received knowledge with the phrase of speech *nii zxa* (they say).

(1) Gifts for the Godparents 2014

```
1    Benné Òlla:  #Me'e# (.) peèro de múccho signifikasyón.
                  me'e    pèro de  múcho significasyón
                  little  but of   much  significance
                  Little! (.) but of much significance.
```

2   Benné Òlla: ↑Máa lò né mbálle↑.
                  má=lò=né   mbále
                  greetings=2s=ACT3o compadre
                  ↑*Greetings Compadre*↑.
3   Benné Òlla: Mbálle li'i lò mbálle noo li'i lò
                  BO turns to godparents gestures to each with right hand
                  mbále   li'i=lò mbále   no   li'i=lò
                  compadre   PRO=2s   compadre and PRO=2s
                  You compadre and you comadre
4   Benné Òlla: Xhii nekka tòkko íññi::.
                  BO gaze to bird holds with both hands
                  T gaze to bird
                  xhi   ne-aka tòko íni⁵
                  how   STA-be one   animal
                  How it is one animal::.
5   Benné Òlla: ↑Cheè maà noo paà nii á nzoo kyéere tòkko:::::
                  séñña↑

                              -|BO gaze to T

                              ----|T gaze to BO smile
                  che   mà   no   pà   ni=á   n-zo   kyere tòko   séña
                  well mother and father say=1s STA-come want   one   sign
                  Well Mother and Father I say there is coming up a:::: sign
6   Benné Òlla: peèro tòkko íññi ↓díkki.
                  ------|T averts gaze from BO to left (smiling) raises
                        L-hand to chest
                  pèro tòko íni   diki
                  but   one animal   feather
                  but (as) one plumed ↓animal.
7   Benné Òlla: Nekka ↓nóo
                  ne-aka nó
                  STA-be that
                  Be ↓that
8   Benné Òlla: li'i í netee balóoro é
                  BO moves bird toward N
                  ------------------|N reaches to take bird
                  li'i=í   ne-te   balóro=é
                  PRO=3ANIM STA-come value=3o
                  its value comes
9   Benné Òlla: en el #passo# nii zxa,
                  ------------------|BO releases bird R-hand then pointing
                      gesture toward T
                  T lowers hands then raise open palm upright R-hand toward BO
                  en el   paso ni=zxa
                  in the pass say=3DIS
                  in the passing say the people,
10 Toòmbálle: T touch BO hand lower together
11 Benné Òlla: peèro (.) skwaa' nekka né ta.
                  -|BO holding eye gaze on T L-hand over R-hand pointing gesture
                  pèro skwa'   ne-aka=né=ta
                  CONJ like.this   STA-be=ACT3o=always
                  and it is like this always.
12 Toòmbálle: Chettza lò mbálle. (.) Chettza lá lò mbálle.
                  -|T raise L-hand gaze past BO-L head nod
                  ------------------|T raise R-hand gaze past BO-R head nod
                  chetza=lò mbále   chetza la=lò   mbále
                  thanks=2s compadre   thanks already=2s   compadre
                  Thanks comadre. (.) Thanks compadre.

48   *Saying and Doing in Zapotec*

```
13  Benné Òlla:    °Skwaa' nekka né ta°.
                   ------|BO body torque
                   -----------------|BO head turn left toward T direct gaze
                   kwa     ne-aka=né=ta
                   this    STA-be=ACT3O=always
                   °It is like this always°.
14  Toòmbálle:     T body torque-R to N (speaks with head flip toward crowd)
```

The ritual phrase of the Benné Òlla *skwaa' nekka né* (It is like this) in 11 and 13 is what people use to accept gifts. This and the thanking gestures of the Toòmbálle in 12 and 14 in the direction of the gift line mark the end of this gift giving sequence (a joint action of offer-acceptance). We would expect the ritual to normally go on to the next giver and gift. As the Benné Òlla moves to deliver his denouement, the joint action appeared to him to be complete. Benné Òlla emphasizes the humility of giving a single gift saying, "instead of several they give one" in 15, another clear parallel to the text that guided Toò Fabiano's narrative.

```
15  Benné Òlla:    En el pásso de, (0.3.) báryos, (0.6) ↓dette tòkko. (0.3)
                   íññi díkki nii zxa.
                   |BO turns to T raises both hands palms facing hands
                     apart,
                   --------------|BO L-hand left
                   --------------------|BO raise 2-hands front with palms facing
                   -----------------------------|BO hands alternate down beats
                      |lowers both hands
                   en   el    páso   de   báryos   dete   tòko   íni    díki   ni=zxa
                   in   the   pass   of   several  pass   one    bird   give   say=3DIS
                   Instead of (0.3) several (0.6) (they) ↓give one. (0.3)
                   bird gift say the people.
16                 T points past N and utters directive to put bird there
                   BO turns to take bird-2 at this point being presented by A
17  Benné Òlla:    Stókkwe?
                   ---|BO grabs bag and lifts bird-2
                   stókwe
                   Another?
18  Alfonsa:       Áà,
                   áà
                   Yes,
19  Benné Òlla:    °Níngye' stokko é nèé'°.
                   -|BO head turn toward T/N
                   nínge'       sH-tòko=é           nèé'
                   thing        another-one=3o      now
                   °Now another one°.
20  Benné Òlla:    Chòkko beeròlla akka xle'e wa.
                   |BO hands bird-2 to T
                   -------|T grabs bird-2 with both hands
                   chòko    be#ròla          aka     x-le'e=wa
                   two      CLAS#male.turkey  be     POS-PRO=2PL
                   Two turkeys are yours.
21  Benné Òlla:    BO releases bird-2
22                 N interacting with bird-1
23                 T head point behind N utters directive to put bird-1
                     there
24                 BO body torque-L gaze to A who holds bird-3
```

25 Benné Òlla: °Chòkko beeròlla nekka kwénda' beè zxa nèé' la°?
                  |BO thumb point back toward T
                  --|A gaze to BO
                  choko be#ròla   ne-aka kwénda'   bè=zxa nèé'=la
                  two   CLAS#male.turkey STA-be gift.pleasure PL=3DIS now=Q
                  °Two turkeys are gifts for them now?°

26 Alfonsa: Tàkko í [tàkko í 0.
                  BO reaches for bird-3
                  tàko=í   tàko=í
                  four=3ANIM   four=3ANIM
                  Four of them [four 0.

27 Benné Òlla: [Tàkko (.) ↑Aà wenno.
                  -|BO head nod, takes bird-3
                  ----|A head nod
                  tàko à   weno
                  four oh   good
                  Four (.) oh good.

28 Benné Òlla: BO turn-R step toward T
29 Toòmbálle: T (holding bird-2) head turn to BO stumble-L
30 Benné Òlla: Nii zxa (0.4) nii zxa (0.2) ↓#tàko# í jdette kwénda' nèé'.
                  -----------------|BO nod
                  ni=zxa   ni=zxa   tàko=í   r-dete   kwénda'   nèé'
                  say=3DIS   say=3DIS   four=3ANIM HAB-give gift.pleasure now
                  They say (0.4) they say (0.2) ↓#four# of them are given
                      as gifts now.

31 Benné Òlla: ↓Áà paà.
                  áà   pà
                  yes father
                  ↓Yes father.

32 Toòmbálle: Tii? Tii zxa nóo nii zxa skwa'?
                  ti   ti=zxa   nó   ni=zxa   skwa'
                  who who=3DIS that say=3DIS like.this
                  Who? Who of them says it is like this?

33 Benné Òlla: Paà: taà wa nii: nzoo kyè oo (.) benné á ka'a aà
                  -------|BO R-thumb point back-R
                  ----------------------|BO turn-L 180° grabs bird-3 with
                      R-hand
                  --|BO L-hand
                      shoulder A
                  pà: ta=wa   ni   nzo#kè   o   bené=á   ka'a   à
                  father which=2PL   say stand#up um   person=1s here   oh
                  Father which of yours says it stands so, um, my people
                      here, oh

In 16 we see some of the business of accommodating, or dealing with, the material gifts. Toòmbálle points to Noòmbálle indicating a place to put the live turkey held in a mesh bag (which he repeats a second time in 23). Turning to his assistant, Benné Òlla sees a second bird and asks, "Another?" while taking it. His assistant affirms and he then turns to do the voicing of the gift, "Now another one. Two turkeys are yours." and passes the bird to Toòmbálle (19–21). While two turkeys contradicted Benné Òlla's commentary that gifts are one, it is a constraint that is tolerably violated and he goes on with the ritual. By 24 Benné Òlla turns to his assistant to see another turkey. With the third turkey coming, Benné Òlla issues an understanding check, "These two are gifts for them now?" (25), as a way of probing whether this third bird is the beginning of a new gift sequence from another giver. The assistant (Alfonsa) tells him there are four turkeys. Benné Òlla turns to Toòmbálle and passes the information emphasizing in breathy voice the number four, "they say #four# of them are given as gifts now" to which Toòmbálle responds with a question, "Who of them says it is like this?" We can see the incident develop across several moves in the transcript. Beginning with the introduction of the third turkey in 24, a series of repairs are initiated: first with Benné Òlla's understanding check in 25 and then the response of Alfonsa. What she tells Benné Òlla transits the participant chain of the ritual ecology through him to Toòmbálle. Finally with Toòmbálle's question of "who" in 32, the incident becomes the business at hand. The participants step out of the ritual frame to fully deal with the incident of the four turkeys that stopped the ritual. One way this can literally be seen is the bodily actions transcribed in the subsequent line. The men break from the focused multi-participant configuration (what Adam Kendon 2009 termed the "F-formation") in which the ritual has been carried out, and turn to the audience to look for who offered such a gift (33). Benné Òlla's talk indicates this ongoing search, asking, "Which of yours says it stands so?" Then as Alfonsa (Daniel's helper and the groom's sister) steps forward with a knowing smile, "Who" becomes apparent to Benné Òlla, indicated in his news uptake index "oh." Alfonsa, in the falsetto voice of respect I have described previously (Sicoli 2007, 2010a), smiles and affirms, "It is like this."

```
34  Alfonsa:      ↑Áà ⱼ[skwa' nekka né kwa'↑.
                  -|A gaze to T smile
                  Áà    skwa'        ne-aka=né    kwa'
                  yes   like.this    STA-be=ACT3o this
                  ↑Yes it is like this ↑.

35  Benné Òlla:   ⱼ[Kwénda (.) nokkwe xoombále wa nokkwe xoombále wa.
                  |BO open-hand point beyond A becomes |I-finger point,
                  ---------------|BO head turn R to T head turn gaze
                                past A
                  kwénda              nokwe zxo-mbále=wa    nokwe
                  gift.pleasure this  POS-compadre=2PL      this
                  zxo-mbále=wa
                  POS-compadre=2PL
                  Your compadres your compadres give this gift.

36  Alfonsa:      ⱼ[↑Nekwénda↑ (.) ↑Kwénda kon permisyón↑. (.) Tòkko kwénda.
                  ---------------------------|A head nod
                  -------------------------------|A head nod
                  ne-kwénda      kwénda         kon  permisyón  tòkko
                  STA-gift.pleasure gift.pleasure with permission one
                    kwénda
                    gift.pleasure
                  ↑Gifting↑ (.) ↑A gift with permission↑. (.) One gift.

37  Toòmbálle:    ₖ[Áwwa? ₖ[So né mbálle:? Skwà' mballe:::?
                  T head flip gaze to A-------------|gaze to No
                  áwa    r-tzo=né    mbále       skwà'     mbále
                  yes    HAB-go-ACT3o compadre   like.this compadre
                  Yes? It goes like this comadre? Like this comadre?

38  Novio:        ₖ[Áà (.) ningye' nekka né toòmbálle.
                  --------|No enters frame walking from R gaze to T
                  ----------------|BO gaze to N
                  áà     ninge'  ne-aka=né    tò#mbále
                  yes    thing   STA-be=ACT3o godfather
                  Yes this thing is so godfather.

39  Benné Òlla:   Nii [kláa wa.
                  -------|BO head nod
                  ni     klá=wa
                  say    clear=2PL
                  You all clarify this.
```

```
40 Novio:            [Tonno nii:: benné oxxo kaà txee (0.35) nokkwa nekka
                      boluntáad txee.
                     No gaze BO R-hand up palm-L---------|No hand beat down
                     -------------------------N takes bird-2 from T
                     tono   ni    bené    oxo    kà      txee    nokwa   ne-aka
                     if          say     person  grand   this    then    this     STA-be
                     boluntád   txe
                     will       then
                     If the Benné Òlla says it's OK ther (0.35)
                     this is my will then.
```

At this point it is essential to think about the tangling of roles in the situation of the gift ritual, the larger wedding in which it is embedded, and the everyday relations of kin and ritual kin that link the participants. Alfonsa is acting as an assistant to the Benné Òlla and is his cousin as well as sister to the groom and thus part of the family unit—the family being the social group that bears gifts and gains reputations in such exchange. Her falsetto voice in 34 marks a shift from her previous utterances as assistant, which were in modal voice. With it she becomes a gift giver, standing on behalf of her family. The *beè toòmbálle* (godparents of the wedding) in this ritual are in everyday life *xombálle* (co-parents), sharing ritual responsibilities with the bride and groom as godparents in support of each other's children. This relationship is referenced by Benné Òlla in 35, the answer to the question "who" in 32. The temporal development of his recognition is embodied as his less distinct open-hand point becomes an index finger point to the bride and groom. In 36 Alfonsa asserts that this is, if permitted, one gift. But who is the permission sought from? As the gift *offer* must be *accepted*, permission must ultimately be granted by the recipient, but in 37 we rather get repair initiations from Toòmbálle questioning Alfonsa if what he sees being offered is true. At this point the groom enters to answer, "Yes, this is so." As the groom approached, several guests and family members gathered around to listen (Figure 2.4). The Benné Òlla directs the parties to clarify the

Figure 2.4 The groom reframes the gift as not four turkeys but two for the godfather and two for the godmother.

situation. In the groom's next turn (40), he specifically refers to the potential permission of the Benné Òlla to allow this gift. The person of the Benné Òlla embodies the ethical judgment on acceptable gifts. His social position has the agency to adjust the norm to resolve the incident. Now let's look at the rhetoric of persuasion the groom develops in clarifying his family's gift and the responses of Toòmbálle and Benné Òlla.

```
41  Novio:       Chòkko í:: li'i lò noo chòkko í noòmbálle á paara nóo
                 nokkwa naa nearkì' á toòmbále.
                 --|No R-hand forward toward T---|No R-hand left toward N
                 -------------------------------|N takes bird-2 from T
                 -|No R-hand forward palm facing T
                 chòko=í    li'i=lò     no     chòko=í    nò#mbále=á   para   nó
                 two=3ANIM  PRO=2S      and    two=3ANIM  madrina=1S   for    that
                 nokwa      na          ne-arkì'=á        tò#mbále
                 be(sit)    appear      STA-heart=1S      godfather
                 Two of them for you and two for my godmother that is
                     where my heart sits godfather.

42  Novio:       Áà kwà' nekka né toòmbále.
                 N nods (2x)
                 áà   kwà'   ne-aka=né    tò#mbále
                 yes  this   STA-be=ACT3o godfather
                 Yes, it is like this godfather.

43  Toòmbálle:   Áà skwa' tzyáà ra mbálle xo/xonno ri'i wa skwa'.
                 BO passes bird-3 to T
                 ----|T takes bird-3 from BO
                 áà   skwa'      tzyáà=ra   mbálle    xono    ri'i=wa    skwa'
                 yes  like.this  just=EXCL  compadre  because make=2S    like.this
                 Yes just like this compadre! Be/Because you make it like this.

44  Novio:       A'a.
                 No head shake
                 a'a
                 No.

45  Novio:       A'a [ákka né txee toòmbále
                 No head shake
                 a'a  H*-aka=né     tò#mbále
                 no   POT-be=ACT3o  godfather
                 No that it be like this then godfather.

46  Benné Òlla:  [Iñní li'kki qee nekka tòkko nóo
                 BO pushes bird-3 lightly pulls hand back F-shape
                 iní    li'ki   qe    ne-aka   tòko   nó
                 bird   give    that  STA-be   one    that
                 Bird-giving is one (but)

47  Benné Òlla:  loo loo [bicchà nóo ri'i #sáa# í. Ri'i #sár# í.
                 ------------|BO gaze to eyes T
                 --------------------|BO palm down
                 -----------------------------------|BO hand up then down
                 lo     bichà   nó    ri'i.sár=í   ri'i.sár=í
                 face   day     that  use=3ANIM    use=3ANIM
                 on a day that (you will) use them. Use them.

48  Novio:       [Áà kwà' nekka né toòmbále.
                 No nods
                 áà   kwà'   nékka=né     tò#mbále
                 yes  this   STA-be=ACT3o godfather
                 Yes, it is like this godfather.
```

The *novio* restates the terms of the gift not as four turkeys as declared by Benné Òlla in 30, but as two gifts of two, distributed to two individuals, "Two of them for you and two for my godmother." This is itself a bending of the truth. Since wedding gifts are attributed to families and not individuals, reducing the gift to two and two constructs each gift as closer to the ideal one, and parallel to the tolerably generous gift of two. Of course the amount of turkeys remains the same, which is why we can see the reduction of the gift as rhetorical, created performatively in words. The groom then declares that this is where his heart sits, the heart in Zapotec, and for many other indigenous Mesoamericans being the center of emotion, and will. In 42 we see the first of what will be several iterations of the utterance *Áà kwà' nekka né toòmbálle* (Yes, it is like this godfather) with affirmative head nods by the groom (note that the talk of this turn echoes the godfather's question in 32: "Who says it is like this?"). The groom's repetition of this phrase a few turns later becomes a rhythmic mantra of repetitions until the godfather verbally accepts the gift, closing the joint action of offer-response and putting the ritual back on its tracks. This acceptance does not come right away in words, but we do begin to see movements of acceptance across the participants. In 43, the godfather issues an affirmative interjection *Áà* in response to the groom's reformulation of the gift as two and two, and an emphatic statement *skwa' tzyáà ra mbálle xonno ri'i wa skwa* (that it is like this! [*ra* marking exclamation] because you compadre are making it like this). While this verbal acceptance nudges the ritual back toward its tracks, it is not fully accepted at this point. (It is conditional and there is still the matter of the birds in hand.) The groom reiterates again the ritual phrase that it be like this, and step by step the birds are handled. First, in 41 we see that just after the groom gestures to the godmother and declares that two of the birds are for her, she takes the second turkey that the godfather has been holding. Then in 43 where the godfather expresses reluctant affirmation verbally he takes the third turkey from the Benné Òlla. The Benné Òlla then makes a declaration that reemphasizes that the norm for the gift is one. "Bird-giving is one," he says, but advises the godfather to take and use them one day in the future. Along with these words the Benné Òlla gently pushes on the third bird held by the godfather, in the direction of where the godmother has been storing the gifts. Here the permission that was sought of the Benné Òlla is granted. But everyone is still waiting for the verbal acceptance of the gift from the recipient. Until this happens, the groom continues repeating his rhythmically resonating declarations, "Yes, it is like this godfather," which we see in 48 and again in 49 with the acceptance coming in 50.

```
49 Novio:       Áà kwà' nekka né toòmbálle.
                ----|No nods
                áà      kwà'    ne-aka=né       tò#mbále
                yes     this    STA-be=ACT3o    godfather
                Yes, it is like this godfather.
50 Toòmballe:   Chettza láa lò toòmbále,
                T nod to BO----------T gaze to N
                chetza=lá=lò            tò#mbále
                thanks=already=2s       godfather
                Thank you, godfather,
51 Novio:       Áà [k
                N nods
                Yes th/
52 Toòmbálle:   [↑Peèro nóo nekka nokkwa.↑ (.) ↑Nóo nekka nokkwa↑.
                T raise L-hand palm to right toward No then toward A
                ----|T head up bows forward toward No then toward A
                pèro    nó      ne-aka      nokwa   nó      ne-aka      nokwa
                but     that    STA-be      this    that    STA-be      this
                ↑But that it be this that it be this↑.
```

53 Novio:	Áà kwà' nekka né toòmbálle.
	No bows forward to T
	----------------T turns gaze to A bows to A
	áà kwà' ne-aka=né tò#mbále
	yes this STA-be=ACT3o godfather
	Yes, like this godfather.
54	((chorus of thanks giving in falsetto voice register))
55 Novia:	Na moves forward bows/head nods toward T

Deferring to the Benné Òlla's permission to accept the gift that he just received, the godfather first thanks the Benné Òlla with a nod to him in 50. Then turning his body toward the groom, the godfather speaks to the groom who stops his rhythmic repetitions in mid-sentence to listen to the godfather. In 52 the ritual acceptance is issued with a respectful raised pitch, "But that it be this," raising his hand as he has in the past gift acceptances and bowing to the groom. The acceptance is a watershed moment. The groom repeats one last time, "Yes like this godfather," which resonates now with the godfather's verbal acceptance and then there is a chorus of falsetto-voiced utterances of thanks from the groom León, his sister Alfonsa, and the bride Carmela, who steps forward toward the godparents and bows to them.

With the incident resolved the interaction moves back into the matter of giving and receiving gifts.

56 Benné Òlla:	BO takes bird-4 from A
57 Alfonsa:	A nudged from behind by beer case turns around
58 Benné Òlla:	**Boluntáad beè zxa nokkwa lá.**
	boluntád bè=zxa nokwa=lá
	will PL=3DIS this=already
	Their will already.
59	BO moves bird-4 toward T
	A reaches for beer case from person frame-R
60 Benné Òlla:	**Boluntáad beè zxa nokkwa lá.**
	T takes bird-4 from BO
	boluntád bè=zxa nokwa=lá
	will PL=3DIS this=already
	Their will already.
59 Alfonsa:	A takes beer case from person frame-R
60	T turns-R N takes bird-4 from T/BO

The Benné Òlla takes the fourth turkey from the assistant, and then she is nudged from behind by a case of beer as the next gift comes into view. The incident frame (the side sequence resolving the trouble) and the ritual frame (of gift giving) are overlapping still. The Benné Òlla makes a declaration that the gift of turkeys was their will (using the plural that indicates that, while the groom and godfather were the spokespersons, the gift is between families). Before the next gift can be passed and voiced, there is still the issue of the turkeys. The godfather takes the fourth turkey from the Benné Òlla who is repeating again that this is their will and the godmother immediately takes the fourth turkey (though the godfather is still left holding the third turkey). At the same time the beer case is being passed from a guest to the assistant Alfonsa.

```
61 Alfonsa:      A'á.
                 A body torque-R
                 a'a
                 INT
                 Here.
62               A body torque-R nudge BO with beer case
                 ---------------|BO gaze A, body torque-L, grabs beer
                     case
64 Toòmbálle:    T turn-L toward BO/A
65 Benné Òlla:   Níngye' tòkko::: ↑refrésko paara ekkyè í nèé'.
                 BO lift beer case
                 ----------|turn R face T
                 nínge'  tòko  refrésko      para  ekè=í      nèé'
                 this    one   refreshment   for   head=3ANIM  now
                 This a ↑refreshment over and above the animals now.
66 Toòmbálle:    Ne/ ↑Nekka txee mbálle↑.
                 T nod-|head turn R ((looks for N))
                 ne-aka   txe  mbále
                 STA-be   then compadre
                 Wai/↑Wait compadre↑.
67 Benné Òlla:   Áà.
                 BO nod
                 áà
                 yes
                 Yes. ((BO goes on voicing attributes of the gift))
68               T head turn-R (to N) hand raise to wipe neck
                 Alfonsa turns to Na gives a big smile
```

Alfonsa interjects *aá* (here) and nudges the Benné Òlla for him to take the beer case. He then turns to the godfather to voice the gift and saying in 65, "This is a refreshment over and above the animals now," the gift coming from the same family! While the ritual has moved on the godfather is still holding a turkey. A bit overwhelmed by this he says disfluently (with a self repair) ↑Wai/Wait compadre.↑ in falsetto voice and then turns right looking for the godmother's help with the turkey. He raises his hand to wipe sweat from his neck visibly hot under the collar, or embarrassed, by the quantity of gifts. As Gloria Goodwin Raheja (1988) observed in *The Poison in the Gift*, the obligation in accepting a gift is like an "inauspicious" affliction. The Benné Òlla goes on describing uses of the gift of the beer case, and Alfonsa turns to her sister-in-law, the bride, flashing a satisfied smile, having achieved, it seems, pragmatic, and emotional affect, with this gift of already too many turkeys, and then some.

What does this show us about offers? First is that in comparison to the narrative of the wedding I recorded with Toò Fabiano in 1998, we can see from parallel speech act formulations that the interaction is semi-scripted with the dialogue of the Benné Òlla and the recipients following ritual norms. These norms/texts/scripts for offering relate to moral dimensions of humility and the social communion of friendship. People I talked with about why the wedding gift of four birds created such a disruption often referenced the normativity of "one" in the response, and that there is some flexibility depending on the will of the bride and groom to give a second.

When the bride and groom, the godparents, and the families of the bride are from our town, the norm is that after the mass, they go to the godparents' house, after that to the bride's house with the gifts for the couple, and then they give those gifts when arriving at the house of the groom. At night when it's time to say goodbye to the godparents [at the godparents' house again], they give a jar of food (mole), a basket of tortillas, one or two turkeys, and a case of beer or soda, a little more or less depending on the possibility or will of the bride and groom. Oh, and a bottle of Mezcal. Like this is the giving of gifts to the godparents: a jar of mole, one basket of tortillas, one bottle of mezcal, and, if possible, one turkey, and if there's no turkey, a chicken. These gifts are given by the bride and groom to the godparents for the favor of sponsoring the wedding.

Giovani's description emphasizes the few types of gifts that are given to godparents, and of these types it is commonly *one* of each, with the exception that sometimes two turkeys are given. In the video though double the amount of turkeys (or four times depending on how one counts) created an incident where this moral norm itself became the object of an interactional side sequence. The temporal progress of the ritual was put on hold and the morality of the gift was brought to center stage in which the potential debt created in accepting this gift had to be negotiated. How this was done is telling about how language weaves its way through time and social relations in Lachixío. The groom's rhetoric involved discursively reducing the gift, previously formulated by Benné Òlla as "four," to two turkeys for the godfather and two turkeys for the godmother. More than a mere play with words, this creative accounting could enter into the common ground as a "true" state of affairs that all could feel matched the expectations of gifts to the godparents. This allows for another obligation to be met: the obligation to accept a gift and the social relation it entails.

How are moral constraints on the realization of relations and reputations negotiated in offers? In the first place, large enough violations of expectation are met with initiations of *repair*, marking the happening as an incident to be remedied. But we also see in the transcript that the obligation to accept is asserted through repetition, as with the groom's rhythmic repetitions of the phrase "Yes, it is like this" that itself resonates with the godfather's sought-after ritual response of acceptance, "That it be this."

But rather than the sole mark of a moment, the language of offers and their acceptance is part to multimodal assemblages that develop in time and space. The passing and accepting to which grammatical constructions are connected are not necessarily performed at the same time with the words spoken. They can be but do not have to be simultaneous or strictly adjacent. We saw this clearly in the fact that before the godfather gave a formal verbal acceptance of the gift, he already began accepting turkeys passed from Benné Òlla and in turn passed them to the godmother. As accepting material gifts involves both talk and the material transfer of the object, there is not a single "synchronic" moment of acceptance, but rather we see acceptance taking place in a region of time assembled across the mutually elaborating semiotic modalities.[6] However, that speech in an assemblage may hold performative value that physical action does not is revealing of what Webb Keane (2005) has called "semiotic ideologies." The on-record acceptance that the interaction has been working toward is a verbal formulaic construction, though it is itself accompanied with ritual body movements of bowing and hand gestures. The pragmatic effect of this composite utterance to change the world is made clear in the immediately subsequent actions of all the participants. Beyond the resonance of the groom with himself and the godfather, we also see parallelism across multiple participants including the Benné Òlla, and the groom's sister Alfonsa. Others in the family join in when the gift is finally accepted where a chorus of resonating falsetto-voiced utterances of thanks erupts, creating in the listener a joint effect (and affect) of overtones, and to the viewer of parallel bodies in visible acts of co-deferment. Together the multiple offers of multiple parties illustrate offers as collaborative joint actions, negotiated in the moment with an eye toward the future obligations that are created with the joint commitment of acceptance.

Now let's turn from the formal ritual of a wedding to the "little rituals" of everyday life, which Haviland (2009: 21), inspired by Goffman's *Interaction Rituals* (1967), observed are places that resonate "echoes of more thoroughly regimented, formulaic, and contextually bound ways of using language."

2.2 Half-a-Taco: Offers that Resonate across Participants and Iterations that Reduce the Burden to Accept

Like the more formal gift exchange at the wedding, everyday offers often have multiple animators in Lachixío. The re-animations involved verbal and gestural characterizations of the gift and its material transfer. An offer initiates a sequence in which it is relevant to accept or reject the object or action. Either response will complete the sequence, though, if the closing act is not performed, the joint action is left incomplete. The little ritual is left in a state of liminality. Side sequences or additional offers may fill the space between offer and acceptance. In the example of offering dinner to a guest we will examine in this section, iterated offers resonate across hosting family members, and even continue to be iterated after verbal acceptance is achieved. Such iterated offers are common in Lachixío and perform an ethic of care and hospitality that is characteristic of a good life, a good family, and is a source of pride to many in the community. These moral dimensions pervade the little rituals of everyday life.[7] One thing that Pedro's collaboration on this project did was create visiting events where Pedro and sometimes his wife or daughter were guests in others' homes. Given the ethic of hospitality in Lachixío, Pedro often received offers of food, drink, and comfort. This participatory dimension clearly directed my attention to offers and shaped the focus of this research.

In this video segment, Pedro is visiting the house of his neighbors Flavio and Kacha, a husband and wife, who live adjacent to his parents at the edge of the village. He went to Flavio and Kacha's house multiple times over two days and recorded several hours of video including dinner preparation and consumption, breakfast, gossip, storytelling, and child socialization events on their patio, and chores. Flavio's mother is present in several videos as are several of Flavio and Kacha's children. On the evening of late July when this video was made, Pedro also had tentatively made plans with me to return to my house to talk, and it was already getting late.

As this segment opens, Pedro is expressing some doubt as to whether he will make it back to see me before I go to sleep and thus if we would have to wait until the morning for our meeting. He is explaining this when Kacha offers that he stay for supper. It is about forty minutes into the recording. The food initially offered is one taco.[8] As an initiating act of a sequence of joint action, the offer creates an obligation to respond, with a preference for accepting. This must be weighed in this situation with the social relations between Pedro and me (about a kilometer away), his video-recording responsibilities to the project we were collaborating on, his habit of filling up a sixty-three-minute DV video cassette before leaving a setting, and the social relations of the present interaction, which include obligations of being together in dialogue and the stacking of joint commitments that that entails. The last two commitments (to the sixty-three-minute format and receiving the food offer in copresence) were weighted to his staying longer, and that is what he did.

The offer in 2 is multimodally accomplished: Kacha places tortillas down on the table near Pedro while saying to him ↑*Odàkko éttà né Béttò*↑ (↑Eat a taco Pedro↑) uttered in the falsetto honorific voice. Pedro accepts in the next turn, also in falsetto ↑*Áà chettza láa lò txee Káccha:*↑ (↑Yes, thank you then Kacha↑). This could be the end of the sequence, but before he finishes, Kacha speaks in overlap with a second offer, ↑*Dàkk:o éttà né Béttò*↑ (↑Eat a taco Pedro↑).

(2) LMSMVDP20Jul0904 (40.00–40.33)

Pedro is seated just out of frame on the left.

```
1 Pedro:    Àsta ye'e xáa lèé
            -K walks out-of-frame toward P with tortillas
            -F gaze on P-----------
            ásta      ye'e       xa        lèé
            until     tomorrow   how       name
            ...(or then) I'll do this tomorrow, um

2 Kacha:    ↑Odàkk:o éttà né Béttò↑.
            -K (puts tortillas on table near P)
            L*-o-dàko?        étà=né              Béto-L
            IMP-CMP-eat       tortilla=ACT3o      Pedro-CLAS
            ↑Eat a taco Pedro↑.

3 Pedro:    ↑Áà chettza lá lò [txee Káccha:↑.
            áà        chetza=lá=lò         txe       Káccha-L
            yes       thanks=already=2s    then      Kacha-CLAS
            ↑Yes, thank you then Kacha↑.

4 Kacha:                      [↑Dàkk:o éttà né Béttò↑.
                              L*-dàko           étà=né              Béto-L
                              IMP-CLAS.eat      tortilla=ACT3o      Pedro-CLAS
                              ↑Eat a taco Pedro↑.
```

One thing you may note is the use of imperative grammatical form in Kacha's offers. We will see this quite a lot in the data where imperative formed directives (commands) are common vehicles for offers and also requests (as we will see in Chapter 3). Her directive form is a strong imperative built on the completive aspect morphology that I have described previously as contrasting with a weaker imperative built on the potential mood morphology (Sicoli 2007, 2010a). Before Pedro replies to this second offer, Flavio joins in to make the offer to Pedro as well.

```
5  Flavio:    ↑Àkko tele'e éttà txee Béttò↑.
              ------|F drops gaze
              L*-àko    te-le'e  étà         txe    Béto-L
              IMP-eat   IND-half tortilla    then   Pedro-CLAS
              ↑Eat half a taco then Pedro↑.
6  Pedro:     Chettza lá lò txee Fláviò.
              chetza=lá=lò          txe    Flávio-L
              thanks=already=2s     then   Flávio-CLAS
              Then thank you Flavio.
7  Flavio:    Àkko tele'e Béttò peèro
              L*-àko    te-le'e    Béto-L         pèro
              IMP-eat   IND-half   Pedro-CLAS     but
              Eat half Pedro but
8  Pedro:     Eèro àkkwá éttà tele'e txee ra Fláviò!
              èro    H*-àko=á    étà         te-le'e txe=ra      Flávio-L
              but    POT-eat=1s  tortilla    IND-half then=EXCL  Flávio-CLAS
              But I'll eat a half then Flavio!
9  Flavio:    Kyènne Béttò àkko te[le'e né Pablò.
              -----------------------|F raises gaze to P--------|F
                     drops gaze
              L*-kene    béto-L       L*-àko   te-le'e=né    Béto-L
              IMP-insist Pedro-CLAS   IMP-eat  IND-half=ACT3O Pedro-CLAS
              (We) insist Pedro, eat a half Pedro.
10 Kacha:                              [↑Odàkko [tele'e né Béttò↑.
                                       -|F raises gaze to ?
                                       L*-o-dàko     tele'e=né      Béto-L
                                       IMP-CMP-eat   IND-half=ACT3O Pedro-CLAS
                                       ↑Eat a half Pedro↑.
11 Pedro:                                       [°↑Áà chettza txee ra↑°
                                                áà   chetza   txe=ra
                                                yes  thanks   then=EXCL
                                                °↑yes thanks then↑°!
12 Kacha:     ↑Chékkye^ nzyaa↑ lò °txee°.
              chéke     nzya=lò    txe
              then      STA.go=2s  then
              ↑A little later↑ you go °then°.
```

The multiple offers, by multiple participants, increase the intensity of the social pressure for acceptance, yet at the same time, and reminiscent of the groom's move in the wedding, Flavio reduces the offer. Flavio says, ↑Àkko tele'e éttà txee Béttò↑ (Eat half then Pedro) in 5 as if Pedro had said no. Flavio also uses a directive form, but uses the less forceful potential mood form. The grammatical difference patterns across gender in these offers. While Kacha continues to use stronger completive-based directives, Flavio consistently uses weaker potential-based directives. Kacha's stronger directive form is, however, juxtaposed with the high-pitched voice of the respect register, a multimodal discordance that attends to two social actions at once.

Pedro graciously accepts Flavio's offer in 6, but like with Kacha before, Pedro's acceptance is followed immediately with a second offer by Flavio to eat a half which Pedro accepts on those terms saying, "I'll eat a half then!" Now Flavio follows Pedro's acceptance in 9 with another iteration of the offer, "[We] insist Pedro, eat a half, Pedro" and Kacha then speaks in overlap with Flavio making yet another offer to eat half-a-taco. Pedro accepts again in the next turn. In the last line Kacha says, "A little later you go." The rhetoric of reduction from the offer of a taco to "half a taco" affords Pedro the opportunity to both manage his relationship with his hosts by accepting a sign of the whole gift in its part and potentially keep his prior commitment to meet with me. Though Pedro makes no hurry in eating, he eats more than just a half-a-taco, and didn't come to visit me until the following morning. So we see here, like with the groom, that the reduction is a ritual means of discursively reducing the burden of accepting. At the same time, the rhythmic parallelism of iterated actions across time, across the participants of the setting, and the imperative grammatical forms intensify the offer. As a guest in Lachixío turning down an offer is difficult and dispreferred. The multimodal, multi-participant assemblage through which everyday offers like this are made, and accepted, constructs an ethic of amicable sharing, building social bonds and family reputations.

As part of the participatory methodology of the project, I set up a playback dialogue with my friends David and Giovani who viewed the video and talked about what was going on. Between them they decided to depict for me how food offers go in Lachixío by enacting several skits. Like with Toò Fabiano's narrative about the form of the wedding, David and Giovani's performances display several parallels that reveal their understanding of the cognitive and moral orientations guiding social interaction between families and friends who visit.

2.3 "Saying and Doing"

One of the things the interaction in the previous section shows is that even if an offer is accepted, the sequence may still be characterized by further iterations of the offer. Thus in their doing, offers achieve and display something more than the practicality of getting food on the table. In linking the saying of the verbal offer, the verbal response of acceptance or refusal, and the doing of actions with the material objects exchanged, relationships are being built. While in linguistic theory talk and action are commonly thought to be unproblematic mirrors of each other, not explicitly theorized, and ignored in linguistic text collections made through audio-only media capture, the video-recorded segments, and the discussions of my collaborators, support that there is a creative and symbolic dimension to how the modalities of encounters are aligned and juxtaposed by participants in the temporality of the event. We see this in Kacha's combination of respectful voice with more forceful imperative forms and the verbal reduction of turkeys or tacos to reference less than the whole actually being given. Across the chapters of this book we will see more examples where words and actions are creatively combined into discordant assemblages.

During video watching sessions, David and Giovani discussed how insistence and repetition of offers are customs of Lachixío. They talked about the video segment between themselves, and then talked with me about what they saw going on, what they felt was important or representative of Lachixío culture. In these sessions, Giovani also initiated skits that depicted naturalistic interactional sequences where he and his younger brother took on the role of a host and a guest. The first was about how many offers a host might give to a guest before allowing the sequence to end without acceptance. The second depicted several polite refusals before accepting. And the third depicted the offering of more food to guests already eating at a fiesta.

Refusals of food offers are commonly phrased as declarations of having already eaten as in David's response in 2.

```
1 Giovani:     Àkko txèkka éttà Béttò.
               L*-àko txèka étà       Béto-L
               IMP-eat food  tortilla Pedro-CLAS
               Eat a taco, Pedro.
2 David:       A'a chettza lá lò. Odàkko lá né.
               A'a chetza=lá=lò       o-dàko=lá=né
               NEG thank=already=2S CMP-eat=already=ACT3o
               No, thank you. I have already eaten.
```

Repetitions of offers may proceed from offering to eat in general, to offering just one food item, like a taco, to offering less than one, like half-a-taco. This is also common when inviting someone first to drink, then reducing the offer to just one beer, or one shot of mezcal, and subsequently to half a beer or half a shot. Such offers with their reductions are then often repeated for additional rounds. David again refuses Giovani's offer to just eat half in 7, elaborating his earlier claim of having already eaten with the specificity of having eaten just before arriving, and framing the proposition as the truth with *de líi* (lit. of upright) to emphasize that it is not just rhetoric.

```
7 Giovani:     Màsse tele'e né àkko txee.
               màse tele'e=né    àko txe
               more half=ACT3o   eat then
               Then eat another half.
8 David:       A'a de líi odàkko ìnza éttà nzellá.
               a'a de-lí         o-dàko ìnza étà      n-zelá
               NEG of-upright CMP-eat just tortilla STA-come
               No, I truly just ate before I came.
```

In the skit it was after three offers that Giovani reduced the offer to half. The half-offers were also then done three times. In response to each offer-initiation, David repeated that he had just eaten before arriving. The refusals all included tokens of negation, and finally the offerer (Giovani) repeated "no" (line 13) as an acknowledgment of the refusal, paused, and then said, "OK," but he made one more attempt asking, "Why not eat a bit more before stopping the offers."

```
13 Giovani:    A'a. (0.6)
               No.
14 Giovani:    Bweno txee xhinnó láa àkko lò màsse txèkka é txee?
               bweno txe  xhinó  lá   àko=lò màse  txèka=é  txe
               good  then why   neg  eat=2s  more  food=3o  then
               OK then why not eat a bit more then?
```

15 David: De líi chettza lá wa lè'kka li'i odàkko txèkka nzellá.
            de-lí   chetza=lá=wa   lè'ka li'i o-dàko txèka
            of-upright thanks=already=2PL   also when CMP-eat food
            n-zelá
            STA-come
            It's true. Thank you all. I just ate before I came.

David answers one more time thanking the host and referencing the truth of the proposition about having eaten before arriving. It is notable that his pronoun use scales his referent not for the singular server, but in the plural thanking the offerer's family by saying *chettza lá wa* (thank you all). While the offer is animated by any individual in the position to do so, the moral reputation built goes beyond the individual to that of the family. As the refuser's work to represent the truth about having already eaten would indicate, refusing food when one has not eaten would produce a discordant relationship between words and world, which could be an affront to amicable social relations. In another video of the corpus, a family gossips about a person who rarely accepts offers. Notably the gossip also scaled up to reference the family of the person.

After this example, Giovani and David performed another skit of how, even when somebody accepts a food offer, offers continue to be made, ensuring that they have their satisfaction of tortillas, salt and lime, chile, enough food on their plate, and so on. This sequence looks very similar to what we have seen. Multiple offers are made before and after acceptance. Additionally Giovani and David noted that offerers may tell the guest, *láa zhìkkí lò* (don't you be afraid) and *láa txénno arkì' lò* (don't worry your heart) as part of the formulations of the offer. I have experienced these very assurances over the years.

Offering more food in the everyday world also parallels offers of more food during ritual events like family parties. For example, during a fiesta the woman of the house, or her kin who are helping, will come to a table where guests are eating to offer more food. Leading into a third skit, Giovani said,

> Another example that happens a lot here. During a fiesta when the compadres arrive. Even though they have food on their plate. They just serve them food again. They come to serve the plate another time. And another time there's the denial "No, that I still have" but the woman then (.) *saying . and . doing* ((G gestures a plate filling motion)) so that before the person who is eating can notice the woman is already serving food. That's a sure thing. That's the custom of the people.

Giovani illustrated that the saying of the offer and the doing of filling the plate are done simultaneously, and he stressed this point several times during his depictions and our conversations.

The theoretical understanding of sequence organization in conversation analysis is that an adjacency pair, like the offer-acceptance, happens in order, and to the extent that people also attend to the material offered, the object is prototypically transferred after the acceptance. But here the simultaneity of doing the plate filling with the verbal offer truncates the sequence and cuts off the possibility for real refusal. Both the offering and the receiving depict the moral virtues of the host and the guests to complete the joint action that composes the gift exchange, even though they will run through verbal scripts of denial and insistence. Laura Ahearn's work in Nepal suggests another way that saying and doing can be misaligned: pretending not to notice what is going on until it is too late to refuse. In Nepal the recipient of insistent offers of alcohol will often act as though she does not see the host coming to refill the glass and then "has to" drink it since it's already in the glass (Laura Ahearn p.c. 2017). There also we see an obligation to accept. Interestingly, in this Lachixío example, even though the sequence has been compressed, the receiver still does the verbal work of accepting the offer in the end, after the gift has already been exchanged. As David and Giovani performed their improvised dialogue to illustrate what was just narrated, we see an ethic of acceptance played out that was further described by Giovani as follows: "Practically there's the obligation, out of respect, to eat the food, and to accept the food that is being offered." Here it is clear that in Lachixío the gift creates an obligation to accept. The obligation is motivated out of respect for the future relationship with another, a future with causal relationship to the present. Examining the talk Giovani and David animated at the imagined fiesta, we see ways that the language is tied into the joint actions of relationship building, and we learn something more about how the burden to accept is made less burdensome by what I have referred to as a rhetorical reduction. With the gift of four turkeys and the gift of half-a-taco the burden reduction is accomplished by literally reducing the gift offered (at least in words), in this example the reduction is achieved by scaling up the "definition of the situation" (Goffman 1974). We see this form of reduction is happening in lines 12 and 13. Rather than reducing the gift through what is offered as in the previous examples, rhetorical reduction is accomplished here by broadening the scale, here, through pronominal use. Giovani shifts from the second-person singular pronoun with which he has been imploring the guest to eat, to the second-person plural saying the equivalent of "Don't worry, eat well there are many of you (pl) eating." It is after this that he gets the verbal acceptance in 14.

Playback—Skit 3

11 Giovani: ↑Odàkko éttà odàkko éntzà' shinnó' nokkwe láa txénno
              arkì' lò fwérte dàkko láa nóo↑
              L*-o-dàko   età   L*-o-dàko éntzà' shinó   nokwe
              IMP-CMP-eat tortilla   IMP-CMP-eat food   because um
              láa   txéno   arkì'=lò   fwérte   dàko=lá   nó
              NEG   worry   heart=2s   strong   eat=already that
              **↑Eat a tortilla, eat food because, um, don't you worry
              eat heartily already that**
12   (0.5)
13 Giovani: dàkko waxxhi wa nekwaa ràkko wa ka'a.
              dàko   waxhi=wa   ne-kwa   r-àko=wa   ka'a
              (CMP)eat many=2PL   STA-be(loc) HAB-eat-2PL here
              there's many of you here eating.
14 David: ↑Áwwà. Chettza lá lò. Chettza lá lò.↑
              áwà   chetza=lá=lò   chetza=lá=lò
              yes   thank=already=2s thank=already=2s
              ↑Yes. Thank you. Thank you.↑

Several methods of assembling knowledge articulate in our account of how talk and action weave together through offers in Lachixío. This analysis has brought together varieties of participatory research including narrative, video recording and analysis of spontaneous real-life interactions, playback dialogues and interviews, and theatrical performances intrinsically enacting social actions. Before closing this chapter consider another offer that introduces some complication to our understanding. The social roles of the participants are reversed from what we've seen so far. In the next example, a guest offers a gift of her labor to the hosts, creating a set of conflicts that, through the video analysis, we can see play out along the multimodal dimensions of the interaction.

2.4 Mary's Offer to Wash the Dishes

On the evening of July 2, 2009, Pedro was recording video while visiting neighbors accompanied by his wife Mary. It was the night before the combined kindergarten, elementary school, and middle school graduations and many families in Lachixío were busy preparing for the next day's celebrations of their graduating students. In the house Pedro was visiting, the matriarch and her daughter-in-law were working to prepare a mole sauce for the graduation party the next day. The men (father and son) were sitting exchanging local gossip. Pedro sat just outside of the frame to camera left. The interaction I draw your attention to is between Mary, the elder woman of the house who I am calling Náolla (Zapotec for grandma), and her daughter-in-law Lydia. As in the video in section 2.2, Pedro and Mary are visitors, which puts them in the social position to be on the receiving end of offers of hospitality. Despite this role, Mary makes an offer to wash the dishes. As we've seen in the previous sections, offers proffered create an obligation for acceptance, and this in turn creates social relationships of solidarity and family reputations. Mary's offer raises moral conflicts, though. The fact that she offered should be met with acceptance, but it is also a divergence from the role for the guest. These two constraints shape the multiple trajectories of this interaction. Examining the transcript, we can see the participants managed the constraints along different modalities. As the skits of the previous section showed us, the saying and doing of interaction are not redundant but are what Goodwin (2011, 2017) calls "mutually elaborating." Attention to talk alone, whether in attempt to analyze the grammar, or to analyze the conversation, is inadequate in itself here because the talk and structure of the interaction emerged with the whole of the multimodal assemblage. The participants have in their experience a gathering of talk, bodies in motion, action with objects, and the being in futuro of participants' orientation to the relations, obligations, and reputations coming into being in the present moments of interaction.

(3) LMSMVDP02jul09 (20.17–21.33)

```
1  Mary:        ↑Xá' tzyáà. Taà níngyè' nèé' nísso↑?
                -----------------------------------------|M grabs bowl
                ----------------|N raise gaze to M furled brow then
                    drops gaze
                --------------------------------------------|L raise gaze M
                H*-xa'a   tzyáà  tà     níngyè'  nèé'  níso
                POT.scrub just   which  thing    now   aunt
                ↑I'll just scrub. Which things (need washing) now, aunt↑?
```

```
2  Lydia:      ↑Xhii waà' nèé'↑?
               -----------|M shows bowl containing food scraps
               |N raise gaze M furled brow
               -L continues gaze M
               xhi  wà'   nèé'
               how  this  now
               ↑What's this then↑?
3  Lydia:      ↑Aà::↑ (1.3)
               -------|L raise r-arm hand on head
               -------|N lowers gaze
               ↑Oh::↑
4  Lydia:      ↑no'kwe::↑
               -L scratch head, looks at finger, looks to left, rocks to stand
               ↑Um::↑
```

In 1, Mary's first offer to wash the dishes is issued to the elder woman Náolla using the honorific kin term *nísso* (aunt) in the falsetto voice register and in a formulation that uses the active verb *xaʼa* (to scrub). During her utterance, Mary also grabs a dirty bowl. Her offer receives no immediate uptake. Náolla looks to Mary with a furled brow and then back at her work, and Lydia first asks, "What's this then?," and answers her own question with an exaggerated news uptake token, "Oh" and then a token of disfluency,

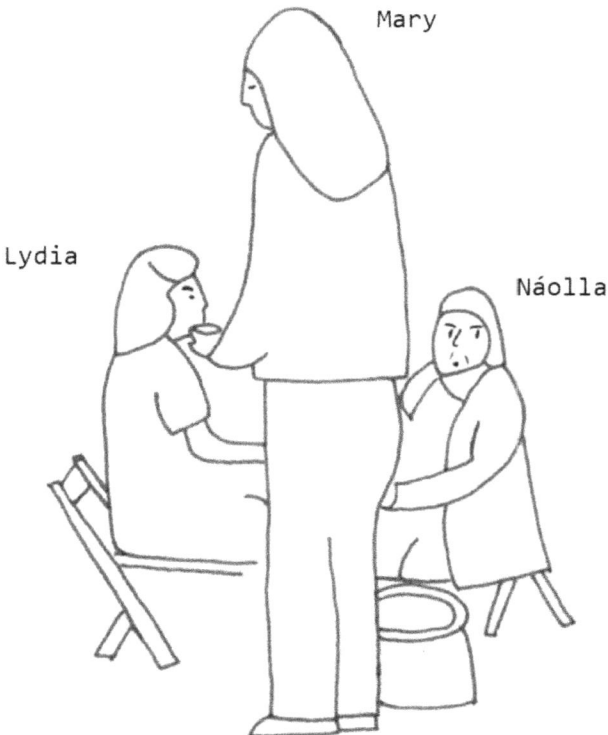

Figure 2.5 Mary gathers dishes.

"Um," while slowly standing. Here, the disfluency is a sign that Mary's offer has become an *incident* and that we should take a close look at what happens next.

```
5   (0.7)
6   Lydia:      °Xa' goo [oora lò°?
                |L stands face stove
                |M stands
                |N lift gaze to L
                xa'a#go  ora=lò
                scrub#?  now=2s
                °You (want to) scrub now°?
7   Náolla:              [Ekkyè sa'a' tzyáà cho'o né.
                --------|N r-hand point|stove---|gave to M
                ekè      sa'a'    tzyáà    cho'o=né
                head     together just    gather=ACT3o
                Just stack them up together.
8              (0.5)
9   Lydia:     ↑Masse lò tzyáà junto é cho'o né txee↑.
               ------------------------------------------|N lift gaze
                 bowl
               |L turns left toward M shows bowl
               masse=lò   tzyáà  junto=é     cho'o=né   txe
               even.if=2s just   together=3o gather=ACT3o then
               ↑Even if you just put them together, just gather them then↑
10  Lydia:    ↑Yà kooro sa'a' tzyáà txee Máarì↑.
              --------------------------------L places bowl on table
                near M
              --------------------------------M moves to get
                bowl
              yà    koro     sa'a'    tzyáà  txe    Mari-L
              all   stacked  together just   then   Mary-CLAS
              ↑Just stack them all together then Mary↑
11  Mary:     ↑Yà kooro sa' é txee↑.
              -M walk toward bowl
              yà    koro     sa'a'=é    txe
              all   stacked  together=3o then
              ↑Stack them all together then↑.
12  Lydia:    ↑Yà kooro sa'a' tzyáà txee↑.
              ----------------------|turns back to chair r-hand
                scratch head
              yà    koro     sa'a'    tzyáà  txe
              all   stacked  together just   then
              ↑Just stack them all together then↑.
13  Lydia:    L gaze right to M
14  Lydia:    ↑Nekka waa né Máarì↑.
              |L drops gaze and sits to work with chiles
              ne-aka    wa=né          mari-L
              STA-be    take.out=ACT3o Mary-CLAS
              ↑That's all to take out Mary↑.
15            -M moves bowl, collects dishes
```

After a pause, Lydia picks up Mary's verb of "scrubbing" saying, "You want to scrub now" in a hushed voice and standing to act. This gets Náolla's attention, who in 6 turns her gaze to Lydia and in 7 says to just stack them up together, changing the terms of the offer to what would be the initial step in a washing sequence, but not accepting the offer to scrub. Lydia also reduces the offer in the same way, following Náolla's lead. In

9 she says to *just* gather the bowls together and in 10 to *just* stack them all together. In her embodied action, she participates in an embodied form of accepting by grabbing one bowl to pass to Mary (to stack). Where in the previous examples we have seen offerers changing the terms of the offer to reduce the burden of accepting, here both recipients of the offer are working to change the terms of the offer. Mary goes along with this rhetorical reframing indicated by her repetition of agreement in "stack them all together then," and Lydia does the third turn repeat that characterizes agreement in Lachixío (see Chapter 5 on functions of such resonating repetitions). But Lydia importantly reinserts the word *tzyáà* (just) of her original formulation that Mary had left off. Then Lydia tells Mary that there's nothing more to take out. Mary finds some more bowls herself.

Stacking dishes is just part of what constitutes the whole of washing the dishes, which entails stacking, rinsing, scrubbing, and rinsing. From this perspective Lydia and Náolla have not accepted Mary's offer on the terms that she made it, which was to scrub the dishes. Mary stacks some bowls and then she asks, "Oh where is the place to wash them?" and points to another bowl near Lydia for her to pass.

```
16 Mary:        ↑Áà kaa paara nóo yekkye né↑?
                -----|M points to bowl near L
                ----------|N gaze up to M
                ----------|L gaze toward (not on) M
                àà      ka      para    nó      yeke=né
                oh      where   for     that    wash=ACT3o
                ↑Oh where is the place to wash them↑?
17 Lydia:       ↑Peero okwàá lá né Máarì↑.
                pero    o-kwàá-lá=né               Mári-L
                but     CMP-get.cold=already=ACT3o  Mary-C.AS
                ↑But it's already gotten cold Mary↑.
18 Náolla:      >↑Ye'e txekkye' wáà (.)< ye'e txekkye' [wáà né Máarì↑.
                ye'e    txeke' H*-wàá    ye'e    txeke' H*-wàá=né    Mári-CLAS
                tomorrow then   POT-remove tomorrow then  POT-remove=ACT3o Mary
                ↑Tomorrow then (.) tomorrow then someone will take them
                   out, Mary↑.
```

This is a bit of a strange question since the sink is outside in plain sight but not if the talk is rather the vehicle for Mary to pursue acceptance of her offer to wash dishes. Remember, her offer was transformed into a request to simply stack them up. Telling her where the sink was would implicitly accept the offer. But this doesn't happen. Rather Lydia says in 17, "But it's already gotten cold Mary," as a way of saying "you shouldn't"—in local beliefs working with cold water when it is cold out can bring illness. We also see no acceptance here from Náolla who declares rather that somebody will take them out tomorrow to clean them. She does this in a hurried delivery, repeating this twice in 18. But Mary goes on to find another bowl and approaches Lydia to get the bowl she pointed to in 16.

```
19 Mary:        [↑Jratto nzía tze'a ínza é nísso↑.
                |M turns and walks to get bowl near N
                -----------------L gaze bowl|left
                jratto      nzía    tze'e=á  ínza=é    nísc
                a.while     return  dip=1s   water=3o  aunt
                ↑In a little while I'll return from
                   rinsing them, aunt↑.
```

20 Lydia:	↑Nyàá é (.) [peero okwàá lá↑.
	---------|L reaches left grabs bowl moves to pass to M
	nyàá=é pero o-kwàá lá
	good=3o but CMP-get.cold already
	↑It's fine (.) but it's already gotten cold↑.
21 Mary:	[↑beè níngyè' kye'e↑
	bè níngyè' '-ke
	PL thing ACT-wash
	↑and those to wash↑
22 Lydia:	↑Nyàá tze'e ínza é txee Máarì↑.
	-|M takes bowl from L
	nyàá tze'e ínza=é txe mari-L
	good dip water=3o then Mary-CLAS
	↑Fine rinse it then Mary↑.
23 Mary:	↑Áwwà Lídià↑.
	↑Yes Lydia↑.
24	(1.3)
25 Náolla:	Peero nekwàá lá ínza.
	|N gaze left (to door)----------------gaze down
	------|L stands, moves past stove for another bowl
	pero ne-kwàá=lá ínza
	but STA-get.cold=already water
	But the water's already gotten cold.

In 19 Mary says, "In just a little while I'll return from rinsing them." Notice that Mary has switched verbs in the different iterations of her offer. The original offer in 1 was *xa'a'* (to scrub), the iteration in 16 after getting some reduced uptake of her offer by Lydia and Náolla was *yekkye* (to wash) but which received indirect refusals by Lydia and Náolla bringing up the inappropriateness of washing when it's already cold out, and the statement in 19 uses *tze'e ínza* (to rinse). We see here another way to reduce offers to become acceptable, this one drawing on the value of the semantic space of closely related lexical items with different entailments of effort or agency. Scrubbing is reduced to washing, and then reduced to just rinsing. Mary gets Lydia to give more bowls, and in 20 we get the clearest verbal acceptance of the reduced offer to rinse the dishes: "It's fine" while passing a bowl to Mary, but in synchronicity with the passing of the bowl, Lydia reasserts that it has already gotten cold and in overlap with this, having gotten a weak acceptance, Mary slides back up the scale of activity using a verb of washing again in 21 indicating to Lydia to pass more dishes to *kye'e* (wash). Lydia responds by reasserting the terms on which she accepted the offer *nyàá tze'e ínza é txee Máarì* (fine rinse it then Mary) to which Mary quickly agrees with "Yes, Lydia." Náolla, however, continues to show resistance to this in 25, stating, "But the water has already gotten cold," and then turns her gaze out the door and holds it on the cold, dark night (Figure 2.5).

26	(2.2)
27 Lydia:	Nokkwà laa nya'a.
	L hands bowl to Mary
	n-okwà=lá '-ni=á
	STA-get.cold=already ACT-say=1s
	It's getting cold already I do say.
28 Mary:	Áwwà nísso.
	|M takes bowl from L
	Yes aunt.

| 29 | Lydia sits down and she and Náolla work without talking. Mary turns to stack bowls up on the table. Mary picks up the stack of bowls, turns, walks off frame to the left and out of house. |

In 27 Lydia repeats Náolla's assessment that it's already gotten cold to which Mary simply agrees. The women go silent while Mary stacks up all the bowls and then carries them outside, where she proceeded to scrub the dishes, returning about twenty minutes later.

In examining this dialogue through multimodal transcription, we are drawn to notice that there are different ends to the talk and action with objects gathered together in a complex assemblage. Consider how in 27 Lydia gives a reason for Mary to not wash dishes, saying it is cold out already, while at the very same time handing a bowl to her. Lydia thus rejects the offer verbally but accepts it in her embodied action. We see this intermodal discord across multiple moves. The verbal dimension is attending to a ritual dimension of not expecting or asking guests to do household chores, but the exchange of objects involved in accepting the offer is nonetheless taking place.

This example shows us several things. First, we see that offers have a social life in which they grow, occurring multiple times in multiple forms as the social relations entailed in their offering and acceptance are worked out. As in the other extracts presented in this chapter, the participants worked to reduce the burden to accept by shifting the scale of the gift or shifting the frame. In this case Lydia and Náolla first tried to scale down the gift offered, saying first to not do all the dishes, and then rather than accept an offer for the complete washing sequence, they tried to reframe the offer to merely doing the first part of a washing sequence—the stacking of the dishes. In this way the semiotic relation is like synecdoche. The first part of an action of a sequence can stand in for the whole sequence (e.g., the ritualized intention movements of a child's arms-up display signaling "pick me up" or the bared teeth display of canids signaling threat [Tomasello 2008]). If Mary would do just the first part, she could signal doing the dishes. Mary took up this incremental acceptance but rather than ending there, she used this place in the dialogue to continue working toward a verbal acceptance. Mary continued to press her case for doing more than just stacking and introduced rinsing, going further along the chain of actions involved in a dish washing. In her iterated attempts she used the affordances of substitutable vocabulary related to doing dishes. She reduced the effort she was offering from "scrubbing," to "washing," to "rinsing." With her gift framed as just rinsing she finally gets a verbal acceptance to go ahead and rinse them (explicitly resonating "rinsing" as the term of acceptance). What we also see in this example is *intermodal discord*: the dissonant resonance between semiotic dimensions. A lot of work is being done on the verbal dimension to mediate, reduce, and not accept Mary's offer on her terms, which itself contradicts with her role as a guest. But at the very same time, Lydia and Mary are working to gather the dishes. Thus two "lines" or modes of ritual action are being performed in the time and space of the ongoing interaction. It displays for us the semiotic ideologies that put the verbal on record differently than the embodied action. The talk here is doing what Goffman (1967) called ritual facework, and the action with objects is fulfilling the obligation to accept an offer once it is made, reminding us of Edward Sapir's observation that "one may express on one level of patterning, what one will not or cannot express on another" (1949: 543). I add to this that the relationship between semiotic dimensions is itself a level of organization with emergent properties where different elements contribute to creating an ecology for the interpretation of the others. Together they facilitate a world of social action which requires us to examine multimodal, multi-participant assemblages where the future of social relations, obligations, and reputations causes action trajectories in the present.

2.5 Concluding Remarks

In sum, offers involve the mediation of social actors negotiating the debts, obligations, and social relations of their future self in the present—a being in futuro. Offers in Lachixío are iterated, often many times, by multiple offerers and come with an obligation to accept. Iteration by multiple offerers scales up the source of the offer to come from a family rather than individual. And where repetition increases pressure to accept, second and third offers generally come with some reduction of quantity, definition of the situation, or through lexical choices reflecting scalar semantics that reduce (at least a sense of) the future burden taken on by acceptance. Offers are joint actions. The offer not yet accepted or rejected is like a ritual in a liminal state. Beyond this we saw that rather than the prototypical sequence organization of offer-acceptance-transfer of object/service, variable orders are found including simultaneity of the pair-parts and out of order "sequences." The talk and action with gift/objects cannot be assumed to take place in normative sequence. And talk and action cannot be expected to mirror each other in stance or purpose. Where they do not mirror each other, I introduced the term "intermodal discord," which contrasts with the generally assumed mirroring that I term "intermodal harmony." In moments of intermodal discord, saying and doing can be at cross purposes, or more simply work to different ends. If we only had the text of these interactions transcribed as a written document in the way that so much language documentation and ethnographic representation proceeds, our analysis would be, in the weakest sense, inaccurate, and in the strongest sense, unethical, failing to represent the participants' knowledge and practice with the multidimensional whole to which the participants had perceptual access—the position from which they formulated their language use.

3

Recruit

In developing the notion of "language games," the philosopher Wittgenstein wrote, "It is easy to imagine a language consisting only of orders and reports in battle.—Or a language consisting only of questions and expressions for answering yes and no. And innumerable others.—And to imagine a language means to imagine a form of life" (Wittgenstein PI 1958: 19). This chapter examines the language of recruiting of another's actions in Lachixío. As with our examination of offers in Chapter 2, our scope of engagement includes the sequence of recruitment and its response as joint action. The scope is also multimodal to include participants' integrated techniques of body motion, and actions with objects of material culture. The three video segments in this chapter are all mundane solicitations (for water in two cases and a drink of soda in one), but as we saw in Chapter 2 where everyday offers created social obligations and built reputations, our focus on mundane recruitments informs our interpretation of social relations present to and jointly created in interaction and provides insights into the workings of Lachixío Zapotec grammar.

Recruitments are a family of social actions designed to solicit the gift of another's action. This can be achieved by a number of speech acts such as requesting, commanding, hinting, begging, pleading, and even offering, similar to those we examined in Chapter 2, though with a scale of difference. The term "recruitment" covers the ground of speech acts called "directives," which Searle (1979) and Goodwin (2006) and others have used to categorize actions whose goal is to get someone to do something (see Floyd et al. 2020 and Kendrick and Drew 2016 for development).

Directives and requests differ in that directives involve one participant *telling* another what to do where requests involve one participant *asking* another to do something. Craven and Potter (2010: 437) sketched the difference as directives serving to "actively reduce or manage contingencies during the delivery" (the first-pair part of an adjacency pair), while requests are "structurally designed to project non-compliance" (the second-pair part of response). The basic contrast is grounded in a display of speaker entitlement in which directives treat the contingency of their fulfillment as under the control of the initiating participant rather than as a resource of the responding participant—that is to say that it is a grounded and revealing sign of the power of one participant over another.

Such formal differences of the language of recruitments are a worthwhile focus of social analysis. The public signs of the grammar of recruitments point beyond themselves to aspects of the social formation in which they are used. As such the grammatical forms used are themselves incomplete signs open to the ecology of collaboration between people in interactions. They require an approach to language that engages language as suspended in this social ecology. As with the other joint actions examined in this book, I demonstrate that actively reflecting on how recruitments are said and done in actually occurring interactions is an important tool for ethnographers and linguists to both discover and better come to understand the interdependence of linguistic and social relations as woven together by participants in joint encounters. For both our languages and our other social institutions, the social situation is what Frederick Erickson (2004a) has called, the "construction zone of history."

3.1 Social Relations of Entitlement, Contingency, and Agency

Recruitments are often formulated through the grammar of *modally modified questions*, in utterances such as "Would you get me a glass of water?" or "Could you move back?" Such forms for recruitment focus on the contingency and willingness of the recipient to grant the action. As the first-pair part of an adjacency pair, they create what the American philosopher Charles Peirce has called a semiotic *rheme*, a sign of potentiality for the space it opens for response (1955: 103–4), the response being an *interpretant* sign of the recruitment initiation. By formulating the recruitment as a request, it places control of the contingency for fulfillment with the recipient, who is then discursively framed as having the agency to gift or not gift her action. Directives, in contrast, that tell, rather than ask, still require a response to complete the joint action initiated, but the second-pair part that constitutes the response is not framed by the first-pair part as a choice of the recipient. Hints couched in declarative statements like "There are no tortillas" and "I wonder if you could give me advice" are also recruitment formulations, but ones that "fish for" offers as a response. And offers in a first-pair part position may simply present a material object with the expectation that the responder use it to comply with the recruitment's purpose, the intentions of the bearer understood from a common-ground cultural value of the thing.

People can engage the affordances of these variable forms of recruitment when an initial attempt is not responded to in a way that matches the issuer's entitlement (or own sense of entitlement). When a recruitment is repeated multiple times over a dynamic interaction, the grammatical form of the recruitment may be shifted from request forms to directive forms, as Craven and Potter (2010: 426) have pointed out, illustrating the real-time play of grammar as indexically creative of social relations (Silverstein 1976).

To some degree all conversational actions that make a response relevant involve a factor of recruitment since one participant's utterance compels attention and response. As interpretant signs, response forms are also constrained by preferences projected by the move to which they respond. The enchronic timescale introduced in Chapter 1, where paired actions are evaluated for their effectiveness and appropriateness in an interactional moment, is also a place of moral commitment (see Enfield 2013; Erickson 2004a). Chapter 2 illustrated this point in how offers obligate the recipient not only to respond but in Lachixío offers also obligate the recipient to accept. The acceptance is a public sign of a social relationship and the taking on of the social obligation that the gift signifies. Offers and recruitments illustrate moral dimensions of Lachixío sociality (see also Sicoli 2015) which link exchanges in an interaction to perduring reputations built and sustained over timescales that extend beyond the scale of the interaction.

I illustrate here that examining the fine details of recruitment sequences has methodological value for ethnography because like offers, recruitments have as part of their dynamic teleology, or end directedness, the building and maintenance of social relations. The dynamic is parallel to Marcel Mauss's argument that the giving of a gift is a foundational social act "bringing about and maintaining human relationships between individuals and groups" (Evans-Pritchard 1950). Soliciting a gift, recruitments are in a sense the opposite arrangement of sociality from offers. Where in an offer, one agent is making their behavior available for another's benefit, a recruitment solicits the gift of the recipient's action at the prompting of the initiator. For the recipient, recruitments make relevant a response of either fulfillment or denial. Furthermore, fulfilling a recruitment entails an offer as subsequent action. So if you ask or tell me to pass the salt, the fulfilling action would entail my *offering* you the salt in some way. A crucial difference between the offers we examined in Chapter 2 and these offers is the sequential position. Whereas the offers discussed in Chapter 2 are first-position offers (in the sense that they expect and constrain response), the fulfillment of recruitments are second-position offers. They do not necessarily have the same trimmings of a first-position offer as they are rhematically constrained semiotic *interpretants*—their being oriented to a prior sign-action where an offer is an appropriate response.

Recruitments then are moves that make relevant a subsequent move of a second participant for the benefit of another (either the first or a third).[1] The recruitments we see in the Lachixío video corpus are mostly *directives* that can take several grammatical forms based on the morphology of the potential mood or the completive aspect (Sicoli 2010a). The potential is a grammatical mood that can translate as a subjunctive and relates to a speaker's belief that something would likely happen, though not with the certainty that would be implied with a future tense construction. The completive, in contrast, is a verb aspect that marks an action as having already happened. Both of these set up a relation of words to world in which the speaker indicates a possible future or an event as having already happened, thus making it relevant for a recipient to change the world to fit to the truth conditions of the utterance. In Peircean terms, the potential mood and completive aspect directives embody the potentiality of Rhematic signs, and their responses are interpretants that transform them to become Dicent signs of actuality. They are signs that orient to a future relying on a human prosociality to pull the world into the timespace, and also in this case, the chronotope,[2] indicated in the first-pair part. As such they are not imperatives in the narrower sense that we know in English and many other Indo-European languages (of which there is no comparable independent grammatical form in Lachixío Zapotec), but potential mood and completive aspect directives conventionally function in a way that they can be translated as weak and strong imperatives. Their unity as quasi-imperatives in Lachixío is supported by a low-tone accent that can combine with the segmental morphology of the potential mood and completive aspect to more clearly mark it as a directive.

Speakers have described potential mood utterances as more polite or respectful than completive aspect utterances, and furthermore that completives are often used in reissued directives (Sicoli 2010a). This chapter's examination of grammar actualized in the play of social life illustrates that across reiterated directives speakers often shift grammatical forms making visible the contrasting social value of the potential mood and completive aspect inflections, which is difficult to elicit. Examples also include other forms of recruitment, including questions and declarative hints.

3.2 Recruitments in a Comparative Pragmatics

Part of my goal in the explication of the joint actions named in the central chapter titles of this book is to contribute the ethnographic case of Lachixío to a comparative pragmatics. This chapter specifically examines how Lachixío Zapotec speakers repeat and redo recruitments in the conversational interactions of the video corpus. In studying the details of recruitment in Lachixío, there is also an ethnographically particular goal of using pragmatic actions that distribute agency across participants of an assemblage to understand the social relations intersecting it (such as the social roles and hierarchies of age or gender as action contingencies). Toward the goal of a comparative pragmatics I generally follow the terminology developed on the "Human Sociality and Systems of Language Use" (HSSLU) project directed by N. J. Enfield (2010–15) as it has developed comparable corpora across different world languages. At the broadest level of granularity, recruitments can be defined as actions that make relevant and are followed by the actions of *fulfillment* or *rejection*, though for subtypes I will also make references to *compliance* for directives and the *granting* of requests.

Recruitments have mostly been studied with reference to request sequences (Curl and Drew 2008; Heinemann 2006; Merritt 1982; Schegloff 1979; Lindström 2005; Taleghani-Nikazm 2006; Vinkhuyzen and Szymanski 2005; Wootton 1997) and directives (Craven and Potter 2010; Goodwin 2010; Mondada 2013; Rosaldo 1982; Wootton 1997). Broadening our perspective to be more inclusive than requests is important for recognizing action solicitation as a generic aspect of human sociality that is comparable across sociocultural settings and languages.

Variation in grammatical forms of recruitment is present in most scholarly observations of actions that have been labeled "requests" or "directives." In such studies we tend to see category leak involving speech acts such as imperatives, interrogatives, and modally mediated sentences. Floyd et al. (2014) found such variation in eight languages[3] in which each language corpus showed use of imperatives, interrogatives, and declaratives, with imperatives being the most common recruitment form (see also Mondada 2013 on imperative formatted recruitments). Brown and Levinson (1987), Curl and Drew (2008), Craven and Potter (2010), Ervin-Tripp (1976), Heinemann (2006), Wootton (2005), and Zinken and Ogiermann (2011) all examined speaker's choices between forms of recruitments as signs of a speaker's assessments of the recipient's contingencies for fulfillment, and the speaker's entitlement to a requested object or action. Curl and Drew (2008) argue that relations between contingency and entitlement provide more power of prediction for what grammatical forms to expect than either politeness theory developed by Brown and Levinson (1987) or appeal to institutional settings.

When speakers make a request using modal verbs (Could you . . .) and declarations of want or need (I'd love a glass of water), they treat their request as noncontingent (the conditions for granting being met) and themselves as relatively entitled to the object or action. By contrast, requests prefaced with "I wonder" or "If possible" construct requestors as lacking entitlement or knowledge of the contingencies for fulfillment. Directive forms would index an even lower contingency. The less contingency on a recipient's ability or willingness to fulfill the request, the more likely it will be formulated as a directive such as "pass the salt" when the salt is next to the recipient on the table, rather than a modal "would you get me some salt" which would be more fitted to a speech situation in which the salt had been left in the cupboard or the recipient of the request is otherwise occupied.

More than politeness or simple acknowledgment of entitlement or contingency, speakers' formulations of recruitments show strategies and tactics to navigate social situations. Heinemann (2006) examined requests posed as positive and negative questions in Danish as indices of the requestor's stance on their entitlement to the action. When using positive interrogative request forms, a requestor orients to the request from a stance of low entitlement. Vinkhuyzen and Szymanski (2005) show that variation in customers' choices between requests formulated as "I need . . ." declaratives and "Can you make . . ." questions is grounded in a customer's knowledge of what types of services a shop provides. The sensitivity of social actors to these forms reflects speaker understandings of contingencies on the ability to grant a request including its imposition or face threat (Brown and Levinson 1987; Goffman 1955). Thus, the grammatical choices involve the intersection of relationships of politeness, power, and the destabilization of power.

As speech events are intersected by multiple trajectories of human sociality, relations of politeness, entitlement, and contingency cannot be interpreted solely from the grammatical forms that are made public in discourse but also require that microanalysis of conversational sequence and grammatical forms be integrated with an ethnographic perspective. Consider how we saw in Chapter 2 that offers demonstrating a family's politeness to a guest often used the most forceful imperative forms, which in isolation (or from an outsider perspective) might appear impolite. We must carefully consider the particularities of the means and ends of local grammatical and cultural practices when comparing the generalizations drawn from previous studies that relate entitlement and contingency directly to grammatical forms.

While many studies emphasize variable politeness or contingency in association with grammatical forms (with imperative forms claimed to be universally more direct and less polite), some studies have looked at such mappings as culturally variable. Irvine (1980) noted that translating unmarked requests from Wolof (of Senegal) to unmarked request forms in English resulted in mistranslations. To a similar end, Zinken and Ogiermann (2013) showed functional correspondences between grammatically different forms in Polish and English. And Mondada (2013) showed that French directive forms used during video game co-play related to coordinating ongoing action rather than being seen as impolite. Wootton (1997) and Zinken and Ogiermann (2013) relate the use of imperatives to recruitments designed for ongoing action and contrasting with interrogative forms used to initiate departures from an ongoing action. But Zinken and Ogiermann also report differences in the frequency of imperatives and interrogatives between Polish and British English corpora. Irvine (1980: 3), in an argument that is just as salient today, suggested that pragmatic analysis be coupled with ethnographic analysis stating, "One cannot understand the pragmatics of requests by looking only at their linguistic forms and inferring pragmatic intentions such as degrees of politeness" (see also Rosaldo 1982 for a parallel argument). Imperative forms used for directives, requests and offers need to be examined locally for how they relate to social coordination, contingency, politeness, and social hierarchies involving relational identities between speakers and recipients coupled in multimodal interaction.

3.3 Recruitment, Multimodality, Phylogeny

Recruitments are phylogenetically quite ancient semiotic actions that themselves must precede language, if we consider both what great apes do when food sharing, or that when taught to use sign language or lexigram boards, great apes' speech acts are very close to 100 percent directives/requests. Michael Tomasello describes requests as "prototypically [involving] only you and me in the here and now and the action I want you to perform, [which can be done through] combinations of natural gestures and/ or linguistic conventions," thus requiring only a kind of "simple syntax" (2008: 244). Requesting food can be achieved with a simple open-hand palm-up gesture, even though humans may formulate grammatically complex requests. However, all recruitments, including requests, directives, and other actions that recruit actions, indicate aspects of the participants' social relations through their patterned formulations. Thus a focus on the form of recruitment and the openness of that form to the social environment provides important tools for our analysis.

As existentially bound to the here and now, recruitments can be achieved through talk, through action, or through composite utterances that integrate multiple modalities. Figure 3.1 shows such an action-only recruitment: a mother holding out an empty pitcher toward her daughter. This is an offering posture, but as we will examine in more detail next, it was used to recruit the action of the child.

Offering the empty pitcher was intended as a recruitment of the girl to fetch more water which the mother needs for her current project preparing *eekòkkò 'masa* (corn dough) for tortillas (an everyday activity in Lachixío). There are a number of ambiguities for the interpreter of her posture which embeds both actions of "offering" and "giving," as well as "showing." Accepting her gift would entail actions of "taking" and "releasing" (see work of Kidwell and Zimmerman 2007 on ambiguities and nesting in action recognition where perspective can matter). In this case the mother's reliance on the visual channel with no accompanying utterance resonating her intention resulted in a misunderstanding, and a subsequent need to reassert the request when it was not fulfilled. While the girl recognized the offer of the pitcher as recruiting her

Figure 3.1 A material recruitment for water.

to take it, she did not interpret it as a directive to fetch more water. Rather she put it away and went off to play. It shows us that while recruitments like requests can be done solely through embodied action, the role that utterances play even in the well-grounded here and now of copresence importantly narrows the range of possible futures in joint action sequences.

3.4 Multiple Directives to Fetch Water

In this first set of extracts, we see multiple recruitments initiated by a mother, Angeles, to get her daughter, Sofía, to fetch water. We see in this example shifts between different grammatical resources each time the recruitment is attempted. The first recruitment in this segment was a successful sequence of the form: SUMMONS→ACKNOWLEDGEMENT→DIRECTIVE→FULFILLMENT (example 1). The daughter brought water for the mother. But a second directive for more water failed to be fulfilled and this led to several utterances through which the mother reissued and repaired the recruitment. The initial problem with the second recruitment (example 4) is based on a problem of form coherence, a discordant relationship between the semiotic modalities that played a role in the mis-ascription of the action for which the mother recruited the daughter.

In Figure 3.2, Angeles is making tortillas with her mother-in-law and aunt. Her daughter Sofía is facing her from the foreground.

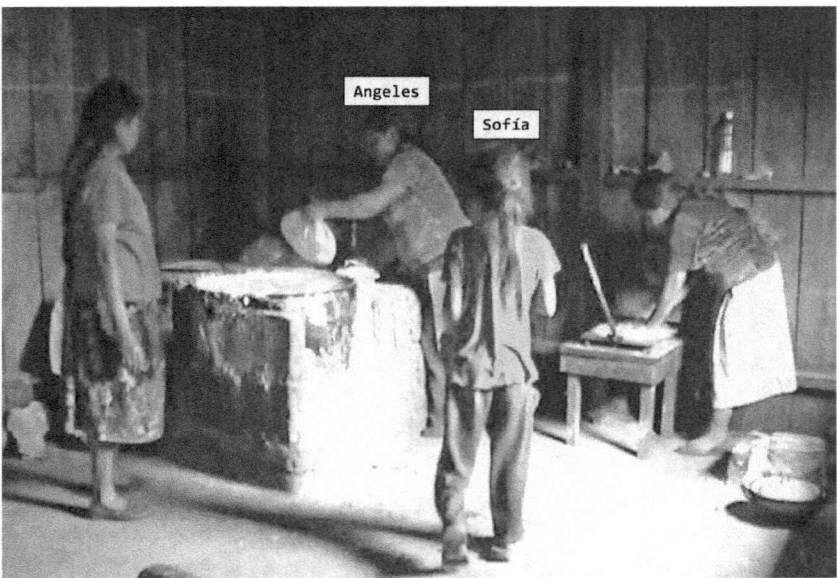

Figure 3.2 Tortilla making in a Lachixío kitchen.

(1) LMSMVDP24Jul0903 (4:53–4:58)

```
1  Angeles:   Sofía:. ((S is outside the kitchen))      SUMMONS
              Sofía.
2  Sofía:     Eè?                                       ACKNOWLEGEMENT
              Huh?
3  Angeles:   Lìkkì' ínza itta no á.                    DIRECTIVE
              L*-likì'      ínza    ita=no=á
              IMP-(POT)give water   relax=INSTR=1s
              (You) would give water so I can soften
                 (the dough).
4  Sofía:     Áà.                             (First Sign Of)
              OK.                             FULFILLMENT
```

In 1 Angeles issues an attention getting summons to Sofía as a pre-recruitment. Sofía responds from outside the kitchen to show her availability. Angeles issues a directive in 3, *Lìkkì' ínza itta no á* ([You] would give water so I can soften [the dough]), which uses the segmental morphology of the potential mood (here ø) and the optional low-tone imperative marker. As I described earlier, the potential mood is the less forceful of the two framings for imperatives. Sofía shows uptake verbally with an affirmative interjection *Áà*, and shortly after this we see her fulfill the terms of the recruitment. She delivers a pitcher of water to her mother at the stove.

Sofía comes into frame and offers the pitcher to her mother with the interjection *Aá* (here) and asks what she is going to do with it. The mother takes the pitcher but does not answer the girl's question. In addition to her work with the masa, Angeles is occupied with a conversation she is having with her mother-in-law who is cooking the tortillas (text not included in the transcript). Sofía turns toward the door and politely closes the interaction declaring that she will be leaving, having complied with the directive: "I'm going already. I already brought the water." In my experience, it is common to hear explicit declarations of fulfillment like this in Lachixío, especially by children when complying with adult directives.

```
(2) LMSMVDP24Jul0903  (6:20-6:54)
5                   (2.6)
                    S walks into frame from left.
6   Sofía:          A'á máa.
                    S walking toward A with pitcher
                    Here ma.
7                   (1.0)
8   Sofía:          Xhii jri'i lò é?
                    A reaches for and takes pitcher turns back right grabs bowl
                    xhi   r-ri'i=lò=é
                    what  HAB-do=2s=3o
                    What are you doing with it?
9.                  (4.2)
                    A walks across to table
                    S turns around walks
10  Sofía:          Nzaa lá né. Obikki láa ínza.
                    |S turns head over left shoulder toward A then walks out
                       of frame
                    n-za=lá=né              o-biki=lá          irza
                    STA-go=already=ACT3o    CMP-put=already    water
                    I'm going already. I already brought the water.
```

Next Sofía gets involved in an activity with her toddler brother at the edge of the video frame. It is early in the recording, and she points out the camera to him using whisper-voice directives to "look" (Sicoli 2010a). During this time Angeles uses the water to soften the dough and clean out a bowl. She takes a drink from the pitcher, rinses her hands, and then pours the remainder into a bowl.

Angeles then issues the presentation interjection *A'á*, while thrusting the empty pitcher toward Sofía (Figure 3.2). *A'á* is like saying 'Here' in English or *Ten* (have) in Spanish, though unlike these Indo-European words, *a'á* does not have non-interjection referential uses. Being an interjection for object transfer in both offers and requests, Angeles's utterance is certainly ambiguous. This multimodal formulation of the mother's second recruitment (pitcher presentation + presentation interjection) creates a problem of understanding. While Angeles intended her presentation of the pitcher as a recruitment for more water, Sofía was not sure what to make of it. As with an open-hand palm-up gesture as recruitment, extending the pitcher toward Sofía is an embodied action tied to the here and now. Interpretation requires an inference of its relevance in the action environment, given the materiality of its instrumental form for holding and transporting water *and* its currently empty state. To compound the lack of clarity, Angeles then verbally initiates an unrelated sequence in 17 asking Sofía if she has already eaten. At the same time, she reiterates her presentation of the empty pitcher, thrusting it toward Sofía again as an immediate second recruitment—this time without any verbal interjection. Angeles's physical recruitment attempt and verbal question about food illustrate a moment of intermodal discord (Sicoli 2013) in which the words and physical action are not reflections of each other but are doing two different pragmatic actions. Sometimes these relate to contextualize each other, like in Chapter 2 where intermodal discordance embodied two contradictory responses to an offer as part of the same sequence. But in Angeles and Sofía's case the two actions belong to two entirely different sequences. Both are first-pair parts issued along separate modalities in temporal overlap: one a recruitment initiation and the other a pre-offer.

```
(3) LMSMVDP24Jul0903  (6:43-6:54)
   15 Angeles:      A'á.
                    |A holds pitcher in direction S
                    Here.
   16               (0.6)
                    |S turns gaze to A
   17 Angeles:      Odàkko lá [lò éttà la?
                    |A holding pitcher in direction S |thrusts pitcher
                        slightly forward
                    o-dàko=lá=lò           étà=la
                    CMP-eat=already=2s     tortilla=Q
                    Did you already eat?
   18 Sofía:                 [Stokko é la?
                              sH-tòko=é=la
                              another-one=3o=Q
                              Another one?
   19 Sofía:        Stokko é la?
                    |S takes pitcher from A holds gaze at end of question
                    ----------------|A turns and walks back toward stove
                    sH-tòko=é=la
                    another-one=3o=Q
                    Another one?
   20               (0.7)
   21 Angeles:      Ràkko lá lò éttà la?
                    r-àko=lá=lò        étà=la
                    HAB-eat=already=2s tortilla=Q
                    Are you eating tortillas?
   22               (0.9)
   23 Sofía:        Ràkko [lá á lé'e.
                    ----------------|S walks out of frame swinging pitcher
                    r-àko=lá=á          H*-le'e
                    HAB-eat=already=1s  POT-like
                    I would like to be eating.
   24 Angeles:            [Éttà konna yéxxo ràkko lò la?
                           étà      kona    yéxo   r-àko=lò=la
                           tortilla with    cheese HAB-eat=2s=Q
                           Eat a tortilla with cheese?
   25               ((Sofía exits frame to left))
```

Not surprisingly, Sofía initiates repair in 18 by asking a question to check her understanding of the interaction: "Another one?" she says. This is in overlap with Angeles's question about having eaten, and in 19 Sofía immediately repeats her question as a second understanding check while at the same time accepting the pitcher being offered to her. Though Sofía's utterance is clearly a question marked by the Lachixío interrogative enclitic *la*, Angeles seems to consider Sofía taking the pitcher while saying "another one" as committing to fulfilling the recruitment sequence. She does not answer Sofía's question but forwards the second line of action asking if Sofía is going to eat. Sofía responds that she would like to eat, and Angeles moves to verbally offer a specific food item, "Eat a tortilla with cheese?" During subsequent talk about what to eat, Sofía walks out of frame swinging the empty pitcher. What we see next shows that while Angeles thinks they are jointly committed to the second recruitment, Sofía has not taken the embodied recruitment sequence to be a second directive to fetch water. Ten minutes goes by and Sofía has not returned with water—a task that should only take a minute or two with the spigot located outside the house in the courtyard. Angeles makes a second attempt to recruit the water from Sofía.

(4) LMSMVDP24Jul0903 (18:47-18:52)

26 Angeles:	Sofía::.((who is outside)) Sofía.
27 Sofía:	Eè? Huh?
28 Angeles:	Tèe chi'ccha ínza itta no' á mâ. L*-te g-ri'cha ínza ita=no=á mà.á IMP-(POT) come CAUS-pour water relax=INSTR=1s daughter.1s *(You) would come so I can pour water to soften (the dough) my daughter.*
29 Angeles:	Áà. OK.

Like in the first extract, her effort begins with a summons as a pre-recruitment to get Sofía's attention, which she gives in 27. We see Angeles's next recruitment attempt in 28 "(You) would come so I can pour water to soften (the dough) my daughter." This follows a similar pattern to the very first recruitment when Sofía was outside. Angeles is explicit about her instrumental use of water to soften the dough and also inflects the directive with the potential mood morphology, though there are two important variations that mark this as a reissued directive. First, Sofía's mother does not direct her to "bring water," as she did with the first recruitment. She rather directs her to "come," which presupposes her belief that the previous recruitment (lines 15–23) is already in their common ground. The intensification of the reissued directive is further evidenced by Angeles invoking their kin relation through the person address term *mâ* (my daughter), and the support role a daughter is obliged to provide her mother in the kitchen. Together these lexical choices display the strengthening of the force of her directive. Sofía shows uptake in next turn position *Áà* (OK). After about thirty seconds, Sofía has still not come with the pitcher to fulfill the recruitment (she can be heard in a conversation outside the house, so it is not contingent for her to easily comply at this point, having to extract herself from a competing joint commitment with another person), and in the next iteration (now the third iteration of the second recruitment) the directive takes on new grammatical features. Angeles first frames her next move as an action that is being done again. She does this in 31 when she addresses Sofía by name and uses a reported speech verb to reference her own prior dialogue and explicitly mark this as a second attempt, *Sofía nii á* (Sofía, I said). However, Angeles does not quote herself exactly but rather transforms the directive from the potential mood form *tèe* to the stronger completive form *otèe*, also reiterating the person reference.

```
(5) LMSMVDP24Jul0903 19:28-20:13
31 Angeles:      Sofía nii á:.
                 Sofía    ni=á
                 Sofía    say=1s
                 Sofía I said.
32               (1.0)
33 Angeles:      Otèe Sofía.
                 L*-o-te           Sofía
                 IMP-CMP-come      Sofía
                 Come Sofía.
34 Sofía:        Nzee lá á kwa'a lá á.
                 n-ze=lá=á           kwa'a=lá=á
                 STA-go=already=1s   be(loc)=already=1s
                 Here I'm going already.
35               ((Sofía walks into frame without pitcher and then off
                   again to get the pitcher off a table [audible] and to
                   fetch water))
36               ((At 20.06 we hear Sofía's footsteps returning with the
                   pitcher of water))
37               ((At 20.08 she appears in left frame walks to her mother
                   at the metate and then hands her the pitcher saying:))
38 Sofía:        Oyáà lá né.
                 |S hands A the pitcher and turns to walk back
                 o-yáà=lá=né
                 CMP-go=already=ACT3o
                 I went for it already.
```

The completive aspect in 33 characterizes an action as already completed, placing a moral burden on the recipient to make the world fit the words (and particularly the verbal aspect). In response, Sofía calls from out of frame that she is going and already there (doing it). Sophia is outside, not visible to Angeles. Accordingly, Sofía makes use of the verbal channel to provide feedback describing her action that would, if visible, be a sign that fulfillment is underway. Sofía walks into the frame briefly to get the pitcher off a table then she leaves the frame to go fetch the water. When she returns with the filled pitcher, she verbally marks the closure of the recruitment sequence saying, *Oyáà láa né* (I went for it already) and then turns to walk outside again.

As Sofía had to come in to get the pitcher, it is clear that she did not understand the earlier embodied recruitment attempt (example 3). We see here through the iteration of recruitment attempts the play of Lachixío Zapotec lexicon and grammar—shifts from potential mood to completive aspect, ellipses, references to social relationship, and the use of constructed dialogue of a previous recruitment to mark the action as being done again. My compadre Daniel first described the sequenced morphological upgrades in elicitation sessions in 1998 when I asked him about the difference between the two forms of directives he had given on different occasions. His account was that the potential form was what you say the first time and the completive was what you would say when redoing a directive not complied with. This is not to say that completive formed directives are not ever used in first attempt directives; they can be, and as such may certainly relate to the social position of the issuer of the directive. (Recall that in Chapter 2 a woman was offering a guest a taco using the completive form, but her husband was offering the same taco using the potential.) But in reissued recruitments both the unprompted practice and elicited metapragmatic description of Lachixío speakers demonstrate that the relationship between these grammatical forms is one in which the completive aspect additionally indexes that the directive is one being reissued. Corpora of unprompted practice are especially important for contrasts where introspecting speakers do not think of an example and decide the morphological choices are "the same." This sequence supports arguments by both Craven and Potter (2010) and Curl and Drew (2008) that repeat directives make more explicit the entitlement of the issuing participant to the recipient's compliance.

The next section also shows repeat recruitments, though in this case the social relations embodied in the participation formation are reversed. A child makes multiple recruitments attempts from adults and the sequence plays out quite differently.

3.5 A Child Requesting Soda

This section and section 3.6 could be alternatively titled "How to Ask for a Drink in Lachixío," echoing Charles Frake's article in the (1964) *American Anthropologist* special issue on the *Ethnography of Communication* where Frake argued that asking for a drink in *Subanun* requires knowledge of culture that goes well beyond sentence grammar (see also Irvine 1980, "How Not to Ask a Favor in Wolof"). This extract of a child's multiple requests for a drink in Lachixío provides several insights into Lachixío family organization, age-grade rank hierarchy, work-reward ethic, and ideologies of language forms appropriate to requesting. These different social trajectories all intersect this dialogue that took place during a break from farmwork. The sequence forces us to complicate the generalization supported by the last extract that repeat recruitments show upgrading of entitlement. Because of the age-grade social relations present to the speech event, this example shows a shift in utterance form that is only successful when moving down on a scale of entitlement.

The participants in this video are seen in Figure 3.3. The little boy (Efraín ~ Ef), who repeatedly tries to initiate the recruitment of a cup of soda, is seated between the two women: Andrea, his grandmother, and Elvia, his aunt. This is Pedro the cameraman's family. Pedro is the boy's uncle and Pedro's father Táolla (on the right) is the boy's grandfather. The boy's sister Laura is between Elvia and Táolla. The family is working in their milpa to do the second (and last) weeding of the season after which the corn and beans will be tall enough and the squash broad enough to shade out competing plants. The early summer is a time of intensive labor in Lachixío that involves the family working together in fields that can be more than a kilometer from their house. The youngest children accompany the family but do not generally work, though in this video Efraín, who is not expected to work in contrast to the older Laura, is invited to help his grandfather plow (see Chapter 5). This rank and gender difference is also seen in other videos of the family working where the older daughter works and the younger son plays. During playback interviews about this sequence, a custom was explained that workers are all offered food and drink before any nonworking individuals are. This rank difference enters into the way the recruitment sequence develops and illustrates for us that beyond grammatical forms, recruitments presuppose and performatively

Figure 3.3 A family takes a break from weeding in the milpa.

reproduce rank relationships, speaker identities, and everyday ethics. In this way our focus on the formal and functional ties between recruitments and the social situation leads to sociocultural insights beyond entitlement and contingency.

The family is taking a lunch break, eating sandwiches and working through a three-liter bottle of cola. The little boy has not been served a drink yet, though everyone else has. He reaches for a cup in the bucket and in the process nearly knocks over the bottle of soda. During this time a number of offers to drink are being made to Pedro, Sofía, and Táolla. The form and repetition of the offers are like the offers we looked at in Chapter 2; they are repeated whether they were refused or accepted, and they are issued by multiple participants. Among these offers the boy issues multiple utterances which probably would be taken as requests in many European or American households where adults accommodate their behavior to children as has been described by Ochs and Schieffelin (1984). But his attempts are ignored until the boy changes the form of his utterance. Sequences like this could be effective in a child's developing sociolinguistic knowledge, learning how to request appropriately and important distinctions in Lachixío grammar by whether his utterances are taken to be an object for response or not.

```
(6) LMSMVDP28Jul0905 05:07-05:12
1 Pedro:   Xèé ricchi' bí'yyah kattze no' [móodo laxxho wa beè níngyè'.
           -Ef reaches in bucket leaning toward him bumping soda bottle
           xèé#richi'      H*-bi'ya katze    no'o'    módo laxho=wa bè
           good.while#poke POT-see    wherever there.is way   finish=2PL PL
              níngè'
              thing
           With a little work we'll see where you're going to finish these
           fields.
```

```
2   Táolla:                       [((whistles to stop oxen))
3          (2.0)
           -A takes soda bottle from near bucket places on ground near P
           -Ef takes cup out from bucket at same time
```

There are several recruitment attempts as the boy tries to get a drink of soda. In the first iteration, he reaches for a cup himself in the red bucket. Having the instrument of the cup would in itself make relevant an offer of soda as he would display the material affordance for receiving the drink. The sign has the incompleteness of a rheme that is open to the possible future in which someone fulfills the function of the cup (much like the parallel affordance of the empty pitcher). Holding the empty cup here would be an indirect request, particularly in the kairos of a time for drinking that the rest of the family is involved in. However, the boy's move does not get taken up as a recruitment by his grandmother Andrea who merely rescues the falling bottle of soda and moves it out of reach from the boy, effectively denying his hint of a request.

```
(7) LMSMVDP28Jul0905 5:12-5:15
4   Pedro:       ((responding to offer of more drink))
                 A'a níngyè' tòkko [básso wa nèé'.
                 -P holds cup toward A
                 a'a    ningè'   tòko    báso=wa      nèé'
                 NEG    thing    one     cup=2PL      now
                 No, here is your cup now.
5   Elvia:                          [Níngyè' lá é paà.
                                    --|P gaze toward Ta
                                    níngyè'=lá=é       pà
                                    thing=already=3o   paɔa
                                    Here pa.
6   Pedro:       Laa waà lá nèé'.=
                 -P holds cup toward A
                 la   wà=lá              nèé'
                 NEG  drink=already      now
                 I'm not drinking now.
7   Andrea:      =Xee laa [ɨwà lò?
                 -|A reaches for cup from P
                 xe     la    wà=lò
                 full   NEG   drink=2s
                 Enough? You're not drinking?
```

In 4 Pedro is refusing an offer from Andrea, which she issued just prior to the beginning of the transcript. In 5 Elvia offers more drink to Táolla who has been the one driving the oxen and plow. The workers, including the girl, were drinking and being offered more drink until they would indicate (multiple times and in multiple ways) that they were satisfied. Having the instrument for receiving food or drink in Lachixío can always be interpreted as a recruitment to offer. Countering that affordance, Pedro and (later) Táolla give their cups back. In a similar way, an empty bowl or plate at a meal creates the material conditions to receive additional food offers, and good reason to leave a morsel in one's bowl as a sign of satisfaction.

In playback interviews, Lachixío viewers emphasized that only workers drink first, which explains why the boy has not been offered any drink at this point. Pedro returns his cup to show he is finished, and he declares clearly in words that he is returning the cup and is not going to drink more. The intermodal harmony of saying and doing works together to amplify the force or veracity of declaration by aligning world and words. If he had only said he had enough but continues to hold the cup, the intermodal discord would be enough to prompt more offers. Andrea follows asking, "Enough?" and repeating Pedro's proposition, "Your're not drinking," as an understanding check. In 8 the boy starts repeating *weè né* (drink it) over and over in temporal overlap with Andrea in 7.

```
(8) LMSMVDP28Jul0905 5:14-5:21
    8 Efraín:      [₁>weè né weè né [₃weè né weè né weè né<
                   -Ef flipping empty cup around nudging A in leg with it
                   H*-wè=né             [...]
                   POT-drink=ACT3O      [...]
                   >drink it drink it [₃drink it drink it drink it<
    9 Elvia:       [₂Xee! Láa wa lò? No' ka'a láa é.
                   -|P gaze to Ta------|P gaze to cup
                   xe     lá    wà=lò       no'o'     ka'a=lá=é
                   full   NEG   drink=2S    there.is  here=already=3O
                   Enough? You're not drinking more?
                        There's more here.
   10 Táolla:      >Weè lá wa. Weè láa wa<.
                   Ta walk in frame from R and sets cup on ground
                   wè=lá=wa      [...]
                   drink already=2PL [...]
                   >you all drink you all drink<
   11 Efraín:      >weè né [₃weè né weè né [weè né weè né °weè né...°<
                   >drink it drink it drink it drink it drink it °drink
                          it...°<
   12 Táolla:      [₄Weè lá wa.
                   wè=lá=wa
                   drink=already=2PL
                   You all drink.
   13 Elvia:              [₃No' lá é.
                          no'o'=lá=é
                          there.is=already=3O
                          There's still more of it.
   14 Táolla:      [₄Láa waà né dètte waà. [₃Stome'e' weè ì.
                   lá     wà=né         L*-dete   wà      sto-me'e'   we=ì
                   NEG    drink=ACT3O   IMP-pass  drink   a.little    drink=3M
                   I'm not drinking more. Give him ((Pedro))⁴
                   a little more to drink.
```

Efraín's babbled utterance is out of cadence with the ongoing interaction, coming in the middle of Andrea's syntactic, prosodic, and pragmatic units. It is misfit to the constituencies of the interactional moment, given what we know from the work of Ford and Thompson (1996) on grammar and interaction units, and Erickson (2004a) on the ecological rhythm of a dynamically ongoing speech situation. This is the boy's second attempt to get a drink of soda, a transformation that moves his recruitment from the form of hinting by having the cup ready, to formulating a verbal directive. Filling the ready cup on the basis of its affordance alone would index a high entitlement to an offer of soda. Having to now say something to reissue the recruitment would be a reduction in entitlement. But the boy's utterance itself is not like any of the adult utterances we have seen. It repeats indefinitely as if babbling. Copresently performed with the boy's utterance, he is flipping the cup about in his grandmother's field of vision and nudging her with it. She is ignoring him.

Elvia does an understanding check of her father's rejection of her offer to drink more and then makes another indirect offer by stating that there is more to drink. Táolla rejects by redirecting the offer to the group saying, "you all drink" in 10 and again in 12. In 11 the boy again chants *wéè ne* repeatedly (drink it, drink it drink it drink it . . .). Again there is zero uptake from Andrea or anybody else around the boy. Elvia reiterates the offer to her father once more repeating, "There's still more of it." Táolla declares that he is not drinking more, and he suggests that they give more to Pedro (but he did not suggest that they give to the boy). Like Pedro earlier, Táolla returns his cup indicating his satisfaction in an intermodal harmony of declaration and embodied action. He sets his cup on the ground as a display that he is no longer drinking.

```
(9)LMSMVDP28Jul0905 5:21-5:24
15 Efraín:      [₁>wéè né [ⱼwéè né wéè né [ₖwéè né wéè né wéè né<
                                           ((shifts to whining nasality))
16 Pedro:                                 [ₖA'a láa waà láa né nii á
                                          a'a   lá    wà=lá=né              ni=á
                                          NEG   NEG   drink=already=ACT3o   say=1s
                                          No I'm not drinking, I say.
17 Elvia:       Weè lá la?
                -P gaze at L
                we=lá=la
                drink=already=Q
                Do you want to drink more?
18 Laura:       m'mh?
                -L head shake
19 Táolla:      Láa waah lò la?
                --------------|L finishes her cup
                lá wà=lò=la
                NEG drink=2s=Q
                You don't want to drink?
```

The boy continues with his vocalizations, though he is losing steam as his voice quality degrades to a whining nasality with little segmental articulation by the end of 15. In 16 Pedro reiterates that he is not drinking more (responding to Táolla's suggestion that he be offered more). Elvia then offers Sofía a drink asking if she wants more. She gets a negative response both with a minimal bilabial nasal token, *m'mh*, and a head shake. This is followed by the grandfather asking the same question of the girl. Throughout all of this offering though, the boy is being left out, and his multiple attempts at recruitment are being ignored. Several turns are omitted here in which another sequence runs where the adults and Sofía talk about whether a related work party in another field has yet taken their drinks and why Sofía's fear of snakes keeps her from going over there to check.

```
(10)  LMSMVDP28Jul0905 (5.49-6.24)
      ((Several turns omitted))
30 Efraín:      Wàá tome'e' refrésko?
                -Ef waves cup near A gaze to A
                wè=á     to-me'e' refrésko
                drink=1s a-little soda
                I drink a little soda?
```

31 Pedro:	Áww:à.⁵ Y:es.
32 Andrea:	-picks up her cup and gives Efraín a sip then finishes her cup herself. A then takes soda bottle and serves herself another cup to hand to Efraín.

Because Sofía refuses to check with the other work party to offer them drink, it is still left open whether all the workers are satisfied, and it is at this time that we get an utterance from the boy that is actually responded to as a request and recruits an offer of soda from his grandmother. He utters a linguistically well-formed declarative *Wàá tomeè' refrésko?* (I drink a little soda?), uttered with rising intonation (a Spanish-sourced question intonation frame that is taking a foothold in the Zapotec of Lachixío), while waving his cup near his grandma again. We hear Pedro give an emphatic affirmative interjection *Áww:a* (Y:es), and this time Andrea fulfills the request immediately giving him a sip from her own cup. Then she pours more in her cup and gives it to him. Note that she does not give him his own drink in his own cup, something he is still not entitled to (especially as it is left unresolved whether the workers in the next field have drunk). The boy has shifted his utterance form from a babbling bare directive with an indefinite subject *wèè né* to a well-formed declarative proposition with rising intonation that marks him as the subject and explicitly refers to a named object. Shifting to a question form would mark a reduction in entitlement particularly since questions lean toward the request pole. Andrea rewards his linguistic well-formedness and his pragmatic appropriateness with the immediate granting of his request, regimenting a cultural competence with language. But when we consider the ongoing influence of and shift to Spanish in the region, this example intriguingly also shows that the Spanish intonation pattern for marking polar questions is allowed to pass, supplanting the Zapotec interrogative particle *la*, which we saw in the adult polar questions. The paired relationship of the moves in the recruitment-response joint action is one of moral evaluation relevant to studies of contact-induced language change (Sicoli, 2020). We see where people sanction language form and where they do not.

One thing this set of examples shows us is that while we know requests can have a simple form grounded in the here and now (as with open-hand palm-up gesture or a declarative hint), we see in the missing next pair part of either fulfillment or rejection that recruitments are incomplete considered from the perspective of the individual speaker's utterance where they are rather recruitment-initiations. Their issuance and response forms come open to each other, and the space between is intersected by numerous trajectories of sociality. Form matters as it interfaces with social relations and purposes and the ontological trace of these trajectories carry forward in the social life of the participants. For the boy, there is socialization being done in the milpa developing his cultural competence with the simple yet highly symbolic act of getting a drink, and of the finer grained learning of the pragmatics of requesting in Lachixío.

3.6 A Family of Recruitments for Water

In this segment, we will track another series of repeat recruitments for a drink. Though rather than being repeated by a single individual, this recruitment is passed from one

Figure 3.4 Recruitment of water at a family dinner.

participant to another. A family is seated around a table having dinner. *Toò* Pedro is the father (not the same Pedro as my collaborator), Mariana the mother, Inez the daughter, and Rodrigo the son (Figure 3.4). We will see both age and gender hierarchies in play as the recruitment goes through several transformations when passed from one family member to another, and that the two men together produced a multi-participant, multimodal recruitment that finally directs the youngest daughter Inez to go get water. We will also see the multimodally discordant responses of Inez through which she creatively both complied with and pushed back against the gender hierarchy folded into the ultimate recruitment and which declares her agency over the terms of its fulfillment.

```
(11) LMSMVDP07Aug08 7:47-7:53

1 Pedro:      Tomaà nezhoxxo éttà kwà' #aà#.
              ---| P gaze towards I---------| P gaze to bowl
              --------------| R gaze to P
              to-mà   ne-zhoxo    étà         kwà'  à
              much    STA-toast   tortilla DEF      INT
              These tortillas got very toasted #ahh#.
2             (4.4)
              -R gaze to I
3 Inez:       Nezxe'e xe'tta é.
              ------------| I quick gaze to P returns gaze to bowl
              ne-zxe'e    xe'ta=é
              STA-hot     very=3o
              It got very hot (the stove).
4             (2.34)
5 Pedro:      Tome'e' ínza lakka no né.
              -| R gaze to P-------------R gaze to I ((through 14))
              -| I gaze toward P/R
              to-me'e'    ínza    laka=no=né
              a-little    water   lower=INSTR=ACT3o
              A little water will help one get it down.
```

```
6               (2.68)
                -| I quick gaze to M then to bowl
                -| M quick gaze to P then to bowl
```

In 1 of the transcript Pedro issues a declaration, "These tortillas got very toasted #ahh#," which functions at one level as a critical assessment, especially with the harsh-voiced #ahh# with which he punctuates the utterance. After a four-second pause Inez (who made the tortillas) declares only that the stove got very hot. Her response claims no responsibility for overcooking the tortillas but rather locates the cause in the stove. The Zapotec utterance *Nezxe'e xe'tta é* uses a third-person pronoun object, =*é*, and an intensifier *xe'tta* (very) on a stative inflected less-active predicate *-zxe'e* (get hot). This is used by Inez rather than its more active pair *-txe'e*, which would entail an agent. As such there is no causing subject (i.e., the cook) present in her sentence.

Pedro goes on to make an assertion in 5, "A little water will help one get it down," using an instrumental suffix indicating water as a tool with which to swallow the dry tortillas (this is the same instrumental suffix Angeles used to categorize water as an instrument to soften the corn dough in example 4). In many families people do not drink until the end of the meal, so just suggesting a drink of water during the meal is potentially a criticism of the food. To both these turns, Pedro gets no response seen in the long pauses in lines 2 and 6. The expectation that the daughter should be offering water at either of these points can be read from the brother's gaze to her in lines 2 and 5. The latter gaze he holds through 14. This is a very long time and stands as a clear sign-action to mobilize her response consistent with the analysis forwarded by Stivers and Rossano (2010) which argues that mobilizing response is an important social dynamic for gaze (see also Rossano, Brown, and Levinson 2009). The recruitment of water for Pedro goes through several iterations. The first is line 1, "These tortillas got very toasted," which can be considered a "hint" as Pedro uses an assessment to make relevant an offer. In this way, it is a high entitlement act. It is also potentially face saving because he would not have to do the dispreferred action asking for it. Line 5 is the second iteration, "A little water will help one get it down," which is goes beyond the hint to specifically mention a solution using water as an instrument that would remedy the problem of the dry food. These turns also do criticizing, and in neither turn does Pedro specify that he be the beneficiary of the recruited action. Line 1 only mentions the tortillas, and in 5 the implied beneficiary could be everybody sharing the meal at the table. In the silent pause of 6 (the second time an offer would be relevant), the two women make quick glances to others at the table and then to their bowls: Mariana to Pedro and Inez to Mariana.

```
(12) LMSMVDP07Aug08 7:54-8:00

7  Mariana:    Kyáá ínza we' pa' lò Rodrígò.
               ------------------| M gaze to R
               ------------------| P reaches for cup and lifts

               kyáá      ínza     we'     pa-'=lò           Rodrigo-L
               go.and    water    drink   father-POS=2S     NAME-CLAS
               Go and get water for your father to drink, Rodrigo.

8              (0.8)
               -| P moves cup [toward I
               --------------| I smiles gaze toward M
```

```
9  Rodrigo:              [Kyáà jre'e Job.
                         -----| P holds cup in frcnt of face of I
                         kyáà      r-re'e   job
                         go.and    HAB-do   nickname
                         You go do it Sis.
10                 (2.49)
                         -I laughs, puts spoon down, wipes hand on napkin, turns right
                         -R smiles gaze on I
```

It is in 7 that we see the first action that can be clearly recognized as an explicit recruitment. Pedro's wife Mariana issues a directive to the son using an andative form (go and . . .) with an explicit benefactor and named addressee, "Go and get water for your father to drink, Rodrigo." But instead of Inez, she addressed the directive to Rodrigo. Rodrigo is the next youngest at the table and the one who finished eating, in contrast to Inez who still has a full bowl of food. This move illustrates both a high entitlement of Pedro as Mariana is animating a recruitment that he has not made explicit himself, Mariana's entitlement to direct Rodrigo, and also the lower contingency of Rodrigo to fulfill the recruitment since he is the only one finished eating. What we can begin to see next is that the directive is coproduced by multiple participants not only sequentially (through the transformations from participant-to-participant) but also simultaneously in embodied action as Pedro reaches for the cup during Mariana's utterance (Figure 3.5).

```
7 Mariana: Kyáà ínza we' pa' lò Rodrígò
           ------------------|P reaches for cup and lifts
           Go and get water for your father to drink, Rodrigo.

8          (0.8)
                         -|P moves cup  [toward I
                         --------------|I smiles gaze toward E

9 Rodrigo:               [kyáà jre'e Job
                         [You go do it Sis.
```

Figure 3.5 Mariana passes directive to Rodrigo who issues verbal directive to Inez in synchronicity with Pedro's material directive with the cup.

Examining the timing of Pedro's action initiation and Mariana's utterance in 7, we see that Pedro initiates his action prior to the end of Mariana's utterance. He does so at a transition relevance place (TRP) seen in the possible turn completion after the second-person pronoun. This is the union of the completion of a syntactic unit, a phonological word, an intonation unit, and a pragmatic action (see Ford and Thompson 1996 on interaction units and TRPs). It is also before the onset of her next turn construction unit, "Rodrigo," a summons that selects the son verbally, and whom she also selects with gaze at the onset of his name. The whole turn is formulated like a "garden-path sentence" that leads one on to an interpretation that is then disaffirmed over the course of the utterance's temporal development. Pedro would not have necessarily known to whom Mariana's use of the pronoun referred when he lifted the cup. Upon lifting the cup he begins to move it toward Inez. In 9, Rodrigo verbally redirects the request to Inez, "You go do it Sis" (Figure 3.5).

Now if we only had the text transcript of the audio, it would simply sound like the recruitment was being passed from mother to son to sister. But with the video we can rather see that the action of Pedro was already initiated during the mother's utterance when Pedro picks up the cup. And in 8 Pedro is already beginning to move the cup in the direction of Inez when Rodrigo issues his directive in 9. In the multimodal transcription, we see the next iteration of the recruitment as co-performed between Pedro in his embodied action and Rodrigo voicing the request in a verbal utterance. The father and son jointly author the next iteration of the recruitment redirected toward Inez (an interparticipant intermodal harmony that amplifies the social obligation). Inez's response is multimodally complex.

```
(13) LMSMVDP07Aug08 8:00-8:08
11 Inez:        Púuro li'i á noo xhinne?
                -| I takes cup, gazes back to R
                puro   li'i=a    no    xhine
                pure    PRO=1S  and    why
                Why is it always me?
12              (1.31)
                -| I turns in seat
13 Rodrigo:     Le'kka lá lò nóo nekka lò ona'a.
                le'ka=lá=lò       nó    neka=lò    ona'a
                now=already=2S    that  be=2S      woman
                Now it's you because you're a woman.
14              (0.86)
                -| I stands
15 Inez:        Ricche' tzyáà jarra kye' jre'e.
                --------------------------------| I puts cup hard on table
                riche'   tzyáà   jarra    ke'   r-re'e
                fill     just    pitcher  DEF   HAB-do
                (I'll) Just fill the pitcher.
16              (1.04)
                -| P gaze back toward I
                -| R gaze up toward I
```

As we move forward, we see a moment of intermodal discord where, in words, Inez is resisting the recruitment asking, "Why is it always me?" but in action she is accepting it by initiating the actions it would take to fulfill. She takes the cup and turns in her seat to get up. The metapragmatics of gender in the family interaction are made explicit in Rodrigo's response to Inez's question in 13. He says, "Now it's you because you're a woman." Inez stands, further complying with the recruitment, but makes a verbal move to re-term her action saying, "(I'll) Just fill the pitcher" in 15 punctuated by expressively slamming the cup down on the table—the very cup that was dangled in her face as part of the co-agentive recruitment jointly initiated by the two men. While Inez's taking the cup from her father is a move that projects fulfillment of the recruitment, she soon after rejects the terms of the men's recruitment by animating the semiotic affordances accumulated in the interactional history of the cup. Her resistance to the recruitment while also projecting fulfillment is a double-voiced action that complies with the order while discursively pushing back against it (Bakhtin 1981; Voloshinov 1986). The already complex constitution of this recruitment is made more complex in the discordant relationship between its multiple interpretants illustrated in Figure 3.6 using an illustrative form that I borrow from Paul Kockelman (2007). Using Kockelman's (2007) dimensions of agency, we can say that she complied with the *residential agency* of her body but resisted with the *representational agency* of her verbal proposition over that action.

We can also view discordant interpretants from the perspective of the cup—as sign. The cup has a materiality in its form, function, commodity history, and its current valence of emptiness that provides it with qualitative affordance to be taken up into semiosis. This is parallel to the material recruitments we saw with the empty pitcher in section 3.4, and Efraín's presentation of the empty cup in section 3.5. However, a sign-object has a social life that develops as the object is taken into subsequent sign relationships across the turns of the sequence, transforming its value from recruitment, to fulfillment, and then to resistance. The father holds the cup first as a sign grounded

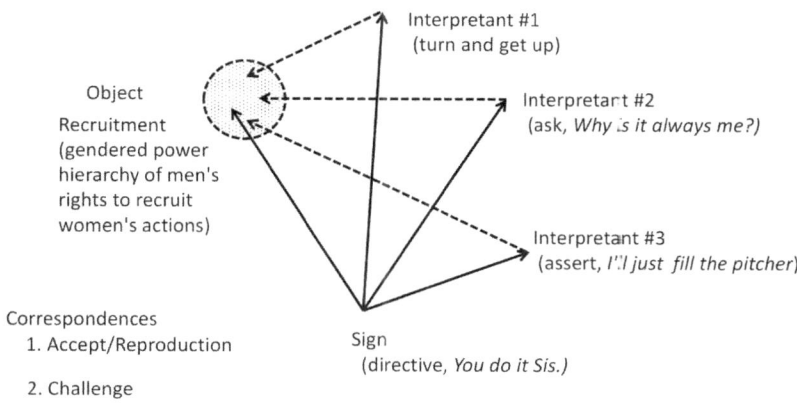

Figure 3.6 Sign-object interpreted through three interpretants that produce an intermodal discord between energetic interpretants that reproduce the value of the sign-object and representational interpretants that contest it and subsequently transform it by scale shifting.

in its instrumentality, but then it enters a new sign relationship for recruitment (lifting up) and selecting the recipient through its movement (toward Inez). As the sign value of the cup develops in time, it marks Inez's compliance when she accepts it, but at that point it moves out of the agentive control of the father and enters into a new sign relation to show Inez's resistance. Her transformation of the value of this cup from the father's intended value involves setting it so firmly on the table that there is an audible crescendo as the bell shape of the empty cup amplifies the impact of the now moment. This assertion of her own agency is met by silent gaze from both Pedro and Rodrigo in 16. During playback interviews in Lachixío the acoustics of the cup striking the table were on separate occasions met with laughter by the participants. The semiosis of the cup as directive then transformed to resistance is represented in Figure 3.7.

Inez brings water about two minutes later, setting the pitcher down next to Pedro who pours himself a cup of water. Mariana is offering her son Rodrigo more food which he rejects saying, "I'm finished." Inez sits down and begins to eat again. Pedro is the only one drinking water. He notices that he is the only one drinking, and asks the others once if they are going to drink water and a second time in the negative, "You all are not going to drink?" as if a realization of the discordance between pitcher's social value and its singular use.

Recruitments are fraught. They are joint actions that threaten the face of the initiator as well as the responder. The initiator must make claim to some level of entitlement to the action of the responder. The responder must yield some agency in complying. It is the recruitment of the recipient's action for someone else's benefit that makes the joint action of recruitments a revealing intersection between language and social life. Recruitments are face threatening to the responder for working against an individual's "desire to be unimpeded," or negative face (Brown and Levinson 1987). To fulfill your request, for instance, I must exert my labor for you. To reject your request,

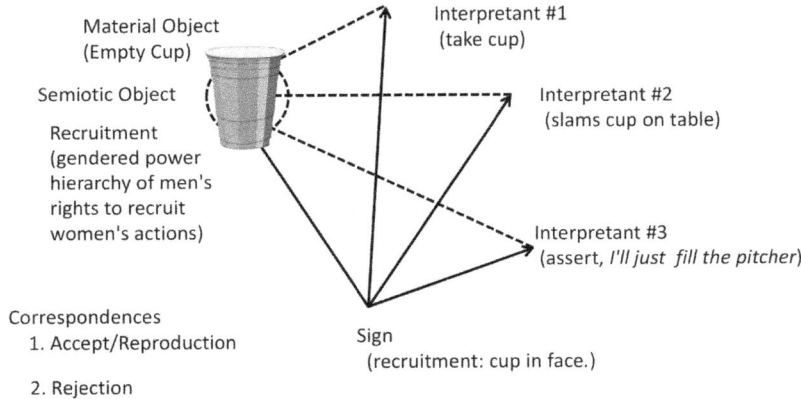

Figure 3.7 Material affordance of empty cup used as directive interpreted through three interpretants that subsequently accept, reject, and then transform the action represented in the sign-object.

I must respond in a way that may be face threatening for both of us. But in strict social hierarchies, like the one Inez finds herself in, rejection is not really a valid option. The recruitments in this dinner table conversation have tended toward the imperative/directive pole in which entitlement and contingency are controlled by the initiator. However, as we saw in Inez's performance, this does not rule out the possibility of creatively resisting such power hierarchies using multimodality to develop what James Scott (1990) would call a "hidden transcript" and de Certeau (1984) and Garfinkel (1967) tactical action.

In sum, we saw two ways that responses to recruitments can be done. In the first, the mother passed the recruitment to the son who then passed the recruitment to the daughter. This moves down the family generational hierarchy and across the gender hierarchy. Pedro made relevant an offer through the perlocutionary effect of declaring the tortillas were overcooked and that water would help get them down. Mariana issued a verbal recruitment in the form of a directive to her son and the son-with-father recruited the daughter who was youngest and lowest ranking at the table (see Ochs and Schieffelin 1984 as well as Rosaldo 1982 for passing directives within a rank hierarchy like this). As the end of the directive chain, Inez was not in a position to pass on the recruitment any further, and given the social relations present at the table, she was not in a position to reject either. Her response is creatively intermodal as she moves to comply with her body but also protest with her words in a discordant configuration of interpretant signs. She is here resisting the "field of constraints" (Heritage and Raymond 2012) created by the directive form by using the multimodal affordances to create a double-voiced action. Where Bakhtin pointed to double voicing in novelistic dialogue, here I claim that voices can be distributed across modalities in copresent interaction, and that through such discord, Inez is able to simultaneously comply with and reject the recruitment. This illustrates a way of response, which builds resonances between modalities with emergent affect at the scale of their assemblage, drawing on the temporal affordances of both simultaneity and sequence. This is parallel to the intermodal and interparticipant resonance between the father and son to jointly initiate the recruitment, one by moving the cup, and the other by co-temporal utterance.

Inez's action illustrates for us an important relationship between structure and agency afforded in the process of semiosis with potential for multiple interpretants. Inez shows us a means of resistance to structures of power grounded in our capacity for and immersion in multimodal discourse. Through video analysis, we make visible a type of structuration that was adumbrated in Sapir's characterization of the locus for culture in an individual's negotiation of and adjustment to structure and which may itself have effect on the transformation of society. However small the change accomplished in this interaction, we can acknowledge, as some participants in playback interviews did, that her practice is not isolated but part of an ongoing historical transformation. Lachixío is a community in the midst of many social changes, and Inez's resistance is part of that change which we are able to see, interpret, and work to understand through a fine-grained examination of the multimodal assemblages of recruitments, built from diverse elements of talk, body movement, actions with objects, and the resonances between them.

3.7 Concluding Remarks

The three video sequences of this chapter each demonstrated how recruitments developed and transformed across iterations and how the grammatical and multimodal formulations of the moves connected to social relations of entitlement, contingency, and politeness. In the first set of extracts, a mother initiated the recruitment of her daughter but without a fitted response the initiation for the joint action of recruitment-fulfillment was left *open*. Across the iterations we saw the grammatical form of the utterance cycle through potential- and completive-formulated directives to index increased assertions of entitlement. We also saw other lexical and grammatical means that characterized repeat directives as "recruitments being done again," particularly ellipses of the requested object, the addition of person reference, reference of deontic role through kin term, and framing the subsequent directive as reported speech. In the second extract, a child's request went through several iterations that reformulated it to rather display a reduction in entitlement. Directive forms issued through babbling repetitions were completely ignored, while a latter request formed as a declarative question with rising intonation was immediately fulfilled. Others only joined in the action of getting him a drink after first establishing it was becoming pragmatically appropriate, and when the verbal morphology was well formed but passing on the lack of the Zapotec polar question sentence particle. The mother-daughter interaction with the water pitcher supports the general observation in the conversation analysis literature that repeat recruitments construct or draw attention to the greater entitlement of the recruiting initiator; this example from the picnic in the milpa shows us that this observation needs to be tempered by attention to other social vectors that intersect the speech event, including social rank, role, and appropriateness. The boy's social rank as a nonworking child, a work-reward ethic, ideologies of politeness for appropriate request forms and the right time to ask, as well as routines of doing language socialization (e.g., ignoring), are critical for our understanding of how this recruitment played out, and why the grammatical form that indexed reduced entitlement was ultimately successful.

In the recruitment for water at the family dinner, we saw entitlement and contingency to be relevant but also had to look beyond these, to include the gender-power hierarchy and the historical trajectory of its change in Lachixío. The multimodal transcript analysis showed the agency for recruiting the action of the daughter to be distributed between the father's embodied action with the empty cup and the son's co-temporal verbal directive. The daughter's response showed both fulfillment and resistance to performing the gender-power hierarchy through the joint action in which she became implemented by creatively duplicating responses across modalities displaying at once compliance and resistance in the intermodally discordant assemblage.

In this chapter, and the last, I have argued, in part by the illustration of a method, that joint actions are exemplary sites for investigating intersections of language forms with social relations, and that the multiple social vectors that converge in joint actions are productively approached in their multimodality. This union requires serious thinking about linguistic signs as, by their nature, open to the contingencies of human sociality, and to their dynamic transformation over time and across the cognition of multiple participants. The semiotic process brings disparate types of participants and modalities into resonances of harmony and discord with emergent effect and affect. To bring the linguistic practice of talk together with the techniques of bodily gestures, and the technology of cultural objects in complex assemblages of mutual causality, and to make those relations noticeable for readers, I have grounded my transcription theory and analytical practices in a Peircean formulation of the sign as emerging through an ongoing dialogic dynamic. The value of this framework has perhaps been most visible in developing an understanding of the process in which the material affordances of the cup were taken up as sign and transformed over several semiosis cycles in the speech event. Though often less striking, this process is to be found with the life of any sign in discourse, a reality for signs pointed to in Derrida's notion of *iterability* (1988) (himself building on Peirce's concept of the interpretant) but which we can more explicitly ground in the interpretive process of semiosis and the resonances afforded in joint action.

Through the interpretive endeavor of multimodal ethnography, we make visible (and more broadly *sensible*) a dialogic process through which a sign-object projects possible interpretants, some of which become actual (and meaningful) in subsequent and public responses. In new cycles of semiosis this interpretant itself becomes the material for a new sign-object which again projects paradigms of possible interpretants and enters new potential and actual sign relations. This biosemiotic process is what Favareau (2008) has called "collapsing the wave function" building upon metaphors of quantum theory. This current work shows additionally that what it collapses to may itself be multiple and that relations emerge that engage each other through the logic of resonance—a double existence as both reproduction and transformation. Upon its utterance the linguistic sign offers itself to be shaped by response. Each participant's interpretation produces the sign's transformation as it does its replication. This is an important affordance of the dialogism of semiosis that makes possible both linguistic and social change through everyday joint actions. As we move into Chapters 4 and 5, we shift scales from an order of activity directed to building social relations to an order where building social relations builds possibilities for intersubjectivity, examining the always-available response move of *other-initiated repair* and the collaborative work to build *resonances* between interactional moves.

4

Repair

The anthropologist Gregory Bateson developed an understanding of mind beyond the individual and in connection with larger environmental process. He wrote, "The total self-corrective unit which processes information, or, as I say, 'thinks' and 'acts' and 'decides,' is a system whose boundaries do not at all coincide with the boundaries either of the body or of what is popularly called the 'self' or 'consciousness'" (Bateson 1972: 319). The chapter examines the repair of interaction as such a system emergent from the joint actions we've been examining in the previous chapters. Long before "intersubjectivity" was a named problem debated by philosophers, psychologists, and anthropologists, it was the prerequisite for the doing together of collaborative actions. As Duranti (2010) has argued, intersubjectivity is not just the achieving of mutual understanding but also "an existential condition that can *lead* to shared understanding" (Duranti 2010, emphasis in original). While this potential to lead to something has been presented at times as *nature* or the inhabiting of the shared objective world (Husserl 1989), intersubjectivity has also been seen as largely a practical problem to be solved in interaction (see Sidnell 2014 and Edwards 2021 for reviews). In thinking about intersubjectivity along with the practical problem of interactional repair in this chapter, I follow a line of research in ethnomethodology that, rather than viewing intersubjectivity as a transcendent ability of one individual to stand *in the place of* another, understands intersubjectivity as how individuals can *stand with* others relying on a public sign system they have built together as their common property. Following Bateson, as quoted earlier, we might then see intersubjectivity as emergent in taking up a relational position to another in an ecology of mind whose ontology lies beyond individual cognition in a social and distributed cognition—an order of life emergent from cooperative action and characterized by self-repair, itself a qualisign of life in the autopoiesis of Varela and Maturana (1998). Bateson, like Peirce (CP 5.128), understood mind to not be necessarily limited to, or reside within, single organisms. From the perspective of the multi-participant, multimodal ecology of interaction, we invert Husserl's question: "If we start from individuals (i.e. monads), how can we explain the formation and existence of community" (Husserl 1931; 1960, §55, cited in Duranti 2010: 25). Life is experienced in part-whole relations of social connection. Humans are never not suspended by webs of biocultural and social relationships, from the fetal dependency, extended infancy and childhood, to a lifetime of kin relations and multi-participant interactions in which ego is emergent with alter. Rather than the individual as starting point, an approach from the perspective of joint action asks how the subjective is emergent with the intersubjective.

Interaction analysis has followed Alfred Schutz's rejection of Husserl's philosophical problem of a transcendental intersubjectivity, to treat intersubjectivity's "achievement and maintenance as a practical 'problem' which is routinely 'solved' by social actors in the course of their dealings with one another" (Heritage 1991: 54). Though importantly for Husserl, intersubjectivity was not limited to a product of interaction, but seen as a precondition for it (Duranti 2010). To have mutual understanding, we have to start with "the possibility of exchanging places, of seeing the world from the point of view of the Other" (Duranti 2010: 21), such as is necessary in the simple joint action of picking up and moving a table together. Husserl saw a precondition for intersubjectivity in *nature* as something that we all share together. But this may assume nature is not variably perceived and inhabited through semiotic means and sensory access to different body-environment relations. Part of an ability to *stand with* another involves a coming together of perceptual, actable worlds, such as referred to by Jakob von Uexküll's *umwelt*, the phenomenal world of an organism characterized in the semiotic dimensions of an environment perceivable through use value and including the affordances of objects and the actions of other organisms (Uexküll 1934). Repairs of reference as we will see in this chapter are often provoked by differential perceptual access to a sensible field presupposed in a turn formulation. Participants may first need to achieve a sharing of access to "nature" before the conditions exist for intersubjectivity. In other words, we may first need to do the work required to stand with the other before we can attempt to stand in the place of the other.

Where this chapter engages intersubjectivity as standing with others to get something done together, whether it be collaborative action, shared reference, mutual, or partial understanding, Chapter 5 on resonance will focus on practices of doing what the other does, and the work such action does to build an interindividual order of doing-with. I would like you to notice how both repair and resonance emerge from the basic social actions of offering and recruiting we examined in the previous chapters, and I work in both this chapter and the next to illustrate how our attention to these universally available actions provides a privileged vantage on how the grammar and vocabulary of a language are fitted to this order, built up in the dialogic steps and joint goals of interaction. They themselves become part to the whole of the living process of the cooperative semiosis of the interaction.

Intersubjectivity is more than a successfully shared reference but also joint activity. A repair sequence is both a joint activity itself and a mechanism to regulate the achievement of intersubjectivity in the superordinate joint activity of the interaction into which the repair is inserted. On conversational repair, the biosemiotician Donald Favareau (2008: 198) wrote:

> Instead of merely being a *propositional* "error-correcting" mechanism interactional "repair" is used by participants to meaning-making interaction as a resource whereby the question of "what constitutes the semiotic order *per se*" at any given moment is abducted, accessed, and creatively engaged with by each individual agent. As such, it is the inescapably available "reality check" against which both public and private understandings must live or die, succeed or fail in a network of relations that includes, but far exceeds the individual system-using agent, i.e., in

the public domain of interactively constituted sign-exchange whereby meanings are created, negotiated and, most importantly for human beings, cooperatively sustained. (Emphasis in original)

Favareau (2008: 197) asks us to "appreciate how the naturally emergent system of talk-and-interaction makes publicly available the means by which its participants can and do validate and invalidate each other's 'understandings' of what is happening at the current moment." Languages have grammatical and lexical resources adapted to these socially cognitive tasks. Because these resources function beyond and between individuals they can only be engaged for study in dialogic speech ecologies of actual conversations. We will also see, as in the previous chapters, that these grammatical and lexical resources are paradigmatically associated with gestures and actions with objects, and syntagmatically incorporated into multimodal configurations of copresent interaction. These relations are rendered intelligible through methods of video analysis and multimodal transcription.

The previous chapters illustrated offers and recruitments in conversational ecologies where linguistic acts were simultaneously socially pragmatic actions. Through offers, moral subjects, family reputations, and social obligations were constructed. Recruitments managed material relations of entitlement and contingency, even at a basic turn level, where a request places the contingency with the responder to reply. We also saw in Chapters 2 and 3 that linguistic forms prototypical of recruitments, like imperatives, could be used for offers, which is to say that forms associated with pragmatic actions can themselves stand in as signs for other or additional social actions.

Dingemanse and Enfield (2015) draw upon a contrast between the social actions of offering and requesting to develop a typology of conversational repair. When one person initiates repair on another person's speech he or she can take two strategies: (1) request that the other speaker redo or remedy something problematic (a turn, a turn construction unit [TCU], or linguistic constituent like a noun reference) and (2) offer some candidate understanding, or a guess at what the problematic turn or sequence was trying to do for the other speaker, offering this into the on-record dialogue for confirmation or disconfirmation by another speaker. We see in conversational repair how basic actions of human sociality that offer for another or recruit from another provide a scaffold for emergent functions in interaction. This is a central point that I argue in this book: the human social world and our built environment are emergent from more basic actions of human sociality that afford them. Thus an important task of describing a language involves identifying and describing how grammar and vocabulary are worlded with these very human social actions.

Reflecting on foundational work of Emanuel Schegloff, Gail Jefferson, and Harvey Sacks (1977) and Schegloff (2000), Jack Sidnell describes conversational repair as "an organized set of practices through which participants in conversation are able to address and potentially resolve . . . problems of speaking, hearing, or understanding" (Sidnell 2010: 110). Repair can be self-initiated or other-initiated and can occur by a speaker on his or her own turn—for example, false starts, change in word choice, or waiting to get the attention or gaze of a listener (Goodwin 1980). Repair can be initiated by another speaker after the turn of a previous speaker (Schegloff 2000), or after next turn (Schegloff 1992, 1997). Work on repair can also take the perspective of how a repair initiation is remedied. Curl (2005) examined how repetitions used as resolutions to repair can be phonetically differentiated from the trouble source (there the prior parallel turn upon which repair has been initiated).

Like recruitment, issuing repair on the speech of another speaker can be a fraught action because it may threaten the face of another speaker (Goffman 1967; Brown and Levinson 1978), pointing researchers to repeatedly recognize a cross-cultural preference for self-initiated repair (e.g., Schegloff, Jefferson, and Sacks 1977; Moerman 1977). Self-initiated self-repair avoids the need for another to intervene.[1] Much trouble in talk may, however, just be accepted without initiating repair, a threshold of "good enough" understanding set to avoid threatening face or disrupting the progression of a conversation. Yet a cross-cultural study of repair found that repairs are still quite frequent, with one occurring every 1.4 minutes of talk on average across numerous world languages (Dingemanse et al. 2015).

Goodwin (1981) has argued that whenever repair is employed, the stops and starts, redoings, and replacements of repair provide a rich stimulus of language input for children learning a language. If we would only look at language in dialogue, we see that "poverty of the stimulus" arguments (e.g., Chomsky 1980) are the result of failing to take into account the way repair and other aspects of dialogic language-use publicly point learners to relevant units of language, normative and nonnormative phrase structures, constituents and sub-constituents, and allowable substitutions of paradigmatic categories. Thus also for language documentation, description, and linguistic theory, the intersubjective orders of repair and resonance constructed between people are an always important means of grammatical depiction and analysis. This chapter on *repair* and the next on *resonance* are about the richness of the stimulus of dialogue in embodied interactions.

I focus on other-initiated repair rather than self-repair consistent with the theme of joint action.[2] Other-initiated repair initiations and their remedies form what Goffman (1981) and Jefferson (1972) called "side sequences" because they divert the course of a conversation from the ongoing topic to handle some emergent matter (see also Chapter 2). Levinson (2013) has shown that side sequences can be embedded recursively within any stretch of talk. The side sequence of other-initiated repair begins at the point where a speaker initiates repair. This is referred to as T0. At T0 the progress of the conversation is put on hold to deal with the trouble of a prior turn referred to now as T-1. The type of trouble (and often stance) can be indicated by the form of repair initiation used. The prior speaker (or sometimes a third speaker) resolves the trouble in a new turn or interactional move referred to as T+1. Example (1) shows the three-part routine as it may play out in American English (Schegloff, Jefferson, and Sacks 1977) and shows a common resolution of full repetition of the trouble source for this type of repair initiation.

```
     (1)
            A:   Were you uh you were in therapy with a private doctor?
            B:   yah
     (T-1)  A:   Have you ever tried a clinic?
   → (T0)   B:   What?
     (T+1)  A:   Have you ever tried a clinic?
            B:   ((sigh)) No, I don't want to go to a clinic.
```

Other-initiated repair is a joint-action routine that can get taken up after any turn in a conversation (Schegloff 1982; Levinson 2013), and every language has lexical and grammatical devices functioning for repair (Dingemanse, Torreira, and Enfield 2013). Repair initiations can be *open* to interpretation by the prior speaker or *restricted* narrowing the focus on the trouble. Open repair can be initiated with a minimal form interjection like "Huh?," an object or manner question word like "What?" or "How?" or a formulaic phrase like "What/how did you say?," and polite formulas like "Pardon me?," "Excuse me?," or "I'm sorry." (Dingemanse and Enfield 2015). Paul Drew (1997) has defined open repair as leaving unrestricted what the problem is with the prior talk. An *open* repair initiation merely makes a request that the speaker of T-1 do something to remedy some nondescript problem, leaving it open to the speaker just how to do it. By contrast, initiations of *restricted* repair orient speaker and listener toward a particular trouble of T-1 and narrow the action of the prior speaker to provide a remedy in T+1. Restricted repairs use grammatical affordances of content questions, or a speaker offering a possible understanding, to provide the speaker of T-1 with an indication of just what the trouble is, like the restricted requests "Which tree (did you mean)?," "Peter who?," or candidate offerings like "Did you say, over at Jane's house?" Offers of understanding, like this last one, often repeat or paraphrase what the speaker of T0 thinks they heard for confirmation or disconfirmation by the prior speaker.

Other-initiated repair is a stable environment for comparing the grammatical and lexical resources of languages because, outside of monologic speech and oppressively inflexible power hierarchies, it is an always-available dialogic action routine that follows a universal three-part format, but it can only be implemented through the grammatical, lexical, and embodied resources of a particular language in interaction. My presentation here draws on comparative linguistic work on conversational repair (Dingemanse and Enfield 2015) and, as discussed later in this same section, the work was coded and is presented in a way that facilitates further cross-cultural research.

Dingemanse and Enfield (2015) developed a typology of other-initiated repair based on prior literature and comparative conversation analysis, which recognized repairs to occur universally in a three-turn sequence that pivots on the repair initiation move (T0), as we have seen earlier. The dimensions of repair are both retrospective and prospective. A repair initiation is retrospective in that looking back from T0, a speaker either leaves open what the trouble of T-1 is or restricts the indication of trouble in some way. At the same time, a repair initiation is prospective in that T0 functions as either a request for the next action of the prior speaker who should then provide some remedy in T+1 or T0 will offer something for the prior speaker to now confirm or disconfirm in T+1 (Figure 4.1).

Dingemanse and Enfield (2015: 105) explain the figure as follows:

The distinction between open and restricted type format is retrospective: it is about the nature and location of the trouble in prior turn. The distinction between request and offer type formats is prospective: it is about the nature of the response that is relevant in next turn. The two dimensions together define three basic types of formats for repair initiation: (1) open request, (2) restricted request, and (3) restricted offer.

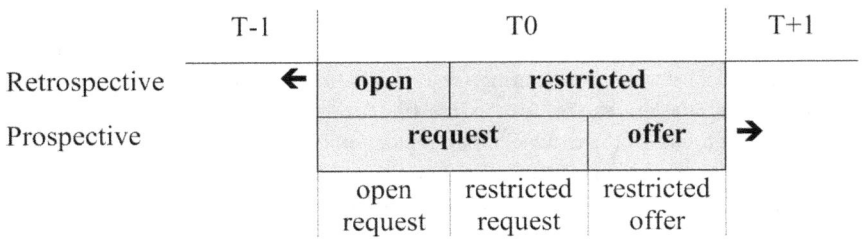

Figure 4.1 The retrospective and prospective dimensions of conversational repair (after Dingemanse and Enfield 2015: 105).

Comparative work on conversational repair has discovered that the range of ways to initiate repair is built from a limited variety of grammatical, prosodic, and lexical resources with a great deal of overlap, yet with language-based differences in the relative frequency of repair initiation types used in local linguistic practice. The linguistics of repair requires primary descriptive work then to examine how a particular language's resources are fitted with this joint activity. Repair provides an important vantage on how language elements take their shape and function through practical actions to build and repair intersubjectivity. Table 4.1 shows basic format types for other-initiated repair and the lexical items and constructions that can characterize the open and restricted initiation types.

My method of engaging other-initiated repair for this chapter involved applying a coding scheme based on the retrospective (open vs restricted) and prospective dimensions (offer vs request) and the basic format types. The coding scheme was developed as part of the ERC funded project *Human Sociality and Systems of Language Use* (HSSLU) directed by N. J. Enfield and published as "A Coding Scheme for Other-Initiated Repair Across Languages" (Dingemanse, Kendrick, and Enfield 2016), which I had previously implemented in coding repair on the *Sochiapan Chinantec Whistled Speech Corpus* (Sicoli 2016). The HSSLU project documented and analyzed casual conversation for comparison across ten languages.[3] The everyday life dialogues of the Lachixío Zapotec Conversations Corpus make it a relevant dataset to compare.

I worked with several student assistants coding 13.75 hours of the corpus identifying repair initiations then coding qualities of T0, T-1, and T+1. The student assistants were trained on the tasks and instructed to code liberally, sometimes overidentifying turns as repair initiations. I then went through their coding, checking every repair by going back to the original transcribed video to exclude items that were not repairs and check that all repairs in a video were identified. I also had a few students code the same files to check inter-coder reliability. Students generally identified almost all of the same repairs with variation on the number of falsely identified repairs. I met with the students regularly to discuss questions throughout the coding and to conduct data sessions on select segments and consulted speakers in playback interviews.

In the coding scheme, the trouble source T-1 was identified as whether it was a first-pair part of an adjacency pair, a second-pair part, or other, and whether it showed self-repair, was in overlap with another utterance, or if there was otherwise

Table 4.1 Basic format types for other-initiation of repair (after Dingemanse and Enfield 2015)

Open type initiators request repair by indicating a problem with the prior talk, leaving open what or where the problem is.
- *Interjection* (often) with questioning intonation.
- *Question-word* from the paradigm of question words in a language. Usually a *thing* interrogative, sometimes a *manner* interrogative.
- *Formulaic.* Expressions (constructions) not incorporating in interjection or question-word, often managing social relations or enacting politeness.

Restricted type initiators restrict the problem space by locating or characterizing the problem in some detail.
- *Request type* (asking for specification/clarification). Typically done by content question words, often in combination with partial repetition.
- *Offer type* (providing a candidate for confirmation). Typically done by a repetition or rephrasing of all or part of T-1.
- *Alternative question.* Repair initiator that invites a selection from among alternatives.

---

noise in the channel that may have influenced intelligibility. The repair initiation T0 was coded for position in a possible set of repairs (first or only, second attempt, etc.), whether it was open or restricted, the type of open (Interjection, Question word, Formulaic), whether it involved repeating any or all of T-1, included a content question word, made confirmation relevant, showed added marking of T0 function (generally explicit marking of a yes/no question with the polar question enclitic *la* or referring back to the prior speech act with a phrase like (o)*nii lò* (you say[ed]), and whether T0 is simple (doing one action generally in one sentence or less) or part of a complex turn doing repair and something else and/or composed of multiple sentences. The remedy T+1 was coded for whether it repeated any of T-1, and if so, whether dispensable items were left off (this could be person address, temporal reference, extraneous parts of a clause, etc.). The coding further queried if T+1 was a modified version of T-1 (even though not repeating words or phrasing, it may have been semantically parallel), confirmed or disconfirmed T0, and if it showed added marking. Added marking in Lachixío Zapotec amounts to stance or epistemic marking often using verbs of speech in more-active or less-active forms, verbs of sight, and pronominal reference (see Chapter 5).

The quantitative results of the coding are presented in Tables 4.2 and 4.3. There were 250 repair initiations in 13.75 hours of video which averaged one repair every 3.3 minutes. Open-class repair amounted to 34 percent of the total number of repair initiations and restricted repair 66 percent including both offer and request types. Repair initiations were approximately equally divided with 31.6 percent open requests, 31.6 percent restricted requests, and 34.8 percent restricted offers in the raw count. When initial attempts at repair were separated from subsequent attempts, noninitial repairs were seen to be mainly handled by restricted repair initiation, with a substantial increase in restricted offer format (Figure 4.2, Table 4.3). This is a robust parallel with cross-cultural findings on the subsequent pursuit of repair (compare Dingemanse and Enfield 2015).

Table 4.2 Repair Initiators and Their Frequencies in 13.75 Coded Hours of Conversation

Type	Subtype	Raw frequency/ proportion (%)		Initial frequency/ proportion (%)		Subsequent frequency/ proportion (%)	
Open 34% (n = 84)	Interjection	79	31.60	76	30.40	3	1.20
	Content question word	0	0	0	0	0	0
	Formulaic	5	2	5	2	0	0
Restricted 66% (n = 166)	Request (asking specification)	79	31.60	69	27.60	10	4
	Offer (providing candidate or correction)	87	34.80	63	25.20	24	9.60
	Alternative question	0	0	0	0	0	0
Total (n = 250)		250	100	213	85.20	37	14.80

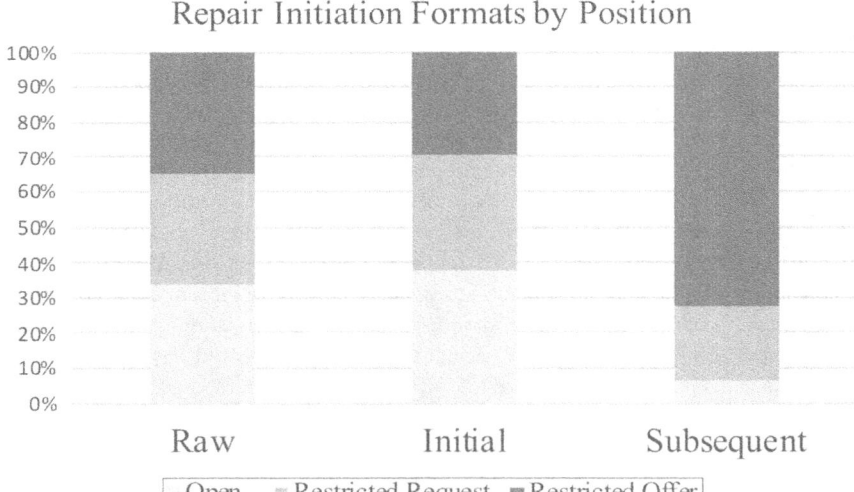

Figure 4.2 Repair initiation formats by position.

Another parallel cross-cultural finding is informative on Meso-America as a cultural and linguistic area. While many world languages use content question words for object (what) or manner (how) for open repair, there was no occurrence of a content question word used as minimal utterance to initiate open repair in Zapotec. This is parallel to what Brown found when coding repair for Tzeltal Maya (Dingemanse, Torreira, and Enfield 2013) (unrelated to Zapotec of the Otomanguean language family but cohabitants of an area with millenia-long histories of multilingual relations). In the Lachixío corpus the only uses of *xhii* (what) and *xekka* (how) as minimal utterances to initiate repair were for restricted repair, picking out the subject, object, or manner of doing something as trouble source. Another content question word *xaa* only occurred

Table 4.3 Repair Initiation Forms and Their Frequencies in 13.75 Coded Hours of Conversation

Subtype	Lachixío Zapotec	Gloss	All (%) (n = 250)	Initial (%) (n=203)	Subsequent (%) (n=37)
Open			(n = 84)	(n=81)	(n=3)
Interjection	Eé?	Huh?	90 (n = 76)	90 (n=73)	100 (n=3)
	Aá?	Huh?	4 (n = 3)	4 (n=3)	0 (n=0)
Formulaic	Xaa nii lò?	How did you say?	6 (n = 5)	5 (n = 5)	0 (n = 0)
Restricted			(n = 166)	(n = 132)	(n = 34)
Request	Xhii?	What?	6 (n = 10)	5 (n = 8)	5.9 (n = 2)
(n = 79)	Tii?	Who?	5.4 (n = 9)	6.3 (n = 9)	0 (n = 0)
	Xonga?	When?	2.4 (n = 4)	3 (n = 4)	0 (n = 0)
	Xekka?	How?	1.2 (n = 2)	0.75 (n = 1)	2.9 (n = 1)
	Kaa?	Where?	13.3 (n = 22)	15.9 (n = 21)	2.9 (n = 1)
	Maa?	To where?	1.2 (n = 2)	1.5 (n = 2)	0 (n = 0)
	Taa?	Which?	18 (n = 30)	18.2 (n = 24)	17.6 (n = 6)
Subtotal			(n = 79)	(n = 69)	(n = 10)
Offer	Repeat+la?	Repeat+PolarQ	21.7 (n = 36)	18.9 (n = 25)	32.3 (n = 11)
(n = 87)	Repeat?	Repeat	10.3 (n = 17)	9 (n = 12)	14.7 (n = 5)
	Other+la?	Other+PolarQ	9 (n = 15)	9 (n = 12)	8.8 (n = 3)
	Other (conf. relevant)	Other (conf. relevant)	6 (n = 10)	5.3 (n = 7)	8.8 (n = 3)
	Other (correction)	Other (correction)	5.4 (n = 9)	5.3 (n = 7)	5.9 (n = 2)
Subtotal			(n = 87)	(n = 63)	(n = 24)

in formulaic phrases like *Xaa nii lò?* (How did you say?) to initiate open repair, and while not occurring in the corpus as a minimal turn form, collaborators said *xaa* could be used alone, though the example they provided indicated a surprised stance rather than interactional trouble (see example [8]). There were also no alternative questions used for restricted repair, though such a construction is possible.

Table 4.3 shows the forms used for initiating repair. For open-class repair, interjections were by far the most common way of initiating repair. Interjections amounted to 94 percent of open repair, with 90 percent of these made with a front central vowel *eé* and a few occurrences of a lower back vowel *aá*. The dominance of open repair, though, is only a fact about first attempts at repair. In subsequent repair restricted formats predominate. Subsequent repair only showed three cases of open repair (1.2 percent) and notably two of the three were by a toddler who only used open repair, and the third also expressed shock in addition to doing repair. A formulaic expression *Xaa nii lò?* (How did you say?) was also used to initiate open repair 6 percent of the time. Though this formula is the way that I was taught by Zapotec consultants to prompt repetition during elicitation sessions, it is actually rather rare in natural discourse. The most frequent content question words for restricted request repairs were *kaa* (where) (22 percent), *taa* (which) (18 percent), *xhii* (what) (6 percent), *tii* (who) (5.4 percent), *xonga* (when) (2.4 percent), *xekka* (how) (1.2 percent), and *maa* (to where) (1.2 percent) (percentages are of all restricted forms including both offers and requests).

Repair initiations in the form of offers were most frequently of the form of a partial or total repeat of the trouble source (T-1) explicitly marked as a yes/no question by the addition of the polar question enclitic =*la* at 21.7 percent of restricted repairs, which broke down to 18.9 percent of first attempts and increasing to 32.3 percent of subsequent repairs. Polar questions composed with the enclitic in Lachixío Zapotec do not show rising intonation. The next most common was to repeat all or part of the trouble source with no explicit morphological marking (10.3 percent), which also increased substantially to 14.7 percent in subsequent repair attempts. Repeats like these often had rising intonation. Producing a formulation that is explicitly marked as a polar question and that does not repeat from the trouble source amounted to 9 percent of all repairs. Producing a formulation that does not repeat and does not mark question function morphologically yet still makes confirmation relevant amounted to 6 percent of all repairs. The final type of offer in the data was to produce a formulation that does not repeat from the trouble source and performs the function of repair not by eliciting confirmation but merely by correcting the public record (an other-repair). We will see examples of several of these in the paragraphs that follow.

Figure 4.3 shows the distribution of open and restricted repairs across the files coded for this chapter, and Figure 4.4 shows the distribution of offers versus requests for the initiation of repair. Thirteen of seventeen files showed more restricted repair than open repairs. The coding category of noise during T-1 is informative here. The few files that showed more open repair also had more background noise creating problems of hearing that were commonly targeted with open-class repair (rather than problems of reference or understanding).

Figure 4.4 plots requests versus offers. In most videos requests far outnumber offers, though a few show a close to even split. Offers outnumber requests in two videos and one video only has offers. Such extensive offering was part of a routine of checking understandings using resonating repetitions that we will examine in Chapter 5.

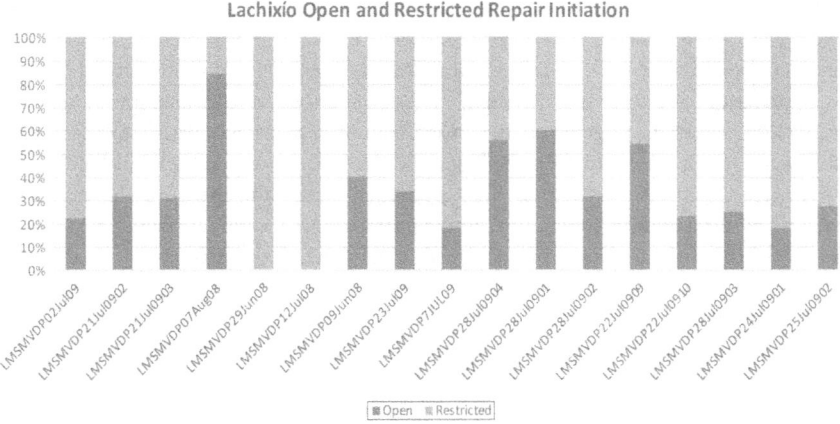

Figure 4.3 Lachixío Zapotec open and restricted repair initiation.

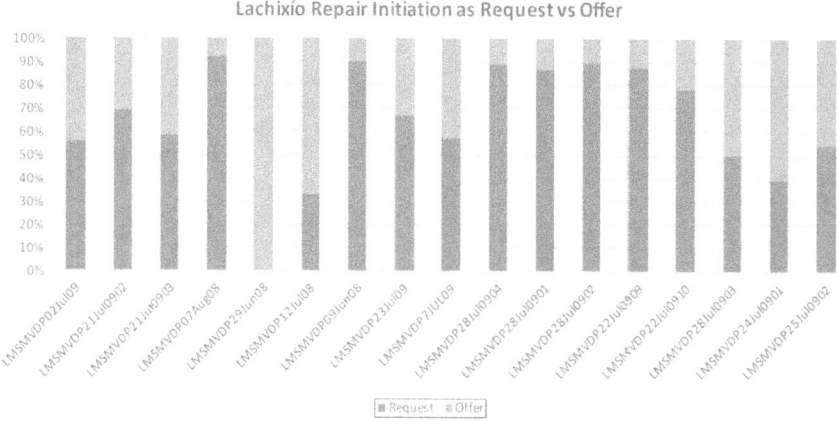

Figure 4.4 Lachixío Zapotec repair initiation as request versus offer.

I will turn now to exemplifying the affordances of Lachixío Zapotec for repair first looking at recruiting repair and then offering repair.[4]

4.1 Recruiting Repair

4.1.1 Open-Class Requests

Open-class repair initiations indicate some unspecified trouble and recruit the agency of the prior speaker requesting that they take some action to repair, but leave open how the response should be formulated. The remedy of open-class repair initiation can range from full or partial repeat to modified repeats where full or partial repeats have additional items added to them, and to reformulations in which the intention of the speaker is displayed through other lexical and/or syntactic means.

4.1.1.1 Open-Class Interjections: Eé?

Almost all cases (90 percent) of open-class repair were initiated with *Eé?*, typically with rising pitch. Consider example (2). In this scene, Andrea and three others are pulling weeds next to a house, and Angeles is sitting on a rock, embroidering. In their ongoing talk around the time of this repair, they are lamenting the lack of rain and how it has been affecting the growth of the fields and gardens.

```
(2) LMSMVDP28Jul0904 47:49.50
1 Angeles:    Puuro tomaà ska' sii bée ri'yya á.
              -Ang sits embroidering. And bent over pulling up plants
              Puro    to-mà    ska'a'   r-tzi       bée      ri'ya=á
              purely  much     yet      HAB-affect  sunlight see=1s
              It's just that the sun's already affecting them a lot,
              I see.
```

2 Andrea: Eé?
              -|And stands holding a small tomato plant
              Huh?
3 Angeles: Tomaà ska' sii bée ri'yya á.
              to-mà   ska'a'   r-tzi   bée   ri'ya=á
              much   yet   HAB-affect   sunlight   see=1s
              The sun's already affecting them a lot, I see.
4 Andrea: Áwwà nii á.
              áwa   ni=á
              yes   say=1s
              Yes I say.

Angeles says that "it's just that the sun is already affecting them a lot, I see." To which Andrea issues open-class repair with *Eé?* We see the remedy repeats almost all of the trouble turn but leaves off as "dispensable" *puro*, an adverb that I translated as "it's just that" that framed the trouble source turn. The remedy (T+1), however, includes the same sight-based epistemic framing *ri'yya à* (I see) indicating firsthand observation in support of Angeles's opinion. Andrea's response of agreement *áwwà* is framed by her own opinion epistemic phrase *nii á* (I say).

Open-class interjections are minimal utterances that are understood to have evolved parallel forms across languages to fulfill their function (Dingemanse et al. 2015). Such minimal turn formulations act to initiate a sequence of repair yet do not take over the floor. As Goffman (1963: 34) pointed out, one of the challenges is to "employ a sanction that will not destroy by its mere enactment the order which it is designed to maintain." In other words, the goal is to fix a problem in the conversation without derailing the conversation itself. But consider example (3). Pedro is talking with elders Felicita and Francisco who are working to repair saddles. Felicita's bodily engagement and eye gaze are on the saddle during this sequence, but at the same time, she is holding a conversation with Pedro who is off-screen by the video camera. In much of their conversation, Pedro is speaking in the respect register referring to her as *Nísso* (aunt), and Felicita is often also using his name at the ends of her utterances.

(3) LMSMVDP25Jul0902 01:00:04.185

1 Felicita: Xhii wà' nóo kaakaa nèé' xhi'i Béttò?
              xhi wà'a' nó   ka#ka   nèé' xhi'i   Béto-L
              how this   that where#where   now use   Pedro-CLAS
              What's this that getting used everywhere now, Pedro?
2 Pedro: Eé Nísso?
              Huh, Aunt?
3 Felicita: Xhii wà' nóo kaakaa⁵ nèé' xhi'i?
              xhi wà'a' nó   ka#ka   nèé' xhi'i
              how this   that where#where   now use
              What's this that getting used everywhere now?

In the Zapotec corpus, person references were found to be added to open-class repair initiations moving them up in scale, just slightly, beyond minimal responses. Lachixío Zapotec stands out from the comparative literature on repair this way. Because the open-class repair initiation is not utterance-final, it supports an analysis that this lexical item has a rising lexical tone, not just rising intonation.

The other case of an open-class repair initiation with a person reference occurs during a conversation where an adult addresses a boy as "my son" in a multiparty interaction. *Pâ* in the masculine and *Mâ* in the feminine are terms of affection used with children in a parallel way parallel to that in which honorific kin terms are used for respect to elders.[6] They are often appended to utterances of direct address. In the exchange in example (4), Efraín (about three years old) is using honorific vocabulary with Elvia. Like in the previous example, the formulation of a turn with a person reference after open-class repair is in moments of dialogic resonance like this where each participant has been referring to the other regularly by name or title in the ongoing conversation).

(4) LMSMVDP28Jul0901 00:35:33.250

```
1  Efraín:    E'nna tòko nóo me'e' olàá nii á so'kko á Elvia a'á.
              -El looking down rubbing her eyes
              -Ef picks up corn ear holds out toward El
              e'na              tòko   nó    me'e'   o-làá         ni=á
              respected-mother  one          that    small   CMP-take out  say=1s
                  r-zo'kko=á    Elvia  a'á
                  HAB-shell=1s  Elvia  look
              Respected mother I found one that's small, I say, for me to
                  shell, Elvia, look.
2  Elvia:     Eé Pâ?
              --------|El lifts gaze to Ef
              Huh my son?
3  Efraín:    Naà tòkko nóo me'e' skà'.
              -Ef turns gaze from ear to El, holds ear closer to El then
                 starts to shell the corn into bucket
              nà       tòko nó   me'e'   skà'
              mother   one       that    small   still
              Mother here's one that's small still.
```

4.1.1.2 *Formulaic Open-Class Repair*: Xaa nii lò?

Consultants in elicitation have pointed to the formulaic question *Xaa nii lò?* (How did you say?) for repair rather than the interjection. This formulation is, however, rather rare in natural corpora. In 13.75 hours it occurred only five times, amounting to 2 percent of all repairs and 6 percent of open-class repairs. By contrast, there were seventy-nine interjections achieving open-class repair initiation. Of the five formulaic uses, four were by the same person in the same video, one was preceded by the open class *Eé?*, and two were preceded by *nóo*, the complementizer (that). In example (5), repair is initiated with *Nóo xaa nii lò?* (That what did you say?).

(5) LMSMVDP28Jul0901 00:31:26.500

```
1  Andrea:   Xella bicchi kaà íiña'a Xhiñña Dáññi nee nóo [xaa lèé
                neláa oriñña wà' nèé' nii á.
             -A looking down to bowl Elv fixing shawl on her head
             r-zxela     bichi   kà     i#na'a      xhina#dáni    ne
             HAB-appear  dry            truly       CLAS#milpa  El.Rincón  because
                 nó   xa  lèé   ne-lá o-rina     wà'   nèé'  ni=á
                 that how name just  CMP-arrive this  now   say=1s
             It's looking truly dry in the milpas of El Rincón because
                 this (the rain) has just arrived now, I say.
```

2 Efraín: [Wáa níngye' nee zo'kko á tókko é txee. Wáa níngye'
              stokko é.
              Ef presents a husked corn to Elv------------Elv gaze to Ef
              H*-wàá   nínge' ne   zo'ko=á   tóko=é txe
              POT-take.out thing   because shell=1s one=3o then
              H*-wàá   nínge' sH-tòko=é
              POT-remove   thing   another-one=3o
              Remove this thing because I shell one then.
              Remove this thing from another one.

3 Elvia: Enzírkeè nèé' là chée bì'yya á nii á.
              -----|Elv takes husked corn from Ef and begins to shuck it
              enzi#rkè   nèé'#là ché   bì'ya=á ni=á
              over.here wait   intend see=1s say=1s
              Let's see, wait, I want to see it, I say.

4 Elvia: Nóo xaa nii lò?
              -Elv shucking the husk off the corn
              nó   xa   ni=lò
              that how say=2s
              That what did you say?

5 Andrea: Xella bicchi iiña'a Xhiñña Dáñni nóo neláa oriñña kìyyo.
              -A and Elv looking down to bowls and shucking corn
              r-zxela   bichi i#na'a xhina#dáni nó   ne-lá
              HAB-appear dry   CLAS#milpa el.Rincón that just
                o-rina   kìyo
                CMP-arrive rain
              It's looking dry in the milpas of El Rincón because the
              rain has just arrived.

In the transcript of the sequence in (5), we can see that that the repair initiation is not immediately adjacent to Andrea's turn that is referred back to as the trouble source. Andrea and Elvia are kneeling on mats on the patio shucking corn and talking about rain. The boy with them, Efraín, initiates a sequence unrelated to Andrea and Elvia's discussion. Elvia responds to Efraín and takes the corn ear he asked her to shuck, and then, while shucking the corn, issues the repair on Andrea's interrupted turn. The repair here not only requests repetition but brings Andrea and Elvia back into their dialogue, which had been interrupted at the point of the clause juncture *nóo* (that) and put on hold while Elvia dealt with the side sequence initiated by the boy. In this way, the formulation using the complementizer before the open-class formula *xaa nii lò* first restricts repair to the second clause beginning with the complementizer, then makes an open request about that clause.

Another point to note about this example is that in 5 Andrea leaves off several dispensable items in the reformulation of her prior turn in 1. These include the adverb *kaà* (truly), causal conjunction *nee* (because), and self-reporting phrase *nii á* (I say), as well as not repeating her own self-repair *xaa lèé* (how's it called) that characterized the second clause of 1. It also replaces the pronoun *wà'* with the noun *kiyyo* (rain) that repairs Andrea's own vague reference with a definite reference. This achieves enough intersubjectivity that the participants together move on in dialogue. After this Elvia goes on to talk about how the possibility of the milpas drying up before the corn fruits is always a worry.

4.1.2 Restricted Requests

Restricted requests are most often initiated by specifying an ontological category with a content question word: *xhii* (what) for thing, *xekka* (how) for manner, *tii* (who) for person reference, *xonga* (when) for time, *kaa* (where) and/or *maa* (to where) for place, and *taa* (which) for a choice among alternatives made relevant in the prior discourse. Each of these question words can occur as a minimal turn relying on the other speaker to make indexical links to the prior discourse and remedy the trouble. While often occurring alone as a minimal turn unit, the question words can also be part of a larger constituent that makes these relations explicit. The dialogic use of question words is generally missed in elicited data, introspective "syntactic" accounts, or monologic "texts" that most often form the data for linguistic grammars. In such methods content question words are analyzed for their syntactic role within isolated sentences of single speakers such as how the wh-word "what" relates to an NP gap in a sentence, for example, what$_i$ are you bringing [NP$_i$]? However informative it is to examine the monologic syntax of question words, the fact that content question words so frequently tie speakers' turns together through conversational repair (e.g., one-third of all repair initiations in Lachixío) makes imperative the analysis of their dialogic syntax through corpora of actual conversation.

4.1.2.1 Restricted Request: **Xhii?** *(What?)*

In many languages "what" can function for either open-class or restricted repair (Dingemanse et al. 2015). In languages like English and German the contrast is often marked with rising intonation on the open-class repair initiation and falling intonation on the restricted class (Egbert, Golato, and Robinson 2009). In the Lachixío conversation corpus, there were no occurrences of the thing content question word *xhii* (what) or the manner content question word *xaa* (how) being used for open repair. Where *xhii* did occur for repair initiation, responses further specified the reference of a subject or object that in the trouble source may have been left un- or under specified. Such responses show us that the token was functioning as a restricted request rather than open request. *Xhii* additionally didn't occur with steeply rising intonation like the open-class interjections but rather level or slightly rising pitch. I present one transcribed example here.

```
(6) LMSMVDP28Jul0902 00:55:48.803
1 Mary:      Nezhìkki nóo beè é nóo ngottxò' letta é lè'kka.
             M head turn-R to S then front to work
             ne-zhìki      nó    bè=é   nó    ngotxò' leta=é    lè'ka
             STA-frighten        that   pl=3o        that    rotten  among=3o   also
             I'm nervous that there are rotten ones among them also.
2 Sofia:     Yaññí tzyáà wà' nèé'.
             yaní    tzyáà   wà'   nèé'
             select   just    this   now
             Just pick this out now.
3 Mary:      Xhii?
             -----|N head turn-R to S
             What?
4 Sofia:     nóo ngottxò' kwà'.
             nó    ngotxò'   kwà'
             COMP  rotten    that
             Those rotten ones.
```

In example (6) Mary and Sofia are in the process of making tortillas. In a series of videos recorded by my collaborator Pedro, his wife Mary and mother Sofia undertake the process of making *éttá yaà* "*tortillas a mano*" (hand-made tortillas) from shelling the corn to cooking *nílla* "*nixtamal*" (corn kernels cooked in water and lime [CaO]), to making *eekòkkò* "*masa*" (corn dough), patting them round, pressing them into form, and cooking the tortillas on the *íllyà* "*comal*" (clay griddle). In the background is the fact that they are doing so as a service to the municipal authorities. Mary is Sophia's daughter-in-law and is supporting and learning from Sofia. This is conversationally apparent in Mary's frequent questions, and Sofia's knowledgeable responses, which we'll see in Chapter 5, are partially constructed in her use of epistemic marking on repetitions. In this example, Mary and Sofia are shelling corn (removing kernels from the dried ears). In 1 Mary expresses that she is nervous that there is rotten corn among those she is adding to the bucket to make the *nixtamal*. Sofia responds that she should just look for and pick them out, formulating her reference using a demonstrative pronoun *wà'* (this). Mary responds with a restricted repair initiation *Xhii?* (What?), turning her head to Sofia to wait for the answer. Mary's formulation specifies that the trouble lies in her recovering the reference of the demonstrative pronoun. Sofia responds that she is talking about those rotten ones (that Mary had already topicalized).

After 4 the sequence goes on with Mary asking Sofia, "Now?" repeating another part of Sofia's turn in 2 as a second repair of the offer type we'll see in section 4.2. Sofia answers that they can look for them when they put the corn in water to boil, and Mary says, "Oh when put on to boil they come to the top of the water then," which Sofia affirms by saying, "Yes, they float," the repair sequence participating in a larger sequence conveying the traditional knowledge used for identifying good corn seed and for preparing tortillas.

4.1.2.2 Restricted Request: Xekka? (How?)

There were two examples in the 13.75 hours coded in the corpus where a participant used the *manner* content question word *xekka* (how). One is presented here and another can be seen in the data for Chapter 6. In example (7) Sofia and Mary are pressing and cooking tortillas in Sofia's kitchen house. It's dark and the oak fire under the *íllyà* "*comal*"(griddle) is filling the house with smoke.

```
(7) LMSMVDP23Jul09 00:05:17:480
1 Sofia:   Xhà'lla lá stome'e' áttze enzí chò'.
           -S gaze to right, head point right, then gaze down to tortilla press
           L*-xha'la=lá    s-to-me'e'       átze      enzí#chò'
           IMP-open=already another-a-little kitchen   over.there
           Open another bit the kitchen over there.
2 Mary:    Xekka?
           ------|M gaze to S
           How?
3 Sofia:   Enzí chò' txee txó'o eezhe'e ka'a.
           -S gaze to right, head point right (2x), gaze to tortilla press
           enzí#chò'    txe    gH*-yo'o   e#zhe'e      ka'a
           over.there   then   POT-enter  CLAS-clarity here
           Over there then so it will clear in here.
```

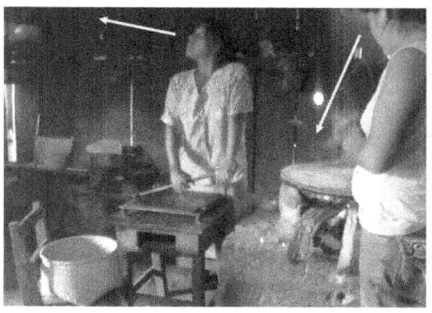

1 Sofia: Xhà'lla lá stome'e áttze enzí chò'.
Open another bit the kitchen over there.

3 Sofia: Enzí chò' txee txó'o eezhe'e ka'a.
Over there then so it will clear in here.

Figure 4.5 Sofia head/gaze points toward window while Mary's gaze is down (left), and Sofia redoes her turn with a second head/gaze point with Mary in joint attention (right).

4 Mary: **Ajjá.**
 -M walks out of frame to left and opens the window
 Uhuh.
5 Sofia: **°Xhà'lla fwértè xhà'lla áttze°.**
 -S gaze down opens tortilla press
 L*-xha'la fwértè L*-xha'la átze
 IMP-open strong IMP-open kitchen
 °*Open it wide, open the kitchen*°.

Sofia recruits Mary to open the window with her reference formulated as a deictic expression *enzí chò'* (that direction). With her hands busy on the tortilla press, Sofia makes a head point toward the window, but at this time Mary is looking down at the tortilla cooking on the *comal*. Mary asks *Xekka?* (How?) and turns her gaze to Sofia. Sofia's response starts again with *enzí chò'* and provides a reason, and it is again accompanied by a head point which, now with Mary's joint attention, makes for a successful reference (Figure 4.5). Mary agrees and walks out cf frame to the left and opens the window. Across the repair sequence Sofia and Mary have developed a shared *umwelt*, creating the potential for their intersubjectivity.

Another word *xaa* meaning "how" was not found in the corpus functioning for restricted request. This is the same word in the formulaic question phrase *Xaa nii lò?* (How did you say?) that functions for open-class repair. But *xaa* was not found in use as a minimal response-token in 13.75 hours of conversation. When I asked my collaborators from Lachixío about this, I was told that *xaa* could be used just like *xekka* but an example was not immediately forthcoming. After a bit of thought and discussion between the son, who I had been instant messaging with about this question, and his father, I was given this example (8).

(8)
1 Gerardo: **Nèé' cháa Béttò.**
 nèé' H*-cha Béto-L
 today POT-marry Pedro-CLAS
 Today Pedro's getting married.

2 Romano: Xaa!
           How!
3 Gerardo: Áwwà. Eskye' né.
           áwà eske'=né
           yes like.this=ACT3o
           Yes. It's like this.

Rather than an open request initiator or a restricted request, *xaa* here is functioning as an interjection of surprise prompting a declaration of veracity rather than repetition, further specification, or correction. The example was provided in written form and the exclamation mark was in the original, rather than a question mark. I would predict that 2 would likely be uttered in breathy voice, which, as we will see in Chapter 5, can function on repetitions to indicate surprise/disbelief and prompt a declaration of veracity or epistemic expansion (see also Sicoli 2010a).

4.1.2.3 Restricted Request: Tii? (Who?)

The ontological category of person is indicated by the content question word *tii* and is found in the corpus as a minimal response, as a specifier in referring to humans, and in reference to nonhumans (some plants). In example (9), Mary and Sofia are talking about getting breakfast when they finally finish making all the tortillas for the municipal authorities.

(9) LMSMVDP23Jul09 00:21:37:320

1 Sofia: °Láa ri'i á bi'yya xhii dàkko sílla' ni'i á í°.
           -S gaze on M
           lá ri'i=á   bi'ya xhi   dàko#síla'   '-ni=á=é
           NEG make=1s sign what eat#breakfast ACT-say=1s=3o
           I don't know what we'll eat for breakfast, I do say.

2 Mary: Xhii eenze'e jdo'o beè ì jree (0.5) tzò' állà zé'e eskye'?
           ---------------------------|M head turn-R to gaze on S
           xhi e#nze'e   r-do'o   bè=ì r-re   tzò'o' álà
           what this.topic HAB-insert PL=3M HAB-move back   plank
              zé'e   eske'
              there.DIST like.this
           **What's that that the vendors put in (their tacos) over
              there behind the planks?**

3 Sofia: Tii?
           -----|S picks up tortilla cooking on comal
           Who?

4 Mary: Beè olla móobil.
           -S checks bottom and drops tortilla back on comal
           -M follows tortilla movement
           bè ola   móbil
           PL city.people   mobile
           **The mobile city folk (taco selling street vendors in the
              cities).**

Mary asks a question about what the taco vendors in Oaxaca put in their tacos (that make them delicious). Her turn is formulated with three pronominal references: (1) *what* is in the taco (*xhii eenze'e* [what that we've talked about before]), (2) *where* she is referring to *tzò' állà zé'e* (*tzò' állà* [behind the boards] referring to street taco stands and *zé'e* [there] at some distant [out of sight] location), and (3) *who* (*beè ì jree* [those who move]). Sofia's restricted request *Tii?* makes clear that the person reference is the trouble source. In response, Mary becomes more specific, replacing the third-person pronoun *i* with a noun *olla*[7] that refers to Spanish speaking people of the city and replacing a rarely used Zapotec verb of motion *-re*[8] with a Spanish loan adjective *móobil* (*móvil*) meaning mobile in her remedy in 4, *beè olla móobil*.

The interrogative pronoun *tii* can also be used to question possession. Example (10) shows repair questioning for whom the tortillas are intended by asking, *Tii éttà?* (Whose tortillas?). Mary and Sofia are shelling corn facing the same direction with Mary slightly in front of Sofia. Sofia laments in the creaky voice register of commiseration declaring, "We're through making their tortillas." Mary requests clarification of whose tortillas in 2 and Sofia responds the tortillas of the authorities.

(10) LMSMVDP28Jul0902 00:16:59.220

```
1  Sofia:    ~La'xxò a'wa éttà' beè ì~.
             -------|M slight head turn toward S
             ʕ-laxò=a'wa    étà-'       bè=ì
             ACT-finish=1PLI tortilla-POS PL=3M
             We're through making their tortillas.
2  Mary:     Tii éttà?
             Whose tortillas?
3  Sofia:    Éttà' beè ostísya bayya.
             Étà-'      bè ostisya   baya
             tortilla-POS PL authority go
             The tortillas going to the authorities.
```

Figure 4.6 Sofia (left) turns to Andrea saying, "Many spines here are getting on me."

Spontaneous conversational environments present the opportunity to examine ontological classification as actually used rather than as ideally represented in interview settings. *Tii*, which translates to Spanish as *quién* and English as "who," can be used for other life forms (on such *ontological crossing* see Sicoli 2016a). While it might not surprise some non-Zapotec readers that *tii* can be used with animals, example (11) shows a repair that applies the person category to *ayya* the *nopal*, or prickly pear cactus. Young Sofia, Andrea, and Elvia are working together to pull weeds next to their house (Figure 4.6). The area Sofia (not the same Sofia as 10) is working had been used earlier by Ariana to cut cactus needles off *nopales* in preparing them for eating.

(11) LMSMVDP28Jul0904 00:20:58.5

```
1 Sofia:     Kwálla' nzokkó éttxè beè eenze'e li'i á.
             -S pulls cactus needles from knee turns head to look at Andrea
             kwála' n-zokó étxè    bè e#nze'e    li'i=á
             many  STA-sit needle  PL this.topic PRO=1S
             Many needles here are getting on me.

2 Andrea:    Tii éttxè nii á?
             ti  étxè  ni=á
             who needle say=1s
             Whose needles, I say?

3 Sofia:     Éttxè beè no'kkwe xhaa lèé nii kaà eenze'e.
             étxè  bè no'kwe xha lèé ni  kà  e#nze'e
             needle PL um    what name say truly this.topic
             Needles of um, I truly don't know what name this has.
```

Sofia's response shows us that *tii* here is taken to refer to the type of cactus. Her response additionally tells that she doesn't know or remember the name for this relatively common plant food, reminding us that ethnobotanical knowledge is shrinking across the generations of Lachixío Zapotec speakers.

4.1.2.4 *Restricted Request:* Xonga? *(When?)*

Repairs can also restrict a request to the ontological category of the time when something happened. In example (12) the restricted request *Xonga?* (When?) is responded to with a when-relative clause. Angeles's family is washing clothes and talking. Angeles is describing a dream she had involving a jícara (gourd bowl) and a goat.

(12) LMSMVDP22Jul0909 00:26:35.67

```
1 Angeles:   Xhiwwa nóo otzanna' wà' skwa' nii arkì' á peèro nzaa loo
                biccha ke' zhíkka zé'e nii xkallà' nii á.
             xhiwa nó  o-tzana' wà    skwa'      ni   arkì'=á    pèro
             why   that CMP-jump this  like.this  say  heart=1s   but
             nza   lo   bichà ke' zhíka zé'e ni  xkalà' ni=á
             go    face day   that jícara there say  dream  say=1s
             Why did that jump that way, I wonder? And the jícara is gone
                since that day that I dreamt it, I say.

2 Jorge:     Xonga?
             When?

3 Angeles:   Txónno láa skà' àtí chíppà.
             txóno  lá  skà' ati chípa-L
             when   NEG yet  die goat-CLAS
             When the goat hadn't yet died.
```

The conversation proceeds to discuss what the dream is trying to say and makes associations between the goat and a deer that had been hunted at the time.

4.1.2.5 Restricted Request: *Kaa? (Where?)*

Asking "Where?" was the second most common restricted request in the corpus. In example (13) repair is initiated because of missing the ground of deictic reference which we can see in the multimodal transcript, though not in the talk by itself. Mary and Sofia are shelling corn together. They have got through the ears that are of good quality and plan to feed the rejects to the animals. Mary asks which are left to do (Figure 4.7).

```
(13) LMSMVDP28Jul0902 00:13:44.58
1 Mary:      Taa kò' la nèé'?
             ta    kò'=lá      nèé'
             which rub?=already now
             Which to do now?
2 Sofia:     Noxxo rkyè' stokko é.
             -|S head/gaze pointing (but M not looking)
             noxo    rkyè'   sH-tòko=é
             lying   there   another=3o
             There's another lying there.
3 Mary:      Kaa?
             Where?
4 Sofia:     Asta noxxo cho'.
             -|S points (moving hand into M's peripheral vision) then
                quickly returns hand to shelling corn.
             asta     noxo    cho'
             toward   lying   that
             That lying over there.
5 Mary:      Reaches forward for a large ear of corn lying in front of her.
```

Sofia's reply in 2 is formulated using a deictic, *rkyè'* (there), in the phrase *Noxxo rkyè' stokko é* (There's another lying there), and she includes a head point since her

2 Sofia: Noxxo rkyè' stókko é.   4 Sofia: Asta noxxo cho'.
          There's another lying there   That lying there

Figure 4.7 Trouble in unseen head/gaze point, Remedy with hand point into visual field.

hands are busy shelling corn. Mary, however, is seated facing the same direction as Sofia and slightly in front (Figure 4.7), and Mary does not see the head point. Such a deictic action requires a shared visual field for this indexical sign to be interpretable. Mary requests repair *Kaa?* and Sofia in 4 reformulates her prior turn. This time she points with her hand which she raises briefly into the peripheral field of vision of Mary before returning it to the task of shelling corn saying, "That lying there." Jointly achieving successful reference through this repair sequence, Mary reaches forward and grabs the ear of corn. This example illustrates clearly how the dependencies between talk and embodied action can both lead to trouble and be combined to repair reference to place.

4.1.2.6 Restricted Request: **Taa?** *(Which?)*

Initiating repair with *taa* was the most frequent form for restricted requests in the corpus, amounting to 38 percent of all restricted requests. In many cases *taa* is used as the initial element of a larger constituent, frequently repeating a noun of the trouble source turn requesting further specification (e.g., which bag?), though often it is used as a minimal response form as in example (14) from a video of brothers working together to fix a bicycle that we will examine in more detail in Chapter 6.

With this example, note that there is a long pause in speech while David walks around the bicycle to move himself into a position to direct his attention on the multipart assemblage Danny is holding before issuing the repair initiation. The utterance *Taa?* (Which?) here is fit to a multimodal configuration of objects and attention.

```
(14) LMSMVDP09Jun08 00:10:48.00
1  Daniel:   A'á tèe na'ttze níngye' ka'a tèe na'ttze níngye' ka'a.
             -Dan (seated) holding assemblage in hand
             a'á  L*-te     na'tze  ninge' ka'a  L*-te     na'tze  ninge' ka'a
             INT  IMP-come  grab    thing  here  IMP-come  grab    thing  here
             Hey, come grab this thing here. Come grab this thing here.
2  David:                                                         Taa?
             -Dav walks to Dan around rear of |bicycle
                                                                  Which?
3  Daniel:   Níngye' tèe na'ttze.
             ----------------|Dav grabs part of assembly (Figure 4.8)
             ninge'  L*-te     na'tze
             thing   IMP-come  grab.
             This thing come grab.
```

In cases when two *taa* repair initiations are issued in a sequence of extended repair (where a repair sequence is extended because the first was not deemed enough to regain intersubjectivity), the first was greater than minimal, the second was minimal. Example (15) depicts this evolution of the which-question from a form that combines which plus repeat to a minimal token *Taa?* and is also followed by a third repair initiation. Sabina, Kacha, and their family are looking at photos.

Figure 4.8 David grabs parts assemblage after repair on Daniel's recruitment.

```
(15) LMSMVDP21Jul0903  01:00:45:236
1 Sabina:    Tii kye' endò' nìyyo me'e' kye' nii á?
             ti   ke' endò'  niyo me'e' ke' ni=á
             who  DEF child  man  small DEF say=1s
             Whose is this? This little boy, I say?
2 Kacha:     Taa endò' nìyyo?
             ta     endò' niyo
             which  child man
             Which boy?
3 Sabina     Endò' nìyo me'e' kye' o endò' ona'a nokwà' la?
             ----------|K bends forward----------K gaze to photo
             endò' nìyo me'e' ke' o  endò' ona'a nokwà'=la
             child man  small DEF or child woman that=Q
             That little boy. Or is this a girl?
4 Kacha:     Taa?
             Which?
5 Sabina:    Ènno nzokkó xombóllo.
             èno  n-zoko       xombólo
             who  STA-be(sit)  sombrero
             The one in the sombrero.
6 Kacha:     Níngye' la?
             ninge'=la
             thing=Q
             That one?
```

7 Sabina: Áà.
              Yes.
8 Kacha: Tii txee kaà endò' nokwà'? Aà: endò' nokwà' Néllà.
              ----------------------------|K stands, turns gaze to photo
              in hand
              ti   txe   kà   endò' nokwà' à   endò' nokwà' Néla-L
              who then truly   child this   oh child this   Nélla-CLAS
              Whose then is this child truly? Oh, that child's Nella's.

In this extract, Sabina asks a question, "Whose is this? This little boy." Kacha, who has been standing nearby, asks, *Taa endò' nìyyo?* (Which boy?), and Sabina uses a definite reference to indicate a little boy in the photo. But then Sabina wonders aloud whether that is a girl. During Sabina's turn, Kacha bends forward to put her gaze on the photo. Kacha holds her gaze and asks again *Taa?* (Which?) using a minimal form, the form having evolved now that "the boy" is firmly established in common ground. Responding to Kacha's question, Sabina expands her reference by using a relative clause *Ennò nzokkó xombóllo* (The one in the sombrero), providing an indexical detail from the photo to ground Kacha's attention. Incrementally moving forward in the joint activity of repair, Kacha now offers an understanding check. She points to a child in the photo and says, *Níngye' la?* (That one?), offering a candidate for confirmation or disconfirmation to which Sabina responds with a token with confirmation. Kacha repeats Sabina's question from 1, as if thinking about it for a moment, and then issues a realization token *Aà* (oh) and states that the child is Nella's.

This last example of extended repair shows both the evolution of a which-question across multiple iterations and a subsequent instance of an offer type of repair initiation. We turn to a detailed look at offering repair next.

4.2 Offering Repair

Open requests put the bulk of the agency for repairing trouble on the speaker of T-1, and restricted requests distribute the agency between the speaker of T0 (narrowing the trouble) and the speaker of T-1, who then moves to resolve the trouble. Offering repair distributes agency though in this case the speaker initiating repair in T0 formulates a candidate understanding as a repair initiation to which the other speaker (of T-1) only has to respond with a yes (confirmation) or no (disconfirmation). Repair offers are of two types: offering for confirmation or offering correction. The first type makes confirmation or disconfirmation relevant. The second type is what is considered a true "other-repair" where the remedy is offered in the next turn position. Other-repair is very rare in Lachixío, so I focus here on other-initiated self-repair.

4.2.1 Offering for Confirmation or Disconfirmation

4.2.1.1 *Offers that Repeat Prior Speaker with Polar Question Enclitic =la*

Repetition of a part of T-1 with the addition of the polar question enclitic =*la* both ties the repair to some relevant part of T-1 and makes explicit that this is a request for confirmation (or disconfirmation). In example (16) Andrea and Elvia are husking and shelling corn.

```
(16) LMSMVDP28Jul0901  00:50:05.620
1 Elvia:     Fréssa nóo nyàá nii á naà nóo letta yoò beè Laura nii á.
             frésa       nó    nyàá       ni=á   nà    nó   leta  yò
             strawberry  that  beautiful  say=1s mother that among land
                  beè  Laura ni=á
                  PL   Laura say=1s
             (There are) Beautiful strawberries I say, Mom, that are on
                  the land of Laura's family, I say.
2 Andrea:    Fréssa la?
             frésa=la
             strawberry=Q
             Strawberries?
3 Elvia:     Àwwà.
             Yes.
```

Elvia makes a statement that there are beautiful strawberries growing on the land belonging to Laura's family. Andrea issues repair by the repetition of strawberries with explicit polar question morphology *Fréssa la?* During this exchange, neither participant diverts their gaze or embodied activity away from their work with the corn (Figure 4.9).

Figure 4.9 Neither participant diverts their embodied activity as Andrea (left) offers repair *Fréssa la?* (Strawberries?).

Repair initiations repeating negative formulations of T-1 are logically met with negative response as affirmation as in example (17).

```
(17) LMSMVDP23Jul09 00:15:29:800
1 Sofia:    Lèkka eekòkò éttà nèé'.
            lèka    e#kòkò   étà          nèé'
            not.be  CLAS-masa tortilla    now
            There isn't any tortilla dough now.
2 Mary:     Lèkka é la?
            lèka=é=la
            not.be=3o=Q
            There isn't any?
3 Sofia:    A'a.
            ----|M walks out of frame to L (gets more masa)
            No.
```

There are several examples in the corpus of the realization token *Aà* (oh) being preposed to repeat plus polar question enclitic. Example (18) patterns similarly in that Adrian asks a question which when answered prompts repair by offering a near total repetition plus polar question and which is preceded by the realization token *Aà*.

```
(18) LMSMVDP29Jun08 00:08:31:000
1 Adrian:   Xhii skwélla nekye'e Qella?
            xhi    skwéla   ne-ke'e    Qela
            what   school   STA-write  Angélica
            At what school is Angélica studying?
2 Giovani:  Xhaa lèé ra? Paara enferméera jri'i nokwà' estudiáar.
            -----------------------------------------------|G head
             turn to A
            xha   lèé=ra      para enferméra  r-ri'i    nokwà'   estudiár
            how   name=EXCL   for  nurse      HAB-do    be.there study
            What's it called? To be a nurse (she's) there studying.
3 Adrian:   °Aà paara enferméera jri'i ndxò estudiáar la°?
            -|A head nod up |down---------|A head nod (2x)
            à     para enferméra   r-ri'i=ndxò   estudiár=la
            Oh    for  nurse       HAB-do=3F     study=Q
            Oh, to be a nurse she's studying?
4 Giovani:  Áwwà.
            Yes.
```

4.2.1.2 *Offers that Repeat Prior Speaker*

Repair can also be offered by repeating part or all of a speaker's prior turn making confirmation or disconfirmation relevant without the added marking of the polar question enclitic as in example (19). Seated on a patio outside of Kacha and Flavio's house, Flavio is sharpening his chainsaw.

```
(19) LMSMVDP21Jul0903 00:01:02:000
1 Kacha:    Nékka' nóo ochekkò' mótto ì látta.
            néka'      nó    o-chekò'   móto=ì         láta
            yesterday  that  CMP-cut    chainsaw=3M    can
            It was yesterday that his chainsaw cut a can.
```

2 Sabina: Látta?
              láta
              Can?
3 Kacha: Lá[tta ochekkò' a'a.
              láta   o-chekò'=a'a
              can   CMP-cut=already
              A can got cut already.
4 Flavio: [Tòkko biséera nóo enta tetzo' ákkà txee.
                  tòko   biséra nó   enta   te-tzo' ákà   txe
                  one   visor   that come   back   tree   then
                  A band that came around the the tree.
5 Sabina: Nya'á.
              '-ni=á
              ACT-say-1S
              I do say.

Kacha tells the story to Sabina of why Flavio is sharpening his chainsaw. She says that it was yesterday that his chainsaw cut a (metal) can. Sabina repeats "Can?" which makes confirmation relevant. Kacha affirms by saying it was a can that got cut. In overlap with Kacha, Flavio clarifies that it was a metal band around the tree. Sabina shows her appreciation of the event by the formulaic *Nya'á* (I do say). Then Kacha continues the story telling how sparks flew when he hit it and that's when the chain lost its edge and why Flavio's sharpening it.

4.2.1.3 *Offers that Do Not Repeat Prior Speaker with Polar Question Enclitic =la*

Repair can be offered with new information rather than by building a turn with repeated information. Like with repeats these can be explicitly marked for confirmation or disconfirmation with the polar question enclitic or not marked as such. When not marked as an explicit polar question, confirmation may still be relevant if the repair is checking an understanding. Or confirmation may not be relevant if the repair is doing correction (other-repair).

Pronominal reference where the indexical link to prior discourse is not apparent can often prompt repairs where a speaker offers a candidate noun as the explicit reference of a pronoun from a prior turn.

(20) LMSMVDP24Jul0901 00:26:11.99

1 Elvia: Entxè ra! Kállò kye' ello owàá í becchò níngye?
            -E gaze forward-|E bend head forward gaze to lower structure
            entxè=ra   kálò   ke' elo o-wàá-í   bechò nínge
            last.night=EXCL how.many this where CMP-remove=3ANIM   turkey thing
            Last night! How many turkey an animal pulled out from this side?
2 Roberto: Bichoò la?
            ----------|E raises gaze to R
            bi-chò=la
            CLAS-coyote=Q
            Coyote?
3 Elvia: Mhmm.
            -|E nods
            Uhuh.

In the trouble turn in example (20), Elvia uses the animal pronoun *í* to refer to the animal or animals that killed their turkeys by pulling them through the wall of their enclosure. Roberto who has recently arrived to the scene and is asking questions about the project offers repair *Bichoò la?* (Coyote?) as possible referent for the pronoun. Elvia confirms in her next turn. While this formulation does not repeat anything from the trouble source, Roberto had heard coyote mentioned in some talk prior to Elvia's turn.

The next extract (21) involves two repair offers made in novel terms in lines 2 and 4.

```
(21) LMSMVDP21Jul0903 00:07:21:880
```

1 Flavio: Ákkà kaà nzée kyeeniì beè ì Eenze'e txee ra!
              áka   kà   nzé ke#nì   bè=ì e#nze'e   txe=ra
              tree truly went plant PL=3o this.topic then=EXCL
              Trees, truly they went to plant. This is it then!

2 Sabina: Enza akyée lá enta beè ì txee?
              ----------------|S gaze up to K
              enza   a-ké=lá   enta bè=ì   txe
              direction low=already come PL=3o then
              From down low they already came then?

3 Kacha: Enza akyée lá enta beè ì txee.
              enza   a-ké=lá   enta bè=ì   txe
              direction low=already come PL=3o then
              From down low they already came then.

4 Flavio: Stangwáa la?
              sta-ngwá=la
              a.while=Q
              A while ago?

5 Sabina: Áwwà añi káa nóo retxée lá nee txónno nzee lá oyáà á
              tyénda.
              --------------------|S gaze to K-----------------------
              -----|S nods
              áwà ani#ká nó   re-txé=lá   ne   txóno nze=lá
              yes must.be that late=already because when went=already
              o-yáà=á   tyénda
              CMP-go=1s   store
              **Yes, it must be that it was late already because they
              were going when I went to the store.**

Sabina, Kacha, and Flavio are talking on their patio. They saw some townsfolk returning who are in service and were wondering together whether they were returning from *ákkà kyee niì* (tree planting) or from *bijilánsya* (vigilance), being on watch patrol (both possible service roles). Flavio suggests they were coming from planting trees in 1. To this Sabina offers an understanding check in novel terms. She says, "They came from down low then?" which would be logically consistent with their having gone in the direction to plant trees. Being on watch rather involves looking after logging equipment up on a mountain, so returning would contrastingly be from up high. Kacha confirms this with a repetition of the proposition in 3, "From down low they already came then." To this Flavio asks *Stangwáa la?* offering (a while ago) for (dis)confirmation. Sabina affirms this in next turn saying that it was already late when she saw them when she went to the store.

4.3 Multiparty Repair

Most of the examples we've seen can give the impression that repair is a dyadic phenomenon resolving trouble between two persons, but as we've seen with offers and recruitments, multiparty interactions involve the production and resolution of intersubjectivity across the ecology of the speech situation often involving the contributions and interaction of more than two participants. In this section I want to discuss segments where more than two people were involved in repair sequences. One way this can happen is if two present speakers issue repair on a trouble source. This is the case in example (22) where Angeles and Elvia both issue an open-class repair initiation at the same time on Jorge's prior turn formulation (Figure 4.10).

```
(22) LMSMVDP22Jul0909 00:28:58.89
1  Jorge:     Tomaà ndzeendzee í nii beé ì ra!
              te-mà  n-tze#n-tze=í           ni   bè=i=ra
              much   STA-walk#STA-walk=3ANIM  say  PL=3M=EXCL
              They say that it roams about a lot!
2  Angeles:   [Eé?
              -----|Ang head turn-L to J
              Huh?
3  Elvia:     [Eé?
              ------|E head turn-R to J
              ------|And head turn-R to J
              Huh?
```

Figure 4.10 Angeles, Elvia, and Andrea turn heads in synchrony toward Jorge.

4 Jorge: Ndzee í xho'o í ni'í beè ì noo ndzee í ásta díkki enza
                   laabe zé'e.
                   ---------------------------------|J head point to town
                   center
                   n-tze=í   r-cho'o=í   ni'í   bè=ì   no
                   STA-walk=3ANIM HAB-go.out=3ANIM house   PL=3o   and
                   n-tze=í   ásta   díki   enza   labe   zé'e
                   STA-walk=3ANIM toward   whole   direction   center there
                   **It walks out of their house and walks all the way to the
                   town center there.**

Angeles and Elvia's synchronous response (lines 2 and 3) indicates a convergence of perspective on a turn that was both underspecified and surprising to them. Further synchronization is seen in Andrea's head turn at the same time as the repair initiations of the other two women. While the women were washing clothes, the three of them had been talking about a deer that a family had kept in a corral in the past. Angeles asked if the deer was still there and Elvia confirmed that it was. Jorge adds in 1, "They say that it roams about a lot!" Both Elvia and Angeles then issue, in the same moment, an open-class repair interjection *Eé?* (Huh?), and Jorge redoes his action of 1 in 4, expanding with details.

In a more complex example of multiparty repair, multiple repairs are issued by multiple speakers in example (23).

(23) LMSMVDP07Jul09 00:44:58.90

1 Sofia: Nékka' báyya ríñña' oyáà arólla' bicchà nékka'.
                   -A looking at S----|F head turn-R to S
                   néka'   báya rína' o-yáà   a-róla'   bichà   néka'
                   yesterday   go   work   CMP-go measure-half   day   yesterday
                   Yesterday I went to work in the middle of the day, yesterday.

2 Alfonsa: Aà::[::
                   -A leans forward toward S
                   Oh::::

3 Fabiola: [Xhii ríñña'?
                       xhi   rína'
                       what   work
                   What work?

4 Sofia: Ríñña' Káarà:.
                   rína'   Kára-L
                   work   Kara-CLAS
                   Kara's work.

5 Alfonsa: De zé'e xhii kaà ori'i lò txee?
                   de   zé'e xhi   kà   o-ri'i=lò   txe
                   of   there what   truly   CMP-do-2S   then
                   And there what truly did you do then?

4 Fabiola: Aà. Nóo oyáà choxxhí lò yéttzà la?
                   à   nó   o-yáà   choxhí=lò   yétza=la
                   oh   that CMP-go   husk=2s   corn.ear=Q
                   Oh. You went to husk corn?

5 Sofia: Entxè' oyáà choxxhí á yéttzà otxee lá oriñña loo óora kye' entxè'.
                   ---------------------------------|S quick head turn L and back
                   entxè'   o-yáà   choxhí=á   yétza   o-txe=lá   o-rina
                   last.night   CMP-go   husk=1s   corn.ear   late=already   CMP-arrive
                   lo   óra   ke'   entxè'
                   face hour   this   last.night
                   **Last night I went to husk corn I arrived later already than
                   this time now, last night.**

```
6  Fabiola:   Aà:
              -F head turn to front
              Oh:
7  Alfonsa:   Ahaà:
              -A nods then bows head
              Uhuh:
```

In 1 Sofia makes the surprising contribution to the conversation that yesterday she went to work in the middle of the day (meaning late). Fabiola issues a restricted request targeting the noun "work" looking for something more specific by saying, *Xhii ríñña'?* (What work?) and Sofia responds *Ríñña' Káarà* (Kara's work) Though while the parties to the conversation know where and with whom the work was, the question of what work is still open. Alfonsa formulates this as an explicit question that acknowledges how the person reference was recoverable as a place reference (another common ontological crossing), "And there what truly did you do then?" Fabiola offers an understanding check, "Oh. You went to husk corn?" which then results in Sofia redoing 1 and expanding in response to the chain of repairs, "Last night I went to husk corn I arrived later already than this time now, last night" during which Sofia turns her head and gazes in the direction of the place reference implicit in multiple turns of the extract (Figure 4.11).

Figure 4.11 Sofia turns her head and gazes toward her implicit place reference (line 5).

Sometimes the assumptions made in collaborative actions can be wrong. Example (24) is a case where a multiparty repair itself needed to be corrected. Jorge, Elvia, Andrea, and Angeles were talking about a fiesta that was happening in a town a few hours away. Jorge had been there but not the three women.

130 Saying and Doing in Zapotec

(24) LMSMVDP22Jul0909 00:22:15.68

```
1  Jorge:    Púuro tzyáà dáññi zxenne xhii nekka Xhiñña' dáññi nii á.
             ------------------------|J head turn-R open hand arm
                 sweep up
             púro  tzyáà  dáni     zxene xhi  ne-aka  xhina'#dáni  ni=á
             pure  just   mountain big   how  STA-be  el.rincón    say=1s
             It's all big mountain like how it is in El Rincón I say.

2            (10.0)
3  Andrea:   Nyàá láa ndzoo é loo:=
             nyàá       lá    n-tzo=é    lo
             beautiful  COMP  STA-be=3O  face
             Is it more beautiful than in=

4  Angeles:                      =xhiñña' dáññi?
                                  xhina'#dáni
                                  el.rincón
                                  =El Rincón?

5  Jorge:    Eé?
             ---|J slight head turn-R to Ang
             Huh?

6  Angeles:  Nyàá ndzoo é loo xhiñña' dáññi la?
             nyàá       n-tzo=é    lo  xhina'#dáni=la
             beautiful  STA-be=3O  face el.rincón=Q
             Is it as beautiful as El Rincón?

7            (1.5)
8  Andrea:   Nyàá láa ndzoo é loo Xombéttò la?
             -|And raises gaze from wash basin to front
             ----------|J head turn-L to And
             nyàá       lá    n-tzo=é    lo    Xombéttò=la
             beautiful  COMP  STA-be=3O  face  San.Pedro=Q
             Is it more beautiful than in San Pedro?

9  Jorge:    Nyàá láa ndzoo é.
             -|J turns gaze to front
             -|And turns gaze down to wash basin
             nyàá       lá    n-tzo=é
             beautiful  COMP  STA-be=3O
             It is more beautiful.

10 Andrea:   Nyàá láa ndzoo é la?
             nyàá       lá    n-tzo=é=la
             beautiful  COMP  STA-be=3O=Q
             It is more beautiful?

11 Jorge:    Áwwà.
             Yes.

12 Jorge:    Nyàá láa ndzoo é áwwà.
             nyàá       lá    n-tzo=é    áwà
             beautiful  COMP  STA-be=3O  yes
             It is more beautiful, yes.
```

Angeles asks, *Xhaa nzoo eenze'e?* (How is this place?). Jorge describes it as being by a large mountain like in El Rincón (the ejido or communal land of Lachixío several kilometers to the south). About ten seconds go by containing another brief mention of the mountain by Jorge and an unrelated comment by Elvia and a few seconds of noise that obscures another utterance. The sound clears up again at an important moment in which we see a failed collaborative completion that is met with the correction of other-repair. Andrea begins a question formulated as a comparative: *Nyàá láa ndzoo é loo:* (Is it more beautiful that at:), drawing out the relational noun *loo* (face) used to mean on or at. During the moment of her hesitation before adding her intended place reference noun, Angeles does a "collaborative completion" (Bolden 2003) assuming Andrea's reference was going to be El Rincón, a place that had already been topicalized in Jorge's description in 1. Jorge issues an open-class repair interjection *Eé?*, and Angeles redoes her and Andrea's parts as a combined whole, "Is it as beautiful as El Rincón?" Jorge doesn't immediately respond, and Andrea then looks up from her work and redoes the move from 3 that she didn't complete. She says, *Nyàá láa ndzoo é loo Xombéttò la?* (Is it more beautiful than in San Pedro?)—another beautiful town in the mountains to their north. After Andrea corrects Angeles's assumption of her intention, Jorge goes on to answer Andrea that the town he is talking about "is more beautiful." Andrea then offers an understanding check and Jorge confirms.

4.4 Concluding Remarks

Collaboration to repair intersubjectivity in conversation is accomplished by the universal means of offering public signs of understanding and recruiting further action on behalf of a prior speaker through requests that are formulated as either open or restricted. In the examples presented in this chapter, we have seen that the joint action of repair is built upon the foundations of human prosociality we examined in the previous chapters: the social actions of offering and recruiting that manage and build human relationships. This makes an important claim about the relations between language as something we do and human sociality, including its development and evolution. While we can imagine an interactional ecology with offers and recruitments but without repair as we see in great ape food sharing, we could not do conversational repair without already doing offering and recruiting. This relationship demonstrates an implicational hierarchy associated with emergent ontologies.

This examination of repair has provided for many insights on the Lachixío Zapotec language that can only be gained in the study of actual dialogue that mattered in the life of the speakers. In this engagement, we see question words at work in a dialogic ecology where content question words help speakers work with the practical problem of intersubjectivity. We also see many uses of pronouns and from frequent repairs of reference how fraught pronominal reference can be. Many referential troubles are rooted in lack of common perceptual ground and are remedied with the assistance of gaze, points, and common focus on objects. This chapter illustrated several examples of what we can consider the adjustment between life worlds to augment their resonance, creating a "contact zone" (Haraway 2008) of shared *umwelten* (Von Uexküll 1934). Remedies to repair reference were seen to either work to make a visible action more noticeable, or redoing it to fit with a deictic verbal component that another person did not get. Repair could also involve a shift from deictic reference to abstract symbolic reference (as I have illustrated in the cases presented in Sicoli 2016a). The fact that speech is also tied to body movements like gesture, body torque, gaze, and actions with physical objects reaffirms the imperative that speech corpora of events where speakers have copresent access to each other's bodies and actions with objects be produced through video and not as audio-only recordings to attend to a whole of which talk is an incomplete part.

In some of the repairs, it looked like something else was also going on, reminding us that repairs may be, and often are, multifunctional, accomplishing simultaneous actions or functioning as the vehicle for another action. For example, we saw Elvia issue an open-class repair initiation as a go ahead to continue a conversation from a turn that was interrupted by a child. There are also other speech tokens that look like the open-class repair initiation *eé* being made of a similarly minimal phonetic form but serving different ends. Their minimal form may in fact be related to Goffman's imperative that some items must intervene in a conversation without derailing the conversation (Goffman 1967). Another interjection, *eè*, with falling tone is often translated to Spanish as *a poco*, a positive minimal response like "Really?". Its form may help show appreciation without taking the floor away from the other speaker. There is also *eé* used to pressure a response. It is not used after a turn to issue repair but may be issued as a minimal turn when having issued a first-pair part to another and not getting a response. Doing so pressures the other by saying *Eé?* as if a response was made but not audible and in need of repair. Like the directives discussed in Chapter 2, the moral imperative here is for the interlocutor to make a world that matches the words.

Another place to question whether repair is about an actual problem of hearing, speaking, or understanding is with some offers of understanding. We can question whether the routine of repair may here be serving other ends. In Chapter 5, we engage this question by looking at several functions for repetition across turns, including the building of public signs that diagram the developing knowledge shared in a conversation. As we look at how speakers jointly build resonance into sequences of interaction in Chapter 5, we should keep in mind how analyzing repair teaches us that a joint-action routine can serve ends at multiple scales.

5

Resonate

We have seen many times now in the video and transcript analysis of this book that people build repetition into dialogue in, for example, repairs and remedies, recruitments, and the iteration of offers and responses. The linguist Roman Jakobson saw such recurrent returns as central to the being of language:

> On every level of language the essence of poetic artifice consists in recurrent returns. Phonemic features and sequences, both morphologic and lexical, syntactic and phraseological units, when occurring in metrically or strophically corresponding positions, are necessarily subject to the conscious or subconscious questions whether, how far, and in what respect the positionally corresponding entities are mutually similar. Those poetic patterns where certain similarities between successive verbal sequences are compulsory or enjoy a high preference appear to be widespread in the languages of the world, and they are particularly gratifying both for the study of poetic language and for linguistic analysis in general. (Jakobson 1966: 399)

Reflecting on the prior chapters, we saw recurrent returns to be formative of offers, recruitments, and repairs built between participants. I now focus directly on this process of resonance building asking how and to what ends people build resonances across their interactional moves. I aim to illustrate that the participatory work of resonance building pervasive in human interaction provides a natural history in which to study grammar well fitted to corpora and the goals of documenting language as part of sociocultural life.

Social anthropologist Unni Wikan wrote that "resonance has to do with empathy and understanding, with what fosters comprehension across clefts and boundaries, with enhancing the relevance of matters seemingly out of touch or reach" (2012: 8). The clefts about boundaries between us may be in sharpest relief in communication across neurological difference. Charles Goodwin (2011) describes the successful communication of ideas by a man with limited grammatical and lexical resources due to sever aphasia who nonetheless emerges as a powerful speaker *in dialogue* through a process that involves copresent listener-speakers constructing next actions by operating on his prior utterances and by him operating on theirs Such joint production of *language structure beyond the individual* involves what C. Goodwin (2011: 189) has described as "cooperative semiosis" as a "central locus for the organization of cognition, action, and language practice." Goodwin goes on to say that,

> crucially, for the study of language and grammar, [practices of cooperative semiosis] extend the scope of investigation simultaneously outward, beyond the individual sentence and speaker, and inward, into the range of alternative possibilities for combining and shaping into larger wholes the signs that construct utterances and sentences ... within processes of multi-utterance cooperative semiosis, the actions of participants create an environment where 1) the stream of speech is parsed into discrete, relevant building blocks; and 2) populations of alternative possibilities for combining these signs into larger units are made publicly available. (C. Goodwin 2011: 189, see also C. Goodwin 2006 and 2017).

Also drawing insight from communication across neurological difference, Du Bois, Hobson, and Hobson (2014) examine dialogic resonance between children with autism and adult interviewers in comparison with neuro-typical children of the same age groups. They explicate relationships between language and the human capacity for intersubjective engagement. Examining different types of resonance, they find strengths and weaknesses in the conversational capacity of autistic children. One strength was in using a "frame grab" strategy (reproducing part of the structure and content of a prior utterance) to achieve coherence across conversational moves, but not often assimilating such structure into their own stance that was characteristic of more neuro-typical talk. The talk alignment without stance alignment is described as leaving the neuro-typical interlocutor feeling a lack of intersubjectivity. They write:

> Intersubjectivity is not a given. It cannot be assumed as a simple human birthright, effortlessly in place as a mere correlate of being born and growing up among other humans. Rather it must be achieved through specific acts of communicative engagement, performed with particular others in the dialogic moment. Nor can intersubjectivity remain at the level of broad generalities and abstractions; rather, its outlines must be filled with the specific meanings gleaned from particular configurations of resonating elements, in directly experienced moments of communicative engagement. (Du Bois, Hobson, and Hobson 2014: 438–9)

In "Towards a Dialogic Syntax," Du Bois describes dialogic resonance as "the catalytic activation of affinities between utterances" (Du Bois 2014: 360). Speakers use the parallelism of repetition to create a connection between turns. This produces a field of commonality upon which differences come into focus for noticing and interpretation, highlighting grammatical resources (the syntagmatic) and potential substitutes and contrasts of the lexicon (the paradigmatic) that contribute to the richness of the stimulus in the natural history of interaction. Du Bois (2014: 360–1) writes:

> The patterns that define language emerge from the interaction of particulars, as one utterance follows another, reproducing its pattern in part. The resulting parallelism invites a perception of pairing, generating something new in the

event: a specific resonance of forms and meanings.... The resonance that arises between parallel utterances defines a matrix of relational affinities, triggering analogies which generate an increment of inferred significance in the moment. As one utterance is juxtaposed to another, the structural coupling that results creates a new, higher-order linguistic structure. Within this structure, the coupled components recontextualize each other, generating new affordances for meaning.

Parallelism and repetition are important form components for building emergent resonances. *Dialogic repetition* is where a speaker repeats part or all of a prior speaker's turn in sequential adjacency or near adjacency (i.e., at some scale that affords noticing). Such repetition can be of another individual (cross-speaker repetition) or of the same individual of a prior time and, as we will see in the Lachixío Zapotec data, may involve cycling and recycling signs across several turns blurring the boundaries between the talk of one speaker and another. Where one turn builds on a prior turn by repetition, the sign is both in a new sequential environment and produces a new environment together with the prior turn, as a semiotic interpretant of the former. The qualitative Secondness of the semiotic adjacency of repetition forms a third, higher-order syntactic unit that then projects an emergent function for interpretation in the next moves of talk, and thought, as one moment of joint action becomes the next in the process of semiosis. Dialogic repetition is a type of form-function correspondence that can be considered a subset of a range of cross-utterance (or cross-action) relations where similarity creates a field for the noticing of difference that characterizes an analytical strategy I call *resonance grammar*.

We can see some parallels in Charles Hockett's suggestion that linguists move from thinking about words as particles to thinking about their resonance (Hockett 1987). Hockett argues that morphemes should not be understood in their thingness, or their compositionality, but as they relate to the other items in their set. If we extend this to consider linguistic methods, we can see that elicited or assembled paradigms of linguists' work are sets of resonating frames that bring differences into focus. Repetition in conversation produces a paradigm as it "projects," as Jakobson (1960) wrote, "the principle of equivalence from the axis of selection into the axis of combination," which is to say from the paradigmatic to the syntagmatic (syntactic), but in the practice of language, and its learning, projection can rather work in the opposite way: speakers build resonant structures to project, and comment on, the axis of selection from the axis of combination. While Hockett suggests looking back to Saussure to inform this move to resonance (a relevant observation pointing to Saussure's paradigmatic dimension of language and the analytically important concept of *value*), we will more productively look to Peirce to think about an emergent quality of symbols involving the resonances between the multiple indices that compose them. Referential symbols involve an index of reference, and multiple lateral indices of a semantic field that we learn through substitutions and alternations in dialogue, and from which a sign acquires paradigmatic value (see Deacon 2003). Where Saussure's linguistic and semiological science was ideal and synchronic, Peirce's conception of semiosis is temporally dynamic and dialogic with attention to materiality that provides us with tools to consider the resonances emergent between speakers. In addition, Saussure's (and later generative linguistics') privileging of the arbitrary mode of signification erases the pervasive functioning of iconicity and indexicality in all grammatical function.

For Peirce, signs have a life located in the process and development (growth) of a sign-object relationship for interpreters' in the subsequent interpretant sign, as we reviewed in Chapter 1. Dialogic resonance exploits these developmental and relational properties of the sign. A sign's interpretant, itself a further developed representation of a sign-object relation, is also a sign that can be taken up into further semiosis in ongoing cycles. Dialogic resonance is created as an utterance exhibiting parallelisms with a prior utterance is taken as a sign. The process builds a diagrammatic icon, a sign where parallel parts within a larger whole relate to each other. The parallelism creates a field upon which difference is salient for the noticing, and thus highlighted as a focal element, to achieve a pragmatic action in the discourse. In this way, it is crucial to recognize that studying language outside of its temporality (e.g., synchronic syntax) erases from analytical consideration the very richness of the dialogic syntax that makes language learnable, and the cooperative semiosis that makes it functional.

Peirce's semiosis is accomplished in phases where icons, indices, and symbols have a temporality that is involved in their being as action:

> An icon has such being as belongs to past experience. It exists only as an image in the mind. An index has the being of present experience. The being of a symbol consists in the real fact that something surely will be experienced if certain conditions be satisfied. Namely, it will influence the thought and conduct of its interpreter. (Peirce CP 4.447)

A repetition points to its antecedent by means of iconicity, the retrospective icon recontextualizing its likeness in a higher-order diagrammatic icon, complete with an internally consistent set of indices. The forms become icons of each other brought copresent in an indexical juxtaposition that forms a higher-order syntactic structure. This new unit functions for a symbolic action that is itself prospective in projecting an interpretant and used for a pragmatic function. Dialogic resonance in conversation makes the sign processes of semiosis visible to conversational participants and, fortunately, to researchers.

Though the concept of dialogic resonance is different than repetition because resonance is *emergent between* while repetition is a potential mechanism (among others) to build resonance, the history of work on repetition in grammar is important background. The analytics of repetition was brought into contemporary linguistics in the mid-twentieth-century publications of Roman Jakobson with *parallelism* defining the poetic function in linguistics (1960). Jakobson (1966) pointed to the importance of "recurrent returns" at every level of language. Jakobson sketched a history of parallelism that reached back to the eighteenth-century biblical scholar Robert Lowth, who provided the term "parallelism," but was himself recognizing a mechanism of knowledge and practice among biblical authors. Other scholars have observed parallelism to be organizational in historically independent linguistic traditions, for example, Mesoamerican hieroglyphic inscriptions (Hull and Carrasco 2012), and

Mesoamerican Ritual discourse (Haviland 1996; Cruz 2017), and for the creation of textual authority in Weyewa Ritual Speech (Sumba Indonesia) (Kuipers 1990). Dell Hymes's (1977) "verse analysis" used parallelism to discover the poetic verse structure in Native American narratives represented in Boasian inspired text collections first transcribed as prose paragraphs. In Hymes's influential method for recovering an emic poetics of speech once erased under a prose-normative literary ideology of text collection, "Verses are recognized, not by counting parts, but by recognizing repetition within a frame, the relation of putative units to each other within a whole" (Hymes 1977: 438).

Parallelism and repetition have been important in the study of child language learning and child-directed speech. Keenan (1977) observed how young children often repeat utterances addressed to them. Brown (2000) described dialogic repetition as facilitating children's analysis and use of Tzeltal verbs. De León (2007) described parallelism and metalinguistic play in the emergence of Zinacantec Mayan sibling culture. And Merritt (1982) described repeats in the primary classroom "as windows on the nature of talk engagement."

Repetition, like all aspects of language, is multifunctional. In Tannen's work on repetition (1987, 1989, 1990), she describes multiple functions for repetition in talk and dialogue. She shows that second-turn repeats in dialogue can show listenership (engagement), initiate repair on prior utterance, answer a polar question, request confirmation, provide an acknowledgment or agreement, provide assessment through an affective response, create humor through play, and savor, or appreciate, the significance of a prior utterance. Discourse analysts have shown that repetition is pervasive in dialogue with scholarly work assembled in a volume edited by Johnstone (1994) arguing that repetition serves linguistic, cognitive, and cultural functions. Brody (1986) showed repetition for "contrastive highlighting," M. Goodwin (1983) illustrated repetition for challenge and correction in children's conversations, and for what she called "format tying" through which turns are indexically linked to each other for noticeable effect (1990). Schegloff (1996) argued that repetition can be involved in "confirming allusions." Heritage and Raymond (2005) and Stivers (2005) analyzed the role of repetition in claiming epistemic precedence. Focusing on repetition across speaker turns, Brown, Sicoli, and LeGuen (2010) compared three Mesoamerican languages (Tzeltal, Yucatec, and Zapotec) for their similar discourse practices and functions that themselves are suggestive of a Mesoamerican Discourse Area. In this chapter, I exemplify several of these Mesoamerican discourse functions and others found in the Lachixío corpus.

This brief review supports that repetition is recognized as ubiquitous in talk and dialogue, but it is little recognized how important the human practice of building resonances can be for grammatical analysis. In part this is because of the division of labor that developed historically in studies of language where grammatical analysts have come to work in the domain of the sentence or proposition, and conversation is mainly studied within a branch of sociology. Even within the division of labor of the discipline of linguistics, discourse analysis is rarely considered a "core" area of linguistic study in most departments of linguistics. And where it is represented, there is too often an entrenched opposition between grammatical analysis and discourse analysis—grammatical analysts generally don't do discourse (often defined as being a domain "beyond the sentence") and discourse analysts rarely apply their work to the study of grammatical analysis and to informing theoretical linguistics.[1] This has the unfortunate effect of leaving the documentary linguist in the lurches between inter- and intradisciplinary divisions, less prepared to engage conversational interaction as a primary source for grammatical description. Corpus linguistics could fill some of this gap, but most computational-corpus linguistic work targets "big data" written corpora of "big" languages for the statistical power and scalability it affords, rather than the relatively smaller corpora of language documentation, particularly those of "small" languages. Beyond recognizing repetition and parallelism in discourse, resonance grammar aims to transcend the institutionalized divisions of grammar and discourse to consider an order of syntax beyond the individual, of great utility for documentary linguistics and ethnographers of language, corpus linguists, and with consequence for theoretical linguistics and the study of language learning and development.

5.1 Dialogic Syntax and Resonance Grammar

Where dialogic syntax (Du Bois 2014) represents an emergent dialogic practice through which a speaker recycles another speaker's talk in a way that ties utterance to prior utterance, resonance grammar is intended to more broadly approach resonances participants jointly build within and across any modalities of discourse. The emergent grammar of an interaction may engage dialogic syntax analysis, where the talk itself carries much of the semiotic load, but may also relate talk to gesture, gesture to object of joint attention, gesture to gesture, and so on. Resonance grammar is suited to the study of audiovisual corpora in its openness to multimodality, and more resembles the practice of grammatical analysis accomplished by children as they learn languages through the natural histories of multimodal interactions with others in a world of things. In this chapter, I focus largely on examples toward the dialogic syntax pole to illustrate lexical-syntactic analysis of Lachixío Zapotec though some examples also involve the broader concept of intermodal resonances (as have multiple examples in prior chapters). Chapter 6, "Build," more explicitly engages with analysis of intermodal resonances.

One way analysts can represent parallels and contrasts is visually. Dialogic syntax does this through the *diagraph* aligning resonating elements vertically as I have aligned the interlinear glossing of example (1). In the three-turn sequence, frame resonance can be seen in the identity of items across turns and focal resonances are indicated with underline. In producing parallel frames, the speakers themselves have produced a field for the noticing of two focal contrasts: a pronoun contrast, *é ≠ né*, characteristic of dialogic syntax examples presented in the literature, and a voice register contrast, modal ≠ breathy. Prosodic contrasts like these have not previously been the subject of dialogic syntax analysis. Resonance has the affordances of engaging lexical-syntactic material, but is not limited to that domain. Prosody is in a sense a bridge between dialogic syntax and resonance grammar.

(1) LMSMVDP09Aug0803 00:36:41.75
```
1 Daniel:    Láa likki zxà é.
             lá   liki  =zxà  =é
             NEG  give  =3DIS =3INAN
             They don't give it.
2 Pedro:     #Láa likki zxà é#.
   #         lá   liki  =zxà  =é
   breathy   NEG  give  =3DIS =3INAN
             #They don't give it#.
3 Daniel:    Láa likki zxà né.
             lá   liki  =zxà  =né
             NEG  give  =3DIS =ACT3O
             They won't give it.
```

The natural history of this extract involves Daniel telling his younger brother Pedro about a time that he traveled around southern Oaxaca looking for day-labor gigs with several others from Lachixío. He is describing a difficult time in one town that he characterized as having "bad people" for their lack of hospitality indicated in their not offering a place to sleep. Example (1) highlights a contrast in voice quality that has proven to be highly systematic across conversations and speakers. Breathy voice in the resonant frame of a repetition marks the expression of affect, surprise, disbelief of the face value of the proposition, and regularly functions to recruit an expansion in next turn where the prior speaker provides some epistemic qualification to strengthen and justify the claim, which we see in 3. We also see in 3 that this strengthening involves a second repeat and a shift in pronoun to one that specifies an indefinite active agent (=né).

In Daniel's response to Pedro's breathy-voiced repeat, we see an epistemological strengthening device available in the Lachixío pronominal paradigm illustrating a function for the "indefinite subject acting on object" pronoun né. Intensive, repeated elicitations and interviews about the morpheme failed to achieve reference or depiction of this use. Elicitation with multiple speakers gave the impression that /=né/ and /=é/ were invariably bound to a verb's semantics, but using methods of dialogic syntax on actually occurring discourse, the pronouns were found to be paradigmatically substitutable. In 3 Daniel "upgrades" the pronoun from the third-person inanimate pronoun /=é/ to the active subject on object /=né/. Through the frame resonance of the repetition, this one grammatical substitution produces a focused contrast. Daniel creatively uses a paradigmatic contrast available to him to attribute intention to the subjects: it is not simply that they don't give but that they won't give shifting his characterization from a description of a happening to a moral evaluation as I have analyzed in other work (Sicoli 2015, 2016a). Such examples show a focus on resonance to be a critical tool for linguistic description. The rest of this chapter will present data analyses of dialogic resonance in the *Lachixío Zapotec Conversations Corpus* with attention to the resonances of their jointly produced form, the epistemic relations at issue in their situation, and the insights for Lachixío Zapotec grammatical description.

5.2 The Ringing of Resonance in Lachixío Conversations

While we saw repeats to be a common form of both initiating and remedying repairs in Chapter 4, repetition is far more common than repair in the corpus. In a sixty-three-minute recording of three people sitting side by side (a participant formation that predicts greater repetition in the response system according to Levinson and Brown 2016) (Figure 5.1), there were only 4 clear repairs but 218 dialogic repetitions where someone repeated part or all of the turn of a prior speaker. Quantifying across 8 recordings in which we coded for both repair and repetition, there were a total of 842 dialogic repetitions in 454 minutes. This is a repetition on average every thirty-two seconds of dialogue. In actual practice, repeats may cluster into sequences one after another and, as we saw with repairs and offers, may be part of exchanges of more than two people. In contrast to the 842 repetitions, the same recordings had 120 repair sequences. Of these repairs forty-three were initiated with repeats as part or all of the formulation and eighty were remedied with some type of repeat (full repeat, part repeat, full repeat plus additional material, part repeat plus additional material). Thus in 454 minutes of spontaneous conversation, 123 repeats were in the service of repair and 719 repeats built resonant relations outside of the environment of conversational repair. What is all this resonance building accomplishing in Lachixío Zapotec conversations?

Figure 5.1 Francisco, Regina, and Aurelia sit side by side talking.

An impressionistic description of a conversation in Lachixío Zapotec is that it rings with resonance. Consider an example from the 63-minute video with 218 dialogic repetitions: Regina, Aurelia, and Francisco are talking about a sickness experienced by a friend. Aurelia is affected by the description. In 5 she asks, *Xhii eenze'e?* (What's that?). The response to this question is syntactically parallel to the question formulation.

```
(2) LMSMVDP28Jul0903  00:42:07.88
 5 Aurelia:    Xhii eenze'e?
               xhi       e#nze'e
               what      CLAS#there
               What's that?
 6 Regina:     Iccha eenze'e ta.
               -R still looking to left (away from A)
               icha      e#nze'e=ta
               sick      CLAS#there=always
               The sickness is that always.
```

Diagramming lines 5 and 6 as a diagraph shows the alignments of the resonant formulation.

```
 5 Aurelia:    xhi       e#nze'e
               what      CLAS#there
 6 Regina:     icha      e#nze'e      =ta
               sick      CLAS#there   =always
```

Regina did not have to use the word order she chose in 6. The sentence could have been *Eenze'e iccha tà*. Syntactic priming may play a part in such emergent constructions, and the relationship between priming and dialogic syntax has been acknowledged (Du Bois, Hobson, and Hobson 2014), but where priming is automatic and unconscious, the resonance-building action of dialogic syntax is about formulating syntactic choices that create engagement between speakers. Consider how this conversation continues with two pairs of resonant turn exchanges.

```
 7 Aurelia:    %Eeliccha kàlla' eenze'e txee%.
               -A looking forward
               e#l-icha     kàla'      e#nze'e    txe
               CLAS#NOM-sick truly     CLAS#there then
               %That's truly the sickness then%.
 8 Regina:     Eeliccha kàlla' eenze'e txee.
               -R turns head from left to forward (parallel to A)
               e#l-icha     kàla'      e#nze'e    txe
               CLAS#NOM-sick truly     CLAS#there then
               That's truly the sickness then.
 9 Aurelia:    Lèkka eenze'e kossa nze'kka.
               lèka       e#nze'e    kosa    nze'ka
               not.be     CLAS#there thing   good
               That's not a good thing.
10 Regina:     Lèkka eenze'e kossa nze'kka.
               ---------------------------|A nods
               lèka       e#nze'e    kosa    nze'ka
               not.be     CLAS#there thing   good
               That's not a good thing.
```

In 7, Aurelia offers an affective assessment in a whispered voice, and in 8, Regina repeats the content and form in modal voice. Aurelia again offers an assessment in 9 which Regina repeats in full. By repeating Aurelia's assessments, Regina shows agreement by "doing again" Aurelia's assessment "saying again" the same phrase. The resonating pairs display public signs of intersubjectivity and purpose achieved in the conversation. Additionally, we see Regina's gaze direction come parallel with Aurelia creating an embodied resonance displaying harmony as well.

Resonance building does not just occur in pairs like this but can in fact go on for several more turns as in example (3) from this same video. Regina's comment in 1 became the ground for resonating frames that rang across *seven* turn transitions based on her phrase *Yexxe a' nzaa bicchà* (The days go quickly). In this setting Aurelia, Regina, and her husband Francisco are seated side by side on a bench (as in Figure 5.1) and have been talking about the annual cycle of saints' festivals. The conversation turns rhetorical, sharing the experience of time with each saying how quickly the days go by.

(3) LMSMVDP28Jul0903 00:08:09.00

```
1  Regina:     Yexxe a' nzaa [bicchà xhii le'e bicchà ra!
               -all gazing forward
               yexe=a'a'     nza    bichà  xhi  le'e bichà=ra
               fast=already  goes   day    how  late day=EXCL
               The days go quickly, how late the day is!

2  Francisco:              [Yexxe a'
                            Quickly

3  Aurelia:    Yexxe a' nzaa bicchà ri.
               yexe=a'a'     nza    bichà=ri
               fast=already  go     day=K+AF
               The days go quickly, indeed.

4  Regina:     Yexx::e a' nzaa bicchà.
               yexe=a'a'     nza    bichà
               fast=already  goes   day
               The days go quickly.

5              (1.0)

6  Aurelia:    Yexxe a' nzaa bicchà.
               yexe=a'a'     nza    bichà
               fast=already  goes   day
               The days go quickly.

7  Regina      Yexxe a' nzaa bicchà peèro
               yexe=a'a'     nza    bichà  pèro
               fast=already  goes   day    CONJ
               The days go quickly and

8              (2.1)

9  Regina:     nóo tzyáà ello nàkki benné yexxe a' jdette bicchà nii paà' á.
               nó    tzyáà  elo  nàki  bené  yexe=a'a'   r-dete bichà
               that  just   where strength person fast=already HAB-pass day
               ni    pà-'=á
               say   father-POS=1S
               that when we're healthy the days pass quickly, my father says.

10 Aurelia:    Ixxh::a' jdette bicchà.
               yexe=a'a'   r-dete  bichà
               fast=already HAB-pass day
               The days pass quickly.
```

```
11              (1.5)
12 Regina:      Eenii kaà::
                e#ni    kà
                CLAS#say true
                It's truly said
13 Regina:      Rátto nzaa tòkko lannà rátto nzaa stokko lannà.
                ráto     nza   tòko  lanà   ráto    nza    sH-tòko     lanà
                a.while  goes  one   year   a.while goes   another.one year
                in a little while one year goes by, in a little while another
                    year goes by.
14 Aurelia:     Rátto nzaa ra!
                ráto    nza=ra
                a.while goes=EXCL
                In a little while (it) goes!
15 Regina:      Bi'yya kóoro' nóo:: eenittzí odette eeliññi yettxé ozxe'kka
                    ni'i á
                L*-bi'ya  kóro'   nó    e#nitzí        o-dete    e#lini   yetxé
                IMP-see   truly?  that  CLAS#2.day.ago CMP-pass  fiesta   pueblo
                o-zxe'ka    '-ni=á
                CMP-feel    ACT-say=1s
                Look, I do say that I felt the annual fiesta has just passed
16 Regina:      nèé' kye'
                nèé'   ke'
                now    this
                and right now
17 Regina:      [stokko a'la eeliññi yettxé oriñña nèé'.
                sH-tòko=a'la        e#lini  yetxé   o-rina     nèé'
                another-one=again   fiesta  pueblo  CMP-arrive now
                another fiesta came now.
18 Francisco:   [sto ss
                -|F smiles, laughs through alveolar fricative and rocks forward
                anoth ss
19 Aurelia:     Ay::: stokko a'la eeliññi yettxé oriñña lacchi a'wa nèé'.
                -|R slight smile, head turn left toward (not to) A
                ay sH-tòko=a'la         e#lini  yetxé   o-rina    lachi=a'wa  nèé'
                INT another-one=again   CLAS#fiesta pueblo CMP-arrive valley=1PLI now
                Ay:: another fiesta came to our valley now.
20 Regina:      Stokko a'la né nèé' ta.
                sH-tòko=a'la=né          nèé'=ta
                another-one=again=ACT3o  now=always
                Another one now always.
```

In only twenty lines of transcript, this fragment of conversational life in Lachixío illustrates many dimensions and scales of resonance. There are the full repeats of frame resonance but also the repetition of frames with small additions or changes. The focal link produced in the parallel framing is used as a vehicle to take a stance by building a new sign from the materials of the prior speech. Line 2 is a partial repeat by Francisco of Regina in line 1. In 3, Aurelia fully repeats Regina's phrase, adding the phrase-final enclitic =ri which is used as a marker of knowing affirmation. In 4, Regina produces a focus by indexing *yexx::e a'* (quickly) with a long drawn out medial consonant. Regina then constructs reported speech that she attributes to her father in 9: "In life the days pass quickly." Reported speech itself makes a claim to resonate with prior speech, and because it is something that her father used to say, it has become built up over time through her own experience of its recurrent returns into citable knowledge. Regina leads into this with what I call the *repeat-and-run* strategy, a format tying where somebody builds a frame resonance using the other's words as the starting point for a longer utterance that may take the conversation in a new direction (compare what Bueno Holle 2019 describes as the *chiastistic structuring* of a sequence where an argument-focused utterance followed a predicate-focused utterance with parallel function in Isthmus Zapotec). Like in Regina's formulation spanning lines 8 and 9, *Yexxe a' nzaa bicchà peèro* . . . , the strategy in Lachixío often employs the conjunction *peèro* after the repetition. *Peèro* is a word form borrowed from the Spanish contrastive conjunction *pero* (but); however, in Lachixío Zapotec, *peèro* is often used as a non-contrasting conjunction. Internal to her father's reported speech there is resonance of the form relations the participants have already mobilized, but with paradigmatic substitution of *jdette* (passes) for *nzaa* (goes). In the following line, Aurelia adopts this lexeme in a new resonant formulation *yexxe a' jdette bicchà* (The days pass quickly). I present the diagraphs to illustrate these resonant relations as the speech evolved.

1	Regina:	yexe=a'a' fast=already	nza goes	bichà day		
2	Francisco:	yexe=a'a' fast=already				
3	Aurelia:	yexe=a'a' fast=already	nza goes	bichà day	=ri =K+AF	
4	Regina:	yex::e=a'a' fa::st=already	nza goes	bichà day		
6	Aurelia:	yexe=a'a' fast=already	nza goes	bichà day		
7	Regina:	yexe=a'a' fast=already	nza goes	bichà day	pèro CONJ	
9	Regina:	yexe=a'a' fast=already	r-dete HAB-pass	bichà day	ni say	pà=á father=1s
10	Aurelia:	yexe=a'a' fast=already	r-dete HAB-pass	bichà day		

After a brief pause in 10, Regina adds a proverb about time into the talk. As common knowledge that can be heard and repeated in brief forms that circulate, proverbs themselves are resonant forms of shared culture which in Mesoamerica (and many other places) take authority in the form of a couplet (Haviland 1996). Proverbs resonate with other instances of their use and can be expected to give rise to resonant conventional interpretations. The fact that it occurred to Regina as she dwelled in this dialogue, as well as her recalling her father's speech a few lines earlier, is itself a fact about the role of resonance in memory. Couplets like this have their own internal resonance, and this structure forms the basis for a subsequent repetition by Aurelia. There is a syntactic resonance in the form of an ADVERB-VERB-TEMPORAL NOUN sequence across all forms but in this case with *rátto* (a [little] while) substituted for *yexxe a'* (quickly). The proverb shows a frame resonance and focal contrast among determiners based on the number one: *tòkko* (one) and *stokko* (another). And in 14, Aurelia makes an affective comment by resonating part of the frame of the proverb and adding the exclamative enclitic =*ra*.

4-7	R/A	yexe=a'a fast=already	nza goes		bìchà day	
13a	R:	ráto a.while	nza goes	tòko one	lanà year	
13b	R:	ráto a.while	nza goes	sH-toko another-one	lanà year	
14	A:	ráto a.while	nza goes			=ra =EXCL

After together savoring the proverb through the resonance jointly constructed across turns 13 and 14, Regina then moves the conversation forward with something new but still related to the feeling of time passing quickly. She refers to the endless cycle of ritual obligations to the saints. Her utterance parallels the syntactic structure of the proverb's ONE-ANOTHER contrast. In lines 15–17, Regina says that she felt the annual fiesta just passed and right now another fiesta came. The predictive power of the ONE-ANOTHER syntactic frame set up in the proverb is seen in Francisco starting a turn in overlap with Regina using the same word *stokko* (another). In 19, like in many of her previous moves in this extract, Aurelia resonates the frame of Regina's talk with the addition of a focal element of affective morphology. In this case, it is an affective interjection ↑*ay* and a local place reference *lacchi a'wa* (our valley). The last turn in this extract again displays resonance with a pronoun *né* paradigmatically substituting for the "fiesta of the pueblo" noun phrase. The active indefinite agent coded in the pronoun *né* goes some way toward conveying the active work involved in the offerings to the saints, and the pueblo, that are these festivals. They don't just happen. They have agents in the background making them happen, which is both an honor and a burden. The addition of the phrasal enclitic =*ta* (always) comments on the endless cycling of their recurrent returns.

17	R:		sH-tòko another-one	=a'la =again	e#lini fiesta	yetxé pueblo	o-rina CMP-come		nèé' now	
18	F:		sH-tòko another-one							
19	A:	ay INT	sH-tòko another-one	=a'la =again	e#lini fiesta	yetxé pueblo	o-rina CMP-come	lachi=a'wa valley=1PLI	nèé' now	
20	R:		sH-tòko another-one	=a'la=né =again=ACT3o					nèé' now	=ta =always

Talking about the cyclical round of saints' day festivals also made for other cases where these speakers built resonances. In addition to building intersubjective connections, the resonating frames of talk are well fitted to iconically represent the cyclicity of the ritual calendar. In this next extract, the syntactic structure of a prior speaker is taken as a form to be filled with new content. The sequence highlights the rhematic quality of syntax as a semiotic dimension of form. In Peirce's framework, a rheme is a sign of potentiality. A sentence's syntax is a rheme with internal structure and diagrammatic relations to other instances of such phrase structuring.[2] As we saw earlier, the accumulated uses of form can become influential for subsequent use, such as how the ONE-ANOTHER rheme of the proverb provided grounds for Francisco's prediction of Regina's next move.

Just a few minutes after the previous example, the following exchange took place:

(4) LMSMVDP28Jul0903 00:12:24.52

```
1  Regina:   Peèro aà láa le'e wà' nèé'. (0.5)
             A looking toward (not at) R A| turns gaze forward
             -------|R bows head and shoulders forward
             pèro   à    lá   le'e   wà'    nèé'
             and    INT  NEG  delay  this   now
             And, oh, it won't be long now.
2  Aurelia:  Yexxe a' enta wà' nèé' txee.
             -|R turns gaze toward (not to) A
             yexe=a'a'       enta   wà'    nèé'  txe
             fast=already    comes  this   now   then
             Quickly this comes now then.
3  Regina:   Yexxe a' enta é Orélia.
             yexe=a'a'       enta=é       Orélia
             fast=already    comes=3INAN  Aurelia
             Quickly it comes (the feast of) Aurelia.
4  Aurelia:  Yexxe a' enta wà' nèé'.
             yexe=a'a'       enta   wà'    nèé'
             fast=already    comes  this   now
             Quickly this comes now.
5  Aurelia:  Bicchà txoo oriñña lá Toò Zándo.
             ---------------------------|A head turn-R to R
             bichà    txo     o-rina=lá       tò#zándo
             day      after   CMP-arrive=already  Todos.Santos
             Some days after (the feast of) All Saints already arrived.
6  Regina:   Toò Zándo txo oriñña Sáario.
             --------------------|R bow forward
             tò#zándo        txo     o-rina       Sário
             Todos.Santos    after   CMP-arrive   Rosario
             After All Saints (the feast of) Rosario arrived.
```

Here we see the blueprint of a turn formulation provided by the syntax of a previous turn where resonance is a resource for building connected meanings. Such incremental building can be made visible through the diagraph analysis. The first pair of turns build on an ADVERB-VERB-DEMONSTRATIVE-TEMPORAL rheme with Aurelia adding a temporal adverb (discourse marker) *txe* (then).

```
1  R:   lá                        le'e      wà'     nèé'
        NEG                       delay     this    now
2  A:        yexe=a'a'     enta   wà'       nèé'    txe
             fast=already  come   this      now     then
3  R:        yexe=a'a'     enta=é        Orélia
             fast=already  come=3INAN    Aurelia
4  A:        yexe=a'a'     enta   wà'       nèé'
             fast=already  come   this      now
```

Aurelia repeats the structure of previous turns again in 4 and then in turn 5 fills new content on the rhematic scaffold. I repeat 4 again in this diagraph. In 5, the temporal adverb slot is first filled with *bicchà* (day) and then by *Toò Zándo* (Todos Santos). The verb position *enta* (comes) is then substituted with *oriñña* (arrived). *Wà'* (this) is substituted by *Toò Zándo* in 5 and with *Sáryo* (Rosario) in 6.

```
4  A:    yexe=a'a'                  enta             wà'          nèé'
         fast=already               comes            this         now
5  A:    bichà           txo        o-rina=lá        tò#zándo
         day             after      cmp-arrive=already  Todos.Santos
6  R:    tò#zándo        txo        o-rina           Sá^yo
         Todos.Santos    after      cmp-arrive       Rosario
```

Each step of this dialogue is built from the artifacts of what came before, with such parallelism illustrating a way that conversation, and the knowledge that results from it, is truly a joint activity with emergent properties. Like we saw with repair, more complex social communicative action is composed from more basic human action with the composition taking on emergent function. What came before is a scaffold offered by the prior speaker, which like a gift is accepted and reciprocated. The form is shared over many turns of talk each adding value by the operations of subsequent speakers.

Let's consider several intersubjective functions of resonance building in Lachixío Zapotec. We have already seen in Chapter 4 examples of repetition in initiating and remedying repair, so I will go on from there.

5.4 Resonating Affirmation

A common way of answering a polar question in the affirmative in Lachixío is by repeating the proposition of the question.

```
(5) LMSMVDP09Aug0803 00:28:47.75
1  Daniel:   Kássi láa dò'o' zxa (i') iiña'a txee?
             kási    lá   dò'o'=zxà   i#ña'a    txe
             almost  NEG  put=3DIS    milpa     then
             They don't plant milpas much then?
2  Pedro:    Káss:i láa dò'o' zxa iiña'a.
             P head shake
             kási    lá   dò'o'=zxà   i#na'a
             almost  NEG  put=3DIS    milpa
             They don't plant milpas much.
3  Daniel:   Aà.
             Oh.
```

Daniel formulates a polar question in the negative, "They don't plant milpas much then?" referring to the planting of fields of corn, beans, squash, and other plants in a mutually supportive assemblage. Pedro confirms Daniel's allusion by repeating his formulation in 2 and shaking his head "no," matching the valence of the question. Daniel shows uptake with the change of state token *aà* (oh) in 3.

5.5 Displaying a New Knowledge State by Re-performing Its Sign

Repeating another's talk can be used to display a knowledge state achieved in dialogue after another speaker's turn that answers a question, remedies a repair, or otherwise informs the listener of something new. Such resonating responses can also be used for performing operations on the display of parallel knowledge such as the epistemological challenge of breathy-voiced repeats seen in example 1.

Responses after answers to questions often show the token *Aà* (oh) (as in 3), English oh having also been called the "change of state" token by Heritage (1998) for its marking a new state of informational awareness.

```
(6) LMSMVD21Jul0903 00:23:16.11
1 Flavio:    Nzokkó skà' kaà móttò' wa nèé' la?
             F looking down at chainsaw, P out of frame
             n-zokó=skà'  kà    mótò='=wa         nèé'=la
             STA-sit=yet  truly chainsaw=POS=2pl  now=Q
             Do you all still have your chainsaw?
2 Pedro:     Nzokkó skà' é Flavio.
             n-zokó=skà'=é   Flavio
             STA-sit=yet=3o  Flavio
             Still have it Flavio.
3 Flavio:    Aà nzokkó skà' é nèé' ra!
             à   n-zokó=skà'=é   nèé'=ra
             oh  STA-sit=yet=3o  now=EXCL
             Oh, still have it now!
4 Pedro:     Nzokkó skà' é nèé'.
             n-zokó=skà'=é   nèé'
             STA-sit=yet=3o  now
             Still have it now.
```

In example (6) Flavio asks Pedro if his family still owns their chainsaw. Pedro answers that they do, and as we saw in example (1), the question and answer resonate with parallelisms. Flavio then says, "Oh, you still have it now!" indicating his uptake of this knowledge and additionally marking its affect with the exclamative enclitic *ra*. Pedro affirms in next turn by repeating the proposition again.

While the *Aà* token occurs on some displays of new knowledge, particularly after answers to questions, there are many cases where a display of knowledge gained in conversation is done by repeat alone. Pablo is talking to his grandmother (*Náolla*) about her genealogy. She states, "We were pure family then," which he repeats. The only difference is a deictic shift from her "we" to his "you all," common in cross-speaker repetition.

```
(7) LMSCVDP20Jul0901 00:05:31.18
1 Náolla:    Púuro li'i ro eenze'e txe.
             -------|N index finger point in circular gesture
             ---------------------|N gaze to T
             púro  li'i=ro   e#nze'e    txe
             pure  PRO-1PLX  CLAS-there then
             We were purely family then.
2 Pablo:     Púuro li'i wa eenze'e txe.
             -|T nod
             púro  li'i-wa  e#n-ze'e    txe
             pure  PRO-2PL  CLAS-there  then
             You all were purely family then.
3 Náolla:    Púuro li'i ro eenze'e.
             -|N gaze forward, head bow
```

```
puro   li'i=ro    e#n-ze'e
pure   PRO-1PLX   CLAS-there
```
We were purely family.

Resonances across utterances and their speakers like these put the conversational achievement of shared knowledge on display. The next sections look at resonance with attention to the differing knowledge states of the participants where resonance building is grounded on shared experience, shared cultural knowledge, or asymmetries in knowledge.

5.6 Resonating with Assessments and Informings

5.6.1 Shared Environment

When people are copresent in an environment, common sensory perception can give them shared epistemic access. A prime example is talk about the weather as in example (8) where participants react to a rain storm suddenly coming over the edge of the valley. I had been setting up to work on the elicitation of color terms with Adrian, a knowledgeable elder man, and Giovani was visiting Adrian when I got there. Giovani and Adrian are talking about Giovani's time away at college. Suddenly a rain cloud spills over the mountain rim. Adrian and Giovani are facing the other way, but its presence can be felt in the cool breeze created as the rain displaces the air. Adrian assesses the situation, turning to look to the north, and sees the rain fast approaching (Figure 5.2).

Figure 5.2 Adrian turns to look at the mountain after feeling the cool wind announce the rain, and Giovani follows the direction of his gaze.

(8) LMSMVDP29Jun08 00:19:05.05

1 Adrian: Enta lá kìyyo nii á.=
              -A head and shoulder turn to north
              ----------------|G head turn to north
```
           enta=lá       kìyo   ni=á
           comes=already rain   say=1s
```
              The rain's already coming I say.

2 Giovani: =Enta lá kìyyo yaa. (.)
```
                         =enta=lá         kìyo     ya
                         comes=already    rain     quickly
```
                            The rain's already coming quickly.

3 Adrian: Enta lá kìyyo nèé'. (.24)
```
           enta=lá       kìyo   nèé'
           comes=already rain   now
```
              The rain's already coming now.

Adrian states in 1 that the rain is coming framed by the phrase of speech *nii á* (I say). Giovani, turning his head to the direction of the rain, repeats Adrian's assessment, like we saw with affirmative answers earlier framing it with an adverb *yaa* (quickly). Adrian in turn repeats the frame again substituting the temporal adverb *nèé'* (now) for Giovani's *yaa* (quickly).

5.6.2 Shared History

Where the previous example showed resonance in the display of shared environmental knowledge, a similar yet contrasting epistemic relationship is grounded on historical knowledge, where shared knowledge is from the common ground of cultural experience. The waves of language shift and endangered status of Zapotec in the region is one case in point. In 2008, when this was recorded, almost all children in Lachixío were learning Zapotec as their primary language. Yet people in Lachixío knew that in many nearby communities, the children were no longer learning Zapotec. This common knowledge is the shared epistemic ground for a resonating display of intersubjectivity between Pedro and Daniel in example (9). Pedro and Daniel are seated side by side talking about their travels in the region. Pedro tells Daniel about Zaniza, a town in the historically Papabuco Zapotec area to the west where he worked for a while noting its advanced state of language shift.

(9) LMSMVDP09Aug0803 6:02.890-6:10.5202

1 Pedro: Benné jóbenes, (.85)
```
           bené      jóbenes
           person    young
```
              The youth,

2 Pedro: beè eenze'e eenze'e beè eenze'e láa nii a'la
              beè nze'e dyá'llò.
```
           bè   e#nzè'e      e#nze'e    bè  e#nze'e      lá     ni=a'la
           PL   CLAS#there   CLAS#there PL  CLAS#there   NEG    speak=again
           bè   e#nze'e      dyá'lò
           PL   clas#there   indigenous.language
```
              all of them there, there, all of them there don't speak
              their Zapotec.

3   (0.5)

```
4  Pedro:       Púuro dii stílla [la nii eenze'e.
                -|P gaze toward D, smile
                ---------------|P head nod (3x)
                puro  di#stíla=lá        ni    e#nze'e
                pure  Castilian=already  say   there(topic)
                They speak just³ Spanish there.
5  Daniel:                      [Púu:ro dii stílla.
                                -D nods
                                puro    di#stíla
                                pure    Castilian
                                Just Spanish.
6  Pedro:       Púuro dii stílla la nii enze'e. (.)
                -P nodding, smiling
                púro  di#stíla=lá        ni    enze'e (.)
                pure  Castilian=already  say   there(topic)
                Just Spanish they already speak there.
7  Daniel:      °Púuro dii stílla°.
                púro  di#stíla
                pure  Spanish
                Just Spanish.
```

Pedro states that the youth no longer speak Zapotec (1–2). He goes on to say in 4 that they only speak Spanish there. This turn is performed as an important moment marked off in multiple ways across the semiotic dimensions of the interaction. Pedro creates a dramatic pause in 3, and then as he begins his utterance, he turns his head and gazes to Daniel nodding three times after the name of the Spanish language *dii stílla* (speech [of] Castilians) while holding his gaze on Daniel. Daniel repeats *púu:ro dii stílla* (just Spanish) in 5, which he affectively marks by focusing it with an index of lengthening: *púu:ro* (purely/only/just). Through performative dimensions across modalities, Pedro marked the phrase Daniel repeated as the knowledge he is conveying. In 6, Pedro affirms Daniel's uptake with another repeat. The phrase is repeated one more time by Daniel in 7 marked affectively by whispered voice.

The shared knowledge displayed through the resonating sequence is also a space for a jointly enacted lament of this sociohistorical trajectory of language shift the two share from growing up and traveling in this region, and their moral concern for the future of the language in Lachixío. The dialogic resonance is instrumental in building this moment of empathy. Their conversation goes on after this with Pedro explaining that many years ago while working as a preschool educator in Zaniza, he learned, the community decided by vote in a town hall meeting to speak only Spanish to the children at home. The narrative he heard framed the event as a rupture from an old past to a new future "From this day forward" that itself resonated the "modern" narrative of "progress" so often tied to language shift. The parallel and contrast to the history of Lachixío would be apparent to these interlocutors who know that arguments to stop speaking Zapotec have been made by some teachers arriving since the 1950s and that Lachixío parents met and decided as a community to continue to speak Zapotec at home. At another scale on which resonance acts, the discourse of the teachers was responded to in ways that, along with other social and ideological forces, created parallel responses of language shift in many communities of the region, leaving a few islands with contrasting socialization practices that maintained environments where the indigenous languages continued to thrive at the time of this fieldwork. During my master's and PhD research from 1997 to 2007, resisting this change was celebrated in stories told to me (Sicoli 2011), and in 2008–9 when most of the video recordings for this book project were made, it was exceptional for parents to choose Spanish for child-directed speech in Lachixío. Though by 2018, it could rather be observed as a new norm that young parents in Lachixío were also raising their children in Spanish (Sicoli 2020). This change did not happen by vote but by a slow accumulation of shifts in socialization practices.

5.6.3 Asymmetrical Knowledge

One of the surprising findings of Brown, Sicoli, and Le Guen's comparison of dialogic repetition in three Mesoamerican languages (the Otomanguean Lachixío Zapotec and the Mayan languages Tzeltal and Yucatec) (2010) was that in contrast to the observed uses of repetition in languages like English as represented in the discourse and conversation analysis literature, speakers of the Mesoamerican linguistic area commonly use repeats to display knowledge states that do not include a prior shared dimension. In the conversation from which the extract in (10) is drawn, Pablo and Pedro are seated across from each other at a table. Pablo is telling Pedro about his experience traveling north to the United States a couple of years earlier in search of work with others from the area. The trip was described as one trouble after another and ultimately Pablo returned without finding good enough work to stay. In example (10), Pablo is describing how a bus he was on in northern Mexico went off the road and crashed.

```
(10) LMSMVDP09Aug0802 00:08:02.95
1  Pablo:   Onakkkò' ro auksílyo de eskye' oriñña [ambulánsya beè ì.
            -Pe gaze on Pa
            -Pe gaze on table R-hand circle------|Pa R-hand left to
             right sweep
            --------------------------------|Pa gaze up to Pe
            o-nakò'=ro   auksílyo de eske'    o-rina    ambulánsya bè=ì
            CMP-ask=1PLX police   of like.this CMP-arrive ambulance  PL=3S
            We asked a police officer and like this an ambulance arrived
               for them.
2  Pedro:   -----------------------------------[Pe nods
3           (0.9)
4  Pablo:   Oyaa beè benné ze'e ospitáal beè nóo oyannó á sa'.
            -|Pa gaze to table
            ----------|Pa R-index point up and forward
            o-ya  bè bené  ze'e ospitál bè nó  o-yanó=á       sa'a'
            CMP-go PL person there hospital PL that CMP-go.with=1S REFL
            They went to the hospital, the ones who were traveling with me.
5  Pedro:   Aà ha^HL::
            -Pe nods
            ------|Pa nods
6  Pablo:   °Áwwà° eskye' pyáà stokko see diesióccho
            áwwà   eske'  pyee    sH-tòko  se          diesiócho
            yes    like.this think.1S another-one remaining   eighteen
            Yes, like this I think another eighteen
7           (0.7)
```

```
8  Pablo:      nekka enò nzaa ro.
               -----------|Pa R-hand index point up
               -----------------|Pa gaze to Pe
               ne-aka  enò      nza=ro
               STA-be  who      STA.go=1PLX
               it was who, we were going.
9  Pedro:      Nzaa wa.
               -Pe nods
               nzaa=wa
               STA.go=2PL
               You were going.
```

Pablo tells Pedro that some of his travel companions were injured, and they asked the police to send an ambulance (1). Pedro nods (2) as an affirming backchannel cue (note that, because of the presence of the table, they are facing each other where nods are accessible rather than side by side, where they are less so, as in several earlier examples). Pablo then says that some went to the hospital, and Pedro again responds with a nod and a parallel interjection *Aà ha:* (oh huh) with a marked intonational contour that we can interpret as having made confirmation relevant from Pablo's affirmative response in next position (6). Pablo then says there were eighteen still going north after the accident. Pablo's phrase *Nzaa ro* (We were going) indicates the continuation of the journey after the trauma of the bus accident. This important plot element is what Pedro resonates with. He repeats *Nzaa wa* (You all were going).

Having reached a point in the narrative where the young men continued on their journey, Pablo assesses the good of this tragic story in 10: the good thing is that eighteen of them were able to continue and arrive in the United States.

```
10 Pablo:     Lo bwenno nóo nzaa diesióccho eskye' oriñña ro asta zé'e.
              ----Pa nods-----|Pa head point north----------Pa| gaze to Pe
              ----------------------------Pa| gaze to Pe--Pa| headpoint north
              lo-bwenno nó    nza       diesiócho eske'   o-rina=ro
              it-good     that STA.go   eighteen  like.this CMP-arrive=2PLX
                    asta      zé'e
                    until     there
              The good thing is that eighteen went like this we arrived
                 there.
11 Pedro:     Oriñña wa asta zé'e. (0.4)
              ----------|Pe head point north (blended with nod)
              o-rina=wa       asta    zé'e
              CMP-arrive=2PL  to      there
              You arrived there.
12 Pablo:     Ori'i anna oriñña ro asta zé'e.
              -Pa nods (4x)
              o-ri'i#ana   o-rina=ro        asta   zé'e
              CMP-do#win   CMP-arrive=2PLX  until  there
              We succeeded, we arrived there.
13 Pedro:     Esso.
              -Pe nods
              that
              Exactly.
14 Pablo:     Á:wwà.
              -Pa nods
              Ye:s.
```

15 Pedro: Nelíi kaà né
              ---|Pe eyebrow flash
              -------|Pe gaze to Pa
              ne-lí   kà=né
              STA-upright   truly=ACT3o
              It is certain
16   (0.5)
17 Pedro: waxxhi sufrimiénto nò'o' desde nóo cho'o lò tòkko eeyettxé.
              -|Pe head shake---|Pe gaze down--|Pe gaze to Pa
                        ((a masa grinder starts loudly outside))
              waxhi   sufrimiento nò'o' desde   nó   cho'o=lò   toko   e#yetxé
              much   suffering   be   when   that leave=2s   one   CLAS-town
              there is a lot of suffering when you leave your town.

The place reference in 10 is multimodally complex involving two head points toward the north (the United States) and a distal demonstrative pronoun *zée* used to indicate the far, out-of-sight, location. In 11, we see resonance built in both the verbal dimension and the gestural dimension (Figure 5.3).

Pedro repeats *oriñña wa asta zée* (you all arrived there), again shifting the deictic reference of the pronoun position, and additionally resonates the bodily action also making a head point toward the reference of *zée* (there) (the United States far to the north). The stroke of Pedro's head gesture itself lifts the head and gazes to the north and then the return includes a bending forward of the head and lowering of gaze to blend the gesture with a nod. Pablo responds in 12 *ori'i anna* "we succeeded" (literally

A: Pablo and Pedro Mutual Gaze   B: Pablo Head Point North

C: Pedro Head Point North   D: Pedro Nod

Figure 5.3 Pablo's head point north (B) resonated by Pedro's head point (C) north blended to nod (D).

"we did win") and then repeats the same resonant phrase displayed in Pedro's prior turn *oriñña ro asta zée* (we arrived there). Pedro responds in 13 by nodding with an emphatic *esso*, a lexical item from Spanish meaning "that" and functioning in the region as something like "exactly," and Pablo says "yes" with a parallel nod. These parallel affirmations close this segment of the narrative and Pedro moves to offer "the moral of the story." He says, "It is certain," accompanied with an eyebrow flash and gaze to Pablo and followed by a dramatic pause before continuing, "there is a lot of suffering when you leave your town." While not a couplet formatted proverb like Regina's from example (2), the saying is an expression of known wisdom in the village that relates place, distance, and morality (on this theme in Lachixío discourse and ideology, see Sicoli 2016, Formulating Place, Common Ground, and a Moral Order in Lachixío Zapotec, and on the sayings of Zapotec beliefs see Cruz Santiago 2010).

The repeats in this example are not doing requests for confirmation like earlier repair initiations. The channel is untroubled, and we see actions like Pablo's gaze to Pedro at the end of 8 and 10, which makes Pedro's responses relevant. Pedro is expected to respond at these points, and an appropriate response in the local response system is to repeat a phrase of the prior talk. Since they have good visual access to each other, the repeats are doing much more than audible back-channeling. In cases like these it is apparent that the resonance is marking waypoints on a map of the developing intersubjective territory.

5.7 Contrasts in Morphology across Resonant Frames

We've seen a few cases of stance-taking acts in examples of prior sections, though I want to now focus our attention on this topic. The dialogic semiotic triad in which an interpretant sign (here a conversational move) links to prior sign-object (a prior move) is an environment with an emergent affordance for stance-taking. Resonance often plays an important part in the triadic relation because a prior phrase or action can be repeated to iconically prompt the indexical binding of sign-object and stance-taking metasign. Examples in this section focus on morpheme shifts in otherwise parallel frames that mark different epistemic relations to a message.

5.7.1 Epistemics of Saying and Seeing in Lachixío

Evidentiality marks the source of knowledge of a proposition, and many languages are known to have dedicated morphology to contrast sources of knowledge such as that gained through empirical observation (sometimes contrasting sight with other senses), through hearsay, through inference, and through liturgical texts (see, for example, Aikenwald 2004 on evidentiality). Zapotec languages are not described as having systems of grammatical evidentiality, but in Lachixío conversations source of knowledge is frequently marked, or questioned, indicating an ongoing pragmatic concern with epistemics that is regularly marked with phrases of "saying" and "seeing." Linguists who work on languages with morphological evidentiality have pointed out that using the

Figure 5.4 Sofia sets a tortilla on the comal as Mary assesses the smoke.

term "evidentiality" to refer to these functions in Lachixío conversation may diffuse the research of linguists who have worked hard to define evidentiality in languages where it is grammatically and obligatorily marked. But these systems can often be shown to involve advanced grammaticalization of verbs of seeing and saying, so perhaps the pervasive yet not obligatory concern with source of knowledge in Lachixío represents a cultural ecology in which an evidential morpho-syntax could emerge. The Lachixío verbs of seeing and saying used in these functions do in fact show some grammaticalization since they are used without inflection. In any case, marking source of knowledge is very frequent in Lachixío conversation, and in many cases the source of knowledge is the varied focal part of an otherwise identical frame resonance (Figure 5.4).

```
(11)  LMSMVDP23Jul09  01:01:27.19

1  Mary:    Tomaà jri'i zxénne, berdáa?
            to-mà         r-ri'i      zxéne     berdá
            a.lot         HAB-do      smoke     true
            It's making a lot of smoke, true?

2  Sofia:   Tomaà kàlla' jri'i né ri'yya á          txee.
            to-mà      kàla'      r-ri'i=né         ri'ya=á      txe
            a.lot      true       HAB-do=ACT3o      see=1s       then
            It's truly making a lot of smoke I see then.

   Mary:    to-mà                r-ri'i      zxéne      berdá
            a.lot                HAB-do      smoke      true

   Sofia:   to-mà      kàla'     r-ri'i      =né        ri'ya=á
            a.lot      true      HAB-do      ACT3o      see=1s
```

Example (11) illustrates use and epistemic function for *ri'yya á* (I see) as a response to the statement with the tag question "true?" Mary is assisting Sofia making tortillas and comments, "It's making a lot of smoke, true?" Sofia resonates Mary's formulation with two morphological additions that relate to the truth of the proposition.

Now consider another exchange from the same video. Sofia has just announced that she is going to count the tortillas (to see if they made the quota that would fulfill her family's service obligation to provide tortillas to the town authorities). Looking to what they will do next Mary asks, "Then what's for breakfast I say."

```
(12) LMSMVDP23Jul09 00:21:27.91
1 Mary:    Asta nóo xhii dàkko sillà' nii á?
           asta nó    xhi  dàko silà'         ni=á
           to   that  how  eat  breakfast     say=1s
           Then what's for breakfast I say?
2 Sofia:   %Áwwà nii á xhii dàkko sillà' nii á%?
           áwà   ni=á  xhi  dàko  silà'        ni=á
           yes   say=1s how  eat   breakfast   say=1s
           %Yes, I say, what's for breakfast I say%?
3 Sofia:   %Láa ri'i á be'yya xhii dàkko sillà' ni'i á í::%.
           lá    ri'i=á be'ya         xhi  dàko  silà'      '-ni=á=é
           neg   do=1s  sign          how  eat   breakfast  ACT=say=1s=3o
           %I don't know what's for breakfast I do say it::%.
```

Framing her proposition with a first-person phrase of speaking "I say," the statement is marked as her own opinion. Sofia replies with an affirmative interjection marked with a first-person phrase of speaking *Áwwà nii á* "Yes, I say" and then resonating the rest of Mary's frame including the first-person phrase of speaking *nii á* "I say." This expresses that she is of that same opinion (the two women have been up since before dawn making tortillas without eating). Sofia goes on to say that she doesn't know what's for breakfast resonating the frame again for this new purpose. She preposes the construction, *Láa ri'i á be'yya* (I don't know) (literally, I don't make a sign), and then substitutes a more active first-person phrase of speaking at the end using the active glottalization morpheme on the verb and in an overtly transitive construction *ni'i á í* (I do say it).[4] The phrase of speech "I say" declares opinion without claim to empirical observation. In addition to the "I say" phrase, this example illustrates the more active and explicitly transitive phrase of speech that we've seen many times in the examples of the previous chapters *ni'i á (í)/* (pronounced [nya'á í:]) and which we see in the next example can also occur in a non-overtly transitive structure without the object pronoun *ni'i á*.

Example (13) shows a difference between empirical knowledge and the presence and absence of the use of *ri'yya á* (I see). Flavio, a lumberjack, has seen firsthand the damage from a chainsaw wound. Here Flavio makes an assessment for Pedro that chainsaws are dangerous. He frames this with the phrase of seeing *ri'yya á* (I see).

```
(13) LMSMVDP21Jul0903 00:22:12.26
1 Flavio:  Pelígrò móttò ri'ya á ni'i á Béttò.
           pelígrò     mótò      ri'ya=á     '-ni=á     Béto-L
           dangerous   chainsaw  see=1s      ACT-say=1s Pedro-CLAS
           I see chainsaws are dangerous I do say, Pedro.
```

2 Pedro:	Ay nóo pelígrò móttò nóo nii lò Flávio.
	ay nó pelígrò mótò nó ni=lo Flávio-ʟ
	ɪɴᴛ that dangerous chainsaw that say=2s Flavio-ᴄʟᴀꜱ
	Ay that chainsaws are dangerous that you say Flavio.

The diagraph brings out the contrasts. The first focal difference is in Pedro's interjection *ay* that frames his repeat with a display of affect. But where Flavio uses the verb of seeing, the sight verb is not reproduced in Pedro's resonating repeat as Pedro does not have such direct experience. Additionally, where Flavio uses an emphatic active form of the verb of saying (in addition to seeing), Pedro uses a less-active verb and shifts the deictic reference to second person, indexing Flavio as the source of this information.

Flavio:			pelígrò	mótò		ri'ya=á	'=ni=á
			dangerous	chainsaw		see=1s	ᴀᴄᴛ-say=1s
Pedro:	ay	nó	pelígrò	mótò	nó		ni=lò
	ɪɴᴛ	that	dangerous	chainsaw	that		say=2s

There are at least two other possible contrasts in this framing position that we've also seen in the previous chapters. As we saw in the wedding gift extracts of Chapter 2, *nii zxa* (they say), with variants *nii benné* (the people say) and *nii no* (the elders say), can be used for hearsay and for received wisdom (see Sicoli 2010a). Another phrase of speech with the first-person possessed heart as subject, *nii arkì' á* (says my heart), indicates a feeling or desire. This set of contrasting verbal constructions can be observed at work in the conversational ecology of dialogic syntax. They depict embodied sensory relations to epistemology with seeing as empirical fact, saying by self as opinion, by other people as received knowledge or hearsay, and by the heart as feeling, desire, or emotion.

5.7.2 Phrase-Final Enclitic Morphology

Phrase-final enclitic morphology in Lachixío can mark an utterance as a polar question interrogative =*la*, an affective exclamative =*ra*, an epistemic marker of knowing affirmation =*ri*, and as always so =ta. Of these only the polar question enclitic is easily elicited. The polar question and exclamative enclitics are very common in conversation, while the epistemic marker =*ri*, and always so =ta are rare only occurring a handful of times in almost fifty hours of video-recorded conversation (though several times in the same interaction). We have already seen each of these in the previous chapters, so I will present brief exemplification here (=ta is seen in example 2, line 6 and example 3, line 20 of this chapter and in example 1 of chapter 2, lines 11 and 13).

5.7.2.1 Phrase-Final =la
(14) LMSMVDP28Jul0905 00:08:14.68

1 Táolla:	Yáà tanna' tome' ó'nà' re pâ.
	T out of frame to left
	H*-yà tana' to-me'e' ó'nà' re pà.á
	ᴘᴏᴛ-go touch a.little oxen.team around son.1s
	Go and work a little with the oxen my son.

```
2  Pedro:    Txee tanna' lò ó'nà' la?
             -P gaze to E----------|M gaze to E
             txe   tana'=lò ó'nà'       =la
             then  touch=2s  oxen.team  =Q
             Then you work with the oxen?
3  Marta:    A'nna lò ó'nà' la?
             ----------------|M gaze to oxen
             a'na=lò    ó'nà'      =la
             plow=2s    oxen.team  =Q
             You plow with the oxen?
4  Efraín:   Eé?
             Huh?
5  Pedro:    A'nna lò í la txee?
             ------|P nods
             a'na=lò=í=la    txe
             plow=2s=3ANIM=Q then
             You plow with them then?
6  Carla:    A'nna lò ó'nà' la?
             a'na=lò    ó'nà'      =la
             plow=2s    oxen.team  =Q
             You plow with the oxen?
```

Example (14) occurred when a family was having a picnic taking a break from weeding their *milpa* (Figure 5.5). The grandfather says to the little boy Efraín that he is going to work a little with the oxen. Addressing the boy directly, this is an offer by the grandfather for the boy to learn to plow with the oxen team. The boy doesn't respond, not catching

Figure 5.5 Efraín helps his grandfather work the oxen to weed the milpa.

the indirectness of the offer. Over the next few turns of talk, three different people iterate this offer to Efraín, each of them resonating the frame of the grandfather. They are less indirect, formulating their turns explicitly as yes/no questions with the polar question enclitic. Beside the polar question enclitic, each shows minor additions, subtractions, and paradigmatic substitutions. For instance, Pedro adds a second-person pronoun to the verb *tanna'* (touch) (meaning "work with" here in a common Mesoamerican usage), and Marta substitutes a related but more specific verb *a'nna* (plow) in 3. After Marta's turn Efraín initiates open-class repair *Eé?* (Huh?), and Pedro then resonates Marta's frame substituting the animal pronoun *=í* for the noun *ó'nnà'* (oxen). Carla also resonates this frame with the same noun as Marta. After a couple of more turns of dialogue, the grandfather just gives the boy a directive "get up" and Efraín gets up and joins him.

This example of repetition in child-directed speech illustrates some aspects of the richness of dialogic stimulus for children learning a language. In just a few turns of talk we find nouns and pronouns being swapped and paradigmatically substitutable verbs being exchanged for each other. While the iterations are in a sense doing "the same" action, they do it with such active variation that the affordances of the grammar and lexicon are on display as in the diagraphic representation.

```
Táola:    tana'             to-me'    ó'nà'
          touch             a.little  oxen.team
Pedro:    tana'     =lò               ó'nà'         =la
          touch     =2s               oxen.team     =Q
Andrea:   a'na      =lò               ó'nà'         =la
          plow      =2s               oxen.team     =Q
Pedro:    a'na      =lò               =í            =la
          plow      =2s               =3anim        =Q
Elvia:    a'na      =lò               ó'nà'         =la
          plow      =2s               oxen.team     =Q
```

5.7.2.2 Phrase-Final =ra

We have seen the exclamative enclitic *=ra* mainly in first position (on first-pair parts) in Chapters 2 and 4. In example (15) we see it on a second pair-part. Mary and Sofia are making tortillas, and Mary makes an assessment about the cuff of her pant getting wet last night. Sofia makes a second assessment resonating much of the frame and adding the exclamative enclitic.

(15) LMSMVDP23Jul09 00:08:49.70

```
1 Mary:    Lánna' kye' ri'yya kyeè loo mangérà okwattxà li'i á entxè.
           lána'  ke'  ri'ya#kè#lo     mangérà o-kwatxà        li'i=á entxè
           pants  DEF  see#eye#face    cuff    CMP-make.wet    PRO=1s last.night
           These pants, I can see that I got the cuff wet last night.

2 Sofia:   Aà atti mangérà kàlla' okwattxà li'i=lò entxè ra!
           -S looks at Mary's pants
           à  ati   mangérà kàla'  o-kwatxà        li'i=lò     entxè=ra
           oh given cuff    truly  CMP=get.wet     PRO=2s      last.night=EXL
           Oh, It's certain that you truly got the cuff wet last night!
```

The dialogic syntactic relations are made clear in the diagraph representation. There is a paradigmatic relationship set up between Mary's *ri'yya kyeé loo* (see [with eyes of the face]) and Sophia's *atti* (given), which both have epistemic function. Sophia also adds further epistemic marking with *kàlla'* (truly), and =*ra* takes scope over the resonating frame for exclamative function.

```
Mary:  ri'ya#kè#lo       mangérà            o-kwatxà       li'i =a   entxè
       see#eye#face      cuff               CMP-make.wet   PRO  =1s  last.night
Sofia: ati               mangérà kàla'      o-kwatxà       li'i =lò  entxè            =ra
       given             mangera truly      CMP=make.wet   PRO  =2s  last.night  =EXL
```

5.7.2.3 Phrase-Final =ri

In example (16) we see a phrase-final enclitic that never showed up in elicitation interviews and never in monologic narratives: =*ri*. This enclitic has been described by community members as emphatic agreement, and through consideration of the sequences of spontaneous talk, we see it marks an epistemic stance where a responding speaker makes a claim of being committed to the proposition, often through prior knowledge as in example (3). I gloss this as K+AF indicating affirming from a positive knowledge state following Heritage and Raymond's use of K+ and K− for greater and lesser knowledge in dyadic participation frames (2002, 2005) and use "indeed" as a free translation. Another way that Sofia indicates her commitment to the proposition is that she subsequently resonates Mary's frame two times (without =*ri*) in lines 4 and 5 with low intensity.

```
(16) LMSMVDP23Jul09 00:15:00.14

1  Mary:    Waxxhi beè endò' ndxò.
            -------|S head turn-L to M
            waxhi   bè    endò'=ndxò
            much    PL    child=3F
            She has many children.

2  Sofia:   Waxxhi beè endò' ndxò ri.
            ------------------------|S nods
            waxhi   bè    endò'=ndxò=ri
            much    PL    child=3F=K+AF
            She has many children, indeed.

3           (1.5) S presses tortilla

4  Sofia:   °Waxxhi beè endò' ndxò°.
            -------S head turn-L to M
            waxhi   bè    endò'=ndxò
            much    PL    child=3F
            She has many children.

5  Sofia:   °Waxxhi beè endò' ndxò°.
            -------S head turn-L to M
            waxhi   bè    endò'=ndxò
            much    PL    child=3F
            She has many children.
```

These are just a few examples that illustrate some of the most common morphemes used to contrast dialogically resonant frames.

5.8 Resonance Mediates Disagreement by Building on Agreement

In improvisation theater, there is a strategy for improvising that is referred to as "yes and . . . thinking" that is also often employed in classrooms to value answers by a student and to then build on or redirect the contribution. While overt disagreement is rare in Lachixío discourse, disputes and differences of opinion do occur, and their resolution is something achieved turn-by-turn in conversation.

(17) LMSMVDP21Jul0903 00:02:25:000

```
1 Kacha:    Pyáá chó'o tòkko ayyò' tróssa zé'e.
            pyáá      H*-cho'o  tòko  ayò'  troso  zé'e
            think.1s  POT-go.out one   five   piece  there
            I think we'll get five pieces out of it there.
2 Flavio:   A'a ásta loo púndo ká' é ra!
            a'a   ásta   lo    púndo   H*-ka'a=é=ra
            NEG   until  face  point   POT-extend=3O=EXCL
            No, to the end it will extend!
3 Kacha:    Ásta loo púndo ká' né chó'o ayyò' ra!
            ásta   lo    púndo  H*-ka'a=né  H*-cho'o   ayò'=ra
            until  face  point  POT-extend=3O POT-go.out five=EXCL
            To the end it will extend (and) we'll get five pieces out of it!
```

In example (17), we do see a rare overt disagreement. Kacha, Sabina, Stefan, and Flavio are talking about the work Flavio and his son Stefan are doing to cut planks from a log with a chainsaw. Kacha asserts her opinion that she thinks they will get five planks from the log. Flavio overtly disagrees saying that the planks will extend to the end of the log (implying, since the log is tapered, that they will get less. In another turn of the larger sequence, he suggests four). In 3, Kacha resonates Flavio's assessment, but not his negation, and expands on this in a larger phrase with a repetition of her own assessment in 1, resonances that connect to both Flavio's and her prior turns. Another resonance between Flavio's assessment on 2 and the retort of Kacha in 3 is the parallel framing with exclamative affect.

Since resonance has a role in displaying agreement and mapping the territory of common ground, it can play an important role in mediating disputes and disagreements. This will be important to remember as we examine how disputes around artifact production are resolved in Chapter 6.

5.9 Chiasmus

Chiasmus is a poetic process in which grammatical constructions, words, or concepts are reversed between two halves of a resonant unit. The name itself is taken from "crossing" like the crosswise arrangement of the Greek letter *chi* χ. As a final example, consider the chiasmus demonstrated in example (18).

(18) LMSMVDP21Jul0903 28:43.86-28:48.06

```
1 Naà:   Ozàkkà wa. Salvadór chii tzoò.
         L*-o-zakà=wa              Salvadór  chi    tzò
         IMP-CMP-be.quiet=2pl      Salvador  quiet  sit
         Be quiet you all. Salvador sit quietly.
2 Paà:   Zàkkà Salvadór. Chii kwaa wa.
         L*-zaka                   Salvadór  chi    kwa=wa
         IMP-(POT)-be.quiet        Salvador  quiet  freeze=2pl
         "Be quiet Salvador. You all stay quiet."
```

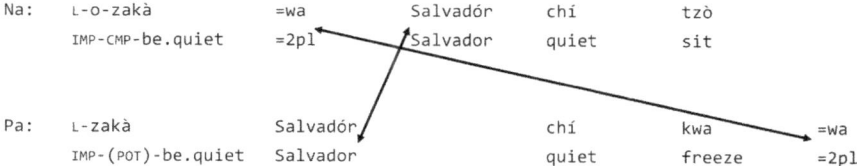

Figure 5.6 Chiasmatic resonance between parents.

In this interaction, the mother and father are outside talking on the patio, and their children are playing loudly with each other in the middle of the conversational formation of the parents. The mother says, "Be quiet you all" and then singles out the oldest child then saying, "Salvador sit quietly." The father resonates her frame but with a chiasmatic syntactic transformation. "Be quiet Salvador," he says, switching Salvador into the subject position where the mother had the pronoun "you all" and moving the second-person plural pronoun to the subject of the second sentence "You all stay quiet." The diagraph in Figure 5.6 is marked with double-headed arrows to show the crossing transformation of focal differences between otherwise parallel frames. In the proximal timespaces of dialogic interaction, two people build and rebuild from lexical-syntactic resources they borrow from each other and recycle (see also Bueno Holle 2019: 103–7 on chiastic structures in Zapotec discourse serving to bind two turns together into a couplet; and more generally in dyadic conversation, see Silverstein 1984) (Figure 5.6).

This example of a crossing transformation across resonant frames is a narrow case of the poetics of chiasmus, but upon reflection, it prompts the more general observation that the logic of dialogic resonance is one of a jointly constructed chiasmatic syllogism. The twinned dynamics of frame resonances that build similarity and focal resonances that build difference complement each other in the emergent, diagrammatical whole. Roy Wagner (2017: 4) describes chiasmatic logic as a *double-proportional comparison* where "two things are compared to each other twice" "creating a self-symmetrical analogical anti-structure in which each of the two comparatives is analogous to the other in the same way that the other is analogous to it." The double-proportional comparison of dialogic resonance is one between parts of the diagrammatic icon—a whole collaboratively built between participants through their dialogue: the focal resonance is the difference between the first and second moves (the discord), and the frame resonance is the similarity (the harmony). Resonance grammar works to understand grammatical patterns through the double-proportional comparison afforded by peoples' joint action in dialogue.

5.10 Concluding Remarks

Resonance building is a frequent joint project in Lachixío conversations. To resonate can be to agree, to signal to go on, to index waypoints on the discursive map of a developing intersubjective territory. A resonating frame can be a field in which to contrast voice, intonation, or morphology, and through which to challenge and demand an account. Resonance can mark scope of epistemic morphology, claim epistemic primacy, question understanding, and initiate repair. Resonance can provide agreement in disagreement. Resonance sparks a moment of connection that invites a search for its relevance. Resonance, in short, is a dimension through which the *genius of a language* (Sapir 1921) does its work of connecting humans in habitual joint actions that, consequentially, puts the workings of grammar on display. Because resonance is dialogically emergent, it cannot be approached through introspection, elicitation, or monologic text collections, but requires corpora of people actually doing their work with language in interactions. As with repair, resonance building in interaction supports Peirce's philosophical convictions that much of human reasoning (and knowledge) is diagrammatic (CP 1.54) and that a mind is not limited to or contained within an individual but is emergent in dialogic process (CP 5.128).

While Jakobson by the mid-twentieth century pointed out the elemental importance of recurrent returns to language and called for it to be an essential focus for grammatical study, parallelism went on to play little explicit role in the canon of grammatical analysis in linguistics since the 1960s. This chapter has, I hope, demonstrated that engaging the pervasive resonance building activity of conversational interaction links grammatical analysis in nontrivial ways to the pragmatics of sociality and intersubjectivity that shape languages over short and long timescales. While periodically, some attention returns to resonances as transformations, including Hockett (1987) as described earlier, or Brown (1968) who wrote that "the changes produced in sentences as they move between persons in discourse may be the richest data for the discovery of grammar," there has been slight effect on paradigms of linguistic theory or language documentation.[5] More recently, Du Bois (2014: 391–2) argued that "the full human capacity for language is realized only when interlocutors engage with one another to articulate the relation between their respective meanings." He goes on to say that "from a cognitive-functional perspective, then, syntactic abstractions may represent grammaticized adaptations to the demands of structural coupling between interlocutors and their utterances. Adaptation to engagement yields a virtuous circle of reproduction, emergence, grammaticization, and affordance." Considering a dialogically emergent syntactic order of language as the whole asks us to think differently about its component parts than when thinking about the parts alone.

In arguing for incorporating linguistic theory into the work of grammar writing, Keren Rice (2006) asks whether the language can tell its own story without the guiding of linguistic theory. In the same volume, Dench and Evans (2006: 27) point to future directions in grammar writing afforded by the technological advances in the real-time recording of discourse. They say that discourse-oriented approaches emphasize parsing, and the interpretation of hearers rather than the sentence generation of speakers privileged in elicitation. But still language is conceptualized more as a conduit for the "successful transmission of meaning" than its coproduction. Dialogic Syntax is an order of linguistic theory that examines not what is "transmitted" between individuals but what is jointly built between them. Resonance grammar approaches, including Dialogic Syntax, foreground an auto-grammatical dimension parallel in goal to the self-representation of auto-ethnography, and the ethnomethodological goal of understanding how participants themselves orient to the activity they are engaged in together.

Resonance grammar is also fitted to the task of understanding "language in its cultural context" as called for by many language documentation funding agencies and a goal of many documentary linguists. Greg Urban (1996: 21) wrote that *replication* is a particularly revealing way to approach the entextualization of language "for it involves an examination not only of the original and copied discourse, but also of the social relationships obtaining between originator and copier," which as we have seen often involves epistemic relations between participants.

Engaging actual interaction for thinking about grammatical description also raises questions about relationships between talk and bodies in interaction, tools and objects, and the many possible configurations, substitutions, and alternations among semiotic modalities. While several examples in this chapter touched on the building of intermodal resonances, in Chapter 6 we explicitly consider how the Lachixío Zapotec language is shaped by, and shaping of, collaborations for the production and repair of material artifacts—language games where the joint production is not an abstract intersubjective territory, but a material object built in the world.

6

Build

On the goal of philosophy of language and in light of the focused logics of language games that had transformed his thinking about language, Wittgenstein wrote, "We want to establish an order in our knowledge of the use of language: an order with a particular end in view, one out of many possible orders; not the order.... The confusions which occupy us arise when language is like an engine idling, not when it is doing work" (1958: no. 132). We have developed an understanding in the previous chapters of how a language and its speakers work toward particular ends of human sociality and intersubjectivity, themselves emergently enabled by our cognitive abilities to cooperate in joint activities. Such joint activity can be as mundane as moving a log *together*, or deciding what to share for breakfast, to the complex collaborations that navigate a ship into port, or land a probe on an asteroid. The building of social and intersubjective relations is itself coordinated multimodally. We previously examined joint actions that build social relations and reputations in the language of offers (Chapter 2) and recruitments (Chapter 3). And we saw how offers and recruitments are themselves components of an emergent order of language use that builds intersubjectivity through the joint actions of repairs (Chapter 4) and collaborative construction of resonances (Chapter 5). Each chapter was informative of how the Lachixío Zapotec language was fit to the generic qualities, contingencies, and purposes of social actions that offer, recruit, repair, and resonate, but which were always accomplished through the historically local semiotic resources in interactions that unfolded in real time among copresent participants. In this chapter, I want to take our understanding of the relationship and intersubjectivity-building work we examined in the previous chapters as background to cast light on the relations between the Lachixío Zapotec language and the built-world of material artifacts. Working within the framework of multimodal semiosis, I examine how the form of the language is itself shaped when involved in building a material environment. We can look at these collaborations as higher-order language games built up from the lower-order language games we have already examined in Chapters 2 through 5. In addition to Wittgenstein's later writings, examining language as it is put to work was suggested long ago by anthropologist Bronislaw Malinowski (1935), who studied the pragmatically oriented language of magic, gardening, and sailing in the Trobriand Islands, as well as in the pragmatism of Peirce (see, for example, *The Essential Peirce: Selected Philosophical Writings (1893-1913)* 1998). The social accomplishment of working together has more recently also been the focus of research on joint and distributed cognition (see, for example, the professional vision of Goodwin 1994, distributed cognition of Hutchins 1995, and joint activities of Clark 2006). A focus on social-material accomplishment is facilitated by current digital video technology which can complement methods of participant observation and goals of grammatical description.

Joint activities involve what Herb Clark (2006) has referred to as a two-tiered structure where we can, on the one hand, look at the coordinated activity itself as a joint activity and, on the other hand, see that the joint actions of interaction also coordinate such joint activity. The latter "allows [people] to arrange, agree on, or coordinate who is to do what, when, and where" (Clark 2006: 128). Joint action is nested within joint actions which are consequential in considering how actions and commitments "stack up" to distribute agency across the human and nonhuman participants of a collaborative activity over the time of the event. With attention to the two tiers of joint activity, we again shift ontological scales in this chapter, to examine how social actions that offer, recruit, repair, and resonate compose coordinated actions through which participants arrive at, and jointly commit to, decisions of what will be done, by whom, when, and how, with what tools, and in which way.

The two video segments presented in this chapter involve people working in teams to collaborate in projects that build some enduring part of their world. First, we will glimpse a fateful, jointly achieved decision in an elderly couple's work fabricating saddle straps. And then, we return to the scene that opened Chapter 1, to examine an extended sequence in which a family works together to improvise a new turkey enclosure the day after a turkey was killed by a predator. When one bad idea begins to be reproduced, we examine the work of negotiation it took to back out of the joint commitments to this idea, and the development of second idea that emerged through interaction. Both of these trajectories left their marks on the enduring artifact.

6.1 Epistemics, Distributed Agency, and the Accrual of Commitments

Multiparty participation in a common project entails that multiple individuals with differing life histories, skill sets, and knowledge of materials and techniques contribute to a common goal. The different individuals may also be invested to different degrees. In collaborative hunting, the different parties may be equally invested in the outcome where the food will be distributed, but in repairing an item that belongs to one individual, the helper will not benefit to the same degree as the owner. Such a helper may be more principally invested in gifting labor to build a social relationship with the owner being helped. The two projects we look at in this chapter show varied relationships: different levels of knowledge about the tasks of fabrication or assembly, and different relationships and responsibilities of the participants to each other.

I will argue here for an ontology of objects in these projects where objects themselves take on participation status with a distributed and contingent agency afforded by their form and relations to the other participants. Symbolic acts of commitment to objects in the local history are important to developing this ontology. Objects can come to exert a contingent influence on choices and decisions as they become signs of the joint commitments accrued over the development of a project. To understand a sequence of actions in a collaborative project, including the decision making that results in coproduced artifact form, it is important to attend to this distributed agency accrued in the joint commitments displayed and referenced in the emergent timespaces of cooperative action.

In addition to form relations and audiovisually marked commitments to them, to understand the persuasive power of objects in joint activities, we must also recognize that some objects have commodity values that need to be taken as background knowledge in the cultural common ground of the participants. They are not simply objects, or objects with a local and immediate interactional history, but types of objects that, not locally produced, generate constraints on material choice. We see in several segments, for example, that rope is a valued commodity that influences choices that shape material formations and the flows of interaction that produce them.

The transcripts of this chapter illustrate the persuasive power of things in human collaborations. Sometimes the things are parts of projects or whole project assemblages, sometimes the things are linguistic constructions or the larger pragmatic assemblage to which they are part. How do things take on a power to coerce and influence actions in their presence? The process-ontology of semiosis presents a way. Paul Kockelman, building on Peirce, illustrated how agency can reside in a form that predicts its use vis-à-vis its user. For example, while not excluding innovative or deviant uses, a tool designed to fit the human hand exerts an agency to be picked up and used with this intention of the designer, an observation crucial to much archaeological interpretation. Also building on Peirce, though mainly through the index rather than on the more complete phenomenology where Kockelman starts, Alfred Gell discussed how art objects can create agentive effects, such as how the form of a painting can lead the eye of an observer across a canvas (Gell 1998). In these cases commitments to producing forms and relations of prior actors, such as in the form of a hammer or a hand axe, a painting, or a sculpture, a structural part of a larger object or building, or a grammatical construction, exert a suggestive influence on how subsequent users commit to interpreting and using the objects (see also Whorf 1941 on how material language form accrues and guides habitual language use and habitual thought).

6.1.2 Joint Decisions and Joint Commitments

Copresent joint action involves joint decision making. Even where one individual may lead the activity, the need for collaboration necessitates that there be ways of convincing or persuading others to come on board. These can be grounded in a social hierarchy, as in a military chain of command, and some rank-focused family structures in which the orders of a higher-ranked individual are not to be challenged. Or they can be grounded in a more egalitarian set of social relations such as how a "big man/big woman" leads, not by directive, but by example—an intrinsic mode of semiosis, where the sign is its referent (Ekman and Friesen 1969). Addressing joint decision making in collaborative activities, Tomasello, imagining a scenario of a collaborative hunt, focuses on how communication strategies may be used to argue for the best course of collaborative action. The types of utterances he imagines range from pointing at animal tracks for another's common ground-based inference of direction of travel to providing an explicit account of prior knowledge hypothesizing a different direction based in an implicit claim that the first inference of direction was grounded on faulty reasoning. Maybe another participant argues that the tracks were not made today, or that there is evidence that someone approaching the problem from a different epistemic state knows better because he or she saw the animals moving in a different direction on another path. Tomasello (2014) sees everyday joint decision making as a rhetorical process through which one must *convince* another of the merits of a particular course of action as preferred to another. A broadly parallel yet specifically distinct view of joint decision making emerges when we work through the data of the videos examined in this chapter. These are actual examples of emplaced collaborations rather than made-up philosophical examples. They provide material to think about persuasion as emergent and distributed in multimodal assemblages with both human and nonhuman participants rather than locating persuasion in an individualized intentional agency of one individual convincing another. The agency for deciding a course of action is not located in one or even all of the human actors, but is distributed across human participants, nonhuman objects with participant status, and in the form of the prior talk and other semiotic action that creates expectations and moral obligations for next moves. Enfield and Kockelman (2017) describe such distributed agency as "flexible and accountable causality." Examining spontaneous sequences in actual joint activities in Lachixío, we see strikingly different modes of argumentation ranging from explicit argumentation in Tomasello's thought experiment to the intrinsic (inherently iconic and indexical) leading by example of big men/big woman described in anthropological literature (Sahlins 1968; Lepowski 1990; and for review, Lederman 1990, 2015). In many acts of convincing, linguistically explicit argumentation is not necessarily the primary persuasive device for achieving a joint commitment to a decision. Where symbolic reference, the assumed high achievement or sine qua non of human cognition, fails, it is readily abandoned for iconic signs that depict, or intrinsic signs that perform the action for a consociate rather than refer to it. Thus, one outcome of my analysis in this chapter is showing that multimodal analysis of actual discourse through which people achieve a joint activity is crucial to philosophical inquiry into collaborative decision making, the art of persuasion, and the reproduction and change of human institutions.

6.2 Symmetrical Social Relations and Epistemic Asymmetry in Saddle Repair

Pedro visited his elderly uncle and aunt. The husband, Toò Francisco, and wife, Toò Felicita, were working together to fabricate saddle cinch straps by recycling woven plastic bags (*kostálle*, Sp. *costal*) originally used for corn seed or fertilizer. During playback interviews in Lachixío, the two were described as being in a relatively symmetrical social relationship. Their shared general familiarity with the task and with each other comes through in the video and the transcript where little talk is exchanged

Figure 6.1 Felicita and Francisco talk about fastening rope to the strap.

that explicitly manages their joint activities, so it is notable when it does. Apart from comments about their materials and out-loud talk about the state of the task, most of the talk was about unrelated things like making jokes, chatting about the cool wind blowing that day, the state of crops, and making hopeful dialogues about what a good rain would do for the crops. While a relatively egalitarian social relationship exists between the couple, it becomes clear over the course of the interaction that Francisco has epistemic authority for tying knots. Extracts (1) and (2) are two of the interactions that involved talk to coordinate their collaboration.

6.2.1 This Rope or the Thick One?

Just before the transcript extract (1) Felicita offers Francisco a *kostálle* that she folded to produce the form of a cinch strap that will fasten the saddle around a burro's belly (see Figure 6.1). As she offers it to Francisco, she says that it needs rope (to lash the end loop which will fasten to one side of the saddle). She then presents him with a choice of two ropes using an either/or grammatical construction.

```
(1) LMSMVDP25Jul0902 46:00-46:24

2  Felicita:   Toò kyè' nèé' oo neròkko xettà é la?
               Fe picks up ropes to her left and begins to separate them
               tò    kè'   nèé' o   ne-ròko  xetà=é=la
               rope  this  now  or  STA-thick much=3o=Q
               This rope now or the one that's a lot thicker?
```

3 Francisco: **Láa ròkko é.**
   ------------|Fr head shake
   lá   ròko=é
   neg thick=3o
   Not the thick one.

4   (0.8)
           Fe separates one rope from another
           Fr bunches folded-over end of strap

When Francisco accepts the *kostálle* Felicita has offered him, Felicita asks him the question in 2 to determine which rope he wants to use. His epistemic authority in the seizing/lashing task is constructed in her offer of the strap to him and in deferring the rope choice to him, though it is important to note that in formulating her question as an either/or construction, Felicita is the one who lays out the grounds for his answer. Felicita's turn is formulated as an alternative question indicating a rope at hand, *toò kyè'* (this rope), and describing a thicker competing alternative, *neròkko xettà é* ([a] much thicker one). Francisco responds in 3, "Not the thick one," which leaves him with the "choice" of "this one."

5 Felicita: **Níngyè' stokko.=**
   Fe pulls cord through hand to hold two ends offering to Fr.
   nínge'   sH-tòko
   thing   another-one
   This other one.=

6 Francisco: = ↑Mm. Áà.
   Fr grabs cord middle
   mm`   áà
   Mhm. Yes.

7   (1.7)
           Fr looks around to his right

8 Felicita: **Toò doññi nzáa é asta aññì xhílla ra!**
   Fr slides r-hand down rope
   Fe holds/lowers end of rope |releases it and picks up end of another rope
   tò   doni n.za=é   asta   ani   xhíla=ra
   rope long STA.go=3o until neck seat=EXCL
   The rope's just long enough to go to the neck of the saddle!

9 Francisco: **Nzaa é asta aññì xhílla.**
   Fr slides r-hand down length of rope to ground
   n.za=é   asta   ani   xhíla
   STA.go=3o   until neck seat
   It'll go to the neck of the saddle.

Felicita separates the rope from a tangle, and then offers Francisco the rope in 5 saying, "This other one" which he evaluates in 6, ↑*Mm* and accepts, saying, "Yes" and grabbing the cord. In 7 though we see that Francisco looks around, taking a couple of seconds searching the area for a third option. He is not fully committed to the cord he just accepted as part of the alternative question sequence initiated by Felicita. He slides one hand down the length of the cord measuring it. Seeing this, Felicita makes an assessment: "The rope's just long enough to go to the neck of the saddle!" In 9, Francisco repeats part of Felicita's assessment, "It'll go to the neck of the saddle." As we saw in Chapter 5, his creation of a second assessment by resonating Felicita's assessment displays a moment of agreement where it seems they align on the truth value of the proposition (or at least an agreed probability assessment) that the rope is long enough. In this way, they developed and then displayed their joint commitment to "this rope."

Francisco spends several minutes applying a multistep process he uses to seize the strap loop with the rope, after which he comments to Felicita that the rope was not long enough. The amount used in the wraps and knots for the seizing task has shortened the working end of the rope so much as to make it inadequate to complete its function. He suggests that a piece be cut to the right length and begins to unwind the work he did. In making the joint commitment to use this rope, both the alternative question format of Felicita's offer and the material presence of the thinner rope with ambiguously adequate length were persuasive. Without intrinsically tying the knot it was indeterminable how much rope would be taken up by the process of the seizing knot. Together we can see how these material affordances shaped the sequence.

There are additionally other joint commitments that are intersubjectively present to the interaction but only indirectly indicated in the transcript. One is a joint commitment to saving rope which we will also see later in the corral building of section 6.3. Without a contemporary local industry of making rope in Lachixío, rope is a commodity that must be purchased from local general stores or through trips to regional markets hours away by bus. Cutting a rope reduces the potential use (or reuse) value of the whole and is thus avoided whenever possible by using scrap materials left over from prior projects. A second background factor is the cultural obligation to accept offers discussed in Chapter 2. The jointly achieved commitment to the short rope segment Felicita offered results in an expenditure of labor and time only to have to untie it and start over with a new rope cut from a longer length. As Clark (2006) pointed out, it is such an accumulative stacking of joint commitments that can be influential in people continuing to pursue less than optimal, or even debilitative, courses of action.[1] The objects of joint actions can develop their own persuasiveness because of a stacking of joint commitments to them developed in a chain of semiosis. The presence of the already made and committed to sign-object provides its own momentum that preferences its continuation or replication as an element of the collaborative project. It would actually require additional work by the other participants to back out of their commitment to such an object, and in this case to literally unwind their entanglement with it than it does to merely go on.

In the next segment, Francisco is finishing seizing the burro's cinch with the new rope, and Felicita is working on folding another *kostálle* for a second cinch strap for a different saddle.

6.2.2 Felicita Asks about Tying the Cinch Ring

In this segment, a dialogue fails to achieve shared understanding of how to attach a cinch ring. Like the previous extract, we can see the epistemic difference as one participant defers to the other for this one task. But this time Francisco is already involved in the seizing process on the first cinch, so he tries to explain how Felicita could do it herself. In the process of explaining, his semiotic action shifts from talk that is referentially symbolic, and pragmatically argumentative, to one which is iconic where he gestures to depict qualities of the action, and finally to an intrinsic semiotic mode, communicating what he means by actually doing it himself in the copresent attention of his consociate.

As we ended the last segment, Felicita had folded the second bag to produce the form for a second cinch strap. Francisco seizes the first strap and declares it finished.

```
(2) LMSMVDP25Jul0902 53.77-55.01
20 Francisco:   Enno chingáo nèé' sí.
                Fe lifts rope and 1-hand slides up to end
                eno   chingáo  nèé'  sí
                who   chingado now   yes
                Yes, fucking got it now.
21 Felicita:    (2.2)
                ------------------------------m`m´m
                Fe lifts gaze to Fr lowers gaze| to strap
22 Francisco:   Onga txe'e' síngye' nóo xokko búrro' noo=
                Fe partly wraps rope around strap loop with 1-hand
                onga#txe'e'   sínge'   xoko   búrro'  no
                (CMP)be#formed like.this clothes burro  and
                Form the burro's clothes like this and=
23 Felicita:    =Láa nóo síngye' rekka níngye' nèé' a'á.
                Fe works 1-hand to opposite end of rope
                -----------------|Fr turns gaze to Fe
                lá   nó   sínge'   re-aka  nínge'  a'á
                NEG  that like.this HAB-be  thing   INT
                =No, that like this the thing is, see?
24              (1.2)
                Fe arcs r-hand with rope end over strap-loop r-to-l raising
                    gaze to Fr upon arc completion
```

In 20, Felicita holds up the rope, measuring it out and then in 21 produces a minimal utterance to get Francisco's attention to a new task turning her gaze to him as well. Such gaze action can function to mobilize response (Stivers and Rossano 2010; Rossano, Brown, and Levinson 2009). Francisco describes what to do in 22, saying, "Form the burro's clothes like this and." Though whatever was being projected by the conjunction "and" is cut off by Felicita with a second-position repair initiation, "No, that like this the thing is, see?," her response indicates that his prior turn was misfit as the response she was seeking to her question in 21. Going on in 24, Felicita moves to manipulate the rope communicating through a depictive iconicity that her question was about the tying of the seizing knot and not about the general shape of the strap for cinching to the burro's belly (Figure 6.2).

```
25 Francisco:   Xaa tzee tzyáà.
                ---------------|Fe lowers gaze to her hands
                ----------------|Fr turns gaze to bench-r
                xa    tze   tzyáà
                how   walk  just
                Just however it goes (however you want it).
```

```
26 Felicita:   Laa yànna' né zekka.
               Fe raises folded strap-loop assembly presenting to Fr
               ----------|Fr turns gaze to Fe's hands
               la   yàna'=né    zeka
               NEG  stay=ACT3o  good
               It won't stay good.
27 Francisco:  Otza'nna (0.4) laa tzyáà níngye' zxe'nna é. (1.0)
               |Fe lowers assembly to lap pulls rope tight around fold
               -------------|Fe raises presenting to Fr again
               -------------|Fr r-hand I-point to fold rotates r-hand
                  beyond folded end, then back to fold
               o-tza'na    la   tzyáà   nínge'  zxe'na=é
               CMP-leave   NEG  just    thing   a.little=3o
               Leave (0.4) just a little bit of it. (1.0)
28 Francisco:  A'á.
               |Fr turns r-hand to wrap two fingers through ring under strap
                  and squeezes against thumb on top.
               -----------|Fe gaze l to far end of strap
               -----------|Fr gaze r to far end of strap
               See here.
29 Francisco:  Paara nóo txee txó'o né xlàkko í.
               Fr I-point l-r along strap length then to Fe's hands with
                  strap assembly
               para  nó    txe   H*-g-yo'o=né              x-làko=í
               for   that  then  POT-CAUS-enter=ACT3o      POS-belly=3ANIM
               So that then it makes it stay on its belly.
```

In 25 then Francisco says, "Just however it goes" taking a stance that Felicita can tie the knot but examining his embodied action he foreshadows what would be involved for him to do it. Francisco turns his gaze to the right side of the bench projecting the location he will move to in 36 to work along with Felicita to fasten the ring to the strap. At 26 Felicita presents the strap-ring assembly holding it up for Francisco to show how she formed it, and she says, "It won't stay good" in a negative assessment of what could be her potential seizing attempt. At 27 she returns the assembly to her lap, working the rope to mime the seizing procedure that will secure the strap around the ring, and then raises the assembly again to Francisco, offering the assembly to him as she did in the previous extract with the first cinch strap. Her miming shows that she

27. Francisco r-hand I-point to fold

28. Francisco turns r-hand to wrap two fingers through ring under strap and squeezes against thumb on top.

Figure 6.2 Francisco's index finger points to fold saying, "Leave just a little bit" (27), and then he turns his hand to depict the cinching of the fold wrapping two fingers through ring and squeezing folded strap held by Felicita.

understands the seizing knot to some extent, though she still defers to Francisco for the actual operation. Rather than taking Felicita's presentation of the assembly as a "giving" action to be responded to with acceptance and taking, Francisco ascribes it as a showing action (see work of Kidwell and Zimmerman 2007 on how a giving action entails a showing action, and can often lead to mistaken action ascription needing remediation). When Felicita raises the assembly, Francisco gestures with an index point to the fold and rotates his pointing hand beyond the folded end and then back to fold saying to "leave just a little bit of it" (just enough folded over to seize it).[2] In 28, Francisco issues a verbal interjection *a'á*, which can be used like "here," "see here," or "like this" and gestures indexically and iconically in explanation of the course of action to construct the seizing knot. His complex gesture turns his right hand to wrap two fingers through the ring under the strap and squeezes the assembly between his thumb on top and two fingers underneath mimes the function of the seizing knot and then provides a reason, "Because then it makes it stay on its belly" in 29.

Felicita's subsequent actions show the indications and explanations of Francisco are not enough to get her to commit to seizing the ring in the strap herself.

```
30 Francisco:  Teme'e' nakki (.) laa tzyáà me'. Zokko né tetzo' é.
               Fe opens and closes fold works rope on open end
               te-me'e'    naki    la   tzyáà  me'e'  zoko=né       te-tzo'=é
               a-little    strong  NEG  just   little thread=ACT3o  a.back=3o
               A little tight (.) just a little. Put it through (and) around.
31 Francisco:  Skwa' tzyáà làá né nèé' skwa' tzyáà koò làá né nèé'.
               Fe opens and closes fold
               skwa'       tzyáà  làá=né              nèé'  skwa'      tzyáà
               like.this   just   leave=act3o         now   like.this  just
               làá=né         nèé'
               leave=ACT3o    now
               Just like this leave it now, just like this leave it now.
32 Felicita:   Peèro (.) [peèro no/
               fe tosses rope end from r-1 with r-hand
               pèro  pèro
               but   but
               But (.) but that/
33 Francisco:           [Peèro ↑zxokka yakkò' kòo é nèé'.
                        Pero   zxoka    yakò'#kò=é       nèé'
                        but    strong   tie#knot=3o      now
                        But tie it TIGHT now.
```

Felicita unfolds and folds the strap around the ring and works the rope end to which Francisco responds, "Just like this, just like this tie it around the loop." Felicita replies in 32, "but, but that," Francisco responds in a parallel form beginning his turn with the conjunction, *peèro* (but) in the resonating "repeat and run" redirecting strategy I described in Chapter 5, "but tie it closed now." Felicita does not and rather presents the assembly again to Francisco:

```
34 Felicita:   Nzenné né síngye'. Nzenné né. Xhikká koò é.
               |Fe presents assembly to Fr
               -----------------|Fr looks r-1 along cinch1 and lifts it
               n-zené=né     sínge'     n-zené=né     L*-zhìka'#kò=é
               STA-grab=ACT3o like.this STA-grab=ACT3o IMP-tie#knot=ACT3o
               It's grabbed like this. It's grabbed. Tie its knot.
```

35 Francisco: #m´m`   (7.1)
              Fr puts down cinch1 on ground to his left moves his body
                along the bench closer to Fe and carefully puts a knife
                from that side of the bench on top of cinch1.
              Fe holds cinch2 presenting to P with prepared fold toward him.
36 Felicita: Nii á ozxella tòkko nóo me'e' láa loo níngyè' nii á.
              Peèro kaa nzaa é toò lèkka tzyáà é loo xhílla nokkwe.
              Fr takes rope end with r-hand and straightens rope to end
              --------------------------------Fe points to ring------
              ----------------|Fe turns head to right, head point
              ------------------------------------Fr| follows Fe's gaze
              ni=á   o-zxela tòko   nó   me'e'   lá   lo   níngè'   ni=á
              say=1s CMP-find one   that small   COMP face thing   say=1s
              pero   ka   nza=é tò   lèka   tzyáà=é lo xhíla   nokwe
              but   where   gone=3o rope scarce just=3o face seat this
              I say I found one that was smaller than that I say. But
                where did it go. It's not here on the saddle.
37 Felicita: Tò-burro' Bítò ra!
              tò-burro-'   Bíto-L=ra
              deceased-burro-POS   Victor-CLAS=EXCL
              (The saddle) of Victor's dead burro!

With Felicita's presentation of the assembly to Francisco in 34, she says, "It's grabbed like this," "tie its knot." Francisco is still holding the first cinch strap which still needs more work. This competing commitment constrains his accepting her offer. His acceptance moves forward in steps incrementally as he first looks right and left along the strap he holds and lifts it to then carefully put it down. He utters #*M´m`* in 35 (a positive affirmation), but does so with a harsh breathy voice that indicates some annoyance. He puts down the first cinch strap visibly backing out of the competing commitment he has to it. Francisco then moves along the bench to his right to get closer to Felicita and the assembly she's holding together (a move that he projected ten lines earlier with gaze to the right along the bench). He goes on to take the rope, which is an intrinsic sign of entering into the seizing activity with Felicita and the strap-ring assembly. Felicita makes a reference to the large metal ring that she folded into the strap and which they are trying to seize, noting that she saw a smaller one earlier but that she can't find it now. Like with the ropes before, the presence of material influences the decisions, troubles, and outcomes of their joint activity. Perhaps Felicita could have seized the strap herself with a smaller ring, and though she knows there is a smaller ring somewhere, she influences Francisco to help seize the strap now rather than stop the project's ongoing progress to start a search for another ring.

Over the next couple of minutes, in a canonical joint activity with reciprocal roles and emergent product, Felicita holds the strap assembly in place while Francisco seizes the fold capturing the metal ring (Figure 6.3). The seizing knot involves more than he indicated to Felicita in his gestures. After Felicita helps him get it started, he takes the strap-ring assembly himself and holds one end of rope with his teeth and the other with his hand and pulls very tight to crimp the strap. This technique provides great force to seize the assembly tight—so much that the creaking sound of the compressing materials were picked up by the microphone.

Figure 6.3 Felicita and Francisco take reciprocal roles working together to seize a ring at the end of a saddle cinch. Felicita holds the strap in place while Fernando seizes it with rope.

This example shows the negotiation of a course of action guided and limited in part by the material objects present in the participation frame, and, importantly, by the material form of a prior utterance (Felicita's either/or formulation). We could also see in the negotiation of who would do the binding operation a division of labor insisted upon by Felicita. Both extracts in fact show Felicita deferring to Francisco for this binding task, indexing an epistemic difference for this part of their joint project of saddle cinch fabrication. The choice of ropes in the first extract and the presence of the large, but not ideal, metal ring in the second exemplify clearly that collaborative decision making in joint activity is more than the articulation of arguments of persuasion. Material objects themselves are participants in the ecology. As participants in the sequence, they exert influence through other participants' joint commitments to them. Agency is distributed this way across the multimodal-multi-participant assemblage of the interaction. Synchronic analysis would fail us here as time process is essential in the ontology. As the time of an interaction proceeds, semiosis links sign-objects to interpretants, which themselves become signs. Joint commitments develop over time and become layered and dependent upon one another making it increasingly challenging to withdraw from a joint activity once it is underway, even if it is ill-fated. The human disposition for collaboration is unparalleled in the natural world affording coproduced artifacts, culture, and language. As we just saw, however, collaboration can also create trouble reaching a pragmatic goal. We further develop this understanding when considering a family building a turkey corral.

6.3 Multidimensional Social Relations in Building a Turkey Corral

Collaborations involve the assessment and recognition of problems and joint decision making to move ahead as a group to solve them. In strict, and corporate, hierarchies, this could involve organizing joint actions through the expected fulfillment of directives, but where hierarchies are not clear or can shift from moment to moment, these decisions, and the joint commitments to them, are negotiated through interactional moves and sequences. The extracts in this section show a family working to build an enclosure for their turkeys. The previous enclosure (or corral) had been raided by a coyote the night before and a turkey was killed. The loss of the turkey was a serious symbolic and monetary loss, making it imperative to build a better enclosure. The purpose of the corral is to house turkeys that are used in ritual exchange and redistribution known in Oaxaca as *guelaguetza* exchange (Beals 1970), *Eeliettzá* in Lachixío. Each household keeps turkeys as a form of banking to pay debts they have incurred in the past, and to loan turkeys, which in-turn creates debts for others. Turkeys are also the possession and responsibility of a household's women, which explains why the women are the ones principally invested in this project with the eldest woman (Andrea) being the most active in ensuring that the corral will protect the turkeys. Nazaria, as Andrea's daughter-in-law, is the most formally supportive of Andrea's actions. There is only tangential participation by the men with Nazaria's husband (Andrea's son) making a few suggestions from off camera at one point and with Pedro working for a while to contribute his ideas but leaving the activity when his suggestions are not taken up into the developing corral structure (Figure 6.4).

Because the prior construction allowed the coyote to push planks aside and prey on the turkey, the family must solve the practical problem of how to attach plank walls to the frame to make the enclosure secure from predation. We can see like in the prior video that the project's materiality and temporal development exerts influence over the terms, outcomes, and argumentation expressed through language and embodied action. This section has four transcribed segments:

6.3.1 How to secure the planks?
6.3.2 Pedro comes to join the task suggesting a potential course of action. Nazaria jointly commits and collaborates with him to reproduce Solution 1.
6.3.3 Andrea brings rope and suggests weaving boards as a competing course of action. Nazaria jointly commits with Andrea, abandoning her prior joint commitment with Pedro. Then Andrea and Nazaria collaborate to weave the top of the boards to the corral frame.
6.3.4 Pedro brings thinner rope and attempts to show on the lower pole that his method uses less rope. His sister Elvia verbally expresses her doubts until Pedro, by intrinsically trying his plan out, comes to also realize it does not use less rope and abandons his idea.

The turkey-corral project is an everyday life example of the concept of *bricolage* mobilized in anthropology by Lèvi Strauss (1966) and of the family as *bricoleurs* who

Figure 6.4 A family works together to build a turkey enclosure.

build from whatever materials are at hand. But where Lèvi Strauss's *bricoleur* was a creative *individual*, we see in this encounter a multi-participant, multidimensional ecology involving human and nonhuman participants collaborating with distributed influence over the shape of the artifact emergent from their joint actions. The materials for the corral are items that are found around the house left over as scrap from house building activity, like cut-off plank scraps and posts, and much of the material from the previous corral which they just tore down. Around the perimeter of the new corral structure forming a backing for the wall, there is also a wire mesh, a commodity manufactured to be used for reinforcing poured concrete floors or roofs. This is a new contribution to the corral design to better prevent the intrusion of predators. Rope and wire, found around the worksite or stored nearby, is used for fastening materials together. Participants walk out of the video frame several times to return with poles, ropes, and planks. Like with the saddle repair project, rope is a valued commodity that is usually in short supply. Several sequences address which rope to use, and how to avoid cutting rope. As with many of the videos, there is music playing from a nearby stereo and the occasional grunt of a pig, call of tom turkeys, or voices of off-screen conversations. In relation to Pedro who set up the camera, Elvia is his sister, Andrea is his mother, and Nazaria is his sister-in-law (daughter-in-law to Andrea). The corral the family fabricated this day stood for eight years and was only rebuilt in 2017 to be repurposed for goats.

The image in Figure 6.5 bears the material indices of two ideas. The lower part of the wall has vertical planks captured behind a pole that is suspended horizontally being tied at both ends (labeled Solution 1). It was proffered and put in place by the participants before the video recording began. Once materially present it presented a source of influence on the talk and actions that followed. It even began to be reproduced as the solution to fasten the top of the planks, and then became something to be argued against, which was challenging because of the trajectory toward reproduction it had developed through the joint commitments of multiple participants. The upper part of the wall in Figure 6.5 shows a rope weave holding the boards in place (labeled Solution 2) which is the material form of the counter solution argued for by Andrea. We will see that these two material indices relate to sequences of talk and action built up from offers, recruitments, repairs, and resonances. One point I make here is that the artifacts of collaborative bricolage have language production associated with them as part of the weave of their natural history. In this section, resonating Wittgenstein's concern, we examine what the shape of an order of language looks like with a particular end in view. Given that the finished project shows indices of multiple construction techniques, we ask, what was the multimodal interaction that produced such complex and contrasting forms? That is to ask, how can signs of ideas become signs of joint commitments, and, in this family project in Lachixío, how is conflict between competing ideas resolved to move the joint project forward together to the final form of a dwelling that displays material signs of the multi-participant interaction that produced it?

Figure 6.5 Two solutions to fastening the planks.

Figure 6.6 Andrea gestures to right indicating the place she is suggesting they put another post.

6.3.1 How to Secure These Planks?

Our first look at this collaboration is through a segment where participants discuss how to fasten the planks to the wire mesh-corner posts assembly. Andrea suggests they need another post. We begin with Elvia responding to Andrea's reasoning with a repair initiation and Andrea's attempt to clarify her points (Figure 6.6).

```
(3) LMSMVDP24Jul0901 1:03-1:30
    5  Elvia:    Láà nóo onii lò [₁xékka nóo
                 --------------------------|N turns head from beyond corral to A
                 Là=á    nó   o-nì=lò         xéka    nó
                 get     that CMP-say=2s      how     that
                 I get that you said how that
    6  Andrea:   [₁Nóo nii á nóo zokkà a'wa [₂bí'ttzà nii á eenze'e tzyáà nii à.
                 --------------------------|A beats palms up then gestures to
                         right and continues talk and gesture to right (Figure 6.7)
                 no      ni=á    nó     zokà=a'wa   bí'tzà    ni=á      e=nze'e
                 that    say=1s  that   seat=1PLI   post      say=1s    that(topic)
                         tzyáà   ni=à
                         just    say=1s
                 That I say that we put a post I say that is all I say.
```

```
7   Elvia:    [ⱼAà nóo nii lò enzí chò' tzyáà akka txee ree né stokko nii lò.
              --|E points and turns gaze beyond the corral |turns gaze
                back to A
              à    nó  ni=lò  enzí  chò'  tzyáà  aka  txe  re=né    sH-tòko
              oh   that say=2s  over  there  just   be   then  MOV=ACT3o  another-one
              ni=lò
              say=2s
              Oh that you say over there then will be put another you say.
8   Andrea:   Ka'a (.) xe'lla eenze'e txee.
              -|A points right arm beyond corral and brings arm back while
                beating with left
              ka'a   xe'la   e=nze'e       txe
              here   send    that(topic)   then
              Here (.) send that then.
9   Elvia:    Áwwà xe'lla ka'a nèé'. (.) Xaa kye'e' otzee arkì' lò txe?
              A still gesturing, A and E hold mutual gaze
              áwà   xe'la  ka'a nèé'  xa  ke'e'  o-tze=arkì'=lò       txe
              yes   send   here now   how  sound  CMP-breathe=h∋art=2s  then
              Yes send it here now. (.) What do you think then?
10            (0.7)
```

The offering of ideas, like the offering of objects and labor that we saw in Chapter 2, is often rhetorically minimized in Lachixío. In 6, Andrea offers an idea saying, "I say that we put a post I say that is all I say." Note that her offer is also a request for joint commitment. This is taken up as new information by Elvia in 7 with the news uptake marker *aà* (oh) and a candidate offering of her understanding of Andrea's suggestion that the corral have

Figure 6.7 Andrea assesses the trouble to be because of a prior joint commitment at the beginning of the project, saying, "Too bad we didn't dig the ground that we just made it like this" while catching a falling board (line 11).

the addition of another post. The argumentative talk is very much about what they have said, or are trying to say, framed with opinion markers like "I say" and "you say." Andrea introduces the idea of using another vertical post to strengthen the corral in 6, but Elvia responds in 7 in the middle of Andrea's turn just prior to the point where Andrea mentions the object, *bí'ttzà* (post). The verb *zokkà* (to set) syntactically projects both a subject and object, and thus Andrea's turn construction unit (TCU) is incomplete when Elvia comes in with her news uptake, displaying understanding before proposition completion. In the multimodal configuration of the time and space of this kairotic moment, Andrea's gesture is enough indication of the referent that Elvia's utterance is well fitted as a response (and thus not met with repair). In 8, Andrea says, "Here, send that then," pointing beyond corral and then back toward the entrance. Because Andrea's gesture sequence resonates with the form of the horizontal pole, it iconically indexes Solution 1. This potentiates the poles' reproduction of itself. Andrea's move is met with overt agreement from Elvia in 9, "Yes, send it here now" and then asking Andrea what she thinks.

Andrea responds with a negative assessment of their project, "Too bad we didn't dig the ground that we just made it like this." And this is where we came into the extract beginning Chapter 1.

```
11 Andrea:    Nóo láa rikki a'wa a'ññí a'wa loo yoò eenze'e nóo skwa'
              tzyáà ri'i a'wa.
              -|A pointing to right, N is moving boards one starts falling
               A pushes falling board back against wire
              nó    lá    riki=a'wa   a'ní=a'wa   lo     yò    e=nze'e    nó
              that  NEG   endure=1PLI dig=1PLI    face   earth that(topic) that
                skwa'    tzyáà    ri'i=a'wa
                like.this just    make=1PLI
              Too bad we didn't dig the ground that we just made it like this.

12 Elvia:     A'a txee?
              a'a   txe
              NEG   then
              No then (not like this)?

13 Andrea:    Síngye' kaà nè lá lixxho jri'i né rì'ya á.
              A pushing board against wire
              singe'   kà    nè.lá    lixho    r-ri'i=né    rì'ya=á
              like.this truly coming  bad      HAB-make=3o  see=1s
              I see that like this it's truly coming bad what we're making.

14 Nazaria:   Kyée kaà né la?
              -----|N gazing at boards
              ------------|A head turn to N
              H*-ke        kà=né=la
              POT-go.up    truly=ACT3o=Q
              Think it will really stay up?

15 Andrea:    Xhe' láa kye' kyee né.
              xhe'   lá    ke'    ke=né
              maybe  NEG   this   go.up=ACT3o
              This may not stay up.

16 Elvia:     ↑Kyée né↑.
              H*-ke=né
              POT-go.up=ACT3o
              It will stay up.

17 Nazaria:   ↑Kyée né↑?
              H*-ke=né
              POT-go.up=ACT3o
              It will stay up?
```

```
18              (0.4)
19 Elvia:       ↑Kyée né↑.
                H*-ke=né
                POT-go.up=ACT3o
                It will stay up.
```

During Andrea's negative assessment, a plank begins to fall over to the side as if the object itself is underscoring the problem (Figure 6.7). Andrea says, "Too bad that we didn't dig the ground [burying the plank ends], that we just made it like this," in 11 which is met with Elvia's offering repair in 12 in negative form, "No then (not like this)?" making relevant Andrea's second assessment in 13. The board falling illustrates exactly the problem with Solution 1 since the boards are not themselves fastened but only standing up between the horizontal pole and the wire mesh. Andrea then pushes the planks against the wire (an intrinsic illustration of what needs to happen) and gives a second general assessment in 13, "I see that like this it's truly coming bad what we're making," that upgrades the epistemics of the action from *saying* (opining) to *sensing* (empirical knowledge) by framing the assessment with a verb of seeing. In the multimodal ecology, the upgraded epistemic stance can be seen as the semiotic interpretant of the intrinsic and material signs of the falling board. Such a fact illustrates how inadequate a "talk-only" transcript of this event would be and the ethical problem of representing copresent action through audio-only inscription. Andrea's pressing the plank to the wire mesh projects the needed solution. Nazaria asks, "Think it will really stay up?" which is a recruitment of response formulated as an interrogative proposition resonant with Andrea's intrinsic gesture pushing the planks up against the wire mesh. Andrea responds, "This may not stay up," which Elvia contradicts with an other-repair "It will stay up." Nazaria repeats Elvia in high-pitch register and with rising intonation questioning whether it will stay up. This is an other-initiation of repair in the form of an offer built through both focal and frame resonance with the form of the trouble source. As a repair offer it makes (dis)confirmation relevant. Then Elvia issues her own resonant second assessment, declaring, "It will stay up."

We see in this example ideas being offered into the project and their merits and shortcomings argued for in a multimodal combination of mutually informing talk and gestures and actions with the material of the developing structure. Repair and resonance building play roles in responses that question, challenge, or support previously stated positions. Some positions are merely asserted rather than argued, and intrinsic actions with objects stand as important signs projecting what the future form and function of the elements of the corral could come to be.

6.3.2 Pedro Comes to Join the Task Suggesting a Potential Course of Action. Nazaria Jointly Commits and Collaborates with him to Reproduce Solution 1

On the recording after 19, we hear Pedro say *kyée txee* (go up then) with a low volume resonating in form with Elvia's assessment that the planks will stay up. Pedro enters from camera right at about 2:30 and Andrea turns and leaves frame to camera left.

Figure 6.8 Pedro steps between Nazaria and Andrea placing hand on planks (line 32).

Pedro asks Nazaria some questions about the construction and she responds, shaking one of the vertical planks to show him the issue intrinsically and by pointing low to the left indicating where the pole of Solution 1 is tied near the base. Andrea returns with more planks and hands one to Nazaria. While Andrea has been away, Nazaria and Pedro have come together to decide on a course of action that would reproduce the pole of Solution 1 to also capture the top of the planks (one that Andrea herself also indicated in 8 but then decided was insufficient but has yet to introduce a different solution). She orients to Nazaria with the developing project between them. At 2:51 we get the sequence in example (4).

(4) LMSMVDP24Jul0901 2:51-3:15

```
31 Pedro:      Píi á
               -P walks around back of N
               pí=á
               think=1s
               I think
32 Pedro:      enta beè níngye' lowáare.
               -|P steps toward corral between N and A places/points hand
                  to planks
               ------------------|A turns gaze to follow P's point
               enta    bè    nínge'   lowáre
               come    PL    thing    place
               these things come here.
33 Andrea:     Xekka wà' ri'i?
               xeka    wà'    ri'i
               how     this   make
               How to make this?
```

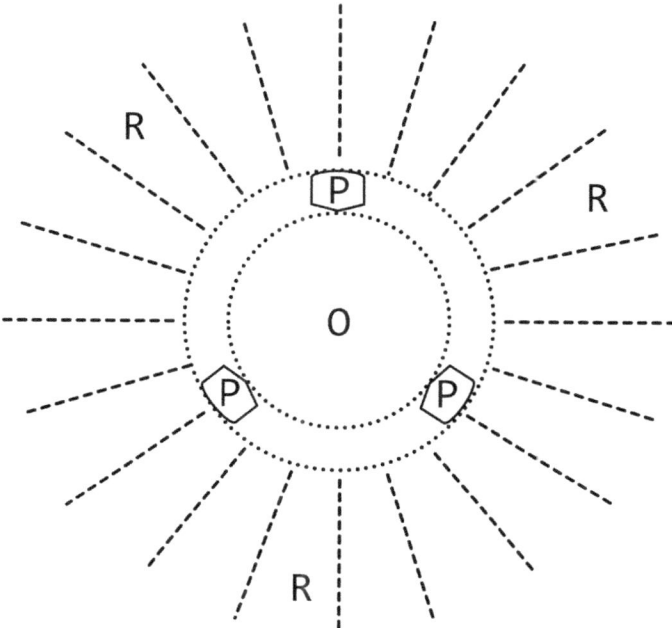

Figure 6.9 Spaces of a focused orientation: Adam Kendon's F-Formation (2009: 235): Participants (P) orienting to a space of common perceptual access (O) defining residual space (R) outside the perimeter of focused participants.

As Pedro comes back into frame, he interjects his opinion, introducing it in 31 with "I think" as he steps in between Nazaria and Andrea (Figure 6.8). In this position, he has effectively put himself in the place that would interrupt any joint project Andrea and Nazaria may be developing. In the terms defined by Kendon (2009), he has stepped into their O-space, a space of mutual access in the ecological orientation of Andrea and Nazaria. In interaction analysis, what Kendon (2009) refers to as an F-formation is an ecological formation that includes the participants, their sensory orientation, and their sensible perimeter (Figure 6.9).

Pedro says, "These things come here," pointing to the planks, and Andrea follows his point with her gaze. Andrea asks, "How to make this?" soliciting his expansion. Pedro then begins to describe what he is thinking.

```
34 Pedro:    Enta níngye' nóo me'e' níngye'.
             enta   ninge'  nó     me'e'   ninge'
             come   thing   that   small   thing
             A thing comes that's small.
35           (0.7)
36 Pedro:    Tonno púuro tzyáà nóo
             tono   puro    tzyáà   nó
             if     only    just    that
             If only (we) just
```

```
37 Elvia:      (0.2) ((Unrelated talk))
38 Pedro:      [Oore nyàá nyàá nóo
               ore     nyàá    nyàá    nó
               or      good    good    that
               Or it would be real good that
39 Andrea:     [Tòkko nakki níngye' nzyaa?
               tòko    naki    ninge'  n.zya
               one     strong  thing   STA.go
               One strong thing goes (here)?
40 Pedro:      Aà nokkwa tzyáà nèé'.
               -|P runs hand to right and left along boards (Figure 6.10)
               aà      nokwa   tzyáà   nèé'
               yes     STA.sit just    now
               Yes it will just sit there now.
```

Pedro's thinking is communicated over several turns that are somewhat disfluent between 34 and 38. In 36, he does not seem to finish his thought, and in 38, he begins to frame a proposition, "Or it would be good that," but at the same time, in overlap, Andrea offers, "One strong thing goes here," which describes Solution 1. This is an understanding check of what Pedro is trying to get at as it makes relevant a yes/no response. Pedro responds in 40, "Yes it will just sit there now," as he iconically gestures its path running his hand across the planks from where he stands toward the right (to where Andrea had previously suggested a second post be set) and back to the left (Figure 6.10). Pedro begins to go on with his hypothetical. At the same time, Elvia comes out through the low doorway of the turkey-corral joking that she twisted her back in the process. Then Pedro begins to make his case.

Figure 6.10 Pedro runs hand to right and left along boards while saying, "Yes it will just sit there now."

41		(1.2)
42	Pedro:	Tonno
		tono
		If
43		(1.9)
44	Elvia:	he.he.he [ozhikka' tettzo'=á.
		|E comes from under doorway header
		|P looks to ground and moves down to grab a rope
		------------|A looks down as P begins to move
		ozhika' te-tzo'=á
		twisted back=á
		he.he.he I twisted my back ((smile voice))
45	Pedro:	kada nó kada nó nza=é síngye' nèé' ni=á tzyáà nó
		kàlo kaà yakà' koò láa tòko nèé'.=
		|P grabs rope on ground, stands and holds rope horizontal
		against planks.
		--|L gaze follow P to rope
		kada nó kada nó nza=é sínge' nèé' ni=á tzyáà nó
		each that each that go=3o like.this now say=1s just that
		kàlo kà yakà' kò láa tòkc nèé'
		how.many where tie.up knot comp one now
		each one that each one that goes like this now I just say
		it's how where each is tied up now.=
46	Elvia:	=Aà nii á nii eskye' kaà nii á.
		|E looks to P's rope placement (his pantomime)
		aà ni=á ni eske' kà ni=á
		yes say=1s say like.this truly say=1s
		=Uh huh I say exactly like this I say.
47	Pedro:	Tii o-ri'i nóo nakka' koò lá níngye ka'a.
		P works rope around front of plank and back of wire frame
		ti o-ri'i nó naka' kò=lá nínge ka'a
		who CMP-make that tied knot=already thing here
		One ties it around the thing here.

Pedro looks to the ground and picks up a rope, then stands and holds the rope horizontally against the planks saying in 45 that each one can be tied now. Elvia latches on to his utterance with an emphatic agreement, "Uh huh I say exactly like this I say," and Pedro says that someone would tie it around the wire frame. He intrinsically demonstrates the tie by working the rope around the wire frame. Both Nazaria and Andrea have had their gaze on his hands as his argument is presented in a multimodal configuration involving speech, gesture, gaze, and action with material objects. It is because of the ecological assemblage of the participants (including the corral and the rope) and the orientation of attention through gaze that Pedro's action is legible for interpretation.

His multimodal configuration, however, has some indeterminacy leading to two possible interpretations. What he may be indicating himself is using the rope to tie each plank to the wire mesh and to the horizontal pole. But Pedro is using an intrinsic semiotic mode to demonstrate the tying with only the rope, and there is no horizontal pole at this point in the upper part of the corral. So another possible interpretation is that rope alone can be used to fasten the planks to the wire mesh. The second interpretation is how the sign further develops for Andrea when she offers Solution 2. But at this point Pedro moves forward with Solution 1. After illustrating his idea with rope in 47, Pedro bends down to pick up a long plank on the ground next to the corral and begins to try to tie it on horizontally like Solution 1. Offering her collaboration, Nazaria grabs the far end of the plank and supports it while Pedro begins to work to tie the plank on with the rope. Andrea sees this sequence of activity between Nazaria and Pedro start and shakes her head slightly in disapproval as she turns and exits camera right (this is subtle and neither Nazaria nor Pedro seem to notice).

Pedro and Nazaria's collaboration (Figure 6.11) is now iterating "Solution 1" (Figure 6.5). Pedro is tying the long horizontal plank against the vertical planks just as the long pole is tied below. Their projected goal becomes an issue in the next sequence where Andrea goes to pursue "Solution 2," which weaves each plank to the wire frame using only rope. What is interesting is that her solution was itself an interpretant of Pedro's argumentation in section 6.3.2, but is not the interpretant he responded with himself. The idea of Solution 2 is truly an emergent co-construction but not the result of an intention to coproduce something together. It is emergent in the sense of being beyond the causal influence of any individual participant. The product of this collaborative moment in Andrea's experience is rather grounded in the process, openness, and indeterminacy of semiosis. For all the participants, the lower horizontal pole that already exists as part of the project is a material index of their joint commitment—an artifact with a presence that imbues it with the ready potential to be taken up as a model, or diagram, for future action. Andrea, however, having already assessed that the corral was being built badly in section 6.3.1, and already knowing that the planks would not stay up with the horizontal pole design, was actively seeking an alternative idea when she questioned

Figure 6.11 Pedro and Nazaria collaborate to iterate Solution 1.

Pedro about his idea. However, the change to an alternative solution requires extra work against the momentum Solution 1 has already gained through the joint commitments between Pedro and Nazaria, and the resonance of their mimesis of the lower pole. In the next segment, Andrea disrupts Pedro and Nazaria's joint activity. In her advocacy for Solution 2, Nazaria claims that Pedro himself gestured toward Solution 2 earlier (45).

6.3.3 Andrea Brings Rope and Suggests Weaving Boards as a Competing Course of Action. Nazaria Jointly Commits with Andrea, Abandoning Her Prior Joint Commitment with Pedro. Then Andrea and Nazaria Collaborate to Weave the Top of the Boards to the Corral Frame

In section 6.3.2, Pedro formulated a multimodal action that for him was to propose a solution that copied the one already in place but for Andrea resulted in an idea to exclude the horizontal pole of Solution 1. In this section, she argues to weave the boards to the wire backing with rope (perhaps it is relevant that Andrea is of a generation of women with experience with backstrap looms of the region and practices embroidery). Andrea's intervention involves interrupting and unwinding the progress that Pedro and Nazaria have made. Pedro, thinking that Andrea had produced the same interpretant as he did, has trouble understanding Andrea, and he initiates multiple repair sequences through which her argument undergoes several transformations. We reenter the interaction when Andrea has just herself reentered the frame with a longer rope and Pedro and Nazaria turn to and look (Figure 6.12). Pedro offers an understanding check.

Figure 6.12 Andrea comes back with a rope and Pedro and Nazaria take notice.

(5) LMSMVDP24Jul0901 4:07-4:51

```
57 Pedro:     Aà. nóo álla (.) nóo chaa ayaa kye' é la?
              à   nó  ála    nó   cha a-ya ke'e=é=la
              oh  that plank that go  up   lift=3o=Q
              Oh. That the planks are held up?
58 Andrea:    Áà nokkwa chaa ello paara nóo nzoo lii nzyàá.
              áà nokwa   cha  elo  para  nó  n-zo      li       nzya
              yes sitting go  where for  that STA-stand correct  nice
              Yes, it goes up there in order to stand there nicely.
59 Pedro:     Wenno txee.
              -|P unties rope
              weno  txe
              good  then
              Good then.
60 Andrea:    Mm 0?
61            (0.75)
62 Pedro:     uhu
```

Andrea's argumentation uses symbolic representational modes and also resonates Pedro's prior speech. As we'll see, she further moves into depictive and then an intrinsic semiotic mode that actually begin to implement Solution 2. Andrea moves into tactile proximity of the corral and disrupts the O-space of Pedro and Nazaria's joint action. Nazaria enriches her communicative attempt using objects of joint attention (the developing corral structure) and gesturing in ways that pantomimes the iterative progression of the weaving action for which she is arguing. She goes on after this to weave the planks herself, intrinsically representing the action in a way that she claims is resonant with Pedro's prior gestures (lines 45–47). Her interpretant was not intended by Pedro but was nonetheless projected by his signs.

One interesting thing about this scene is how it begins: Andrea brings another rope, which in its materiality stands in relation to the interactional assemblage as a sign of an idea distinct from the one Pedro and Nazaria are working on with a different rope (and the horizontal plank they both hold together). Tracking the development of the two interpretants of Pedro's earlier argument, Andrea's rope is a sign that Pedro and Andrea are not holding common ideas, and this underlies the repair sequences we see next. Pedro notices Andrea's rope when he gazes to her just before 57. His utterance begins with a news uptake *Aà* (oh), and he implies that she has brought him a better rope to tie up the plank with a confirmation question, "That the plank stay up?," itself resonating Pedro's utterance upon which he entered into the collaboration, and resonating with the women's connected dialogue about the issue of the planks staying up (14–19). Pedro's offer of understanding makes relevant a yes/no response, and in 58, Andrea responds, "Yes, it goes up there in order to stand there nicely." Though neither yes nor no would contradict either of their interpretations supporting Solution 1 or 2. In this adjacency pair, we see the failure to develop intersubjectivity between Pedro and Andrea. Pedro uses *ayaa kye' é* (it's lifted up) referring to the horizontal plank he and Nazaria are collaborating to fasten. Andrea uses *nzoo lii* (stand up [vertically]) implying she is intending that the rope be used with the vertical planks (not to hang the horizontal plank). Pedro's response in 59, "good then" and his affirmation in 62 verbally indicate agreement. But the ambiguities are numerous and what we see next indicates that the two have not achieved mutual understanding (even acknowledging that intersubjectivity is always partial, their understandings are rather at odds with each other). Pedro unties the rope he is using but does not abandon the horizontal plank. While he seems to be agreeing with Andrea, his action is intermodally discordant.

63 Andrea:	Nokkwe
	nokwe
	this
	Um
64 Andrea:	Yáa axxò é síngye txee lè'kka kye'é nínge' tetzo' rà.
	-| P unwraps last wrap of rope and drops it |-P takes rope offered by A
	yá axò=e singe txe lè'ka ke'é nínge' te-tzo'=ra
	go.and lay=3s like.this then also raise thing back/outside=EXCL
	Go and lay it like this then put the thing up to the surface.
65 Pedro:	Éè? Xhekka?
	éè xheka
	huh how
	Huh? How?
66 Andrea:	Láa zella síngye' la? Oo zella ka'a né la.
	lá zela sínge'=la o zela ka'a=né=la
	NEG want like.this=Q or want lengthen=ACT3O=Q
	(It) doesn't want it like this? Or does it want to be extended?
67 Pedro:	Eé?
	-P turns head to A |
	Huh?
68 Andrea:	Níngyè'.
	|A points to corral
	níngè'
	thing
	This.
69	(0.5)
70 Andrea:	Láa zella álla. Chó'o ka'a la? Oo zella ka'a la?
	-|A walks to corral between P and N (Figure 6.13)
	lá zela ála H*-cho'o ka'a=la o zela ka'a=la
	NEG want plank POT-exit here=Q or want lengthen=Q
	(It) doesn't want the plank. Take it out of here? Or does (it) want to be extended?
71	(0.8)

Andrea goes on in 64 to try to explain that the rope goes on the surface of the planks directly even formulating the lexical construction "lie it" on the surface. At the same time Pedro accepts her offer of the rope. Pedro initiates repair, first communicating his failure to understand with an open-class other-initiated repair token, *Eé* (Huh?), followed by *Xekka* (How?). While in the trouble source of 64 Andrea phrases her intervention as instructions, "Go and lay it like this then put the thing up to the surface." Andrea's contribution in 66 "(It) doesn't want it like this? Or does it want to be extended?" includes a rhetorical shift as she uses the active indefinite agent subject pronoun *né*. Such a framing places subjectivity for the desire in objects here rather than in the person. This is reminiscent of Gell's (1998) analysis of experiencing artwork in response to an agency residing in the object for their effect to lead the gaze of an interpreter. A painting can be talked about as wanting the

Figure 6.13 Andrea steps between Pedro and Nazaria placing hand on planks.

viewer's eye to move across the canvas in a particular way. Such indeterminacy can minimize the interpersonal conflict that the two ideas represent at this point because it comes from a third (and nonhuman) participant. Pedro still does not understand, and he issues another open-class, other-initiated repair in 67. Andrea remedies by pointing to the corral and saying, *Níngyè'* (This). Then Andrea moves into proximity of the corral "in between" Pedro and Nazaria, physically coming between them and disrupting their joint commitment to Solution 1 (very parallel to the way Pedro came between her and Nazaria in section 6.2). With two failed attempts to achieve mutual understanding, Andrea enriches her communicative attempt using objects of the participants' joint attentional space (the developing corral structure), adding iconic gestures along the surface of their project. Line 70 redoes both 66 and 64 with elements expressing what is best for the corral with the implicit subject being the corral, "(it) doesn't want the plank," and by issuing a question, "Take it out of here?" She then repeats most of the second clause of 66 presenting an alternative, "Or does (it) want to be extended?" here the subject being the rope leaving out the pronoun entirely this time. The alternative solution Andrea proposes is now framed as a discovery of what is best for the corral, rather than an individually forwarded idea in opposition to Pedro and Nazaria's joint activity.

At this point Andrea and Nazaria chorus, *Láa zella né* ([It] doesn't want it), a resonant and simultaneously performed sign by Nazaria that she has understood Andrea, publicly marking the moment where she shifts her commitment from the collaboration with Pedro to joining Andrea in arguing for Solution 2 and ultimately committing with Andrea to weaving the boards in place.

```
72 Andrea:      [Láa zella né.
                lá    zela=né
                NEG   want=ACT3o
                (It) doesn't want it.
73 Nazaria:     [Láa zella né.
                lá    zela=né
                NEG   want=ACT3o
                (It) doesn't want it.
74              (0.4)
75 Andrea:      Tetzo' beè álla nóo yakkà' koò beè níngye'.
                te-tzo'  bè  ála      nó   yakà'#kò  bè  ninge'
                back     PL  plank    that tie#knot PL  thing
                On the surface of the planks tie the thing.
76 Nazaria:     A'a.
                No.
```

Andrea expands the explanation of her idea in 75 with the clearest formulation we see so far, "On the surface of the planks tie the thing." In 76 Nazaria says, *A'a* (No), following up with a parallel message to the one in 73 and incrementally adding to the shift in her commitment from Solution 1 to Solution 2.

In 77–79, we see another shift in Andrea's phrasing where she builds rhetorical opposition with a shift into reported speech (see M. Goodwin 1980, 1991).

```
77 Andrea:      Eèro nóo nii lò akka né síngye' nóo nii lò akka né skwa' nèé'.
                A grabs horizontal brace at left. A grabs plank on right
                    and straightens it.
                N reacts and accommodates to A moving brace.
                èro nó   ni=lò  aka=né     sínge'      nó   ni=lò  aka=né
                but that say=2s be=ACT3o   like.this   that say=2s be=ACT3o
                    skwa'    nèé'
                    this.way now
                But that you're saying like this that you're saying this
                    way now.
78              (0.4)
79 Andrea:      Nóo nii lò akka né nóo cho'o ka'a tòkko à ka'a nii lò.
                A makes repeated c-shaped hand gestures moving to her right
                nó   ni=lò  aka=né    nó   cho'o  ka'a  tòko    à   ka'a ni=lò
                that say=2s be=ACT3o  that go.out here  one     SEQ here say=2s
                That you say it's made (so) that (it) goes out here one-by-
                    one you say.
80 Nazaria:     Nokkwa stokko zella é.
                N pulls out brace and stands it up against the corral.
                nokwa   sH-tòko        zela=é
                sit     another-one    want=3o
                It wants another. ((an out-loud declaration))
81              (0.2)
```

Here Andrea constructs Solution 2 as offered by Pedro himself in the last segment where in 45 he said, "Each one that each one that goes like this . . . each is tied up," which

Figure 6.14 Andrea makes repeated C-shaped gestures left-to-right while saying "one-by-one" indicating tying the boards iteratively while Pedro and Nazaria gaze at her gestures.

she reports back with framings of "you say" both before and after Pedro's constructed dialogue in 79 as, "That you say it's made (so) that (it) goes out here one-by-one you say." In this way she frames the idea she is trying to forward as Pedro's (showing semantic resonance between his formulation of "each one each one tied now" and her "one-by-one" construction which arose as an interpretant to Pedro's earlier composite talk-gesture-object actions). In addition to Andrea's constructed dialogue, "That goes out here one-by-one, you say," she pantomimes the iterated tying of planks in place using iterated C-shaped gestures moving to the right along the corral structure (Figure 6.14). Subsequent to this in 80, Nazaria then moves to fully abandon her joint commitment to the collaboration with Pedro and the horizontal plank by physically removing the plank from the project, declaring at the same time, "(It) wants another," as an "out-loud" assessment that publicly marks her abandonment of the joint activity with Pedro.

Andrea now holds the rope in her left hand and pantomimes again depicting the iterated progress of securing the planks with the rope with Pedro and Nazaria watching.

```
82 Andrea:   Nóo kyaa ka'a toò kye'e tòkko nóo nakka koò ka'a.
             A holding rope with 1-hand chopping motion with r-hand
                 moving right.
             P and N watching A's hands
             nó    g-gya  ka'a  tò    ke'e   tòko  nó   naka#kò   ka'a
             that  CAUS-go here  rope  raise  one   that tied#knot here
             That (we) go and here raise a rope that is tied here.

83 Andrea:   Ka'a kye'e ka'a né.
             A reaches r-hand over 1-hand
             ka'a   ke'e    ka'a=né
             here   raise   lengthen=ACT3O
             Here it gets strung up.
```

84 Pedro:	Áwwà txee bi'yya. P moves forward and grabs rope from A áwà txe bi'ya yes then see **Yes then Let's see.**
85 Pedro:	Áà nzaa ya'nna é. P tying rope while A holds board in place áà nza ya'na=é yes go stay=3o **Yes it's going to stay.**

Andrea is clearer in her description in 82 and 83 having now just pantomimed it, perhaps supporting McNeill's argument (1985, 2005) that gesture and speech are parts of the same psychological structure, and which problematizes the commonly assumed typological distinction between the verbal and nonverbal. Here the verbal description is a reflex of Andrea's self-clarification through the pantomime, and is thus as a representational interpretant, a further-developed sign of her energetic embodiment of the action. Her lexical choices become more specific as well where she specifically refers to rope, *toò*, (rather than "it" or "thing") and indicates that the rope be "lengthened/strung up" running to her right and tying knots for each. Pedro seems to commit to Andrea's project now with an affirmation and grabbing of the rope, declaring in 83 that it (the boards) will stay up this way.

Pedro goes on to tie the first plank in place. Andrea leaves the frame to return a few moments later with another plank. Pedro, however, shows himself to still not be jointly committed to the project to which Andrea and Nazaria are now jointly endeavored as he voices a contradictory line of action. He says, "I say it would be better to tie on a pole," first looking at Nazaria (his prior collaborator) and then turning to Andrea as she comes stepping into close proximity. Pedro is still advocating for Solution 1. Andrea takes the rope from Pedro and nonetheless begins to tie the next board in place implementing Solution 2. And then with the help of Nazaria, she works the rope to weave the planks, one by one, to the wire mesh. Pedro watches and in the next minute steps back from the corral a few times until he finally walks to the other side of the corral away from the activity of Andrea and Nazaria to attend to another part of the project.

In this multimodal-multi-participant assemblage with multidimensional social relations, ideas have come from various sources and have been developed through both the contingencies of the project's materiality and the processes of semiosis into which they have been taken up, and developed by Pedro, Andrea, Nazaria, and Elvia. It is Andrea who asserts Solution 2 through a series of rhetorical and physical moves. Over the interactional timescale, we see the persuasive intensity of her suggestion increase through the chaining of semiosis in which subsequent frames of interpretation develop from priors. Charles Goodwin's term "co-operative action" characterizes such building of present action by operating on others and our own prior artifacts. Andrea's argument itself gains its strength from iterated and resonant doings much like the weaving of the boards one by one in a larger structure gives the corral its strength. Her rhetoric is variably formulated as descriptions, directives for action, questions of what's best for the corral, as well as animation of Pedro's earlier speech and gesture. Her use of Pedro's reported speech has some parallels to the "he-said-she-said" accusations described by M. Goodwin (1990, 1980), though in this case Andrea is not reporting a third party's speech but rather the addressee's speech from an earlier participation frame. The choice of reported speech in the sequence constrains the choice of the next move (1980: 682) and establishes "a right to undertake such action" (Emerson 1969: 166 cited in M. Goodwin 1980: 682). Since the earlier Pedro himself said this, the present Pedro would have to do some interactional and moral work to disagree. Andrea is framing Solution 2 as both what the corral wants and what Pedro has already said/done. Moreover, by stepping into the space of mutual attention (the O-space) of the other participants' F-formation, Andrea disrupts their joint activity. At the focus of Pedro and Nazaria's mutual visual attention, Andrea's argumentation shifts to iconically pantomiming the path of the rope. When Pedro later pushes back against the idea again, Andrea increases the intensity of the suggestion by moving from the iconic mode of her pantomime and symbolic mode of her verbal descriptions to an intrinsic mode in which she conveys her meaning by doing it herself. This is similar to what we saw in the saddle repair of section 6.1 when the husband took the cinch strap to tie it himself after multiple failed attempts to communicate how to do it through symbolic and iconic sign modes. Ekman and Friesen (1969: 60) described an intrinsic code as "in a sense no code in that the act does not stand for but IS its significant; the meaning of the act is intrinsic to the action itself" (emphasis in original). The intrinsically coded act is an icon in being qualitatively like the significant; however, rather than just resemble the significant, it shares an identity with it. Yet we must still consider intrinsic action in cases like these semiosis as the sign-object identity projects an icon as its interpretant (such an act is taken to be a sign in Peircean semiosis but would not be intelligible to Saussure's semiology). Perhaps the most persuasive way to both signify and argue for one's contribution to a joint project is to do it yourself. As we saw earlier when Francisco had to tie the seizing knot before knowing the rope was too short, intrinsic semiosis is also a path to knowledge that argues to oneself. While Pedro abandoned Solution 1 after Nazaria removed her joint commitment, he was not fully convinced and returns after a short while to further develop his idea. Using intrinsic sign modes and the lower pole material index of Solution 1, he attempts to argue for others of the merit of his idea, but he ultimately convinces himself that his idea would use more rope and the extra wood to no better end than Solution 2.

6.3.4 Pedro Brings Thinner Rope and Attempts to Show on the Lower Pole that His Method Uses Less Rope

Three minutes have gone by in which Andrea has woven several boards with the collaboration of Nazaria and which continues as Pedro reenters the scene to introduce an idea to secure the bottoms of the boards to the pole that goes across (remediating Solution 1). He states that his method will not use a lot of rope, though by the end of a sequence where he intrinsically instantiates the actions he is describing he becomes convinced that this is not correct. Instead of the explicit verbal debate imagined by philosophers and what Tomasello described as "shared decision making and the giving

Figure 6.15 Pedro picks up a rope beginning to formulate an idea.

of reasons" (2014: 109–14), it is only after intrinsically instantiating the icon of doing it that he himself becomes convinced that his representation does not resonate the material reality of the corral structures and the affordances of the rope (effectively a semiotic Argument interpretant). In this sequence, Pedro recruits his niece Maria to work on opposite sides of the wall with him using a rope he has brought to try fastening planks between the horizontal pole and the wire mesh. During this, Pedro's sister Elvia is teasing him and claiming his plan actually uses a lot more rope (Figure 6.15).

```
(7) LMSMVDP24Jul0901 7:12-8:13
```

90 Pedro: Xhinne beè níngye' íllo kye' nóo (0.3)
           P comes in frame from left gaze goes to ground and bends to
               pick up a cord. E and M turn gaze to P when he bends to
               ground
           xhine   bè   ninge' ilo   ke'   nó
           how   PL   thing   cord   DEF   that
           How this cord thing that

91 Pedro: nyàá nzaa níngye' paara nóo lá kyi'ña waxxhi.
           P picks up cord with both hands
           nyàá   nza   ninge'   para   nó   lá   ki'na   waxhi
           good   go   thing   for   that neg   use   much
           good to not use much of it for this.

92 Maria: Eskye' txee?
           P gaze to E and M. M and E gaze at P
           eske'   txe
           like.this   then
           Like this then?

```
93 Pedro:      Tòkko nóo nii á stocche' nèé' nóo
               P gaze at E and M
               tòko  nó    ni=á    stoche'  nèé'  nó
               one   that  say=1s  a.while  now   that
               Like one thing I said a while ago now that
94             (0.5)
95 Pedro:      nii á tzyáà nóo akyee kyè' síngye' nèé'
               ---------------------------|P steps toward corral
               ni=á    tzyáà  nó    a-ke   kè'   sínge'    nèé'
               say=1s  just   that  down   this  like.this now
               I'm just saying that down low like this now
96             (1.7)
               P walks to corral between E and A
97 Pedro:      nii á tzyáà nó ka'a nza'lá ye síngye' nèé'
               ---------------|P bends and squats
               ni=á    tzyáà  nó    ka'a   nza'lá  ye   sínge'    nèé'
               say=1s  just   that  here   follow  all  like.this now
               I'm just saying just that here (we should) follow (it)
                  like this now
98             (0.6)
99 Pedro:      ásta ka'a
               P moves hands with rope to his right
               E follows P hand movement (holds gaze to 117)
               ásta    ka'a
               until   here
               to here
100 Pedro:     do'o lámbrà kye'. (0.3)
               do'o    lámbrà  ke'
               insert  wire    DEF
               into this wire.
101 Elvia:     Aà:::
               E moves to her left to get view of P's actions
               oh
               oh:::
```

Pedro comes into frame and picks up a cord off the ground, declaring that there is this cord to use and that it would be good to not use much of it. This makes the background motivation of conserving the commodity of rope explicit and also implicitly expresses Pedro's continued lack of commitment to Solution 2. When Pedro comments about the rope, he recruits Maria's potential collaboration with his gaze. Maria is the only one inside the corral. She replies, "Like this then?" offering a form of collaboration in response to Pedro and gives a go-ahead for him to expand. Elvia, who is standing nearby, and Nazaria, who is assisting Andrea, turn to give their attention to Pedro. In 95, Pedro mobilizes his own prior talk from section 4.2, "Like one thing I said a while ago," referring to his conversation with Andrea about the upper portion of the corral wall. He says, "I'm just saying that down low like this," and then he walks to the wall of the corral inserting his body between Andrea and Elvia. Pedro then bends down to begin to intrinsically instantiate what he is describing in talk with the utterances in 97–100, "I'm just saying just that here (we should) follow (it) like this now" "to here" "into this wire," extending his hand holding the cord to his right along the lower pole. To which Elvia in 101 issues a news uptake, *Aà* (oh).

102 Pedro:	Nattze koò ro'o teme'e ka'a ra María.
	---------------------------------|Maria looks down
	natze kò ro'o te-me'e ka'a=ra María
	accept knot mouth a-little here=EXCL María
	Take this knot end a little here Maria.
103	(2.2)
	M squats down inside corral opposite P
104 Maria:	Nekka lò otzi'kki á.
	P feeds cord end between planks to F
	neka=lò o-tzi'ki=á
	STA.be=2s CMP-throw=1s
	Do it I'll throw it back.
105	(0.3)
106 Maria:	Skwa' tzyáà la?
	skwa' tzyáà=la
	like.this just=Q
	Just like this?
107 Pedro:	Púnta tzyáà lèttzá é.
	púnta tzyáà L*-lètzá=é
	tip just IMP-lift=3o
	Just lift the end.
108	(0.6)
109 Maria:	Likki né la?
	liki=né=la
	raise=ACT3o=Q
	Raise it?
110 Pedro:	Áwwà.
	áwà
	yes
	Yes.
111	(0.7)
112 Pedro:	Áà esso síngye' tzyáà ni á nèé'.
	P feeds rope some
	áà esso sínge' tzyáà ni=á nèé'
	yes eso like.this just say=1s now
	Yes just like this I say now.
113	(0.6)

In 102, Pedro recruits Maria's collaboration with the directive, "Take this knot end a little here Maria." Using "a little" here shows once again the explicit minimization of the burden on the recipient parallel in form of offers we examined in Chapter 2. Maria squats to jointly attend with Pedro and indicates her readiness with a vocal action, "Do it I'll throw it back." Pedro has not given any explicit direction to Maria. She offers a collaborative course of action, "I'll throw it back," based on her inferences, and then issues an understanding check in 106 while manipulating the cord. Pedro gives an explicit directive in 107, "Just lift the end," which is a repair initiation on her previous action indicating for her to lift the end up behind and over the structure of the wire mesh before passing it back through. Maria issues a second understanding check on Pedro's repair as a subsequent repair initiation in 109, "Raise it?" to which Pedro replies with an affirmative interjection, "Yes." As Maria begins to comply, Pedro repeats his interjection, "Yes," expanding on the confirmation, "just like this I say now," while he feeds more cord to Maria who feeds the end back. The multiple repairs finally allow the two to converge on an intersubjective and collaborative action while visibly separated from each other by the corral wall. There we see the language game relying more on audible talk along with intrinsic actions with the rope since the participants are blind to each other's bodies but can see and feel the movement of the rope and through that channel can sense each other's action.

```
114 Pedro:    Ka'a tzyáà [xhi'ka kò tzyáà wa' tòkko é kaà nèé'.
              P shifts footing
              ka'a   tzyáà  xhi'ka  kò    tzyáà  wa'    tòko=é   kà    nèé'
              here   just   tie     knot  just   this   one=3o   knot  now
              Here just tie one knot now.

115 Elvia:    [^Aà eske' kà?
              E gaze still on P's hands
              aà      eske'        kà
              oh      like.this    truly
              Oh truly like this?

116 Pedro:    Sollo nóo txoo nzee rekkò' tzyáà é nèé'.
              P tying rope
              solo   nó    txo   nze   rekò'   tzyáà=é   nèé'
              only   that  then  go    cut     just=3o   now
              It's only that then we'll go and just cut it now.

117 Elvia:    #Nzee rekkò' tzyáà né txee#.
              P tying rope ---------|C moves head and torso for view of F
                      behind corral wall
              nze    rekò'   tzyáà=né      txe
              go     cut     just=ACT3o    then
              #Going to just cut it then#.

118 Pedro:    Nzee rekkò' tzyáà né.
              P tying rope
              nze    rekò'   tzyáà=né
              go     cut     just=ACT3o
              Going to just cut it.

119 Pedro:    Asta stokko laabe kye' nèé' xhikka wa stokko nèé'. (0.2)
              P tying rope E looks back on M's side of wall and back to P
                      M changes stance to stand with hand on hips
              asta    sH-tòko      labe   ke'    nèé'   r-chika=wa    sH-tòko
              until   another-one  center this   now    HAB-insert=1PLI another-one
              nèé'
              now
              Toward another at this middle now we'll insert another now.

120 Elvia:    Mm:
              E rocks torso back slightly from hips shifts foot back

121 Elvia:    Aà skwa' txee la?
              |P turns head gaze on C
              aà     skwa'        txe=la
              oh     like.this    then=Q
              Oh like this then?

122 Pedro:    Skwa' nèé'.
              ------|P gaze to his hands
              skwa'         nèé'
              like.this     now
              Like this now.

123 Elvia:    ^Mm:

124           (1.2)

125 Pedro:    Tòkko tzyáà (.) yakkà' koò ka'a.
              --------------|C body torque to gaze inside corral
              tòko   tzyáà   yakà'   kò    ka'a
              one    just    tie     knot  here
              Just tie one knot here.
```

126 Pedro: Asta dikki' ka'a laa é yakkà' koò stokko tetzo' íxxhì kye' nèé'.
             P working with rope
             asta   diki' ka'a la=é   yakà' kò   sH-tòko
             until gather here already=3o tie   knot another-one
                te-tzo' ixhi ke' nèé'
                surface ixtle this now
             Up to here it's tied and tie another around with this rope now.

With Pedro and Maria having attained mutual understanding through the repair sequences, Pedro advances their joint activity that is materializing his idea. He describes his own activity symbolically, "Here just tie one knot now," while he begins to tie a knot. The intrinsic icon is now effective on Elvia who has attained enough recognition of what Pedro means to speak in overlap during Pedro's turn interjecting a sarcastic comment, "Oh truly like this?" Pedro responds to this in 116, expanding his description to what will come next saying, "It's only that then we'll go and just cut it now." Elvia follows in 117 with a harsh, breathy-voiced repeat, #Going to just cut it then#, which expresses disbelief and challenges the prior speaker to support his claim with epistemic expansion (see Chapter 5, and Sicoli 2007 and 2010a on breathy-voiced repeats). Pedro reaffirms his position with another repetition, "going to just cut it," and then produces an expansion to support his position, "toward another at this middle now we'll insert another now." Elvia looks back on Maria's side of the wall and then back to Pedro's side then changes her stance to stand with arms akimbo. She visibly does not seem to be convinced. Elvia takes a step back and issues another oh-prefaced sarcastic understanding check in 121, "Oh like this then?" which Pedro affirms with a repeat, "Like this now," perhaps not catching the sarcasm. Elvia responds, ^*Mm*, a noncommittal minimal response-token but not the affirmation, *Áà* (yeah), which would indicate uptake of his affirmation. She goes on to offer an understanding check as a declarative question in 127 building her offer in resonance with Pedro's prior turn. Using the repeat-and-run strategy, Elvia transforms the final phrase of Pedro's prior turn *tetzo' íxxhì kye'* (around [with] this rope) as *tetzo' íxxhì kye' kwà'* (around [with] that rope) and adding, "Cinch the pine and pull it then?" turning her gaze to Pedro to mobilize his response. He responds in 128 with an affirmative interjection, "Yes," expanding again verbally in 130, "that it get passed around this wire," while gesturing iconically.

127 Elvia: Tetzo' íxxhì kwà' sindxo zhíccho' la i'ngyì no á txee?
             ----------------------------------|P gaze to C
             te-tzo' íxhì kwà' sindxo zhícho'=la i'ngì=no=á   txe
             back   ixtle that cinch   pine=already pull=INST=1s then
             Around with that rope cinch the pine and pull it then?

128 Pedro: Áwwà.
             ------|P gaze returns forward
             áwà
             yes
             Yes.

129   (0.8)

130 Pedro: Nóo dette né tetzo' lámbra kye'.
             P around gesture
             nó   dete=né   te-tzo' lámbra ke'
             that pass=ACT3o back   wire   DEF
             That it get passed around this wire.

```
131 Elvia:    Aà nii a laa nii tzyáà lò skwà' nii á.
              aà   ni=a  la  ni  tzyáà=lò  skwà'      ni=á
              oh   say=1s NEG say just=2s  like.this  say=1s
              Oh I do say don't just tell me this I say.
132 Pedro:    Áwwà.
              áwà
              yes
              Yes.
133           (0.5)
134 Elvia:    ^Wéy::: xekka akka wà.
              C torques body to look inside corral
              wéy    xeka   aka  wà
              INT    how    be   this
              Whoa dude how does it go?
              ((Pedro's idea would do the same weave the women were
                doing in the last segment))
135           (0.5)
```

In 131, Elvia issues yet another oh-prefaced sarcastic evaluation, "Oh I do say don't just tell me this I say," to which Pedro affirms again with an interjection, "yes." This is clearly reminiscent of Heritage's explication of oh-prefaced responses to assessments (1998: 2002) in which "when persons preface a second or responsive action with *oh*, they are commonly understood to have acted in a fashion that problematizes the action to which they are responding" (2002: 197). All of Elvia's oh-prefacing (aà-prefacing in Lachixío Zapotec) seems to indicate that Elvia considers Pedro's formulations to be problematic. We will see that what is problematic is his presupposition that it will use less rope. In 134, Elvia finally upgrades her evaluations by using a lexical choice that goes beyond oh-prefacing with a tense high pitched, ^ *Wéy*:: (Span. *buey*), saying, "^Whoa dude how does it go?" It is already clear to Elvia that the technique that Pedro is advocating will not use less rope than Solution 2 as each board is still being tied. Beyond this, the use of the extra wood in the horizontal pole is made redundant by tying each board separately to the wire mesh. The fact that it doesn't save rope (and wastes wood) is still not apparent to Pedro who continues advocating for his idea in 136 not yet sensing the irony of the multimodal discord between what he is saying and what he is doing.

```
136 Pedro:    Sólaménte skwa' tzyáà paara nóo láa oyaà é waxxhi toò.
              sólaménte skwa'     tzyáà para nó  la o-yà=é     waxhi tò
              only      like.this just for  that NEG CMP-take=3o much rope
              Just this way so that it didn't take much rope.
137 Elvia:    Eskye' síi ra?
              P stands up
              eske'      sí=ra
              like.this  like.this=EXCL
              Like this?! ((sarcastic))
138 Elvia:    Paara nóo laa oyaa é waxxhi toò ra nee tonno skwa' nèé'
              waxxhi toò waà' nèé'.
              P pulls cord out and stands abandoning his idea. (Figure
                6.16)
              para nó   la  o-ya=é       waxhi tò=ra    ne      tono
              for  that NEG CMP-take=3o  much  rope=EXCL because if
              skwa'     nèé' waxhi tò    wà'   nèé'
              like.this now  much  rope  this  now
              That it doesn't use much rope! Because if it's like this
                now (it'll use) a lot of this rope now.
```

139 Pedro: **Áwwà nii á.**
             áwwà ni=á
             yes say=1s
             Yes, I say. ((got it))

Elvia responds in 137 sarcastically "Like this?!" (including the exclamative particle =*ra*), and then makes the irony explicit in 138 with two speech acts: one indirectly reporting his speech, "that it doesn't use much rope!," and the second characterizing the logical outcome of his physical action, "because if it's like this now (it'll use) a lot of this rope now." At the same time it seems Pedro comes to terms with the fact that his idea does not save rope beginning in 137 when he stands up and in 138 when he pulls out the cord he and Maria had worked together to insert into the project. Pedro then closes the sequence, "yes, I say," a turn which includes both an affirmative interjection and an opinion evidential, *ni á* (I say), that he has come to share this opinion.

One thing this sequence shows is that explicit argument and debate played little role in persuasion and decision making. Much of Pedro's persuasive attempt was done intrinsically with parallel talk representing the actions symbolically (an intermodal harmony where talk and action resonate in complementary semiotic modes). Elvia's counter argument was mostly framed as evaluative comments that questioned Pedro's presuppositions but didn't argue for any counter position (though there was one already going on in the speech environment as Andrea and Nazaria worked together on Solution 2). When she finally moved to explicitly make a statement about what the implications of Pedro's actions were, it was simultaneously timed with Pedro's own realization that he used a lot of rope. Rather than a forward-looking argument, her

Figure 6.16 Pedro stands and pulls his rope out abandoning his idea (line 138).

statement can be seen as making explicit the internal state of Pedro's realization which he simultaneously and intrinsically demonstrated by abandoning his commitment to this idea by untying the cord and pulling it out (Figure 6.16). Like Pedro commenting symbolically on his intrinsic action, Elvia's statement is of similar intermodal relation yet one where the multiple modes of action related in a complex sign are distributed across multiple participants.

6.5 Concluding Remarks

The transcripts of this chapter illustrate to some degree the persuasive power of things in human collaborations. These things can be objects, with forms, relations, and contingencies, and these objects can be prior semiotic actions that create something to respond to, answer, accept, agree with, reject, or commit to (kariotic moments of a time to do something in a future constrained by the materiality of the past). I have presented longer, more continuous transcripts of multimodal interaction here than in prior chapters to show the temporal development of joint commitments to collaborative projects, and how objects come into relations with the semiotic actions working to coordinate collaboration, and how these actions shape the form of language as well. This work develops the suggestion of Wittgenstein to establish "an order in our knowledge of the use of language ... with a particular end in view" (Wittgenstein 1958: no. 132). Attending to actual instances of discourse in which people interact to collaborate in a joint activity is a crucial research practice for philosophical inquiry into human thought, action, and language, where we can see material goals develop in the world of things built through interaction. The things built also include human grammars (and their parts), which, like the corral, come to bear indices of the conversations affording their emergence.

In this chapter, we learned from the couple repairing saddles that a form of prior action can limit the forms of response, and from the family building the turkey corral that collaboration with copresent objects relies greatly on indexical, iconic, and intrinsic sign modes and less necessarily on the symbolic. Beyond this we learned how the material index of a (bad) idea itself became a persuasive participant through the stacking of commitments to material, and the analogical pressure to resonate its form in a different but parallel location of the structure. Remediations only achieved success by unwinding the prior commitments and often distributing agency for the change across multiple participants including the things animated by joint commitments. In all the examples talk was most often notably incomplete on its own, through pervasive indexical grounding of deixis, and often paired with, or minimized, in favor of iconic gesturing and intrinsic action with objects. The resonances activated between objects, gestures, and talk were affective of cognition where we found that the talk representing an idea became more precise when the activity was embodied intrinsically. It is through relations of multimodal assemblages that our social, intersubjective, and material worlds are built and experienced. Seeing that objects of joint commitment animate in multimodal interaction, we can ask what dynamic can animate the languages and thing-parts of joint action? The reflection of the final chapter develops a more explicit account of the phenomenology and biosemiotics implicit in Chapters 2–6.

7

Living Assemblages

In his book *Vico and Pragmatism*, Max Fisch addresses reciprocal relations when writing (in chiasmatic form), "The doings and makings by which world and mind are known enter into the making of both mind and world." He goes on to say, "If the human mind could be given at all, it would be in nothing short of the history of human institutions; but that history, like the history of the natural world, is a laborious, secular, incompletable construction" (1986: 223). In a multimodal linguistic anthropology, we ask, how does language ebb and flow with the sensible modalities available for action and interpretation in the paired moments of daily life that scale to become our built worlds? How is language reproduction and change influenced by the fact that language is always part to the wholes of living process emergent between human and other-than-human participants in interaction? This project has worked to depict the Lachixío Zapotec language as (like any language) an incomplete part of multimodal and multi-participant assemblages for which it is formulated to participants' ends and through which its grammar and lexicon have become shaped over the iterated joint actions that breathe life into language. To the ends of depicting a language as living process, this multimodal ethnography of joint actions has brought together participatory and ethnographic methods to produce multimedia records of social encounters that involve the Lachixío Zapotec language. These formed the basis for semiotic analysis of relations emergent in the sequencing and simultaneity of multimodal data, and grammatical analysis grounded in resonances across modalities and across participants' connected moves. To close this examination of language in joint actions in Lachixío, I want to reflect on the place of language in collaborative world-building projects achieved through complex assemblages that connect human and nonhuman of participants into living webs of causality. Here I can reprise the approach I have taken to engage with living language and relate it to the developing field of biosemiotics that connects the life processes of organisms into ecosystems of knowledge—described as a sigma-scientific approach to come "to know," as Kalevi Kull wrote, "what life knows" (2009). I see this goal of biosemiotics as parallel to the anthropological concern with *emic* knowledge (learning to see from the native point of view) (Geertz 1976; Goodenough 1970; Harris 1976; Malinowski 1922; Pike 1967) and to the concern of ethnomethodology to examine how individuals construct together in interaction an enduring sense of reality (Garfinkel 1967, 2002; Heritage 1991). The challenge is to approach documenting and understanding indigenous linguistic knowledge without displaying it through Cartesian ideologies of language and mind but rather in resonance with a concept of indigeneity like that Kyle Powys Whyte described as "how one is situated as an agent in relation to other beings, entities, and systems that exercise different and similar forms of agency" (2016: 146). So this last move is one that I hope reveals a resonance between such an indigenous perspective and biosemiotics bearing on contemporary directions in linguistics and anthropology.

7.1 Multimodal Assemblages and Biosemiotic Relations

I aimed with this project to engage with the Lachixío Zapotec language as living through joint actions that tie multiple participants through multimodal means to collaborative ends. We started by examining generic social actions that *offer* and *recruit*, and then followed offers and recruitments as they themselves were part to higher-order actions that build intersubjectivity in sequences that *repair* and *resonate*. Finally, we turned to the place, form and function of the language of offers, recruitments, repairs, and resonances in building and repairing artifacts of a durable world. In this account, semiotic process and relations emergent through joint actions develop the form of functional artifacts enduring for future uses. Focusing on such process is both metaphor, and more than a metaphor for how languages themselves are made and remade through the little rituals of daily life. Language, like life, derives qualities of its form and relations of its function between the moments of immediate prior relevance and future contingencies, where, working with what is immediately at hand, we select what is next done that then becomes the prior material for future actions in ongoing ontological chains of process.

The theoretical concepts of multispecies assemblages and living semiosis were guides to integrating multimodal, ethnographic, and corpus-based methods in a way that I hope helped the reader-interpreter witness processes that shape language in Lachixío daily life, in ways that themselves guide further appreciation of the rhythms and resonances of social life in this Zapotec community. Starting from the acknowledgment that languages are embedded in multiple scales of time and causality and thus are productively studied in the temporal dynamics that connect the multiple semiotic modalities present to the participants, rather than as self-contained synchronic objects out of time, this project has worked to open our perspective on the everyday work people do toward *the incompletable construction of a language*. Such a being for language in the time and space between participants connected in joint action makes it crucial to examine a language through the ongoing life process of semiosis and the polydimensional relations of its multimodality. This goes beyond what has become the institutionalized domain of linguistic inquiry, and also beyond a concern with individual cognition to those of social, distributed, and extended cognition. In practice, language emerges with multimodal assemblages of joint action, an order akin to what Gregory Bateson (1972) referred to as an "ecology of mind" where mind is not isolatable in an individual's computation, but rather constituted in biosemiotic, part-whole relations between agents and recognizable/actable dimensions of environment. Jakob von Uexküll (1934) referred to such an organism-environment relation as an *umwelt*: the phenomenal world of an organism characterized in the semiotic dimensions of an environment perceivable through use value and including the affordances of objects, and the actions of other organisms. In addition to Uexküll, and Peirce, biosemiotics follows anthropologist Gregory Bateson as one of its acknowledged precursors in recognizing that the boundaries of mind "do not at all coincide with the boundaries either of the body or of what is popularly called the 'self' or 'consciousness'" (Bateson 1972: 319, also 2002). As biosemiotician Wendy Wheeler (2017) wrote, "Mind, itself, is not a material thing. It is made of biosemiotic relations of similarity, difference and interpretation that flow constantly between a body, an environment and some form of living memory." Wheeler's description touches upon the relational elements we discovered through the chiasmatic logic of resonance, where parallel resonant frames of similarity create the material conditions for noticing the differences instrumental for interpretation and action ascription. While some may say this takes us afield of the object of language, I rather see that this ontological process is the nexus of language reproduction and change. Attending to the resonances participants create between their actions and across their sign modalities is a necessary engagement for language description and grammatical analysis. I hope to have also made it a tolerable engagement. My offer to readers in this work was the production of the material conditions that afford glimpses into Lachixío Zapotec's process of becoming in the early twenty-first century, and to articulate a conception of language open to its multimodal transformations. Stitched into embodied encounters, linguistic forms are subject to what is called downward causation in emergent systems theory (Campbell 1974). This is where the higher-order patterns that emerge from lower-order constituent actions affect the shape and fabric of those very constituents.

7.2 Habits Emergent across Temporal Scales

The timescales for a language's pattern reproduction and change link the phenomenally experienced iterations of the practice of daily life with the perdurance of cultural institutions. This has both immediate and enduring effects. For language we find grammatical forms recurring for social, intersubjective, and materially effective purposes. There are long-term effects on a language because recurrent materials resonate across timespaces to canalize themselves into patterns of morphological form and function. Such habit building helps us to link small-scale actions of immediate relevance—what Enfield (2013) called the "experience-near" enchronic scale, Favareau the "immediate-next action space" (2015, 599), and Kauffman, working on a more general question of nature and living systems, referred to as the "adjacent possible" (Kauffman 2000; Kauffman and Gare 2015)—to more durable evolutionary scales, such as the perdurant scale of sociocultural institutions, including languages, which iterate their own forms over time through popular reproduction. I mean popular here to be *with* people and more broadly, the more-than-human participants that collaborate to bring about reproduction through emplaced interactions.

In Peircean semiosis, what is called "Thirdness" refers to patterns, rules, or conventions, or so-called laws, which emerge in the temporal scales of living process to become habits—habits of mind, habits of relation, habits that allow prediction, expectation, interpretation, and which often vitally depend on the actions of others. Such is the semiosis of all life process but for human language, words, signs, and grammatical relations occur at any moment as an exemplar that in dialogic process has a resonance of similarity with prior exemplars and a difference that has the future effect of shapeshifting its habit for an interpreter. Every current use of a linguistic form is tied to both the past and future and is mutable in this way. As we have seen so often in Lachixío dialogue, the forms of language mobilized in interaction are tied through resonances to others' uses. We saw this clearly in Chapter 2 with the family scaling-up offers from the individual animator to the social family through their reiteration by kin. And seen in Chapter 3 where a recruitment was passed from participant to participant, and was finally transformed by the ultimate participant to simultaneously comply with and resist the recruitment. We learned about forms tied through resonance in conversational repairs of Chapter 4, where interparticipant indexicalities of anaphora linked content question words uttered by one speaker to parts of another speaker's utterance, in Chapter 5 with the cross-participant building of dialogic resonances with talk, and in Chapter 6 where resonances linked formulations of talk, actions, and their artifacts. The extracts from the Lachixío Zapotec Conversations Corpus we examined in these chapters display language not in self-contained sentences of an individual speaker but as part of larger wholes collaboratively built through the joint actions of multiple participants. Such an emergent process ontology for language is not visible through sentence-focused syntax, and does not lend itself to explanation by simple appeal to a sentence's "context." Too often, important details are explained away by casual use of the semantically bleached term "context." Beyond context are intimacies between collaborating elements in sensible inter-indexical relations, potential or possible substitutions, and actual transformations between modalities, participants, ends, and means. In my fieldwork and video analysis, I have worked to notice these relations and transformations, and in the representational ethnographic work of this book project, I have worked to make these relations visible for readers' interpretations.

Instead of referring to the commonplace term "context" to describe the complexities of language use, I have chosen to work at a scale of *multimodal assemblages*, which, in the way they connect among different ways of being, are animated as living assemblages. My concept builds on my reading of polyphonic assemblages of Anna Tsing (2015) where diverse species gather into webs of what my colleague Kath Weston (2017) has called intimate relations. An innovation of this book is that it *transiterates* my own prior understanding of harmony and discord in the acoustic signal (Sicoli 2007, 2010a) to the affordances of a multimodal scale that considers relations between the saying and doing of multiparty interactions. Getting a sense of the multimodal through the ecological notion of multispecies *assemblages* has advantages over the often vaguely applied notion of "context" as container, a metaphor misfit to the ontology of mutual elaboration between signs in multimodal discourse. The often-unrecognized metaphorical ground of "context" reduces its usefulness through an erasure of the reciprocal causations, mutual elaborations, and inter-indexical connecting that build webs of relations across modalities and participants through semiotic processes. These processes are like niche construction in biosemiotic ecologies, what Peterson et al. (2018) referred to as involving "mutual mutability" resonating Imanishi (2002), who argued that there is a bidirectional influence of organism and environment where organisms should not be conceptualized as distinct entities from their environments. In a similar way, languages should not be conceptualized as distinct entities from their "contexts," or, as Wittgenstein observed, of the game they are bound up in. Both the concept of *umwelten* and niche-construction productively complicate our understandings of ecological relationships involving reciprocal causality. Beyond this an important generalization is that emergent systems are themselves participants in the constitution of being for their constituents, exerting a transcalar causality in systems reproduction.

7.3 *Umwelt*, Semethic Interactions, and Assembling We-Relations

Theorizing multimodality requires that we move beyond the dichotomizing container metaphor of text and context.[1] Multimodal relations emerge across temporal dimensions of simultaneity and sequence, and the resonances of recurrence. The interpretive, dialogic, and accumulative processes of semiosis take as their whole an assemblage to which elements of language are a part. The semiotic dimensions of a multimodal assemblage do not place any particular code, participant, or organism at the center to be contained in an external environment of context and then transported whole and separable to another container (in another context). From the perspective I have taken in this book, the intercorporeal scene of encounter is one where the degrees of freedom for communication and cognition that we can call its *semiotic carrying capacity* emerge through the affordances of modalities perceptually available and materially appropriated as means toward the ends of interaction. This of course is constrained by the relations of power participants have to make such appropriations in the first place.

We can relate the position of any participant and/or object as part of an assemblage to what in Uexküll's *umwelten* are the units of a perceptual and effector world that link organism to perceptible and actable aspects of a larger-order world through signs. Importantly, the perceptual and effector world is a part-world and not the whole objective world. The variable subjective access to an objective world that *umwelt* captures helps us constrain notions of intersubjectivity most broadly conceived as "an existential condition that can *lead* to a shared understanding . . . rather than being itself such an understanding" (Duranti 2010: 21, emphasis in original). That reading of intersubjectivity assumes a shared objective world where we all share one separate and containing nature, rather than the perspectivism of *umwelten* and its resonance with the ontological turn in anthropology that admits many natures, and partial intersubjectivities between humans, and with nonhuman participants. Sharing some aspects of body plan and perceptual-motor organs with other mammals and vertebrates, but also given relative differences in bodily form, capacities for semiosis, cognition, and evolved and developed habits, we could turn Wittgenstein's famous statement "if a lion could talk, we would not understand him" (PI 223) to address the biosemiotics question of "how could we come to know what a lion knows?" And perhaps state that if an octopus could also talk, we would better understand the lion. *Umwelten* can differ in kind by species attuned over evolutionary timescales to attend to meaningful effects and affordances of the copresent, and how the experiential moments of separate organisms become a kairotic time to act in some interpretable way that connects them. *Umwelten* are in part built through the sign action of other organisms, which is why, though sometimes talked about as a perceptual bubble or surround, *umwelt* is rather a set of relations and connections afforded by evolved habits for semiosis—habits that themselves may include attention to the perceptual and effective habits of others. Where one life form attunes to the signs made sensible through the habits of another, Jesper Hoffmeyer (2008a) has used the term "semethic interaction." The dynamic concepts of both *umwelt* and semethic interaction are helpful for understanding human language as part of the niche-constructing semiotics of multi-participant, multimodal interaction.

In interactional linguistics, the concept of *umwelten* as both diverse and partially overlapping has been taken up at some length by Charles Goodwin (2017). Many years before, Erving Goffman used the term as the title to a section in his essay "Normal Appearances" (1971b). Goffman took a narrower perspective than Goodwin, focusing mainly on *umwelt* in attending to signs of alarm, using it less in Uexküll's sense than as a "metaphor" for certain semiotic phenomena that interested him (see Handler 2012 for discussion). Uexküll's focus for *umwelt* was on the experienced world of organisms, for which the term was taken up by several phenomenologists including Husserl, Heidegger, and Schutz (Goodwin 2017: 260). Schutz used *umwelt* as one division he applied to Husserl's *lebenswelt*, or lifeworld, with *umwelt* representing the "we-relationship" of consociates sharing community through direct experience, and differing from the *mitwelt* of mere contemporaries. For Schutz *umwelt* represents a copresence of space when another is "present in person and I am aware of him as such," "of his body as the field upon which play the symptoms of this inner consciousness" and of time "when his experience is flowing side by side with mine, when I can at any moment look over and grasp his thoughts as they come into being" (Schutz 1980: 163). While Schutz considered the rules of a grammar to be in the sphere of the more distal *mitwelt*, the work represented in this book implores us to consider how grammar, linguistic form more generally, and multimodality work together for the attunement of individuals to share experience in a way that itself affords the collaboration of joint action. This resonates with concerns of ethnomethodology and conversation analysis to study the architecture of intersubjectivity beyond its potential. Intersubjectivity is both afforded and achieved by embodied copresence through a multimodal sensorium, practices of joint attention building and action coordination, action sequencing, repair organization, and language (see Sidnell 2014). My contribution directs attention to the dialogic and intermodal resonances at play in the emergence and repair of language as ontologically generative.

Hoffmeyer has written about human communication (speech in his example but equally relevant from the perspective of multimodal interaction) as an emergent transition for humanity that enabled the sharing of "one large, common umwelt" with the "benefit that it could turn the world into a mystically produced common dwelling place" (Hoffmeyer 1996: 112). For examples of such dwelling construction that are, in my experience, not at all mystical when we examine the relations of time and multimodality in the semiosis of their assemblages, consider the formulation and reformulation of place and object references before and after repair initiations that we examined in Chapter 4. In several cases where a reference was repaired, what was problematic was the assumption of shared sensory attention—a shared, or overlapping, *umwelt*. While two individuals may have been objectively copresent in the frame of video, they demonstrably did not share a subjective spacetime—the we-relationship that permits successful reference in interaction and reveals reference itself to be a joint action rather than contained in a proposition. A multimodal formation of a hand point and deictic pronoun indicating a place or a relevant ear of corn to be husked can fail to become intersubjective if the addressee does not share a sensory ground for interpreting the sign mode. Remedies after repair initiation can work to make the visible action a more noticeable fit with the deictic verbal component, or shift from deictic reference to more abstract symbolic reference (see examples 7 and 13 of Chapter 4, and cases presented in Sicoli 2016a). Importantly, though, semiotic modes can be shifted in the other direction. In arguments to convince another (Chapter 6), we saw that troubles in understanding abstract symbolic reference could be redone by shifting semiotic modes from symbolism to the intrinsic mode of doing an action in the copresence of another as a sign that stands for itself.[2] We also saw that intrinsic action was involved in an individual making their own thoughts clearer to both others and themselves. Where someone was having trouble formulating their idea in words, the use of the semiotic mode of intrinsic action which externalizes the idea performatively through bodies and objects of a material world was then followed by more precise referential vocabulary describing their idea (Chapter 6, examples 6–7). Transformations between and among semiotic dimensions before and after repair initiation show us both the power and the limits of language to produce a common dwelling place where the joint action of communication can happen. With this knowledge, analysis of human language cannot focus merely on relations within self-contained sentences, but must examine resonances built across modalities and participants' interrelated moves—resonances that illustrate how participants build overlapping *umwelten*, a constructed niche, or more accurately phrased, a *built-relationship* to make for the successful joint action of shared reference.

For language to work in the pragmatics of joint action, broader semiotic architecture must construct an intersubjective niche of relationships, which provides the potential for mutual understanding and/or successful collaboration. Multimodality recognizes that *umwelten* can flex and grow, or reduce in dimensionality, and that language ebbs and flows to fit dimensions that become a relevant semiotic ground for sign building and interpretation. Thus, where we share perceptual access to each other's bodies in an interactional encounter, that access includes gaze direction, gestural movement, proximal relations and body orientations, facial gestures, and joint attention to/manipulation of objects. Our *semiotic freedom* (Hoffmeyer 1996: 61) is grounded in the variable degrees of freedom for the joint actions of meaning-making emergent at the perspectival position from which one connects to an assemblage. Such perceptual positions shift from moment to moment, and language has evolved to be open to such contingency.³ Language is a shapeshifter like the *nagual* of Mesoamerican shamanism. Our analysis of language must recognize its ability to transform through and across modalities, and to become something more as modalities link up in an emergent multimodal and multi-participant syntax. *Umwelten* can even shift temporarily when the lights go out, when there is noise in the channel, when one participant diverts attention, where mutual attention is focused on a shared object, and when communication is mediated through different technologies, distances between interlocutors, and participant formations (see Sicoli 2016b). People may go blind during their life and come to a different *umwelt* connected to others through different semiotic dimensions, such as how Tactile ASL supplants Visual ASL among some with Usher syndrome who transition from deaf to deaf-blind during their life histories (Edwards 2014). Technological mediation also shifts the affordances of perception and the modalities of communication. Connection via telephone sets up an encounter to privilege the oral/aural channel, and video conferencing adds some limited visual access. Instant text messaging via analog connections relies on written forms, to which images, emoji, and moving GIFs may be integrated with digital data plans. There is a moral obligation for research that ostensibly aims to represent and understand language, to represent the actual elements and arrangements that enter into the ontologies of human communication and not to privilege one mode of language as "natural" or "primary" (particularly one that suspiciously parallels Western written practices in form). It is not simply that an organism has a particular *umwelt* as an innate biological endowment but that many contingencies are at play in producing semiotic freedom given the carrying capacities of the emergent timespaces of everyday life for semiosis.

Uexküll concludes his book *A Stroll through the Worlds of Animals and Men* with an example of an oak tree as object and environment and contrasts the different *umwelten* of different species that interact with the "same" tree. The human, fox, owl, woodpecker, and bark beetle all sense the tree as something different. The biosemiotician seeking to "know what life knows" would be engaged in folly to describe the tree of the owl in the terms of the knowledge of the bark beetle, or of the human. It is parallel folly to seek to understand the language of a copresent multimodal interaction, where participants have sensory access to each other and their objects of joint attention, through audio-only transcription and linguistic analysis of what was said (as it was to judge sign languages on the terms of spoken language). But analyzing copresent interactions through attention to the spoken/written record is exactly what much of discourse analysis does. Perhaps this would be more suitable where the potential intersubjective dimensions are monodimensional (Hockett 1987) like a short, written example, text message, or utterance mediated via telephone or radio technology, though not really, since the embodied dimensions of using such technologies are erased where analysis is focused merely on the text record. The imperative for representing language in actual instantiations is that analysis be fitted to the *umwelten* of the participants, and the work they do to build resonances with intersubjective potential for connection, communication, and collaboration. Where bodies are copresent with each other and afford shared attention to copresent objects there is attunement that produces a shared *umwelt* through which talk and other semiotic action become intelligible through connection. We saw such an example in Chapter 4 (example 14, Figure 4.8) when David was recruited by Daniel to hold a bicycle parts-assembly, but David holds off initiating repair, "Which?" until walking around to establish an attentional common ground with Daniel. At other times the immediate prior speech sets up such a ground (a summons, a pre-action, a prior action that becomes repeated, all do the work of niche construction to set up a ground for interpretation) (see also Schegloff 2006). In these cases there is not a stable "environment" (environ = surround) or con-text but a mutable set of relations that connect multiple dimensions across an encounter and across encounters. Related concepts from conversation analysis are regulatory actions such as intonation, gaze, and head nods that regulate turn structure and attention, and "frame attunement" which Adam Kendon (2009: 239) described as facing the "problem of establishing what each other's interpretive perspectives are." Frame attunement involves practices like routinization and rhythm (semiotic thirdness), the communication of attention (semiotic secondness relating body orientations), formulaic devices like greetings, ready signals, and the like. "Attention getters" as described by Tomasello (2008) for nonhuman primates similarly create a shared scaffold of attention that produces the potential for intersubjective actions like play and sharing.

Frame attunement through the regulation of nods, gaze, formulaic language, poetic structure, and the parallelism of resonance, are all scaffolding actions or devices that constrain and enable what additional orders of communicative and collaborative goals can be realized. As we have seen across the chapters of this book, joint actions that *offer* and *recruit* scaffold emergent orders of relationships, intersubjectivities, and materialities. Moreover, resonating sequences can be used to scaffold the doing of many more actions. Resonance is involved in affirmations, negations, agreement, the scaling up of offers, reframing of recruitments, just to name a few and the list can go on and on. As we saw in Chapter 5, repetition scaffolds the practice of dialogic syntax (Du Bois 2014) and the analysis of grammar it affords through the dialogic and chiasmatic logic of resonance, a "double-proportional comparison" where "two things are compared with each other twice" (cf. Wagner 2017: 2019). A resonating parallel frame (one comparison of similarity) makes noticeable focal grammatical differences (a second comparison, of difference). The parallelism built from the other's material may be seen as offering a diagrammatic icon that then recruits attention (a noticing) and a search for meaningful difference.[4] Resonances may be built up not only between individuals but between modalities organized in relationships that are harmonic or discordant. We thus can extend Jakobson's observation quoted of Chapter 5 that "the essence of poetic artifice consists in recurrent returns" (Jakobson 1966: 399) to the intersemiotic domain of multimodal configuration and transformation.

Thus, rather than start with separate ideas of core and periphery, or inside and outside, like language and context, we can focus our attention on the mutual elaboration of semiotic dimensions that build an inter-indexical and resonating web of relations. From the perspective of a multimodal assemblage, no single mode of signification is *a priori* privileged, and this works to advance a project of a non-Cartesian science of language. Cartesian practice since Descartes has divided the world into two kingdoms "those of mind and of matter, the cultural and the natural spheres" (Hoffmeyer 1996: 94), with much of contemporary academic disciplines also divided across a dualism with Humanities and Social Sciences representing the kingdom of mind and culture, and the Natural Sciences the kingdom of matter and nature. Pervasively, Cartesianism is also fractally recursive. We are habituated to thinking of language as something inside cultural context, language competence as inside an organism (or a so-called mind-brain) or organism as inside an environment. Biosemiotics "seeks to cross [this boundary between kingdoms] in hopes of establishing a link between the two alienated sides of our existence—to give humanity its place in nature" (Hoffmeyer 1996: 94). The biosemiotic project, then, is parallel to the project of giving language its place in multimodality, and the goal of documenting language as part of sociocultural life, or which I prefer to conceptualize as engaging with language as living process.

As I said in the Introduction, the semiotics of multimodality is not about getting more. It is not adding context to language even though it is misunderstood as such. In a multimodal order, the components from which it emerged are themselves transformed. Human cooperative interaction in general, and multimodal interaction specifically, can be recognized as the locus of a major transition in evolution (Maynard Smith and Szathmáry 1995), and one that is ongoing in daily life activity in which language and symbolic action are themselves emergent.

7.4 Teleodynamics and the Life of Things

Objects have played important roles in multimodal assemblages in this book. From the gifts exchanged in the wedding, the planks and poles of the turkey corral, to the empty pitcher and cups, objects took up roles not just as signs but also as participants. What kind of dynamic is this in which objects (from our material tools to our institutionalized systems of communication) can become guiding participants, including participation that guides its own reproduction? In this section, I want to discuss how the habitual goals coded in the form of objects relate to their sign usage in multimodal interaction. Through the dynamics of joint actions with objects of joint attention, inanimate objects can take on their own participant status animated through a teleodynamic process where objects resonate with the joint commitments of their assemblage-companions to produce qualities we expect of life.

In Uexküll's characterization of *umwelt*, he considered there to be something of objects present in an *umwelt* that is not materially present in sensory perception. This is something *absential*, to use Deacon's term, defining an "intrinsic property of existing with respect to something missing, separate, and possibly nonexistent" and "a defining property of life and mind" (Deacon 2013: 547). Uexküll posed the question, "How do we manage to see *sitting* in a chair, *drinking* in a cup, *climbing* in a ladder, none of which are given perceptually. In all the objects that we have learned to use, we see the function [the effector image] which we perform with them as surely as we see their shape or color" (Uexküll 1992: 358, emphasis in original). A rock used as a hammer stone would take on functional association for its users just as any cultural object takes its use as part of its effector image. Some objects have a conventionally functional form, like the pitcher with its use in the life history of individuals for holding a liquid quantity suitable to a social gathering, and thus while materially similar to a cup, it differs in social value. Such "coding" is a form of *extended cognition* or *externalization*. Henrik Sinding-Larsen (2019) argues that externalization shapes cognitive habits of imagination. Tracing the history of the semiotic system of musical notation, he shows that such an externalization both catalyzed and constrained the Western musical imagination (see also Shayan, Öztürk, and Sicoli 2011 for a resonant argument). Furthermore, Lyre (2018: 831) has recently claimed that "from the point of view of extended cognition . . . it is the possibility of actively structuring the physical environment afforded by the world that significantly drives the development of symbolically structured and linguistically encoded thought." Sharing concern to some degree with my questions on the language of joint actions, Lyre applies his work on extended cognition to developing our understanding of shared intentionality. But as I have mentioned about scholarship on philosophy of language earlier, and as I will for social autopoiesis later, Lyre's argument is built in the abstract, drawing entirely on the made-up examples of always-dyadic interactions, like two people collaborating on a book, or an amnesiac using his notebook as an extension of memory. While thought experiments like those are useful heuristics, I hope this book has made clear the potential and obligation for bringing the grounding of language documentation and practices of ethnography together on questions of intersubjectivity, shared intentionality, we-relations, social, extended, and distributed cognition. Through such a grounding in a science of the concrete (to borrow a phrase from Levi-Strauss 1962), we can rather depict, and thus work to understand, how both potentials for intersubjectivity and the mechanics of its achievement emerge in the dynamics of actual interactions that mattered in the lives of their participants.

It is not just the function encoded in form that makes some objects noticeable and influential. Uexküll notes that other objects with similar form and affordances may be erased from view when not meeting expectations. He refers to this expectational aspect of *umwelt* as the "search image and search tone" where through a history of semiosis with objects we habituate to looking for certain forms when being of a mind to find them. The search tone is so effective that we might not see another actually present solution plainly staring us in the face if it doesn't, as I would say, resonate. Uexküll provides an example of his having become habituated to an earthen jar at a regular lunch with a friend. His acquired expectation of the clay jar had such effect that when it was one day replaced by a glass pitcher, he looked right through the glass pitcher to ask where the water was (Uexküll 1934: 373).

I will focus here on two important involvements for objects guiding a search tone: one involvement is based on morphological resonance and the memory of conventional use, and the other based on commitments that emerge in an interaction and thus more dynamic creative involvement.[5] An object's material qualities relate to affordances for perception and use and its cultural form encodes function. Gibson (1979) in coining and defining the now frequently used term "affordance" argued that affordance entailed a complementarity between organism and environment that dissolved the distinction between them in a way that resonates with Uexküll's *umwelt*, and the notion of *cognition* in Varela and Maturana's work on *autopoiesis*. In autopoiesis the environment and the organism mutually call each other into existence through "enaction" or "co-emergence" (Luisi 2003: 55; Varela and Maturana 1998). The emergent co-constituting and cocreated order pointed to in concepts of affordance and enaction recognizes life and environment as one where "the traditional Cartesian division between matter and mind disappears and where consciousness appears" (Luisi 2003: 55).

The hollow of a gourd for a human, and similarly, the concavity of a leaf for a chimpanzee, affords uses as drinking vessels, and such functional tones can guide one's search and imagination when looking for an instrument to quench one's thirst, or in communicating one's search to another. Intentions can come to be encoded as cultural form. The handle of a hammer fabricated by someone in the past fits the hand of a current user such that when picking one up the hand is guided to the conventional use-relationship. From Kockelman (2007) this would be referred to as in the *residential agency* of the object that is oriented to by an interpreter who may further have *representational agency* over the object (and a way that the interpretive archaeological viewpoint may both resonate in parallel with and differ from those of culturally native tool users).

The second involvement for objects is emergent between the object and the people who together interact in the bricolage practice of spontaneous multimodal interaction. Objects can dynamically take on functions or meanings that are not conventionally coded in their form and only loosely coupled to the conventional history before the interaction. Human joint actions add layers of joint commitment to an object in connection with paired *umwelten* that afford objects a goal-oriented status. When connected to the assemblage of a multimodal interaction through which they become a dynamic participant, objects accumulate something absental that affords self-preservation. We saw several examples of this in Chapter 6. Recall how joint commitments to a particular rope set up by Felicita's response-limiting either-or-formulated offer to Francisco guided his subsequent actions that later had to be undone. More striking is the role a horizontal wooden pole took on in the turkey-corral construction project. In the microhistory of the interaction, one pole placed within a set of relations to the developing corral structure and the people constructing it came to "store" (like a capacitor) intention jointly committed to by the other participants. This intention is activated by those with the historical knowledge to perceive it, and from where, as part of the immediate prior, it can influence their subsequent choices. Favareau (2008) characterizes this as "collapsing the wave function" a quantum shift from the dimension of future probabilities to a present actuality. Through the teleodynamic process of human joint action, objects are endowed with the absental qualities of intentions and commitments. In this way objects, as signs, come to store extrinsic energy with power to persuade other participants and influence futures. This is why I refer to such objects as another type of participant, rather than simply a thing, at such charged moments. In the case of the horizontal pole, resonant energy animated its reproduction. Another pole had recently been taken up into a morphological relationship to the larger assemblage to hold the lower end of the wall planks in place. There it sat as a sign of the social achievement of a solution to the practical problem of attaching the planks. From there it activated a further sign of itself as a solution to the resonant problem of attaching the upper ends. When the first solution was recognized as debilitative for the future of the turkeys and their relations, it still took a good amount of interactional work from multiple participants connected to the assemblage to keep the ill-fated reproduction from happening again.

To reiterate, there are two ways that an object like the horizontal pole can reproduce, and while both involve something absential, one is characterized by its dynamic emergence within the joint action of interaction. In the first case, horizontal poles that capture vertical planks have been seen by the family members in other structures in the region, specifically in kitchen houses which are built loosely to allow smoke to escape. The morphology and structural relations of the construction exist in memory as a potential to be reproduced. The use and memory are icons of each other. Solution 1 was in the first place likely motivated for this resonance with the vertical plank construction form of many kitchen shacks. However, in the multimodal ecology of the interaction, the pole becomes a more dynamic participant, as a material sign of commitments held jointly between multiple persons also connected to the assemblage. The material takes on its own history that resonates with the goals and commitments of the other participants. It is cognitively co-emergent within the distributed order of the assemblage, and not contained in its material itself which, in a reductionist perspective, would only be a piece of wood. Through the energy added by the other participants in its assemblage, the thing comes to have a life of influence, a coexistence in connection with paired *umwelten* where the new affordance emerges. It is not just a template for the future like the memory (a semiotic rheme), but a sign of the existence of commitments in a built-world (a semiotic dicent). As the material sign of commitment, its subsequent interpretation can influence other participants to collaborate in its reproduction.

Multimodal joint action then creates conditions for a synergistic emergence of attributes of component parts of assemblages that are not objectively "in" the parts. The absential quality emerges through what Deacon calls teleodynamic process. Deacon (2013: 552) defines teleodynamics as "a form of dynamical organization exhibiting end-directedness and consequence-organized features that is constituted by the co-creation, complementary constraint, and reciprocal synergy of two or more strongly coupled morphodynamic processes." Human multimodal interactions, conversations, and joint actions with objects demonstrate the strongly coupled reciprocal creation of teleodynamics that breathe life into the emergent products of such interactions, including language. The wooden pole is an object-form that makes the point simply. While vastly more complex, languages are themselves (re)produced through this emergent dynamic both in experience-near interaction and in the long *durée* as perdurant, yet mutable, sociocultural institutions. Words, phrases, and grammatical constructions accrue histories of the joint intentions of collaborative uses that, as signs, exert an influence to reproduce aided by the extrinsic action of their co-collaborators.

In systems theory and biology, synergistic emergence stands in contrast to modularity and reductionism. Where synergistic emergence works with components as part of assemblages, modularity tends toward reduction to seemingly isolatable functions or structures. Wholes that emerge through dynamic connections between species of plants and their mycelium companions have transformed understandings of forests to interspecies collaborations for communication and the sharing of nutrients (Simard et al. 2012). Where life itself is teleodynamic, the synergy of several lives in interaction creates higher-order teleodynamics emergent from the synergisms of their mutual elaboration.

Echoing Bateson, we can work with the concept of teleodynamics as "a pattern that connects" across life sciences and social sciences, and across scales of order. Sinding-Larsen wrote that "higher order teleodynamics can emerge from collaborating colonies of lower-order teleodynamic systems, like multicellular organisms, colony forming organisms, and socially or culturally integrated human institutions" (2012: 24). The related concept of *autopoiesis* has similarly been applied to human social systems as higher-order self-maintaining and reproducing systems that perdure across generations even though individuals themselves come in and out of the system (see Luhmann 1984; Teubner for application to law; Paulson 1988 for application to literature; Mingers 1995; Capra 2002 and Zeleny 1997 to macro-social systems; and Luisi 2003 for a helpful review). While many applications of autopoiesis to human sociality have focused on macro-social systems and institutions, Mingers (2001) draws some explicit attention to embodied and interactional levels of emergence that connect more micro-levels to more macro, exhibiting both bottom-up and top-down constraints. Mingers's levels include *the embodied individual* as a system of enactive/embodied cognition; the *social individual* which through a "double contingency" of expectations (a recursive theory of mind) couples individuals in meaning, emotion, and behavior; *social networks* through which systems of conversation and recurrent interaction within groups couple to a behavioral domain of meaning, legitimation, and power; and a level of *society/organization* where communication establishes society (upward causation) and society in turn structures interaction (downward causation) (Mingers 2001: 115). The work of social autopoiesis, as with cellular autopoiesis makes important observations on the dynamic, recursive self-formation of living systems, but the dynamic is often only approached in the abstract. And while informed by questions of phenomenology that connected biology with the philosophy of Husserl (1931) and Merleau-Ponty (1967), among others, the detailed histories of living through these emergent connections are not described. Scholars of social autopoiesis have tended toward theoretical expositions. I have rather utilized ethnography and the exegesis of actual events through video analysis. Because I am interested in the application of emergent dynamics to the projects of language documentation and ethnomethodologically informed anthropology, I am drawn more to Deacon's related though distinct conceptualization of the characteristic dynamics of life as teleodynamics both as involved in major emergent transitions in evolution and with potential for describing what is emergent in the resonances of multimodal assemblages that take language as their part. Describing teleodynamics, Deacon wrote that "rather than being an abstract description of the properties that living processes exhibit, [teleodynamics] is a specific dynamical form that can be described in quasi-mechanistic terms" and is "not necessarily limited to the biological domain." Teleodynamics as an organizing dynamic of joint action can help make more productive the abstract characterizations of social autopoiesis in works like Mingers (2001). Documentary linguistics can thus develop our theoretical understanding of language as life process when coupled with concrete methods of interaction and grammatical analysis attuned to the semiotic logic of resonance emergent with the orders of dialogic syntax and multimodal interaction.

Through the teleodynamics of multimodal joint actions, objects, linguistic constructions and conventions, and even conversations themselves take on self-sustaining (self-preserving and reproducing) qualities we associate with life. Though unlike organisms which are self-sustaining through their own self-contained teleodynamics, inanimate objects take on such living qualities when taken up as part of larger-order assemblages, more like a virus, which, without its own energy and ability to reproduce itself, ties into the teleodynamic system of an autonomously living cell. Existing as inanimate particles outside their interaction with living cells, they are nonetheless considered agents, and a form of life, for their self-replication when animated in biosemiotic connection to an assemblage of cellular teleodynamics (e.g., referenced as infectious *agents* and also as *means* of horizontal gene transfer). For objects connected to human assemblages of interactional joint actions, the tendency toward self-preservation and replication for participants that begin as objects is not wholly located in the object but rather in it being taken into paired *umwelten* as a sign of commitment to a joint goal, and for a language, of the possibilities for intersubjectivity built into its conventions. Agency for the goal committed to in a joint action is distributed, and, as long as a perceived harmony between goals and the materials-which-evoke-signs-of-the-goals exists, there is a telos of reproduction such that it requires more work to keep it from being reproduced. The horizontal pole of Solution 1 of the turkey corral (in the problem space that was later solved by Solution 2) persisted with the help of Pedro and Nazaria until there became a shared understanding that it was discordant with the goal of the larger assemblage. While Andrea worked the most to convince the party of the discordance, the persuasion only became effective when the corral was represented as an agent wanting another solution, and ultimately with the cooperation of Nazaria abandoning her joint commitment to Pedro and the wooden pole. Words can similarly persist in usage and require some amount of work to change their tendency to reproduce. The masculine pronoun "he" as a generic persisted in English (and still does in some circles) before the work that has gone into drawing notice to discordant relations with the assemblages of its use and intentions. Conversations themselves also take on self-sustaining qualities once they get going, and this is why we have elaborate closing routines to end them (Schegloff and Sacks 1973). This self-sustaining quality of a conversation also gives us some understanding of how sequences of resonant repeats can go on in Lachixío and other Mesoamerican languages for many turns before some additional work is undertaken to shift topic.

In teleodynamic process, form is generated synergistically from the interaction of participants that contribute their energy to the emergence of a new order of relations. Sinding-Larsen (2012: 24) observes that "in general, teleodynamic transitions are rare in evolution, but they seem to appear with an accelerated frequency after cultural evolution took off among humans." Language is considered a major emergent transition for humans, but given the nesting of emergent transitions in our evolution, we should ask to what extent the emergence of language is tied up with emergent transitions to joint action and multimodal interaction? We should also ask if this emergence is ongoing and thus empirically observable? To both of these questions, many cognitive and functional linguists would affirm that we can see the ongoing emergence of language in the multimodal phenomenology of child development where we can see deixis and predication built on embodied acts of pointing and pantomime (Tomasello

2008) and that more complex syntactic embedding emerges in phases built from less complex embedding (Lieven 2014). In considering a language's place in multimodal joint actions, the approach I have taken here views the practical ability for focused joint action through multimodal semiosis as an evolved teleodynamic transition that afforded the teleodynamic transition to language for our species evolutionarily, of our children developmentally, and for the continuous shaping of language form, function, meaning, and use through the iterated and resonant interactions of everyday life. Let's now reflect on the place of languages in the teleodynamics of multimodal joint action through a final review of the book.

7.5 Ongoing Major Emergences that Build Worlds and Shape Languages

I will reiterate one last review of the emergent relations through which we have examined the Lachixío Zapotec language as lived in multimodal joint actions in the early twenty-first century. I have structured the chapters of this book by what are imperatives of human social life "offer," "recruit," "repair," "resonate," "build," and have worked to demonstrate ordered, emergent relations between them which we can observe in everyday interactions but which, through their implicational relationship, are informing of evolutionary relations for language and social action. The universality of these actions at a generic level opens up the possibility for comparison within and across languages and societies, and for exploring and understanding the teleodynamics of social action that build living worlds between the human and nonhuman. Where we can find resonance in generic action, we can notice difference in specific forms of the locally emergent assemblages that provide unique expression of linguistic and cultural distinction. Such a strategy of comparison is itself grounded in the double-proportional comparison of chiasmatic logic, here creating a potential from genera of similarity for difference in specifics. Within the teleodynamics of language in joint actions, we find the self-generated, end-directed, cocreated, self-repairing, and self-replicating characteristics of life.

We explored in Chapters 2 and 3 how offering and recruiting build social relationships and in Chapters 4 and 5 that offering and recruiting organized intersubjectivity-building actions to repair and resonate with another participant. Repair and resonance rest on social actions that offer and recruit in an emergent relationship (an implicational hierarchy). This is important ontogenetically in our development and phylogenetically in our cognitive evolution.

Throughout this book we learned about Lachixío Zapotec language through relations, resonances, and collaborations articulated through the living assemblages of everyday life. We learned for instance facts about imperative grammatical forms not obtainable in introspection or elicitation. An abstract definition of "expressing a command" that might be found in a dictionary or grammar does little justice to the characteristics and distributions of grammatical forms revealed in focused interactions. We found that the imperatives formed through extensions of aspect and mood morphology were the most common formats for offers, and the solidarity and positive reputation building produced through them in the *being* in futuro of intentions and expectations (Peirce CP 2.86). Directing analytical attention on resonances between different participants in multimodal assemblages, we learned important facts about variation between grammatical forms. For example, in the offers in Chapter 2, we regularly found a pattern where a husband consistently used the potential mood formed imperative and a wife the completive aspect. Imperative forms were also the commonplace way of formulating recruitments. With attention on temporal sequences of recruitments, we saw that the potential and completive imperative forms of recruitment could be substituted in sequence where the completive was used as a pragmatic upgrade that indexically marked the utterance as redoing a recruitment that was not complied with and strengthen its force. Moreover, our attention on the language of joint actions taught us to see with Wittgenstein (1958: 19) that a language is a form of life tied with the other participants of its assemblage into the local history of obligations and exchange, the immediacy of entitlement and contingency, and the imagined futures of relationships and reputations. Analysis of joint actions in the Lachixío Zapotec Conversations Corpus also showed both the capability of self-repair examined in Chapter 4 and self-replication of resonance examined in Chapter 5, both characteristics of the teleodynamics of life. Achieved through the practice referred to in conversation analysis as other-initiated repair, repair at the order of the multi-participant, multimodal interaction involves a total self-corrective unit that does not align with what is generally thought of as the self or individual (Bateson 1972: 319). Rather than individual cognition, other-initiated repair is an order of social-cognition, a system of joint action, and a joint activity in itself. Through describing the details of its semiosis with attention to the temporalities of sequencing and simultaneity, we learned about the grammar of questions, including details of the usage of the phrase-final question enclitic to form interrogative questions, its absence in declarative questions, open-class repair interjections, functions for repetition in repair initiation and response, and about elements left out or added to repetition sequences. We also learned a great deal about the use of content question words, and found them to be functioning at an order of relating separate individuals' utterances. In Chapter 5 the ringing resonance of Lachixío conversations illustrated how the recurrent returns that Jakobson pointed to as particularly gratifying for linguistic analysis are collaboratively built by participants in their conversational exchanges and thus provide an unparalleled ethnomethodological and autoethnographic tool for grammatical analysis. This order of resonance building through the joint actions of dialogic syntax is crucial in language development and for linguistic description because for both the child and the linguist, the double-proportional comparison entailed in dialogic syntax brings difference and variation into focus through a scaffold of similarity and connection. Resonating iterations were seen to build up a social order resting again on offers and recruitments as means to the ends of many forms of repair initiation and remedy. Through a pervasive resonance building in Lachixío language use, we also learned about the system of final enclitics for questioning, exclaiming, and marking prior epistemic knowledge, and the ethnoknowledge involved in acts that substitute grammatical and lexical forms as an affordance for the emergent discovery of linguistic paradigms (Du Bois and Sicoli

2016). In the building of material artifacts in Chapter 6, we also worked with the cross-modal resonances that connect talk, gestures, and actions with objects into an order of language working with a particular end in view (Wittgenstein 1958: no. 132).

As a tool for linguistic and cultural description, multimodal video analysis allowed for the close and repeated examination of the scenes of encounter in which joint actions were initiated and undertaken. This allowed us to consider how grammar does the work of human collaboration in actual scenes of life where participants were morally responsible to each other. Grammars are different when part to the whole of different multimodal assemblages that produce their lifeworld. If we were to focus on copresent collaborations with objects of joint attention, we would yield a different grammatical corpus than focusing on collaborations where joint attention is precluded, or when having to produce a scaffold of time and space for the description of the same collaboration in a retrospective narrative. The multimodal whole exerts a downward causation of constraints on its constituent parts. Requests, as Tomasello pointed out, can be simply accomplished with the grammar afforded in the palm-up display where another organism has the evolved capacity to notice such a sign and the pro-social intentions to act on it. The joint-action games that collaboratively assembled the turkey corral were also instructive this way. The fancy trimmings of human language that we would expect to construct arguments convincing another of the merit of an idea were often forgone for the multimodally affective indexical and iconic sign configurations built upon potentials of the perceptual common ground of copresent bodies and objects. Some of the most persuasive actions took the form of intrinsic action as their mode of sign action, doing the action in the presence of the other as a sign. At times we also saw that intrinsically doing an action allowed for subsequently putting the idea into words where it was previously difficult—a transformation from intrinsic to symbolic reference, as if the thinking self needs the doing for the saying.

7.6 Concluding Remarks

This book is one answer to the question what does language documentation informed by the biosemiotics of life look like. It documents the Lachixío Zapotec language as woven through joint actions of everyday life. We glimpse moments of the shared life of a language and its participants as they build a world between them and the artifacts of their joint attention. I have argued that emergent relations among the offers and recruitments important to building human social relations scale to build the joint actions for repairing and resonating intersubjectivities, and these acts scale again to build our artifacts and institutions. Involvement in these emergent relations and transformations fundamentally affects the shape of a language as the language is involved in the building of human-connected worlds. I have aimed to show that such reciprocally causal and emergent process becomes accessible for analysis through a multimodal interaction analysis of video corpora coupled with participatory ethnography that includes the engagement of documentary and playback methods in which community members take agentive participatory roles that direct analysis. Community participants also take central role in creating the possibility for a grammar of resonance focused on the harmony and discord of relations built between participants and among modalities. The starting point for a study of language as life process is not in assuming the difference of language from the natural world, but its similarity. Like life, language is interwoven with the many strands from which ecological wholes emerge. The wholes of a language are multimodal, multi-participant, and temporally dynamic assemblages of mutual facilitation. Thus the questions of language form, function, reproduction, and repair share many concerns with the biosemiotics of all life.

I developed this project with the hope of producing a book to inform theory and practice for both anthropologists and linguists conducting fieldwork and to illustrate how corpus building practices of documentary work can inform theory of language and social-cognition (whether joint, distributed, or extended). The implications of a multimodal ethnography of language are not only in how ethnography aids the goals of multimodal interaction analysis, language documentation and description, but also in how the focused attention that multimodal interaction analysis of video corpora teaches us about the many ways people proffer and respond to each other in life's encounters, providing an essential tool for thick description in interpretive ethnography. Even where language description is not itself the ethnographic goal, attention to the jointness of saying and doing provides a means to learn how people interpret each other and make meaning from each other's actions—actions that are themselves jointly built from at-hand artifacts. To work across such differences, I have taken to thinking about language as an always open and incomplete system emergent within multimodal, multi-participant assemblages and which takes on living qualities from its involvement in the teleodynamics emergent with the joint commitments of human collaboration. We can best approach this sense of language, not by starting with preconceived ideas of language's ontology, but by starting with the complex wholes of actually occurring focused interactions and grounding our approach in the built relations that resonate across assemblages where time provides affordances that are both linear (the simultaneity and sequencing of Kronos) and cyclical (the Kairos of a time for the doing of something) and in the interspace of juxtaposition, and transspace of being here again.

This book developed through participatory research methods informed by my interests as a researcher into the language everyday life interactions, and which followed the interests of a set of collaborating participants who recorded life activities that they imagined to be representational of Lachixío culture. In choosing settings for recording, my collaborator Pedro and his collaborators had much influence on the materials we recorded. But as participants in the videos any specific individual's influence was limited because of the multiple possible directions each event could go at any given turn of dialogue. If another set of people participated, some other directions and events would make up the data of this work. Having intimate experience with the entire corpus as well as more than twenty years of recurrent fieldwork in Lachixío, and through the reflections of community collaborators who have contributed interpretations of examples and analyses in the book, I can say that the depictions of the generic and collaborative actions that offer, recruit, repair, and resonate are representative of a nexus of language and life in Lachixío.

I must also say that while video analysis is better fit to ecologies where participants had audible, visual, and visibly tactile access to each other and perceptible-actable things, a notable limit of the audiovisual record of video is nonvisible touch and the proprioceptive sense of actually speaking/being with a language, something of the felt iconicity described in Tony Webster's work with indigenous poets (2010, 2015). Built up and thus shaped by histories of interactions and uses of language, felt iconicities have resonance with what's been described by Zapotec collaborators as a language's *tono* (Sicoli 2007) and perhaps something like what Sapir called the "feeling tones" of words (Sapir 1929; Webster 2010). Video documentation is a complement not a substitute for ethnography and the relationship building of participation it entails. I hope the engagement over time of your interaction with this multimodal ethnography develops some small sense of the *tono* of saying and doing in Zapotec. Any such understanding is not in the video material itself, but built up through many tiers of participatory action and interpretation that led this work to you and you to this work.

I can also say that we do not see in this book some aspects of life in Lachixío that are common and important. This is in part because of my interest in how language facilitates the everyday joint actions of human life and to contributing a corpus that aids the goal of a comparative pragmatics, but also largely because of the choices made by the participants. Further explorations in the ethnography of recruitments, and specifically requests, could productively look at more formal settings, like petitions to the municipal authorities, requests for godparent sponsorship, or for another's hand in marriage. We also do not see in this book the everyday interactions with computers and social media that youth in Lachixío partake in. I would be remiss to not address the quickly changing cultural, linguistic, and digital landscapes of Lachixío that are mediating much of contemporary life, and how social media can produce certain potentialities for intersubjectivity and circulations of culture unafforded by face-to-face interaction, with consequences for political action and sociocultural transformation as is well known in contemporary linguistic anthropology. To such concerns I hope the theoretical contributions to studying multimodality, resonance, and the language of joint actions in this work are understood as more broadly informing that all interaction is mediated through and with the sensible bodies and things of its assemblages.

At the time we began recording video for this project around 2008, the first internet cafe opened in Lachixío, and about the same time internet was installed for the town authorities, which was made available to community members via wireless signal around the municipal building. People could be seen gathering in a new ethological activity with increasingly available personal electronic devices. Today in 2020 there are numerous internet cafes in both Santa María and San Vicente, and most of the youth in Lachixío regularly visit internet cafes that have become almost as common as small general stores were in the earliest days of my fieldwork. To focus on the language of social media content in Lachixío, though, would be to focus on Spanish-language discourse of written communication. Though if our scope were to include the communication in the living scenes of social media use, the world of the internet cafe at the time of writing would be animated through a mix of Spanish and Zapotec, like it has been in the multi-participant scenes around VHS and DVD videos, television, and radio programs for some years already in rural Oaxaca. Increasingly though, in Lachixío the youngest participants are speaking only Spanish being raised in a multilingual setting but where child-directed speech is increasingly in Spanish (Sicoli 2020). At the same time, a community radio station in San Vicente Lachixío broadcasts occasionally in Zapotec and in 2018, Pedro, now a kindergarten teacher, along with others in the eastern Sola de Vega school district, organized the first *Guelaguetza Infantil* (child guelaguetza) for the region, modeled on the popular annual festival exhibiting Oaxacan indigenous cultures through dance, song, dress, and food. The *Guelaguetza Infantil* included dance and costumes that resonated with what the state celebration does, but also focused attention on the Zapotec languages of the minority of towns of the district that still spoke them with both song and poetry performances, and reciprocally on the greater number that have shifted away from indigenous language use. The global frame resonance of the state's relationship with indigenous tourism along with which the local is mobilized is itself transformative of the Zapotec language in these parts where the language-life once wholly animated through everyday joint actions between people becomes the cultural spectacle of staged performance.

Notes

Orthography and Abbreviations

1   https://www.eva.mpg.de/lingua/resources/glossing-rules.php

Chapter 1

1   See parallel critiques by Vološinov 1986 and also Hymes 1974.
2   I generally use copresent interaction rather than the narrower but overlapping face-to-face interaction that assumes/privileges facing participation formats at the expense of side-by-side (common in Meso-America) or nested bodies (Goodwin and Cekaite 2018; Tulbert and Goodwin 2011).
3   Though transcripts themselves take forms that are constrained by publishing and typesetting conventions and why the affect of viewing video in a data session or lecture is not possible to affect in print, and motivates making available the streamable video materials accompanying this book.
4   For several examples of scholars undertaking and presenting video analysis, see the website *Learning how to look and listen: Building capacity for video based social & educational research* https://www.learninghowtolookandlisten.com
5   Population figures: https://www.gob.mx/cms/uploads/attachment/file/48587/Oaxaca_420.pdf

Chapter 2

1   And contemporary accountings of memory have come to understand that the ways the past influences the present are also mediated and mediator, also triadic, rather than the causal binary set up in the passage quoted from Peirce. See, for example, Newell's work on the affectivness of symbols grounded on the materiality of stored objects (Newell 2018).
2   Godparents of the wedding are often the groom's godparents from childhood, though given the advanced age of the *novios*, the godparents are also in compadre relations with them as they are godparents to each other's children. This relationship enters into the trouble and remediation that takes place in the gift giving ceremony.
3   Wedding gifts are to be of use to the couple (or the parents or godparents) not generally ornamental. Ornamental goods take a special morphological marking in the language =*stílla* from "Castilian" used with items that are for show rather than for use.
4   See Couper-Kuhlen (1993) for development of this point on interactive repair.

5 Lexical item *íññi* is from *Zhílìi* "San Vicente Lachixío" where *íññi* = Santa María *náññi* (animal). Benné Òlla who is from Santa María shifts to use the San Vicente dialectal variant when in San Vicente.
6 Here, this resonates with the work of Goodwin (2011) on mutually elaborating semiotic dimensions, Enfield (2009) on composite utterances, and Raymond and Lerner (2014) on multiple involvements.
7 For more on the moral good of care and hospitality in Lachixío, see Sicoli (2016a).
8 The reader should note that tortillas in Lachixío are the size of dinner plates so one taco can equal a plate of food.
9 The initial /d/ is present in completive-inflected forms of this verb (serving as a marker of its "Class D" category). It occurs mostly with the *o-* completive prefix, though also without the prefix as in line 4 and in some lexical items like *dàkko sillà'* (breakfast).

Chapter 3

1 This then includes actions like "Hand me the shovel" or "Get your father a glass of water" but not something like "Go and brush your teeth" or "Go outside and play," which would rather be a simple imperative with the benefactor of the directed action being the same as the actor conducting it (though admittedly we get into fuzzy boundaries here).
2 Kairotic timespaces and chronotopes are not synonyms. The former involves embodied presence and memory, the latter textuality and intertextuality as developed since Bakhtin. The two can, however, relate in the chain of semiosis, like the relationship between Toò Fabiano's narrative of the wedding and the gifts to the godparents, and how moves like first-pair parts project futures through intertextual recognition.
3 Languages are Lao, Siwu (Ghana), Cha'palaa (Ecuador), Russian, Murriny Patha (Australia), Polish, English, and Italian.
4 This reference was confirmed by Pedro in playback interviews.
5 In a playback interview with Pedro, he said his affirmation here was replying to a parallel sequence with Táolla and not as a response, even though in this place sequentially it does seem to parallel Grandma's embodied affirmation.

Chapter 4

1 Avoiding a possibly face-threatening act of intervention or correction is a preference at play in accounting for extended turn-transition times before initiating other-repair, giving the other speaker one last chance at self-repair (Stivers et al. 2009), though see Sicoli (2016b) for how the whistled speech register of Sochiapan Chinantec actually shows a preference for other-initiated repair.
2 An excellent source for examining self-repair in Zapotec and Chatino is the archive of the Zapotec and Chatino survey, which, given the interview and online thinking speakers were doing in the interview setting that involved translating Spanish language prompts to the indigenous language, included many false starts, self-corrections, and repetitions (https://www.ailla.utexas.org/islandora/object/ailla%3A243980).

3   Languages compared in the HSSLU project and published the 2015 Special Issus in *Open Linguistics* (Dingemanse and Enfield 2015) include Argentine Sign Language (Manrique 2016), Cha'pala of Ecuador (Floyd 2015), UK English (Kendrick 2015), Icelandic (Gísladóttir 2015), Italian (Rossi 2015), Lao (Enfield 2015), Murrinh-Patha of Northern Australia (Blythe 2015), Russian (Baranova 2015), Siwu of Ghana (Dingemanse 2015), and Yélî Dnye of Rossel Island PNG (Levinson 2015).
4   I am not representing every kind of repair in Lachixío Zapotec in this exposition.
5   The repetition of the reduplicated form *kaa kaa* (everywhere) (lit. where#where) supports colloquial uses of reduplication in Lachixío for a scaling up of meaning. Compare *tzee* (walk) with *ndzee ndzee* STA-walk#STA-walk (walk around, wander) (Chapter 4, example [22]) and *nyàá nyàá* good#good (real good) (Chapter 6, example 4, line 38).
6   *Pâ* and *Mâ* are written with circumflex accent for quickly falling tone on short vowel tending breathy, which I think is a fusional result of the junction of =1s with the low tone monosyllabic stem: pà=á or pà-H=á, where -H a junction tone (see Sicoli 2007). Contrast pà-' = á (my father) father-POS =1s where the glottal stop alienable possession morpheme perhaps blocks the tonal transformation.
7   *Òlla*, "Spanish speaking city person," differs from *òlla* in the phrase *Benné Òlla* in Chapter 2 in that the latter has low tone.
8   The verb of motion *-ree* occurs in three Lachixío Zapotec compounds—*ree nzhilla'* (to revolve), *-ree ri'kkò'* (to vomit), *-ree txé' dá'ññi* (to embroider). I have never been successful eliciting it outside of these compound verb forms, although it is attested in other Zapotec languages and reconstructed in Proto-Zapotec. Mary's choice to replace it with a Spanish loan after repair may attest to its low frequency and productivity in Lachixío.

Chapter 5

1   Though there have been some notable forays attempting to demonstrate the importance of interaction to the study of grammar such as in the essays collected in the volume *Interaction and Grammar* edited by Elinor Ochs, Emanuel Schegloff, and Sandra Thompson (1996).
2   The diagrammatic relation between knowledge of syntactic structures built up through a frequency of resonant events and an instance of speech may itself be harmonic (grammatical) or discordant (ungrammatical), with grammaticality judgments being the fit between sign and possible interpretant. There is an important parallel to explore between the way that signs build up such rule-like qualities in the temporally iterated experience of interpreters (as Semiotic Thirds developed over multiple tokens of ever developing types) in Peirce's semiosis and exemplar-based and emergentist approaches in contemporary linguistics that I am developing in a new project..
3   I translated *púuro dii stílla* as "just Spanish" in this sequence rather than "pure Spanish" because the sense of it is more *to the exclusion of Zapotec* and "just" could not be misinterpreted as reference to the ideology of a "pure Spanish."
4   This construction also shows a vowel harmony of the third-person object pronoun e->i.
5   Such insight was present in the earliest conception of transformational grammar as a study of discourse (Harris 1952) but lost when the scope of syntax was reduced to the sentence.

Chapter 6

1. Such as demonstrated in the Milgram experiment where a stacking of joint commitments made extraction from the experiment face threatening even after concluding that the action asked for as participation was unethical (Clark 2006).
2. This segment is difficult to hear. I worked with two separate speakers who when just listening to the segment audio didn't have a good idea of what Francisco said until looking at the video of his hand gesture. With the multimodal information they both immediately gave parallel nearly identical responses. A resonance of action primed their recognition of the words.

Chapter 7

1. There is resonance here with linguistic anthropological literature on "contextualization" as process of relationship building rather than "context" as thing. See important work of Gumperz (1982), Auer 1996, and papers in Auer and Di Luzio (1992), Silverstein (1992), and papers in Duranti and Goodwin (1992).
2. On the meaningful potential of signs that signify themselves see also Kath Weston (2013) for developing the semiotic concept to meta-materiality for signs that refer to themselves where the very physicality of a sign allows it to signify, and also Roy Wagner (1986) who argued that the aesthetic forms of symbols afford their standing for themselves in creating meanings that organize cultural life.
3. On the notion of "evolved open-endedness," see the recent work of Howard H. Pattee and Hiroki Sayama.
4. Computational-corpus linguists might take note of this.
5. Compare Silverstein's relatively presupposing versus relatively creative indexicality (1976).

References

Agha, Asif. 2007. *Language and Social Relations*. Cambridge: Cambridge University Press.
Ahearn, Laura. 2000. "Agency." *Journal of Linguistic Anthropology* 9 (1–2): 12–15.
Aikenwald, Alexandra. 2004. *Evidentiality*. New York: Oxford University Press.
Althusser, Louis. 1971. "Ideology and Ideological State Apparatuses." In *Lenin and Philosophy and Other Essays*, trans. Ben Brewster, pp. 121–76. New York: Monthly Review Press.
Anderson, Leon. 2006. "Analytic Autoethnography." *Journal of Contemporary Ethnography* 35 (4): 373–95.
Auer, Peter. 1996. "From Context to Contextualization." *Links and Letters* 3: 11–28.
Auer, Peter, and Aldo Di Luzio (eds.). 1992. *The Contextualization of Language*. Amsterdam: John Benjamins.
Bakhtin, Mikhail M. 1981. *The Dialogic Imagination*. Translated by C. Emerson and M. Holquist. Austin: University of Texas Press.
Baranova, Julija. 2015. "Other-Initiated Repair in Russian." *Open Linguistics* 1: 555–77.
Bateson, Gregory. 1972. *Steps to an Ecology of Mind*. Chicago: University of Chicago Press.
Bateson, Gregory. 2002. *Mind and Nature: A Necessary Unity*. Creskill: Hampton Press.
Bauman, Richard, and Joel Sherzer. 1974. *Explorations in the Ethnography of Speaking*. New York: Cambridge University Press.
Beals, Ralph. 1970. "Gifting, Reciprocity, Savings, and Credit in Peasant Oaxaca." *Southwestern Journal of Anthropology* 26 (3): 231–41.
Becker, A. L. 1995. *Beyond Translation: Essays Toward a Modern Philology*. Ann Arbor: University of Michigan Press.
Berking, Helmuth. 1999. *The Sociology of Giving*. London: Sage.
Birdwhistell, Ray L. 1970. *Kinesics and Context: Essays on Body Motion Communication*. Philadelphia: University of Pennsylvania Press.
Blommaert, Jan, Ben Rampton and Massimiliano Spotti. 2015. *Language and Superdiversity*. London: Taylor & Francis.
Blythe, Joe. 2015. "Other-Initiated Repair in Murrinh-Patha." *Open Linguistics* 1 (1): 283–308.
Bolden, Galina B. 2003. "Multiple Modalities in Collaborative Turn Sequences." *Gesture* 3 (2): 187–212.
Bourdieu, Pierre. 1972. *Outline of a Theory of Practice*. Translated by Richard Nice. Cambridge: Cambridge University Press.
Bourdieu, Pierre. 1980. *The Logic of Practice*. Translated by Richard Nice. Stanford: Stanford University Press.
Brody, Jill. 1986. "Repetition as a Rhetorical and Conversational Device in Tojolab'al (Mayan)." *International Journal of American Linguistics* 52 (3): 255–74.
Brown, Penelope. 2000. "Conversational Structure and Language Acquisition: The Role of Repetition in Tzeltal." *Journal of Linguistic Anthropology* 8 (2): 197–221.
Brown, Penelope, and Stephen Levinson. 1978. "Universals in Language Usage: Politeness Phenomena." In *Questions and Politeness: Strategies in Social Interaction*, ed. Esther Goody, pp. 56–311. Cambridge: Cambridge University Press.

Brown, Penelope, and Stephen Levinson. 1987. *Politeness: Some Universals in Language Usage*. Cambridge: Cambridge University Press.

Brown, Penelope, Mark A. Sicoli, and Oliver Le Guen. 2010. "Cross-Speaker Repetition in Tzeltal, Yucatec, and Zapotec Conversation." *ICCA 10: International Conference on Conversation Analysis*, (July 8). Mannheim, Germany.

Brown, Roger. 1968. "The Development of Wh Questions in Child Speech." *Journal of Verbal Learning and Verbal Behavior* 7 (2): 279–90.

Bueno Holle, Juan José. 2019. *Information Structure in Isthmus Zapotec Narrative and Conversation*. Berlin: Language Science Press.

Bulleri, Fabio, John Bruno, and Lisandro Benedetti-Cecchi. 2008. "Beyond Competition: Incorporating Positive Interactions between Species to Predict Ecosystem Invasibility." *PLoS Biol* 6 (6): e162. doi.org/10.1371/journal.pbio.0060162.

Butler, Judith. 2002. *Excitable Speech: A Politics of the Performative*. New York: Routledge.

Campbell, Donald T. 1974. "Downward Causation in Hierarchically Organised Biological Systems." In *Studies in the Philosophy of Biology: Reduction and Related Problems*, eds. Francisco Jose Ayala and Theodosius Dobzhansky, pp. 179–86. London/Basingstoke: Macmillan.

Capra, Fritjof. 2002. *The Hidden Connections: Integrating the Biological, Cognitive, and Social Dimensions of Life into a Science of Sustainability*. New York: Doubleday.

Cheal, David. 1988. *The Gift Economy*. New York: Routledge.

Chomsky, Noam. 1980. "On Cognitive Structures and their Development: A reply to Piaget." In *Language and Learning: The Debate between Jean Piaget and Noam Chomsky*, ed. Massimo Piattelli-Palmarini, pp. 35–54. Cambridge, MA: Harvard University Press.

Clark, Herb. 2006. "Social Actions, Social Commitments." In *Roots of Human Sociality: Culture, Cognition and Interaction*, eds. N. J. Enfield and Stephen Levinson, pp. 126–50. New York: Berg.

Clifford, James, and George E. Marcus. 1986. *Writing Culture: The Poetics and Politics of Ethnography*. Berkeley: University of California Press.

Collins, Samuel Gerald, Matthew Durington, and Harjant Gill. 2017. "Multimodality: An Invitation." *American Anthropologist* 119 (1): 142–6.

Couper-Kuhlen, Elizabeth. 1993. *English Speech Rhythm: Form and Function in Everyday Verbal Interaction*. Philadelphia: John Benjamins.

Craven, Alexandra, and Jonathan Potter. 2010. "Directives: Entitlement and Contingency in Action." *Discourse Studies* 12 (4): 419–42.

Cruz, Hilaria. 2017. "Prayers for the Community: Parallelism and Performance in San Juan Quiahije Eastern Chatino." *The Oral Tradition Journal* 31 (2): 509–34.

Cruz Santiago, Emiliano. 2010. *Jwá'n ngwan-keéh reéh xa'gox: Creencias de nuestros antepasados*. Oaxaca: Culturas Populares / Consejo Nacional para la Cultura y las Artes / Secretaría de Cultura, Gobierno de Oaxaca / Fundación Alfredo Harp Helú.

Curl, Traci. 2005. "Practices in Other-Initiated Repair Resolution: The Phonetic Differentiation of 'Repetitions.'" *Discourse Processes* 39 (1): 1–43.

Curl, Traci, and Paul Drew. 2008. "Contingency and Action: A Comparison of Two Forms of Requesting." *Research on Language and Social Interaction* 41 (2): 129–53.

Dahlgren de Jordan, Barbro. 1963. *La Grana Cochinilla*. Mexico: Jose Porrua e Hijos.

de Certeau, Michel. 1984. *The Practice of Everyday Life*. Translated by Steven Rendall. Berkeley: University of California Press.

de León, Lourdes. 2007. "Parallelism, Metalinguistic Play, and the Interactive Emergence of Zinacantec Mayan Siblings' Culture." *Research on Language and Social Interaction* 40: 405–36.

de Saussure, Ferdinand, Charles Bally, and Albert Sechehaye (eds.). 1986 [1915]. *Course in General Linguistics*. Translated by Roy Harris. Chicago: Open Court.
Deacon, Terrence. 2003. "Universal Grammar and Semiotic Constraints." In *Language Evolution*, eds. Morten Christiansen and Simon Kirby, pp. 111–139. Oxford: Oxford University Press.
Deacon, Terrence. 2013. *Incomplete Nature: How Mind Emerged from Matter*. New York: W.W. Norton & Company.
Deleuze, Gilles, and Feliz Guattari. 1987. *A Thousand Platteaus: Capitalism and Schizophrenia*. Translated by Brian Masumi. Minneapolis: University of Minnesota Press.
Derrida, Jacques. 1988. "Signature Event Context." In *Limited Inc*, ed. Jacques Derrida, pp 1–24. Evanston: Northwestern University Press.
Dingemanse, Mark. 2015. "Other-Initiated Repair in Siwu." *Open Linguistics* 1 (1): 232–55.
Dingemanse, Mark, and N. J. Enfield. 2015. "Other-Initiated Repair Across Languages: Towards a Typology of Conversational Structures." *Open Linguistics* 1 (1): 96–118.
Dingemanse, Mark, Kobin Kendrick, and N. J. Enfield. 2016. "A Coding Scheme for Other-Initiated Repair Across Languages." *Open Linguistics* 2 (1): 35–46.
Dingemanse, Mark, Sean Roberts, Julija Baranova, Joe Blythe, Paul Drew, Simeon Floyd, et al. 2015. "Universal Principles in the Repair of Communication Problems." *PLoS ONE*, 10 (9): e0136100. https://doi.org/10.1371/journal.pone.0136100.
Dingemanse, Mark, Francisco Torreira, and N. J. Enfield. 2013. "Is 'Huh?' a Universal Word? Conversational Infrastructure and the Convergent Evolution of Linguistic Items." *PloS ONE* 8 (11): e78273. doi.org/10.1371/journal.pone.0078273.
Drew, Paul. 1997. "'Open' Class Repair Initiators in Response to Sequential Sources of Troubles in Conversation." *Journal of Pragmatics* 28 (1):69–101.
Du Bois, John. 2014. "Towards a Dialogic Syntax." *Cognitive Linguistics* 25 (3): 359–410.
Du Bois, John, R. Peter Hobson, and Jessica Hobson. 2014. "Dialogic Resonance and Intersubjective Engagement in Autism." *Cognitive Linguistics* 25 (3): 411–41.
Du Bois, John, and Mark Sicoli. 2016. *Paradigms Found: Dialogic Syntax as a Grammar Discovery Method for Field Linguistics*. Organized Session at the 90th Annual Meeting of the Linguistic Society of America.
Duranti, Alessandro. 1992. "Language and Bodies in Social Space: Samoan Ceremonial Greetings." *American Anthropologist* 94: 657–91.
Duranti, Alessandro. 2010. "Husserl, Intersubjectivity, and Anthropology." *Anthropological Theory* 10 (1–2): 16–35.
Duranti, Alessandro, and Charles Goodwin (eds.). 1992. *Rethinking Context*. Cambridge: Cambridge University Press.
Edwards, Terra. 2014. "From Compensation to Integration: Effects of the Pro-Tactile Movement on the Sublexical Structure of Tactile American Sign Language." *Journal of Pragmatics* 69: 22–41.
Edwards, Terra. 2021. "Intersubjectivity." *The International Encyclopedia of Linguistic Anthropology*. Wiley.
Egbert, Maria, Andrea Golato, and Jeffrey Robinson. 2009. "Repairing Reference." In *Conversation Analysis: Comparative Perspectives*, ed. Jack Sidnell, pp. 104–32. Cambridge: Cambridge University Press.
Ekman, Paul, and Wallace Friesen. 1969. "The Repertoire of Nonverbal Behavior: Categories, Origins, Usage, and Coding." *Semiotica* 1 (1): 49–98.
Emerson, Robert. 1969. *Judging Delinquents: Context and Process in Juvenile Court*. Chicago: Aldine.
Enfield, N. J. 2009. *The Anatomy of Meaning: Speech, Gesture, and Composite Utterances*. New York: Cambridge University Press.

Enfield, N. J. 2013. *Relationship Thinking: Agency, Enchrony, and Human Sociality*. New York: Oxford University Press.
Enfield, N. J. 2015. "Other-Initiated Repair in Lao." *Open Linguistics* 1 (1): 119–44.
Enfield, N. J., and Paul Kockelman (eds.). 2017. *Distributed Agency*. New York: Oxford University Press.
Enfield, N. J., Stephen Levinson, Jan Peter de Ruiter, and Tanya Stivers. 2007. "Building a Corpus of Multimodal Interaction in your Field Site." In *Language and Cognition Group: Field Manual Volume 10*, pp. 96–9. Nijmegen: Max Planck Institute for Psycholinguistics.
Erickson, Frederick. 1982. "Classroom Discourse as Improvisation: Relationships between Academic Task Structure and Social Participation Structure in Lessons." In *Communicating in the Classroom*, ed. L. C. Wilkinson, pp. 153–81. New York: Academic Press.
Erickson, Frederick. 2004a. *Talk and Social Theory: Ecologies of Speaking and Listening in Everyday Life*. Malden: Polity Press.
Erickson, Frederick. 2004b. "Origins: A Brief Intellectual and Technological History of the Emergence of Multimodal Discourse Analysis." In *Discourse and Technology: Multimodal Discourse Analysis*, eds. Philip LeVine and Ronald Scollon, pp. 196–207. Washington DC: Georgetown University Press.
Ervin-Tripp, Susan. 1976. "Is Sybil There? The Structure of Some American English Directives." *Language in Society* 5 (1): 25–66.
Evans-Pritchard, E. E. 2000 [1950]. "Introduction." In Marcel Mauss, *The Gift: The Form and Reason for Exchange in Archaic Societies*, pp. 1–9, trans. W. D. Halls. New York: W. W. Norton.
Fairclough, Norman. 1989. *Language and Power*. London and New York: Longman.
Fairclough, Norman. 1995. *Critical Discourse Analysis: The Critical Study of Language*. London and New York: Longman.
Favareau, Donald. 2008. "Collapsing the Wave Function of Meaning." In *A Legacy for Living Systems: Gregory Bateson as Precursor to Biosemiotics*, ed. Jesper Hoffmeyer, pp. 169–211. New York: Springer.
Favareau, Donald. 2015. "Creation of the Relevant Next: How Living Systems Capture the Power of the Adjacent Possible through Sign Use." *Progress in Biophysics and Molecular Biology* 119: 588e601.
Fisch, Max. 1986. "Vico and Pragmatism." In *Peirce, Semeiotic, and Pragmatism: Essays by Max H. Fisch*, eds. Kenneth Ketner and Christian Kloesel, pp. 201–26. Bloomington: Indiana University Press.
Floyd, Simeon. 2015. "Other-Initiated Repair in Cha'palaa." *Open Linguistics* 1 (1): 467–89.
Floyd, Simeon, Giovanni Rossi, N. J. Enfield, Julija Baranova, Joe Blythe, Mark Dingemanse, Kobin Kendrick, and Jorg Zinken. 2014. *Recruitments across Languages: A Systematic Comparison: Talk Presented at the 4th International Conference on Conversation Analysis [ICCA 2014]*. University of California at Los Angeles, CA. 2014-06-25 - 2014-06-29.
Floyd, Simeon, Giovanni Rossi, and N. J. Enfield (eds.). 2020. *Getting Others to Do Things: A Pragmatic Typology of Recruitments*. Berlin: Language Science Press.
Ford, Cecelia, and Sandra Thompson. 1996. "Interactional Units in Conversation: Syntactic, Intonational, and Pragmatic Resources for the Management of Turns." In *Interaction and Grammar*, eds. Elinor Ochs, Emanuel Schegloff, and Sandra Thompson, pp. 134–84. New York: Cambridge University Press.
Foster, George. 1965. "Peasant Society and the Image of Limited Good." *American Anthropologist* 67 (2): 293–315.

Foucault, Michel. 1972. *The Archaeology of Knowledge*. New York: Pantheon Books.
Frake, Charles. 1964. "How to Ask for a Drink in Subanun." *American Anthropologist* 66 (6) Pt. 2: 127–30.
Fuentes, Agustín. 2016. "The Extended Evolutionary Synthesis, Ethnography, and the Human Niche: Toward an Integrated Anthropology." *Current Anthropology* 57 (13): S13–S26.
Garfinkel, Harold. 1967. "Studies of the Routine Grounds of Everyday Activities." In *Studies in Ethnomethodology*, ed. Harold Garfinkel, pp. 35–75. Englewood Cliffs: Prentice-Hall.
Garfinkel, Harold. 2002. *Ethnomethodology's Program: Working Out Durkheim's Aphorism*, ed. Anne Warfield Rawls. New York: Rowman & Littlefield.
Geertz, Clifford. 1973. "Thick Description: Toward an Interpretive Theory of Culture." In *The Interpretation of Cultures: Selected Essays*, ed. Clifford Geertz, pp. 3–30. New York: Basic Books.
Geertz, Clifford. 1976. "From the Native's Point of View: On the Nature of Anthropological Understanding." In *Meaning in Anthropology*, eds. Keith Basso, and H. Selby, pp. 221–37. Albuquerque: University of New Mexico Press.
Gell, Alfred. 1998. *Art and Agency: An Anthropological Theory*. Oxford: Clarendon Press.
Gibson, John J. 1979. *The Ecological Approach to Visual Perception*. Boston: Houghton Mifflin Harcourt (HMH).
Giddens, Anthony. 1984. *The Constitution of Society: Outline of the Theory of Structuration*. Malden: Polity Press.
Gísladóttir, Rosa. 2015. "Other-Initiated Repair in Icelandic." *Open Linguistics* 1 (1): 309–28.
Goffman, Erving. 1955. "On Face Work." In *Interaction Ritual*, ed. Erving Goffman (1967), pp. 5–45. London: Penguin.
Goffman, Erving. 1963. *Behavior in Public Places: Notes on the Social Organization of Gatherings*. New York: Free Press of Glencoe.
Goffman, Erving. 1964. "The Neglected Situation." *American Anthropologist* 66: 133–6. doi: 10.1525/aa.1964.66.suppl_3.02a00090.
Goffman, Erving. 1967. *Interaction Ritual: Essays in Face-to-Face Behavior*. New York: Pantheon Books.
Goffman, Erving. 1971a. "Tie Signs." In *Relations in Public*, ed. Erving Goffman, pp. 188–237. New York: Harper and Row.
Goffman, Erving. 1971b. "Normal Appearances." In *Relations in Public*, ed. Erving Goffman, pp. 238–333. New York: Harper and Row.
Goffman, Erving. 1971c. *Relations in Public*. New York: Harper and Row.
Goffman, Erving. 1974. *Frame Analysis: An Essay on the Organization of Experience*. Cambridge, MA: Harvard University Press.
Goffman, Erving. 1981. "The Interaction Order." *American Sociological Review* 48 (1): 1–17.
Goodenough, Ward. 1970. "Describing a Culture." In *Description and Comparison in Cultural Anthropology*, ed. Ward Goodenough, pp. 104–19. Cambridge: Cambridge University Press.
Goodwin, Charles. 1979. "The Interactive Construction of a Sentence in Natural Conversation." In *Everyday Language: Studies in Ethnomethodology*, ed. George Psathas, pp. 97–121. New York: Irvington Publishers.
Goodwin, Charles. 1980. "Restarts, Pauses, and the Achievement of a State of Mutual Gaze at Turn-Beginning." *Sociological Inquiry* 50 (3–4): 272–302.
Goodwin, Charles. 1981. *Conversational Organization: Interaction between Speakers and Hearers*. New York: Academic.

Goodwin, Charles. 1994. "Professional Vision." *American Anthropologist* 96 (3): 606–33.
Goodwin, Charles. 2000. "Action and Embodiment within Situated Human Interaction." *Journal of Pragmatics* 32 (10): 1489–1522.
Goodwin, Charles. 2006. "Human Sociality as Mutual Orientation in a Rich Interactive Environment: Multimodal Utterances and Pointing in Aphasia." In *Roots of Human Sociality*, eds. Stephen Levinson and N. J. Enfield, pp. 96–125. New York: Berg.
Goodwin, Charles. 2011. "Contextures of Action." In *Embodied Interaction: Language and the Body in the Material World*, ed. Jürgen Streeck, Charles Goodwin, and Curtis LeBaron, pp. 182–93. New York: Cambridge University Press.
Goodwin, Charles. 2017. *Co-Operative Action*. New York: Cambridge University Press.
Goodwin, Marjorie Harness. 1980. "He-Said-She-Said: Formal Cultural Procedures for the Construction of a Gossip Dispute Activity." *American Ethnologist* 7 (4): 674–95.
Goodwin, Marjorie Harness. 1983. "Aggravated Correction and Disagreement in Children's Conversation." *Journal of Pragmatics* 7 (6): 655–77.
Goodwin, Marjorie Harness. 1990. *He-Said-She-Said: Talk as Social Organization among Black Children*. Bloomington: Indiana University Press.
Goodwin, Marjorie Harness. 2006. "Participation, Affect, and Trajectory in Family Directive/Response Sequences." *Text & Talk* 26 (4–5): 515–43.
Goodwin, Marjorie Harness. 2010. "Organizing Participation in Cross-Sex Jump Rope: Situating Gender Differences Within Longitudinal Studies of Activities." *Research on Language and Social Interaction* 34 (1): 75–106.
Goodwin, Marjorie Harness. 2017. "Haptic Sociality: The Embodied Interactive Constitution of Intimacy Through Touch." In *Intercorporeality: Emerging Socialities in Interaction*, ed. Christian Meyer, Jürgen Streeck, and J. Scott Jordan, pp. 73–102. New York: Oxford.
Goodwin, Marjorie Harness, and Asta Cekaite. 2018. *Embodied Family Choreography: Practices of Control, Care, and Mundane Creativity*. New York: Routledge.
Goodwin Raheja, Gloria. 1988. *The Poison in the Gift: Ritual, Prestation, and the Dominant Caste in a North Indian Village*. Chicago: The University of Chicago Press.
Gumperz, John, and Dell Hymes (eds.). 1964. "The Ethnography of Communication." *American Anthropologist* 66: (6, part 2).
Gumperz, John J. 1982. *Discourse Strategies*. Cambridge: Cambridge University Press.
Hägerstrand, Torsten. 1970. "What about People in Regional Science?" *Papers of the Regional Science Association* 24 (1): 6–21.
Hall, Edward T. 1959. *The Silent Language*. Garden City: DoubleDay & Company.
Hall, Edward T. 1990. *The Hidden Dimension*. New York: Anchor Books.
Handler, Richard. 2012. "What's Up, Doctor Goffman? Tell Us Where the Action Is!" *The Journal of the Royal Anthropological Institute* 18 (1): 179–90.
Haraway, Donna. 2008. *When Species Meet*. Minneapolis: University of Minnesota Press.
Harris, Marvin. 1976. "History and Significance of the Emic/Etic Distinction." *Annual Review of Anthropology* 5: 329–50.
Harris, Zellig. 1952. "Discourse Analysis." *Language* 28 (1): 1–30.
Haviland, John. 1993. "Anchoring, Iconicity, and Orientation in Guugu Yimithirr Pointing Gestures." *Journal of Linguistic Anthropology* 3 (l): 3–45.
Haviland, John. 1996. "'We Want to Borrow Your Mouth' Tzotzil Marital Squabbles." In *Disorderly Discourse: Narrative, Conflict, and Inequality*, ed. Charles Briggs, pp. 158–203. New York: Oxford University Press.
Haviland, John. 2009. "Little Rituals." In *Ritual Communication*, eds. Gunter Senft and Ellen Basso, pp. 21–50. New York: Oxford.

Heath, Shirley Brice. 1983. *Ways with Words: Language, Life and Work in Communities and Classrooms*. Cambridge: Cambridge University Press.

Heinemann, Trine. 2006. "'Will You or Can't You?': Displaying Entitlement in Interrogative Requests." *Journal of Pragmatics* 38 (7): 1081–1104.

Heritage, John. 1991. *Garfinkel and Ethnomethodology*. New York: Wiley.

Heritage, John. 1998. "Oh-Prefaced Responses to Inquiry." *Language in Society* 27 (3): 291–334.

Heritage, John. 2002. "Oh-Prefaced Responses to Assessments: A Method of Modifying Agreement/Disagreement." In *The Language of Turn and Sequence*, eds. Cecilia Ford, Barbara Fox, and Sandra Thompson, pp. 196–224. New York: Oxford.

Heritage, John, and Geoffrey Raymond. 2005. "The Terms of Agreement: Indexing Epistemic Authority and Subordination in Talk-in-Interaction." *Social Psychology Quarterly* 68 (1): 15–38.

Heritage, John, and Geoffrey Raymond. 2012. "Navigating Epistemic Landscapes: Acquiescence, Agency and Resistance in Responses to Polar Questions." In *Questions: Formal, Functional, and Interactional Perspectives*, ed. Jan P. de Ruiter, pp. 179–92. New York: Cambridge University Press.

Hill, Jane H. 1995. "The Voices of Don Gabriel: Responsibility and Self in a Modern Mexicano Narrative." In *The Dialogic Emergence of Culture*, eds. Dennis Tedlock and Bruce Mannheim, pp. 97–147. Urbana: University of Illinois Press.

Himmelmann, Nikolaus P. 2008. "Reproduction and Preservation of Linguistic Knowledge: Linguists' Response to Language Endangerment." *Annual Reviews in Anthropology* 37: 337–50.

Hockett, Charles. 1987. *Refurbishing Our Foundations: Elementary Linguistics from an Advanced Point of View*. Amsterdam: John Benjamins.

Hoffmeyer, Jesper. 1996. *Signs of Meaning in the Universe*. Translated by Barbara J. Haveland. Bloomington: Indiana University Press.

Hoffmeyer, Jesper. 2008a. *Biosemiotics: An Examination into the Signs of Life and the Life of Signs*. Scranton: University of Scranton Press.

Hoffmeyer, Jesper. 2008b. "Semiotic Scaffolding of Living Systems." In *Introduction to Biosemioitics: The New Biological Synthesis*, ed. Marcello Barbieri, pp. 149–66. Dordrecht: Springer.

Hull, Kerry, and Michael Carrasco. 2012. *Parallel Worlds: Genre, Discourse, and Poetics in Contemporary, Colonial and Classic Maya Literature*. Boulder University Press of Colorado.

Husserl, Edmund. 1931. *Méditations cartésiennes: Introduction a la phénoménologie*. Translated by Gabrielle Peiffer and Emmanuel Lévinas. Paris: A. Colin. (English translation in Husserl, 1970).

Husserl, Edmund. 1960. *Cartesian Meditations: An Introduction to Phenomenology*. The Hague: Nijhoff.

Husserl, Edmund. 1989. *Ideas Pertaining to a Pure Phenomenology and to a Phenomenological Philosophy. Second Book: Studies in the Phenomenology of Constitution*. Translated by Richard Rojcewicz and André Schuwer. Dordrecht: Kluwer.

Hutchins, Edwin. 1995. *Cognition in the Wild*. Cambridge, MA: MIT Press.

Hymes, Dell. 1974. *Foundations in Sociolinguistics: An Ethnographic Approach*. Philadelphia: University of Pennsylvania Press.

Hymes, Dell. 1977. "Discovering Oral Performance and Measured Verse in American Indian Narrative." *New Literary History* 8 (3): 431–57.

Hymes, Dell. 1981. *"In Vain I Tried to Tell You:" Essays in Native American Ethnopoetics*. Philadelphia: University of Pennsylvania Press

Imanishi, K. 2002 [1941]. *A Japanese View of Nature: The World of Living Things*. New York: Routledge.

Irvine, Judith. 1980. "How Not to Ask a Favor in Wolof." *Paper in Linguistics* 13 (1): 3–49. doi: 10.1080/08351818009370491.

Jacob, Michelle M. 2016. *Indian Pilgrims: Indigenous Journeys of Activism and Healing with Saint Kateri Tekakwitha*. Tucson: University of Arizona Press.

Jakobson, Roman. 1960. "Closing Statement: Linguistics and Poetics." In *Style in Language*, ed. Thomas Sebeok, pp. 350–77. Cambridge, MA: MIT Press.

Jakobson, Roman. 1966. "Grammatical Parallelism and Its Russian Facet." *Language* 42 (2): 399–429.

James, Henry. 1969. *The Portrait of a Lady*. New York: Modern Library.

Jefferson, Gail. 1972. "Side Sequences." In *Studies in Social Interaction*, ed. David Sudnow, pp. 294–338. New York: The Free Press.

Johnstone, Barbara. 1994. *Repetitions in Discourse*. Norwood: Ablex.

Kauffman, Stuart. 2000. *Investigations*. New York: Oxford University Press.

Kauffman, Stuart, and Arran Gare. 2015. "Beyond Descartes and Newton: Recovering Life and Humanity." *Progress in Biophysics and Molecular Biology* 119 (3): 219e244.

Keane, Webb. 1997. *Things of Value*. Berkeley: University of California Press.

Keane, Webb. 2003. "Semiotics and the Social Analysis of Material Things." *Language and Communication* 23: 409–25.

Keane, Webb. 2005. "Signs Are Not the Garb of Meaning: On the Social Analysis of Material Things." In *Materiality: Politics, History, and Culture*, ed. Daniel Miller, pp. 182–205. Durham: Duke University Press.

Keenan, Elinor. 1977. "Making It Last: Repetition in Children's Discourse." In *Child Discourse*, eds. Susan Ervin-Tripp and Claudia Mitchell-Kernan, pp. 125–38. New York: Academic Press.

Kendon, Adam. 2009a. "Behavioral Foundations for the Process of Frame-Attunement in Face-to-Face Interaction." In *Conducting Interaction: Patterns of Behavior in Focused Encounters*, ed. Adam Kendon, pp. 239–62. Cambridge: Cambridge University Press.

Kendon, Adam. 2009b. *Conducting Interaction: Patterns of Behavior in Focused Encounters*. Cambridge: Cambridge University Press.

Kendrick, Kobin H. 2015. "Other-Initiated Repair in English." *Open Linguistics* 1 (1): 164–90.

Kendrick, Kobin H., and Paul Drew. 2016. "Recruitment: Offers, Requests, and the Organization of Assistance in Interaction." *Research on Language and Social Interaction* 49 (1): 1–19.

Kidwell, Mardi, and Don Zimmerman. 2007. "Joint Attention as Action." *Journal of Pragmatics* 39 (3): 592–611.

Kockelman, Paul. 2007. "Agency: The Relation between Meaning, Power, and Knowledge." *Current Anthropology* 48 (3): 375–401.

Kockelman, Paul. 2011. "Biosemiosis, Technocognition, and Sociogenesis: Selection and Significance in a Multiverse of Sieving and Serendipity." *Current Anthropology* 52 (5): 711–39.

Kockelman, Paul. 2013. *Agent, Person, Subject, Self: A Theory of Ontology, Interaction, and Infrastructure*. New York: Oxford University Press.

Kohn, Eduardo. 2013. *How Forests Think: Toward an Anthropology Beyond the Human*. Berkeley: University of California Press.

Kristeva, Julia. 1980. *Desire in Language: A Semiotic Approach to Language and Art*. Translated by Thomas Gora, Alice Jardine, and Leon Roudiez. New York: Columbia University Press.

Kuipers, Joel. 1990. *The Power in Performance: The Creation of Textual Authority in Weyewa Ritual Speech*. Philadelphia: University of Pennsylvania Press.

Kull, Kalevi. 2009. "Biosemiotics: To Know, What Life Knows." *Cybernetics and Human Knowing* 16: 81–8.

Latour, Bruno. 2005. *Reassembling the Social: An Introduction to Actor-Network-Theory*. Oxford: Oxford University Press.

Lederman, Rena. 1990. "Big Men Large and Small? Towards a Comparative Perspective." *Ethnology* 29: 3–15.

Lederman, Rena. 2015. "Big Man, Anthropology of." In *International Encyclopedia of the Social & Behavioral Sciences, Second Edition*, ed. James D. Wright, pp. 567–73. Oxford: Elsevier.

Lempert, Michael. 2012. "Interaction Rescaled: How Monastic Debate Became a Diasporic Pedagogy." *Anthropology & Education Quarterly* 43 (2): 138–56.

Lepowski, Maria. 1990. "Big Men, Big Women, and Cultural Autonomy." *Ethnology* 29 (1): 35–50.

Lèvi-Strauss, Claude. 1962. "The Science of the Concrete." In *The Savage Mind*, ed. Claude Levi-Strauss, pp. 1–34. Chicago: University of Chicago Press.

Lèvi Strauss, Claude. 1966. *The Savage Mind*. Chicago: University of Chicago Press.

Levinson, Stephen C. 2006. "On the Human 'Interaction Engine.'" In *Roots of Human Sociality, Culture, Cognition and Interaction*, eds. N. J. Enfield and Stephen C. Levinson, pp. 39–69. New York: Berg.

Levinson, Stephen C. 2013. "Recursion in Pragmatics." *Language* 89 (1): 149–62.

Levinson, Stephen C. 2015. "Other-Initiated Repair in Yélî Dnye: Seeing Eye-to-Eye in the Language of Rossel Island." *Open Linguistics* 1 (1): 386–410.

Levinson, Stephen, and Penelope Brown. 2016. "Comparative Feedback: Cultural Shaping of Response Systems in Interaction." Talk presented at the *7th Conference of the International Society for Gesture Studies (ISGS7)*. Paris France, July 18, 2016–July 22, 2016. http://hdl.handle.net/11858/00-001M-0000-002B-A0D5-A.

Lieven, Elena. 2014. "First Language Development: A Usage-based Perspective on Past and Current Research." *Journal of Child Language* 41 (S1): 48–63.

Lindström, Anna. 2005. "Language as Social Action: A Study of How Senior Citizens Request Assistance with Practical Tasks in the Swedish Home Help Service." In *Syntax and Lexis in Conversation: Studies on the Use of Linguistic Resources in Talk-in-Interaction*, eds. Auli Hakulinen and Margret Selting, pp. 209–30. Amsterdam: Benjamins.

Luhmann, Niklas. 1984. *Soziale Systeme*. Frankfort: Suhrkamp. Reprinted in translation 1996. *Social Systems*. Translated by John Bednarz, Jr. Stanford: Stanford University Press.

Luisi, Pier Luigi. 2003. "Autopoiesis: A Review and a Reappraisal." *Naturwissenschaften* 90: 49–59.

Lyre, Holger. 2018. "Socially Extended Cognition and Shared Intentionality." *Frontiers of Psychology* 9 (831). doi: 10.3389/fpsyg.2018.00831.

Majid, Asifa, Seán Roberts, Ludy Cilissen, Karen Emmorey, Brenda Nicodemus, Lucinda O'Grady, Bencie Woll, Barbara LeLan, Hilário de Sousa, Brian L. Cansler, Shakila Shayan, Connie de Vos, Gunter Senft, N. J. Enfield, Rogayah A. Razak, Sebastian Fedden, Sylvia Tufvesson, Mark Dingemanse, Ozge Ozturk, Penelope Brown, Clair

Hill, Olivier Le Guen, Vincent Hirtzel, Rik van Gijn, Mark A. Sicoli, and Stephen C. Levinson. 2018. "The Differential Coding of Perception in the World's Languages." *Proceedings of the National Academy of Sciences* 115 (45): 11369–76. www.pnas.org/cgi/doi/10.1073/pnas.1720419115.

Malinowski, Bronislaw. 1922. *Argonauts of the Western Pacific: An Account of Native Enterprise and Adventure in the Archipelagoes of Melanesian New Guinea*. London: Routledge.

Malinowski, Bronislaw. 1935. *Coral Gardens and their Magic: A Study in the Methods of Tilling the Soil and Agricultural Rites in the Trobriand Islands. Vol 1: The Description of Gardening. Vol 2: The Language of Gardening*. London: Routledge.

Mannheim, Bruce. 1999. "Iconicity." *Journal of Linguistic Anthropology* 9 (1/2): 107–10.

Mannheim, Bruce. 2015. "All Translation is Radical Translation." In *Translating Worlds: The Epistemological Space of Translation*, eds. Carlo Severi and William Hanks, pp. 199–219. Chicago: University of Chicago Press.

Manrique, Elizabeth. 2016. "Other-Initiated Repair in Argentine Sign Language." *Open Linguistics* 148 (4): 308–14. doi.org/10.1515/opli-2016-0001.

Mauss, Marcel. 1990 [1925]. *The Gift: The Form and Reason for Exchange in Archaic Societies*. Translated by W. D. Halls. New York: W.W. Norton & Company.

Maynard Smith, John, and Eörs Szathmáry. 1995. *The Major Transitions in Evolution*. Oxford: Freeman Spektrum.

McNeill, David. 1985. "So You Think Gestures Are Nonverbal?" *Psychological Review* 92 (3): 350–71.

McNeill, David. 2005. *Gesture and Thought*. Chicago: University of Chicago Press.

McQuown, Norman A. (ed.). 1971. *The Natural History of an Interview* (with contributions by Gregory Bateson, Ray L. Birdwhistell, Henry W. Brosin, Charles F. Hockett, Norman A. McQuown, Henry L. Smith, Jr. and George L. Trager). Microfilm Collection of Manuscripts on Cultural Anthropology no. 95 Series XV. University of Chicago.

Merleau-Ponty, Maurice. 1967. *The Structure of Behaviour*. Translated by Alden L. Fisher. Boston: Beacon Press.

Merritt, Marilyn. 1982. "Repeats and Reformulations in Primary Classrooms as Windows of the Nature of Talk Engagement." *Discourse Processes* 5 (2): 127–45. doi.org/10.1080/01638538209544537.

Mingers, John. 1995. *Self-Producing Systems: Implications and Applications of Autopoiesis*. New York: Plenum.

Mingers, John. 2001. "Information, Meaning, and Communication: An Autopoietic Approach." In *Sociocybernetics: Complexity, Autopoiesis, and Observation of Social Systems*, eds. Felix Geyer and Johannes Van Der Zouwen, pp. 109–23. Westport: Greenwood Publishing Group.

Moerman, Michael. 1977. "The Preference for Self-Correction in a Tai Conversational Corpus." *Language* 53 (4): 872–82.

Moerman, Michael. 1988. *Talking Culture: Ethnography and Conversation Analysis*. Philadelphia: University of Pennsylvania Press.

Mondada, Lorenza. 2013. "Coordinating Mobile Action in Real Time: The Timely Organization of Directives in Video Games." In *Interaction and Mobility*, eds. Pentti Haddington, Lorenza Mondada, and Maurice Nevile, pp. 300–42. Berlin/Boston: De Gruyter.

Mondada, Lorenza. 2019. "Conventions for Multimodal Transcription." https://www.lorenzamondada.net/multimodal-transcription.

Nail, Thomas. 2017. "What Is an Assemblage?" *SubStance* 46 (1): 21–37.
Newell, Sasha. 2018. "The Affectiveness of Symbols: Materiality, Magicality, and the Limits of the Antisemiotic Turn." *Current Anthropology* 59 (1): 1–22.
Ochs, Elinor, Emanuel Schegloff, and Sandra Thompson. 1996. *Interaction and Grammar*. Cambridge: Cambridge University Press.
Ochs, Elinor. 1982. "Talking to Children in Western Samoa." *Language in Society* 11 (1): 77–104.
Ochs, Elinor, and Bambi Schieffelin. 1984. "Language Acquisition and Socialization: Three Developmental Stories and Their Implications." In *Culture Theory: Essays on Mind, Self, and Emotion*, eds. Richard Shweder and Robert LeVine, pp. 276–320. New York: Cambridge University.
Pattee, Howard H., and Hiroki Sayama. 2018. "Evolved Open-Endedness, Not Open-Ended Evolution." Paper Presented at OEE3: The Third Workshop on Open-Ended Evolution at the 2018 Conference on Artificial Life (ALIFE 2018), July 25, 2018, Tokyo, Japan.
Paulson, William R. 1988. *The Noise of Culture*. Ithaca: Cornell University Press.
Peirce, Charles. 1932. *Collected Papers of Charles Sanders Peirce. Vol. II: Elements of Logic*, eds. Charles Hartshorne and Paul Weiss. Cambridge, MA: Harvard University Press.
Peirce, Charles. 1955. "Logic as Semiotic: The Theory of Signs." In *Philosophical Writings of Charles Peirce*, ed. Justus Buchler, pp. 98–115. New York: Dover.
Peirce, Charles. 1998. *The Essential Peirce: Selected Philosophical Writings (1893-1913)*, Vol. 2, ed. The Peirce Edition Project. Bloomington: Indiana University Press.
Peterson, Jeffrey V., Ann Marie Thornburg, Marc Kissel, Christopher Ball, and Fuentes Agustín. 2018. "Semiotic Mechanisms Underlying Niche Construction." *Biosemiotics*. doi.org/10.1007/s12304-018-9323-1.
Pike, Kenneth L. 1967. *Language in Relation to a Unified Theory of the Structure of Human Behavior*. The Hague: Mouton.
Quine, Willard van Orman. 1960. *Word and Object*. Cambridge, MA: MIT Press.
Raymond, Geoffrey, and Gene Lerner. 2014. "A Body and Its Involvements: Adjusting Action for Dual Involvements." In *Multiactivity in Social Interaction: Beyond Multitasking*, eds. Pentti Haddington, Tiina Keisanen, Lorenza Mondada, and Maurice Nevile, pp. 227–46. Amsterdam: John Benjamins.
Rice, Keren. 2006. "Let the Language Tell Its Story: The Role of Linguistic Theory in Writing Grammars." In *Catching Language: The Standing Challenge of Grammar Writing*, eds. Felix Ameka, Alan Dench, and Nicholas Evans, pp. 235–68. The Hague: Mouton de Gruyter.
Rosaldo, Michelle. 1982. "The Things We Do with Words: Ilongot Speech Acts and Speech Act Theory in Philosophy." *Language in Society* 11 (2): 203–37.
Rossano, Federico, Penelope Brown, and Stephen C. Levinson. 2009. "Gaze, Questioning, and Culture." In *Conversation Analysis: Comparative Perspectives*. ed. Jack Sidnell, pp. 187–249. Cambridge, MA: Cambridge University Press.
Rossi, Giovanni. 2015. "Other-Initiated Repair in Italian." *Open Linguistics* 1 (1): 256–82.
Sacks, Harvey. 1972. "An Initial Investigation of the Usability of Conversational Data for Doing Sociology." In *Studies in Social Interaction*, ed. David Sudrow, pp. 31–74, New York: Free Press.
Sacks, Harvey, Emanuel A. Schegloff, and Gail Jefferson. 1974. "A Simplest Systematics for the Organization of Turn-Taking for Conversation." *Language* 50 (4): 696–735.
Sahlins, Marshall. 1968. "Poor Man, Rich Man, Big Man, Chief: Political Types in Melanesia and Polynesia." In *Peoples and Cultures of the Pacific*, ed. A. Vayda, pp.

157–76. Originally published 1963 in *Comparative Studies in Society and History* 5: 285–303. Garden City, New York..

Sapir, Edward. 1921. *Language: An Introduction to the Study of Speech.* New York: Harcourt Brace.

Sapir, Edward. 1929. "A study in phonetic symbolism." *Journal of Experimental Psychology* 12: 225–39.

Sapir, Edward. 1949. "Speech as a Personality Trait." In *Selected Writings of Edward Sapir,* ed. David Mandelbaum, pp. 533–43. Berkeley: University of California Press.

Sapir, Edward. 2002. *The Psychology of Culture,* reconstructed and edited by Judith T. Irvine. Berlin: Walter de Gruyter.

Schegloff, Emanuel. 1979. "The Relevance of Repair to Syntax-for-Conversation." *Syntax and Semantics* 12: 261–86.

Schegloff, Emanuel. 1982. "Discourse as an Interactional Achievement: Some Uses of 'uh huh' and Other Things that Come between Sentences." In *Analyzing Discourse: Text and Talk,* ed. Deborah Tannen, pp. 71–93. Washington DC: Georgetown University Press.

Schegloff, Emanuel. 1987. "Some Sources of Misunderstanding in Talk-in-Interaction." *Linguistics* 25 (1): 201–18.

Schegloff, Emanuel. 1992. "Repair after Next Turn: The Last Structurally Provided Defense of Intersubjectivity in Conversation." *American Journal of Sociology* 97 (5): 1295–1345.

Schegloff, Emanuel. 1996. "Confirming Allusions: Toward an Empirical Account of Action." *American Journal of Sociology* 102 (1): 161–216.

Schegloff, Emanuel. 1997. "Third Turn Repair." In *Towards a Social Science of Language,* Vol. 2: *Social Interaction and Discourse Structures,* eds. Gregory Guy, Crawford Feagin, Deborah Schiffrin, and John Baugh, pp. 31–40. Amsterdam: John Benjamins.

Schegloff, Emanuel. 2000. "When 'Others' Initiate Repair." *Applied Linguistics* 21 (2): 205–43.

Schegloff, Emanuel. 2006. "Interaction: The Infrastructure for Social Institutions, the Natural Ecological Niche for Language, and the Arena in which Culture is Enacted." In *Roots of Human Sociality: Culture, Cognition, and Interaction,* eds. N. J. Enfield and Stephen C. Levinson, pp. 70–96. New York: Berg.

Schegloff, Emanuel, Gail Jefferson, and Harvey Sacks. 1977. "The Preference for Self-Correction in the Organization of Repair in Conversation." *Language* 53 (2): 361–82.

Schegloff, Emanuel, and Harvey Sacks. 1973. "Opening Up Closings." *Semiotica* 8: 289–327.

Schutz, Alfred. 1980. *The Phenomenology of the Social World.* Translated by George Walsh and Frederick Lehnert. London: Heineman Educational Books.

Scott, James. 1990. *Domination and the Arts of Resistance: Hidden Transcripts.* New Haven: Yale University Press.

Searle, John. 1979. *Expression and Meaning: Studies in the Theory of Speech Acts.* Cambridge: Cambridge University Press.

Shayan, Shakila, Özge Öztürk, and Mark A. Sicoli. 2011. "The Thickness of Pitch: Crossmodal Iconicity in Three Unrelated Languages; Farsi, Turkish and Zapotec." *Senses and Society* 6 (1): 96–105.

Sicoli, Mark A. 2007. "Tono: A Linguistic Ethnography of Tone and Voice in a Zapotec Region." Ph.D. Dissertation, University of Michigan. Ann Arbor.

Sicoli, Mark A. 2010a. "Shifting Voices with Participant Roles: Voice Qualities and Speech Registers in Mesoamerica." *Language in Society* 39 (4): 521–53.

Sicoli, Mark A. 2010b. *Lachixío Zapotec Conversations Archive.* https://hdl.handle.net/1839/00-0000-0000-0017-B8CE-B.

Sicoli, Mark A. 2011. "Agency and Ideology in Language Shift and Language Maintenance." In *Ethnographic Contributions to the Study of Endangered Languages: A Linguistic Anthropological Perspective*, eds. Tania Granadillo and Heidi Orcutt-Gachiri, pp. 161–76. Tucson: University of Arizona Press.

Sicoli, Mark A. 2013. "Multi-Modal and Multi-Authored Social Actions in a Lachixío Zapotec Video Corpus." Paper Presented at the 112th Annual Meeting of the American Anthropological Association, Chicago.

Sicoli, Mark A. 2014. "Ideophones, Rhemes, Interpretants." *Pragmatics and Society* 5 (3): 445–54.

Sicoli, Mark A. 2015a. "Agency and Verb Valence in Lachixío Zapotec." In *Valence Changes in Zapotec: Synchrony, Diachrony, Typology*, eds. Natalie Operstein and Aaron Sonnenschien, pp. 191–212. Amsterdam: John Benjamins.

Sicoli, Mark A. 2015b. "Voice Registers." In *The Handbook of Discourse Analysis, Second Edition*, eds. Deborah Tannen, Heidi E. Hamilton, and Deborah Schiffrin, pp. 105–26. Chichester, UK: John Wiley & sons, Ltd.

Sicoli, Mark A. 2016a. "Formulating Place, Common Ground, and a Moral Order in Lachixío Zapotec." *Open Linguistics* 2 (1): 180–210.

Sicoli, Mark A. 2016b. "Repair Organization in Chinantec Whistled Speech." *Language* 92 (2): 411–32.

Sicoli, Mark A. 2021. "Modality, Multimodality." *The International Encyclopedia of Linguistic Anthropology*. Wiley.

Sicoli, Mark A. 2020. "Deliberate Decisions and Unintended Consequences: Ratifying Non-speakers through Code Alternation in Child-Directed Speech." In *Contact, Structure, and Change: A Festschrift in Honor of Sarah G. Thomason*, eds. Anna M. Babel and Mark A. Sicoli, Ann Arbor: Maize Books.

Sicoli, Mark A. N. D. "On the Importance of an Addressee." Unpublished paper, University of Michigan.

Sicoli, Mark A., and Matthew Scott Wolfgram. 2018. "Charles Sanders Peirce and Anthropological Theory." In *Oxford Bibliographies in Anthropology*, ed. John Jackson. New York: Oxford University Press. doi: 10.1093/OBO/9780199766567-0187.

Sicoli, Mark A., Tanya Stivers, N. J. Enfield, and Stephen Levinson. 2015. "Marked Initial Pitch in Questions Signals Marked Communicative Function." *Language and Speech* 58 (2): 204–23.

Sidnell, Jack. 2010. *Conversation Analysis: An Introduction*. Malden Wiley-Blackwell.

Sidnell, Jack. 2014. "The Architecture of Intersubjectivity Revisited." In *Cambridge Handbook of Linguistic Anthropology*, eds. N. J. Enfield, Paul Kockelman, and Jack Sidnell, pp. 364–99. Cambridge: Cambridge University Press.

Silverstein, Michael. 1976. "Shifters, Linguistic Categories and Cultural Description." In *Meaning in Anthropology*, eds. Keith Basso and Henry Selby, pp. 11–55. Albuquerque: University of New Mexico Press.

Silverstein, Michael. 1984. "On the Pragmatic 'Poetry' of Prose: Parallelism, Repetition, and Cohesive Structure in the Time Course of Dyadic Conversation." In *Meaning, Form, and Use in Context: Linguistic Applications*, ed. Deborah Schiffrin, pp. 181–99. Washington: Georgetown University Press.

Silverstein, Michael. 1992. "The Indeterminacy of Contextualization." In *The Contextualization of Language*, eds. Peter Auer and A. Di Luzio, pp. 55–76. Amsterdam: John Benjamins.

Simard, Suzanne, Kevin Beiler, Marcus Bingham, Julie Deslippe, Leanne Philip, and Francois Teste. 2012. "Mycorrhizal Networks: Mechanisms, Ecology and Modelling." *Fungal Biology Reviews* 26 (1): 39–60.

Sinding-Larsen, Henrik. 2012. "Looking With What You Are Looking At: Gregory Bateson and Terrence Deacon as Healers of the Great Divide between Natural and Human Science." Paper presented at the conference *Academic Demarcations: Disciplines and Interdisciplinarity*, University of Oslo, 13–14. September 2012, Retrieved online April 29, 2018 at: https://www.sv.uio.no/sai/english/research/projects/anthropos-and-the-material/Intranet/sinding-larsen-the-patterns-which-connect.pdf.

Sinding-Larsen, Henrik. 2019. "Musical Notation as the Externalization of Imagined, Complex Sound." In *The Oxford Handbook of Sound and Imagination*, eds. Mark Grimshaw-Aagaard, Mads Walther-Hansen, and Martin Knakkergaard, pp. 191–218. Oxford: Oxford University Press.

Smith-Stark, Thomas. 2007. "Algunas isoglosas zapotecas." In *Clasificación de las lenguas indí- genas de México. Memorias del III Coloquio Internacional de Lingüística Mauricio Swadesh*, eds. Cristina Buenrostro, Samuel Herrera Castro, Yolanda Lastra, Juan José Rendón, Otto Schumann, Leopoldo Valiñas, and María Aydeé Vargas Monroy, pp. 69–134. México: Universidad Nacional Autónoma de México & Instituto Nacional de Lenguas Indígenas.

Snelgrove, Corey, Rita Kaur Dhamoon, and Jeff Corntassel. 2014. "Unsettling Settler Colonialism: The Discourse and Politics of Settlers, and Solidarity with Indigenous Nations." *Decolonization: Indigeneity, Education and Society* 3 (2): 1–32.

Stivers, Tanya. 2005. "Modified Repeats: One Method for Asserting Primary Rights from Second Position." *Research on Language and Social Interaction* 38 (2): 131–58.

Stivers, Tanya, N. J. Enfield, Penelope Brown, Christina Englert, Makoto Hayashi, Trine Heinemann, et al. 2009. "Universals and Cultural Variation in Turn-Taking in Conversation." *Proceedings of the National Academy of Sciences* 106 (26): 10587–92.

Stivers, Tanya, and Federico Rossano. 2010. "Mobilizing Response." *Research on Language & Social Interaction* 43 (1): 3–31.

Taleghani-Nikazm, Carmen. 2006. *Request Sequences: The Intersection of Grammar, Interaction and Social Context*. Amsterdam: John Benjamins.

Tannen, Deborah. 1987. "Repetition in Conversation: Toward a Poetics of Talk." *Language* 63 (3): 574–605.

Tannen, Deborah. 1989. *Talking Voices: Repetition, Dialogue, and Imagery in Conversational Discourse*. New York: Cambridge University Press.

Tannen, Deborah. 1990. "Ordinary Conversation and Literary Discourse: Coherence and the Poetics of Repetition." *The Uses of Linguistics* 583 (1): 15–30.

Teubner, Gunther. 1993. *Laws as an Autopoietic System*. Oxford: Blackwell.

Thomason, Sarah G. 2001. *Language Contact: An Introduction*. Washington DC: Georgetown University Press.

Tomasello, Michael. 2008. *Origins of Human Communication*. Cambridge, MA: MIT Press.

Tomasello, Michael. 2014. *A Natural History of Human Thinking*. Cambridge, MA: Harvard University Press.

Tsing, Anna Lowenhaupt. 2015. *The Mushroom at the End of the World: On the Possibility of Life in Capitalist Ruins*. Princeton: Princeton University Press.

Tulbert, Eve, and Marjorie H. Goodwin. 2011. "Choreographis of Attention: Multimodality in a Routine Family Activity." In *Embodied Interaction: Language and the Body in the Material World*, eds. Jürgen Streeck, Charles Goodwin, and Curtis LeBaron, pp. 79–92. New York: Cambridge University Press.

Urban, Greg. 1996. "Entextualization, Replication, and Power." In *Natural Histories of Discourse*, eds. Michael Silverstein and Greg Urban, pp. 21–44. Chicago: University of Chicago Press.

Varela, Francisco, and Humberto Maturana. 1998. *The Tree of Knowledge*. Boston: Shambala.
Vico, Giambattista. 1984 [1744]. *The New Science: Principles of the New Science Concerning the Common Nature of Nations* (Unabridged Translation of the Third Edition (1744)). Translated by Thomas Goddard Bergin and Max Harold Fisch. Ithaca: Cornell University Press.
Vinkhuyzen, Erik, and Margaret Szymanski. 2005. "Would You Like to Do It Yourself? Service Requests and Their Non-Granting Responses." In *Applying Conversation Analysis*, eds. Keith Richards and Paul Seedhouse, pp. 91–106. New York: Palgrave Macmillan.
Voloshinov, Valentin. 1986. *Marxism and the Philosophy of Language*. Cambridge, MA: Harvard University Press.
Von Uexküll, Jakob. 1992. "A Stroll through the Worlds of Animals and Men: A Picture Book of Invisible Worlds." *Semiotica* 89 (4): 319–91. Reprint: Von Uexküll, Jakob. 1934. *Streifzüge durch die Umwelten von Tieren und Menschen*. Berlin: Julius Springer. [English translation 1957] A stroll through the worlds of animals and men: A Picture Book of Invisible Worlds. In *Instinctive Behavior: The Development of a Modern Concept*, ed. and trans. Claire H. Schiller, pp. 5–80. New York: International Universities Press.
Vygotsky, Lev S. 1986. *Thought and Language*. Cambridge, MA: MIT Press.
Wagner, Roy. 1986. *Symbols that Stand for Themselves*. Chicago: University of Chicago Press.
Wagner, Roy. 2017. "The Energy of Liminality." Paper Presented at the Panel on the Work of Victor and Edie Turner at 2017 Meeting of the American Anthropological Association, Washington DC.
Wagner, Roy. 2019. *The Logic of Invention*. Chicago: Hau Books.
Webster, Anthony K. 2010. "On Intimate Grammars with Examples from Navajo English, Navlish, and Navajo." *Journal of Anthropological Research* 66 (2): 187–208.
Webster, Anthony K. 2015. *Intimate Grammars: An Ethnography of Navajo Poetry*. Tucson: University of Arizona Press.
Weston, Kath. 2013. "Lifeblood, Liquidity, and Cash Transfusions: Beyond Metaphor in the Cultural Study of Finance." *Journal of the Royal Anthropological Institute* 19: S24–S41.
Weston, Kath. 2017. *Animate Planet: Making Visceral Sense of Living in a High Tech Ecologically Damaged World*. Durham and London: Duke University Press.
Wheeler, Wendy. 2017. "Ecologies of Meaning and Loss." In *In Other Tongues*. The Dark Mountain Project Website: https://dark-mountain.net/in-other-tongues-ecologies-of-meaning-and-loss/ Accessed August 3, 2018.
Whorf, Benjamin Lee. 1941. "The Relation of Habitual Thought and Behavior to Language." In *Language, Culture, and Personality: Essays in Memory of Edward Sapir*, eds. Leslie Spier, A. Irving Hallowell, and Stanley S. Newman, pp. 75–93. Menasha: Sapir Memorial Publication Fund.
Whyte, Kyle Powys. 2016. "Indigeneity." In *Keywords for Environmental Studies*, eds. Joni Adamson, William A. Gleason, and David Naguib Pellow, pp. 143–6. New York: New York University Press.
Wikan, Unni. 2012. *Resonance: Beyond the Words*. Chicago: University of Chicago Press.
Wittgenstein, Ludwig. 1958. *Philosophical Investigations, Second Edition*. Translated by G. E. M. Anscombe. Oxford: Basil Blackwell.
Wootton, Anthony J. 1997. *Interaction and the Development of Mind*. Cambridge: Cambridge University Press.

Wootton, Anthony J. 2005. "Interactional and Sequential Features Informing Request Format Selection in Children's Speech." In *Syntax and Lexis in Conversation*, eds. A. Hakulinen and M. Selting, pp. 185–207. Amsterdam: Benjamins.

Zeleny, Milan (ed.). 1997. *Autopoiesis: A Theory of the Living Organization*. New York: North Holland.

Zinken, Jorg, and Eva Ogiermann. 2011. "How to Propose an Action as Objectively Necessary: The Case of Polish Trzeba x ('One Needs to x')." *Research on Language and Social Interaction* 44 (3): 263–87.

Zinken, Jorg, and Eva Ogiermann. 2013. "Responsibility and Action: Invariants and Diversity of Requests for Objects in British English and Polish Interaction." *Research on Language and Social Interaction* 46 (3): 256–76.

Index

acceptance 13–14, 39–40, 46–73, 177
   as joint commitment 57
accrual 2, 3, 11, 21, 29, 168–9, 219
adjacency pairs 17, 21, 37, 62, 71–2, 104, 135, 192
affordance 14, 24, 30–7, 85–6, 93–7, 100, 135, 173, 199, 209–17, 219, 223–5
   of grammar 30, 40, 72, 103
   of multimodality 6, 12, 25
   of resonance 138, 155, 160
   of substitutable vocabulary 29, 64–9
   of video 4, 5
agency 12, 21, 52, 68, 72, 74, 89, 93–6, 109, 122, 168–70, 178, 193, 206, 208, 221
   distributed 168–70
   representational 21, 93, 218
   residential 21, 93, 218
assemblage
   ecological 189, 210, 225
   living 207–28
   multimodal 3, 17, 21, 26, 30, 32–3, 38, 56, 64, 95, 170, 206, 208–11, 215–16, 220, 223–4
   multi-participant 3, 8, 23, 70, 178, 197, 207, 225
   multispecies 8, 208, 210
   in philosophy 8
   polyphonic 7–8, 38, 210
autopoiesis 33, 99, 217, 220–1

Bakhtin, Mikhail 93, 95, 230
Bateson, Gregory 5, 9, 99, 208–9, 220, 223
biosemiotics 9–10, 22–4, 29, 32, 38, 206–10, 212, 216, 221, 224–5
bricolage 12, 179–81, 218
built relations 4, 71, 140, 145, 213, 225

Cartesianism 9, 18, 24, 207, 215–16, 218
Clark, Herb 2, 18, 168, 173

cognition 9, 12, 96, 99, 134, 167, 170, 206, 208, 211, 216–17, 220, 223, 225
   distributed 9, 12, 99, 167–70, 178, 208, 217, 219, 225
   extended 208, 216–17, 225
   social 223
context 7, 12, 22–4, 57, 80, 165, 210–11, 215–16
contextualization 5, 24, 135–6
contingency 30, 71–6, 84, 91, 95–6, 101, 214, 220, 223
conversation analysis 21, 25, 37, 62, 96, 103, 152, 212, 215, 223
co-operative action 15, 32, 197

data presentation 5, 25–8
declaratives 28, 72, 74–5, 88, 96, 203, 223
de Saussure, Ferdinand 10, 75, 135, 198
diachrony 10, 75, *see also kairos*; *kronos*; synchrony
diagraph 138, 141, 144–6, 158, 160, 163
dialogic syntax 15–16, 18, 28, 31, 113, 134–41, 164, 215, 220, 223
dimensionality 4, 12, 213
Dingemanse, Mark 101–6, 110, 113
directives 29, 30, 48, 58–9, 71–83, 86, 88, 91–6, 132, 160, 169, 179, 197, 201
discourse analysis 11, 26, 137–8, 214
double-proportional comparison 15, 163, 215, 222
double-voicing 93, 95, 163, *see also* Bakhtin, Mikhail
Du Bois, John 15–16, 18, 31, 134, 138, 141, 164, 215, 223

emergence 11, 24, 28–34, 137, 164, 206, 212, 217, 219–22
enchrony 10–11, 17, 22, 72, 209
Enfield, N.J. 10–11, 16, 20–1, 30, 72, 74, 101–6, 170, 209

entitlement   30, 71–5, 83–101, 223
epistemics   155–78, 185, 203, 223
ethics   10, 39–41, 57–60, 63, 83–4
  everyday   10, 84

Favareau, Donald   9–10, 16, 32, 97, 100–1, 209, 218
fieldwork and methods   3–7, 24–9, 63, 101, 113, 135, 139, 168, 207–8, 220, 225
  participant observation   168
  participatory methods   3–6, 22–5, 57, 60, 64, 133, 168, 207–8, 224–7
  elicitation interviews   6, 28, 82, 107, 111, 139, 149, 161, 164, 222
  playback dialogues   4, 24, 27, 60, 63–4, 83, 85, 94–5, 170, 224
Fisch, Max   18, 207
frame attunement   23, 215

gifts   1, 28–9, 35, 38–56, 216, *see also guelaguetza* and offers
Goffman, Erving   8–9, 12, 39–40, 45, 57, 63, 69, 75, 102, 110, 132, 212
Goodwin, Charles   5, 7, 9, 12, 133–4
Goodwin, Marjorie Harness   5, 11, 137, 195, 198
guelaguetza   1, 43–5, 179, 210, 227

habit (semiotic)   4–7, 9–10, 20, 23–4, 38–9, 164, 169, 209–12, 216–17
Hockett, Charles   12, 135, 164, 214
Hoffmeyer, Jesper   19, 22–3, 28, 32, 212–13, 215–16

icon   1, 10, 19–21, 31, 33, 39, 43, 136, 145, 155, 170, 174, 176, 184, 188, 194, 198–9, 219, 224
  diagrammatic icon   31, 136, 163, 215
  felt iconicity   17, 226
imperatives   58, 60, 73–8, 95, 101, 113, 131–2, 179, 214, 222–3
index   14, 18, 20–1, 26, 50, 72, 75, 86, 96, 135–6, 151, 163, 169, 184, 190, 198, 206
  indexicality   21, 24, 26, 39, 113, 120, 122, 125, 136–7, 155, 170, 206, 223–4, 232
  inter-indexical relations   24, 31, 33, 136, 210, 215

interjections   107–10, 113, 223
intermodal discord   30, 37, 69–70, 79–80, 86, 92–3
intermodal harmony   17, 37, 70, 86–7, 92, 205
interpretant   19–21, 72–3, 93–7, 135–6, 155, 178, 185, 190–2, 196–8
intersubjectivity   28, 99–100, 134, 150, 192–3, 217, 221–22
  as interactional achievement   30, 100, 102, 104, 131, 134, 142, 167, 212
  as potential/affordance   24, 97, 99–100, 115, 134, 211–15, 221
Irvine, Judith   75–6, 83
iterability   9, 17, 22, 29, 30, 57, 60, 69–70, 74, 97, 160, 190, 196–7, 207, 209, 222

Jakobson, Roman   16, 31, 133, 135–6, 164, 215, 223
joint action   1–9, 63, 74, 94–103, 131–2, 135, 163, 167–9, 173, 179–80, 212–27
  incomplete and complete   46–8, 53, 57–8, 93–6
  object ontology in   32, 192, 206, 208, 216–22
joint commitment(s)   7, 29–33, 57–8, 170, 173, 179–81, 190–8, 221, 225
  and the animation of objects   29, 32, 168–9, 178, 181, 206, 216, 218
  competing   81, 177
  disruption of   9, 32, 191, 192, 194, 198
  request for   183
  signs of   7, 17, 168, 181, 190, 196
  stacking (accumulation) of   58, 173, 232

kairos   8–10, 19, 85, 184, 212, 225
Kockelman, Paul   16, 19–21, 93, 169–70, 218
kronos   8–10, 225

language description   5, 209, 225
language documentation   3–4, 6, 25, 35, 70, 102, 138, 165, 217, 220, 224–5
language games   71, 165, 167, 202

Mesoamerican linguistic area   53, 137, 152, 160
morality   6, 10–12, 17, 72, 82, 88, 132, 139, 170, 198
   conflicted   64
   of gifts and offers   39, 45, 55–7, 62, 73
   of representational fieldwork   12, 214
multimodal ethnography   4, 6–7, 25, 32, 97, 225–6
multimodality   4, 11–15, 24–5, 32, 37, 76, 95–6, 138, 208, 211–13, 216, 226

narrative   6, 14, 17, 19, 25–6, 42–8, 55, 60, 64, 137, 151–5, 161, 224
niche construction   7, 22–4, 33, 210–11, 215
   facilitation in   23, 24, 225
   and mutual mutability   24, 210
   reciprocal causation in   23, 24

object (sign-object)   19–21, 30, 32, 39, 46, 93–5, 97, 101, 136, 155, 173, 178, 185, 198, 206, 213, 218
ontological crossing   118, 129
ontology   8–10, 30, 88, 112, 168–9, 214, 225
   emergent   9, 99, 131
   incomplete   3
   intersubjective   18
   of language in multimodal interaction   10, 25–6, 38, 178, 208–11
   of objects   168
   ontological turn   211
Otomanguean language stock   34, 106, 152

parallelism   4, 16–17, 23, 30–1, 37, 57, 60, 134–8, 147–8, 164, 215
Peirce, Charles   7, 16, 18–21, 31, 37–9, 71, 73, 97, 99, 135–6, 145, 164, 167, 169, 198, 209, 223, *see also* semiotics
perspectivism   211
pitch   54, 109, 113, 185, 204
phenomenology   10, 18, 21, 32, 169, 206, 220–1
phonetics   102, 132
phrase-final enclitics   143, 158, 160–1
phylogeny   8, 76–7

poetics   24, 28, 31, 137, 163, *see also* Jakobson, Roman
politeness   75–6, 96, 105
pragmatics   6, 39. 74–6, 88, 93, 164, 213, 226
   comparative   74–6, 226
pragmatism/pragmaticism (in philosophy)   18, 167, 207

reciprocal causation   23–4, 210
recruitments   24, 28–31, 71–98, 167, 181, 185, 208, 210, 215, 223–6
repair/repair initiation   30–1, 45, 50–1, 55–6, 77, 80, 99–132, 137, 140, 184–5, 191–4, 201, 212–13, 222–5
   conversational   17–18, 30, 100–1, 103, 104, 113, 140, 210
   open   103, 106–8, 113
   other-initiated   97, 101–5, 122, 185, 193–4, 223
   reference   6, 24–7, 100, 131, 99–132
   restricted   103–8, 113–14
   self-initiated   101–2
repetition   17, 53–6, 61, 67, 96, 102, 108, 114, 116, 132–44, 147–8, 158, 160, 162, 203, 215, 223
requests   2, 12–30, 58, 67, 71–88, 92–7, 101, 103–22, 129, 131, 137, 155, 183, 224, 226
resonance   4, 6, 15–24, 28–31, 57, 69, 95–7, 100, 102, 111, 131–67, 181, 185, 191, 203, 206–27
   affirming   153. 161
   assessing   2, 69, 74, 137, 142, 149–55, 157, 160, 162, 172–3, 175, 179, 184–5, 196, 204
   chiasmatic   163, 209, 215, 222
   dialogic   15, 31, 111, 134, 136, 139, 151, 163, 209
   discordant   8, 17, 26, 30–1, 46, 60, 62, 77, 89, 215
   focal   18, 31, 138, 163
   frame   18, 24, 31, 138–9, 143–4, 156, 163, 185, 227
   harmonic   8, 17, 26, 30–1, 215
   informing   149–55
   intermodal   15, 17, 26, 32, 95, 138, 165, 205, 212
   interpersonal   15, 95

resonance grammar   135, 138–47, 163–4
resonant frames   155–61, 163, 209

Sapir, Edward   4–5, 9, 69, 95, 164, 226
scale   6–11, 17, 21–3, 29–33, 37–40,
   62–3, 68–73, 83, 93, 95, 97, 100,
   132, 135, 143, 151, 164, 168, 197,
   207–12, 220, 224
semethic interactions   211–16
semiosis   7, 18–25, 31, 93–7, 100, 134–6,
   167, 169, 173, 178, 190, 197–8,
   208–9, 211, 213–14, 217, 222,
   223
semiotic carrying capacity   6, 12, 211,
   214
semiotics   18, 24, 212, 216, *see also* icon;
   index; interpretant; semiosis;
   sign-object; symbol
   argument   20, 174, 192, 198, 213, 217,
      224
   change signals   39
   dicent   20, 73, 219
   Firstness   20, 39
   intrinsic sign   170, 177, 198, 203, 206
   legisign   20
   markers   39
   qualisign   20, 99
   rheme   20, 72, 85, 145–6, 219
   Secondness   20, 39, 135, 215
   sign   19–28
   sinsign   20
   Thirdness   20, 39, 209, 215
   tie signs   39
semiotic scaffolding   22–4, 33
sign language   4, 12, 76, 214
space   2, 8–12, 19–22, 37, 39, 46, 56–7,
   68–9, 72–3, 88, 105, 151, 163, 169,
   184, 187, 192, 194, 198, 208–9,
   212–14, 221, 224–5
speech acts   29, 55, 71, 74, 76, 105, 205
structuration   9, 95
symbol   18–25, 60, 168, 170, 174, 179,
   192, 198, 203–6, 216–17, 229
   as emergent   135, 136, 216
   as a form of life   19, 38, 136
   symbolic reference   131, 170, 174,
      213, 224

synchrony   10, 37, 56, 68, 91, 127, 135–6,
   178, 208, *see also* diachrony; *kairos*;
   kronos
syntax   76, 113, 136, 138, 145–6, 156,
   210, 214–15, 231

teleodynamic process   33, 216, 218–23,
   225
time   7–13, 17, 37, 46, 56, 72–3, 164, 184,
   197, 208–9, 212–13
timespace geography   10, 19–22, 25, 56,
   163–4, 169, 209, 213–14
Tomasello, Michael   28–9, 76, 169–70,
   198, 215, 221, 224
turns/turn-taking   1–2, 9, 11, 53, 90, 93,
   104, 113, 132–8, 142, 145–7, 160,
   188, 221
Tzeltal Maya language   106, 137, 152

Umwelt   100, 115, 131, 208, 211–21
   overlapping (or shared)   115, 131,
      213–14
   paired   218–19, 221
   and perspectivism   211

verbal morphology   68, 96, 112, 117,
   137, 139, 144, 146, 156–8, 160, 176,
   184–5, 213
   completive aspect   58–9, 73–4, 81–3,
      96, 223
   potential mood   59, 73–5, 78, 81–2,
      222–3
Vico, Giambattista   18, 207
video   1–7, 11, 25–9, 39, 45, 79, 92, 95–6,
   101, 104–5, 114, 132–3, 168, 170,
   179–81, 210, 213–14, 220, 224–6
voice quality   87, 139

Wagner, Roy   15, 163, 215
whistled speech   85, 104
Wittgenstein, Ludwig   71, 167, 181, 206,
   211, 223–4

Yucatec Maya language   137, 152

Zapotec-Chatino language family   34
Zinacantec Maya language   137

www.ingramcontent.com/pod-product-compliance
Lightning Source LLC
Chambersburg PA
CBHW070025010526
44117CB00011B/1716